HUBRIS: THE
DONALD ⸱

HUBRIS: THE ROAD TO DONALD TRUMP

POWER, POPULARISM, NARCISSISM

DAVID OWEN

Methuen

HUBRIS: THE ROAD TO DONALD TRUMP

First published in Great Britain by Methuen in 2018
This paperback edition published in 2020

1

Methuen
Orchard House, Railway Street
Slingsby, York YO62 4AN

www.methuen.co.uk

Copyright © David Owen 2020

Excerpts from
The Cabinet's Finest Hour. The Hidden Agenda of May 1940
by David Owen
reprinted with the kind permission of Haus Publishing Ltd.

Tables 12.1 and 12.2 at pages 288-9 are taken from Peter Garrard and
Graham Robinson, eds. *The Intoxication of Power*, published 2016,
Palgrave Macmillan, reproduced with permission of SNCSC.

A CIP catalogue record for this book is available from
the British Library.

ISBN: 978 0 413 77833 8

Typeset by SX Composing DTP, Rayleigh, Essex.
Printed and bound in Great Britain by CPI Group (UK) Ltd, Croydon, CR0 4YY

To Clive Gimson – my teacher, friend and toe-holder

Contents

Acknowledgements

President Trump's election in November 2016 prompted me to review all that I had written about past US Presidents and British Prime Ministers in relation to hubris. Trump is mentioned throughout this book but in some detail in the Introduction and in Chapter 11, *Donald Trump's Populism*. There is a new Chapter 12, Boris Johnson's Populism. Hubris and related conditions are drawn from three previous books. A paperback, *The Hubris Syndrome: Bush, Blair and the Intoxication of Power* published in 2007; *In Sickness and In Power,* published in 2008, followed by an extensive revision in 2016 and *Cabinet's Finest Hour. The Hidden Agenda of 1940* published in 2016. Also the Samuel Gee Lecture I gave on Hubris Syndrome at the Royal College of Physicians (*Clinical Medicine,* 2008; 8: 428-432) and a co-authored paper in *Brain* with Professor Jonathan Davidson of Duke University in the US on 'Hubris Syndrome: An Acquired Personality Disorder? A Study of US Presidents and UK Prime Ministers over the last 100 years' (*Brain,* Journal of Neurology, 2009: Vol 132, 1396-1406). I am indebted to my co-author for his invaluable contribution to my thinking. He was also the lead author of an important article 'Mental Illness in US Presidents' (*The Journal of Nervous and Mental Disease*, Vol 184, No. 1, January 2006) and his book *Downing Street Blues* both of which are quoted in this book.

Where my views remain the same I have not felt it necessary to change the initial text; where new thinking and facts have emerged to change my views over the succeeding years I reflect this.

In addition I have drawn on many articles in medical journals, newspapers and speeches I have given. In a real sense the last 15 years have been work in progress. What has been tragic is how over these years the disillusionment has grown amongst the general public with politics and politicians, as political leaders have distorted facts, lied and played fast and loose with the truth to the point that a form of populism has developed that is mendacious and corrupt. Much of this is linked to personality flaws and changes such as acquired hubris amongst political leaders. This mendacity has been facilitated by social media where the lack of transparency and accountability has to be curbed by global action.[1]

Many people have helped in the discussions that followed putting together this book and to all of them, too numerous to mention over such a long period, I offer my personal thanks. I am grateful to the House of Lords library and the Library of the University of Liverpool, which holds all my personal archives.

Very special thanks go to my wife and literary agent, Debs. Also to Maggie Smart who has worked with me from 1977 when I became Foreign Secretary until the present day. I am indebted to Peter Tummons at Methuen, who published my two earlier books and now this one and to Haus Publishing Ltd for permission to quote from *Cabinet's Finest Hour, The Hidden Agenda of May 1940*.

Any errors of fact or mistaken interpretations are solely my responsibility.

---

1 'Disinformation and 'fake news" Final Report by the House of Commons Digital, Culture, Media and Sports Committee Eighth Report of Session 2017-2019.

Introduction: Hubris, Narcissism and Hubris Syndrome

Many people expect, even want, their leaders to be different from the norm, to display more energy, work longer hours, appear exhilarated by what they are doing and full of self-confidence – in short, to behave in ways that, taken beyond a certain point, a psychiatrist might be tempted to mark them down as hypomanic or manic. So long as those leaders are attempting to achieve what the public wish them to achieve, the public do not want to be told that their favourite leaders are mentally ill. But when they lose the support of their public, it becomes a very different matter. Then the public are ready to use words like 'mad', long discarded by the profession to describe mental illness, as a means of expressing their objection to the way their leaders are behaving.

It is here that things become interesting, at least as regards the health of the body politic even if not of the leaders themselves. This is when a political leader behaves in ways that the public not just disapprove of but instinctively interpret as being the result of a change in mental state: apparent evidence that the leader has 'lost it', has become 'unbalanced', 'unhinged', 'out of control'.

'Hubris' is not a medical term. The most basic meaning, developed in ancient Greece, was simply as a description of an act: a hubristic act was one in which a powerful figure, puffed up with overweening pride and self-confidence, treated others with insolence and contempt. He – and it was usually but not invariably a male – seemed to get kicks from using his power to treat others in this way.

Such dishonouring behaviour was strongly condemned in ancient Greece. In a famous passage from Plato's *Phaedrus*, a predisposition to hubris is defined: 'But when desire irrationally drags us toward pleasures and rules within us, its rule is called excess (*hubris*).'[2] Plato saw this 'rule of desire' as something irrational that drags men into doing the wrong thing through acts of hubris. In his *Rhetoric*, Aristotle picks up the element of desire Plato identifies in hubris and argues that the pleasure someone seeks from an act of hubris lies in showing himself as superior. 'That is why the young and the wealthy are given to insults (*hubristai*, i.e. being hubristic); for they think that, in committing them (acts of hubris), they are showing superiority.'[3]

But it was in drama rather than philosophy that the notion was developed further to explore the patterns of hubristic behaviour, its causes and consequences. A hubristic career proceeded along something like the following course. The hero wins glory and acclamation by achieving unwanted success against the odds. The experience then goes to his head: he begins to treat others, mere ordinary mortals, with contempt and disdain and he develops such confidence in his own ability that he begins to think himself capable of anything. This excessive self-confidence leads him into misinterpreting the reality around him and into making mistakes. Eventually he gets his comeuppance and meets his nemesis, which destroys him. Nemesis is the name of the goddess of retribution, and often in Greek drama the gods arrange the fate of nemesis because a hubristic act is seen as one in which the perpetrator tries to defy the reality ordained by them. The hero committing the hubristic act seeks to transgress the human condition, imagining himself to be superior and to have powers more like those of the gods. But the gods will

---

2 Plato, *Phaedrus*, 238a, in *Euthyphro/Apology/Crito/Phaedo/Phaedrus*, tr. H. N. Fowler, Loeb Classical Library (Cambridge, MA: Harvard University Press, 1914); the Ancient Greek original has been added in italics by the author of this book.

3 Aristotle, *Art of Rhetoric*, tr. J. H. Freese, Loeb Classical Library (Cambridge, MA: Harvard University Press, 1926), 1378b.

have none of that: so it is they who destroy him. The moral is that we should be wary of allowing power and success to go to our heads. The theme of hubris has fascinated playwrights, no doubt because it provides the opportunity to explore human character within highly dramatic action. Shakespeare's *Coriolanus* is a study in it. But the pattern of the hubristic career is one that will immediately strike a chord in anyone who has studied the history of political leaders. The hubristic posture has been described by the philosopher David E. Cooper as 'excessive self-confidence, an 'up yours!' attitude to authority, pre-emptive dismissal of warnings and advice, taking oneself as a model.'[4] Another philosopher, Hannah Arendt, who admired ancient Athens, has written about the shortcomings of its ruler Pericles, who was possessed by 'the hubris of power', and has compared him unfavourably with Solon, the lawmaker of Athens.[5] The historian Ian Kershaw aptly titled the two volumes of his biography of Hitler *Hubris* and *Nemesis*.[6]

Many know Lord Acton's famous dictum, 'Power tends to corrupt, and absolute power tends to corrupt absolutely.'[7] But Acton preceded that with a plea to judge those who hold power by a higher standard than those who do not.

I cannot accept your canon that we are to judge Pope and King unlike other men, with a favourable presumption that they did no wrong. If there is any presumption it is the other way against the holders of power.

---

4 David E. Cooper, *The Measure of Things: Humanism, Humility, and Mystery* (Oxford: Clarendon Press, 2002), p. 163.

5 Margaret Canovan, 'Hannah Arendt as a Conservative Thinker', in Larry May and Jerome Kohn (eds), *Hannah Arendt: Twenty Years On* (Cambridge, MA: MIT Press, 1996), p. 29.

6 Ian Kershaw, *Hitler 1889–1936: Hubris* (London: Allen Lane, 1998); Ian Kershaw, *Hitler 1936–1945: Nemesis* (London: Allen Lane, 2000).

7 Written on 5 April 1887 to Mandell Creighton, author of *A History of the Papacy during the Period of the Reformation*.

The Pulitzer Prize-winning historian Barbara Tuchman wrote that power

> breeds folly; that the power to command frequently causes failure to think; that the responsibility of power often fades as its exercise augments. The overall responsibility of power is to govern as reasonably as possible in the interest of the state and its citizens. A duty in that process is to keep well-informed, to heed information, to keep mind and judgement open and to resist the insidious spell of wooden-headedness. If the mind is open enough to perceive that a given policy is harming rather than serving self-interest, and self-confident enough to acknowledge it, and wise enough to reverse it, that is a summit in the art of government.[8]

Acts of hubris are much more common in heads of government, whether democratic or not, than is often realised and hubris is a major contributor to Tuchman's definition of folly: 'a perverse persistence in a policy demonstrably unworkable or counter-productive'. She continued: 'Wooden-headedness, the source of self-deception is a factor that plays a remarkably large role in government. It consists in assessing a situation in terms of preconceived fixed notions while ignoring or rejecting any contrary signs . . . also the refusal to benefit from experience.'[9] A characteristic of hubris is the inability to change direction because this involves admitting that one has made a mistake.

Bertrand Russell once wrote: 'The concept of "truth" as something dependent upon facts largely outside human control has been one of the ways in which philosophy hitherto has inculcated the necessary element of humility. When this check upon pride is

---

8 Barbara W. Tuchman, *The March of Folly: From Troy to Vietnam* (NewYork: Ballantine, 1985), pp. 32, 33.
9 Tuchman, *The March of Folly: From Troy to Vietnam*, pp. 7, 33.

removed, a further step is taken on the road towards a certain kind of madness – the intoxication of power'.[10]

Watching hubristic leaders, one can ponder whether hubris is a description of a kind of loss of capacity. This pattern is very familiar in the careers of political leaders whose success makes them feel excessively self-confident and contemptuous of advice that runs counter to what they believe, or sometimes of any advice at all, and who start to act in ways that seem to defy reality itself. Nemesis may, though not always, follow.

Whether hubristic behaviour amongst leaders can be linked to certain personality types that predispose someone to act hubristically; and whether, indeed, such personality types create a propensity in those who have them to enter particular careers such as politics, needs more study.

The decision-making of heads of government, engendering folly, in the sense of foolishness, stupidity or rashness, was an issue I faced quite directly on a number of occasions when I was Foreign Secretary from 1977-79 and EU peace envoy to the Balkans from 1992-95. I became fascinated by those leaders who were not ill and whose cognitive faculties functioned well but who developed what I began to describe in medical journal articles as hubris syndrome, in particular in *Brain* in 2009 with Professor Jonathan Davidson, who had previously co-authored an important article on mental illness in US Presidents.[11] Our article was entitled 'Hubris Syndrome: An Acquired Personality Disorder?'[12]

Hubris Syndrome is when leaders who have hitherto been

---

10 Bertrand Russell, *History of Western Philosophy*, 2nd ed. (London: George Allen & Unwin, 1961), p. 782.

11 Jonathan R. T. Davidson, Kathryn M. Connor and Marvin Swartz, 'Mental Illness in US Presidents between 1776 and 1974: A Review of Biographical Sources', *Journal of Nervous and Mental Disease* (2006), vol. 194, pp 47-51.

12 David Owen and Jonathan Davidson, 'Hubris Syndrome: An Acquired Personality Disorder? A Study of US Presidents and UK Prime Ministers over the Last 100 years', *Brain* (2009), vol. 132, pp. 1396–1406.

regarded as broadly 'normal' change their personality and start to behave hubristically simply as a consequence of being in power. In other words, the experience of being in power itself brings about changes in mental states which then manifest themselves in hubristic behaviour. A syndrome happens to someone, it is nature at work, a collection of features, be they signs or symptoms which have a greater chance of appearing together than independently. As work developed on hubris syndrome by definition it seemed wiser not to apply the term to anyone with a history of mental illness particularly an illness associated with hypomania or manic behaviour. This is because hypomania or manic episodes associated with depression were difficult to separate out. It was felt by excluding people with mental illness the term could be reserved for people who were 'normal' at some stage and this fitted in with dropping any association with the term disorder, especially Narcissistic Personality Disorder (NPD).

The behavioural symptoms which might trigger the diagnosis of hubris syndrome typically grow in strength the longer the individual concerned remains in post, whether it is a head of government, a chief executive, head of a university or a headteacher of a school. He or she needs to present, as Jonathan Davidson and I suggest in our article in *Brain*[13] *three or four symptoms from the following list of fourteen before any diagnosis should be contemplated of hubris syndrome and at least one must be amongst the five conditions identified as unique.*

(1)   a narcissistic propensity to see the world primarily as an arena in which they can exercise power and seek glory rather than as a place with problems that need approaching in a pragmatic and non-self-referential manner;

---

13 Ibid, David Owen and Jonathan Davidson, 'Hubris Syndrome: An Acquired Personality Disorder? A Study of US Presidents and UK Prime Ministers over the last 100 years' (*Brain,* Journal of Neurology, 2009:Vol 132, 1396-1406).

(2)	a predisposition to take actions which seem likely to cast them in a good light – i.e. in order to enhance their image;

(3)	a disproportionate concern with image and presentation;

(4)	a messianic manner of talking about what they are doing and a tendency to exaltation;

(5)	an identification of themselves with the state to the extent that they regard the outlook and interests of the two as identical; UNIQUE

(6)	a tendency to talk of themselves in the third person or using the royal 'we'; UNIQUE

(7)	excessive confidence in their own judgement and contempt for the advice or criticism of others;

(8)	exaggerated self-belief, bordering on a sense of omnipotence, in what they personally can achieve;

(9)	a belief that rather than being accountable to the mundane court of colleagues or public opinion, the real court to which they answer is much greater: History or God;

(10)	an unshakeable belief that in that court they will be vindicated; UNIQUE

(11)	restlessness, recklessness and impulsiveness; UNIQUE

(12)	loss of contact with reality; often associated with progressive isolation;

(13)	a tendency to allow their 'broad vision', especially their conviction about the moral rectitude of a proposed course of action, to obviate the need to consider other aspects of it, such as its practicality, its cost and the possibility of unwanted outcomes: a wooden-headed refusal to change course; UNIQUE

(14)	a consequent type of incompetence in carrying out a policy, which could be called hubristic incompetence.

This is where things go wrong precisely because too much self-confidence has led the leader not to bother worrying about the nuts and bolts of a policy. There may be an inattention to detail which can be allied to an incurious nature. It is to be distinguished from ordinary incompetence, where the necessary detailed work on the complex issues involved is engaged in but mistakes in decision-making are made nonetheless.

In *Brain* we left open any relationship between hubris syndrome and Narcissistic Personality Disorder, NPD. In some studies NPD itself has been shown to be surprisingly transient. A large epidemiological study observed a 6.2 per cent lifetime prevalence of NPD, which was higher in men (7.7 per cent) than women (4.8 per cent).[14] Higher rates of bipolar disorder were found amongst those with NPD. These and other reasons make it unwise to diagnose hubris syndrome in these people with a history of depression.

For over a century syndromes of personality were believed to manifest themselves in people by the age of eighteen and stay with them for the rest of their lives. In that important sense hubris syndrome is different in that it manifests itself in leaders in any walk of life only when in power – and usually only after they have been wielding power for some time – and which then may well abate once power is lost. In that sense it is an acquired personality change, a reflection of or an accompaniment to power. The circumstances in which such an exercise of power takes place will clearly affect the likelihood that a leader will succumb to it. The key external factors would seem to be these: an initial appearance

14 Frederick S. Stinson et al., 'Prevalence, Correlates, Disability, and Comorbidity of DSM-IV Narcissistic Personality Disorder: Results from the Wave 2 National Epidemiologic Survey on Alcohol and Related Conditions', *Journal of Clinical Psychiatry* (2008), vol. 69, pp. 1033–45.

of success in achieving and holding power; a context in which there is minimal constraint on the leader exercising such personal authority; and the length of time they stay in power. The medical profession resisted for several decades even the existence of post-traumatic stress disorder, PTSD. How wars wound men's minds and medicine's efforts to heal the damage done is described in Ben Shephard's book *A War of Nerves. Soldiers and Psychiatrists 1914-1994*.[15] Gradually, as more and more hitherto stable young soldiers appeared to have acquired on the battlefield or in the aftermath signs and symptoms of a definable kind, there was a greater and growing recognition that an acquired medical disorder was emerging and needed to be accepted as such and that stress was a major factor.

In 2009 in a lecture at the Institute of Neurology in London honouring the late Professor David Marsden FRS, with whom I worked on beta-blockers at St Thomas's Hospital Medical Unit from 1966-68, I suggested learning more about secondary prevention of post-traumatic stress disorder, PTSD, and the immediate treatment with the beta-blocking drugs. The fact that after a long argument PTSD has been accepted as acquired has undoubtedly helped the claim that hubris syndrome also is acquired. But we need more research.

Acquired hubris syndrome, which instinctively, if imprecisely, people sense is related to power, is just starting to be categorized as a trait and the medical profession, rightly, wishes to be very controlled in its use of language to describe or recognize it. The ICD-11 classification does allow for 'late onset personality disorder' as a diagnostic option which should allow hubris syndrome to be classified. This emphasis on the medical profession does not mean that the issue of hubris is the sole preserve of medicine and should

---

15 Ben Shepard, *A War of Nerves. Soldiers and Psychiatrists 1914-1994* (Pimlico, 2002).

not be questioned and elaborated on by psychologists, philosophers, anthropologists, biologists and lay people as well as the medical profession. Indeed, it is vital in order to increase understanding of hubris syndrome that it is studied in a multidisciplinary way.

How to curb the hubris of leaders, without depriving them of other essential characteristics of leadership, has exercised many minds for some hundreds of years. It is not just a subject that fascinated the Greeks. John Adams, one of the Founding Fathers of America who helped draft the United States Constitution, in *A Dissertation on the Canon and Feudal Law*, published in August 1765, wrote about 'a general knowledge among the people', which he believed meant that 'they have a right, an indisputable, unalienable, indefensible divine right to the most dreaded and envied kind of knowledge. I mean the character and conduct of their leaders.'

Narcissism haunts heads of government, military commanders and business leaders and the latter two are specifically dealt with in Chapters 8 and 9. The word comes from the Greek myth of Narcissus, a boy who could not stop staring at his reflection in a pond, the classic version of which can be found in Ovid's epic poem *Metamorphoses*, written in the first century AD. The most often-quoted use of the word 'narcissism' is Sigmund Freud's, but it tended to change throughout his life. In 1910 Freud wrote a psychosexual biography of Leonardo da Vinci and formed a connection between the myth of Narcissus and the same-sex love of the homosexual. In an important essay called 'On Narcissism' (1914) he described primary and secondary narcissism. Primary narcissism was an instinct 'a measure of which may justifiably be attributed to every living creature'. In 1931 Freud described narcissism in a very short four-page paper called 'Libidinal Types' about the 'normal' personality, defining his three normal types as erotic, obsessive and narcissistic.

The third type (is) justly called the narcissistic type. . . . There is no tension between ego and super-ego (indeed, on the strength of this type one would scarcely have arrived at the hypothesis of a super-ego), and there is no preponderance of erotic needs. The subject's main interest is directed to self-preservation; he is independent and not open to intimidation. His ego has a large amount of aggressiveness at its disposal, which also manifests itself in a readiness for activity. In his erotic life loving is preferred above being loved. People belonging to this type impress others as being "personalities"; they are especially suited to act as a support for others, to take on the role of leaders and to give a fresh stimulus to cultural development or to damage the established state of affairs.

Most of Freud's writing is about personality types that are far from normal but his insights on personality within a normal framework are important. In the 1940s Erich Fromm added a fourth normal personality type, the marketing personality, about people who adapt to the market, a phenomenon first identified and associated with the highly competitive global economy developed in the twentieth century. President Trump might be thought to fit into this category.

The distinguished philosopher Simon Blackburn in his book *Mirror, Mirror. The Uses and Abuses of Self-Love*[16] summarises four different dimensions of narcissism which psychologists have identified: leadership/authority (enjoying being a leader and being seen as an authority), self-absorption/ self-admiration (admiring one's own physical appearance and personality), superiority/ arrogance (overestimation of one's own abilities, underlying themes of superiority and grandiosity), and finally exploitativeness/ entitlement (interpersonal manipulation, expectations of favour,

---

16 Simon Blackburn, *Mirror, Mirror. The Uses and Abuses of Self-Love* (Princeton University Press, reprint edition 2016).

exploitation of others). Blackburn sees narcissism as 'closely allied with demented self-confidence: hubris'.[17]

Allied yes, but as Nick Bouras, Emeritus Professor of Psychiatry, King's College, London, who started his career in Greece, writes:

> Increased awareness of hubris has led to the term not always being used appropriately. A common misconception is that hubris is indistinguishable from narcissism. On the contrary, narcissism is expressed with a blatantly attention seeking, grandiose sense of self-importance, a persistent and burdensome search for admiration and lack of empathy. Excessive narcissism might lead to or coexist with hubris, but the two are fundamentally distinct, the latter characterized by overconfidence, over ambition, arrogance and excessive pride.[18]

Narcissism and self-knowledge as Kets de Vries argues rarely go together. He also writes about narcissistic injury – that is an injury to a person's self-esteem, 'feelings of envy, competitiveness, rage, anger, resentment, revenge and vindication. Amassing money becomes a way to show that you count; it becomes a means of vindication; it can even be used for revenge.'[19]

Michael Macoby, the author of *The Productive Narcissist*, which correctly emphasizes the positive sides to narcissism, writes from his experience as a consultant, business coach and psychoanalyst, 'Narcissists need their followers much the same way politicians need their audience, their constituency.' He credits those he describes as narcissistic Presidents – Lincoln, FDR, Reagan, Clinton – for being

---

17 Roshan Cools, 'Role of Dopamine in the Motivational and Cognitive Control of Behavior', *Neuroscientist* (2008), vol. 14, pp. 381–95.

18 Ed. Peter Garrard, *The Leadership Hubris Epidemic. Biological Roots and Strategies for Prevention* (Palgrave Macmillan, 2018), Foreword by Nick Bouras, p. x.

19 Kets de Vries, *Sex, Money, Happiness and Death. The Quest for Authenticity* (Palgrave Macmillan, 2016), p 258 and 103.

'extraordinary communicators and charmers. Clinton is famous for his ability to "feel your pain", and equally well-known for dropping those who have been close to him.'[20] I do not share Macoby's view of Lincoln as a narcissist.

Mental illness is so common that it is certain to be found in people prominent in politics, the military, business and other professional leadership roles whether in schools or in hospitals and it must never be regarded as an automatic disqualification for a leadership position. President Abraham Lincoln is a most interesting case of how a leader's qualities can be forged through their depression. Few heads of government have borne that affliction for a longer period than Lincoln and yet he refused to be bowed down by it. As a young man he had profound mood swings, more down than up, and even wrote an essay on suicide. 'I may seem to enjoy life rapturously when I am in company. But when I am alone I am so often overcome by mental depression that I dare not carry a penknife.' On 25 August 1838 the *Sangamo Journal* carried an unsigned poem, 'The Suicide's Soliloquy', which points strongly to having been written by Lincoln. By common consent, Lincoln was one of the greatest US Presidents and through all the stress of the Civil War 'he retained an unflagging faith in his country's cause.'[21] Lincoln's character as President was strongly influenced by two major breakdowns and his depression in his twenties became more persistent in his thirties. The author of the book *Lincoln's Melancholy* found evidence of mania, though thinks it is possible that Lincoln had hypomania, characterised by heightened energy.[22] Lincoln had the 'ability to put grudges behind

20 Michael Macoby, *The Productive Narcissist. The Promise and Peril of Visionary Leadership* (Broadway Books, 2003), p. 119.
21 Doris Kearns Goodwin, *Team of Rivals: The Political Genius of Abraham Lincoln* New York: Simon & Schuster, 2005), p. xvii.
22 Joshua Wolf Shenk, *Lincoln's Melancholy: How Depression Challenged a President and Fuelled his Greatness* (Boston: Houghton Mifflin, 2005).

him'[23] which is not a characteristic of a narcissist. He was able to 'form friendships with men who had previously opposed him; to repair injured feelings that, left untended, might have escalated into permanent hostility; to assume responsibility for the failures of subordinates; to share credit with ease; and to learn from mistakes.'

Whether FDR or Reagan were abnormally narcissistic is questionable too for both were blessed with self-deprecating humour which in my experience is not often linked to narcissism. With Bill Clinton, there is an actor quality as with Tony Blair and both have some narcissistic tendencies but they are also empathisers.

Initially many people, particularly in America in 2017, were all too ready to diagnose with great confidence that their new President Donald Trump was suffering from Narcissistic Personality Disorder or NPD. But this came to an abrupt halt following the publication of a letter in the *New York Times* by the Emeritus Professor of Psychiatry at Duke University, Allen Frances, who was the man who had written up NPD in the third edition of the Diagnosis and Statistical Manual of Mental Disorders DSM III. He made it crisply clear that Trump did not have NPD, 'he may be a world class narcissist, but this does not make him mentally ill.' This is because the DSM criterion requires social impairment. Since then, though some speculation of NPD has continued, it has mostly fallen away.

According to Frances, "Most liars aren't mentally ill. Most conspiracy theorists aren't mentally ill. And there's no evidence that Trump is mentally ill. Trump's boorish manners, vulgar speech, and abusive actions make him a national embarrassment and the worst of all possible role models ... He diminishes America, reducing its greatness. But none of this makes him mentally ill ... Medicalising Trump's bad behaviour underestimates him and distracts attention from the dangers of his policies. Trump

---

23 Ibid, Doris Kearns Goodwin, p. xvii and p. 510.

is a political problem, not meat for psychoanalysis. Instead of focusing on Trump's motivations, we must counter his behaviour with political tools."[24]

Narcissism undoubtedly is a general description of President Trump's personality, but it is not a psychiatric disorder by itself. It has been divided into types by Bursten in a study published in 1973.[25] Another classification by Millon is described in the book *Narcissistic Personality*.[26]

Narcissists train themselves from an early age to block out other voices, other opinions, so one of the few voices they trust is their own. John D. Rockefeller, one of the richest men in the world, held intimate conversations with himself, counselling himself, repeating homilies, and warning himself to be aware of moral as well as practical pitfalls before he went to sleep at night.[27]

To the extent that hubris shares common elements with narcissistic and sociopathic disorders, such as impaired decision-making, poor impulse control, poor modulation of aggression and lack of appropriate empathy, the findings of altered dopaminergic, noradrenergic and serotonergic function in these conditions could all be relevant. Frontostriatal and limbic-striatal dopaminergic pathways have been identified as important regulators of impulsive and/or rigid behaviours,[28] and this may reflect deficient motivational or cognitive control.

Pathological gambling appears to show some features of hubris, with impaired risk appraisal. Neurobiologically, pathological

---

24 Allen J. Frances, *Twilight of American Sanity. A Psychiatrist Analyses the Age of Trump* (Morrow 2017).

25 Ben Bursten, 'Some narcissistic personality types', *Int J Psychoanal*. 1973; 54:287-300.

26 Elsa F. Ronningstam, *Narcissistic Personality* (Oxford University Press, 2005), pp. 14-15.

27 Ibid, Macoby, p. 77.

28 Stefano Pallanti et al., 'Serotonin Dysfunction in Pathological Gamblers: Increased Prolactin Response to Oral m-CPP versus Placebo', *CNS Spectrums* (2006), vol. 11, pp. 956-64.

gambling is characterised by abnormal behavioural and neuroendocrine responses[29] and, at least in males, a specific gene.[30] Associations were found between pathological gambling and genes for the D2 and D4, dopamine transporter, tryptophan hydroxylase and the α2c adrenergic receptors, with the dopamine, serotonin and norepinephrine genes each accounting for less than 2 per cent of the variance.[31] The regulation of decision-making and the processing of punishment-related information if impaired may be relevant.[32] One group that are prone to more risky decision-making with misplaced confidence in the correctness of their decisions[33] are those with lesions in the ventromedial prefrontal (vmPFC) and insular cortical regions in the brain, which underpin accurate risk appraisal and decision-making, and in the insular cortex.[34]

Another neurobiological field of research is the role of endogenous steroids in financial risk-taking. In recent studies from a London trading floor which sampled a group of seventeen males under real working conditions, it was found from a trader's morning saliva samples that his testosterone levels predicted the profitability of the day's trades. It was also found that a trader's cortisol rose with both the variance of his trading results and the volatility of the

29 I. Pérez de Castro et al., 'Concurrent Positive Association between Pathological Gambling and Functional DNA Polymorphisms at the MAO-A and the 5-HT Transporter Genes', *Molecular Psychiatry* (2002), vol. 7, pp. 927–8.

30 D. E. Comings et al., 'The Additive Effects of Neurotransmitter Genes in Pathological Gambling', *Clinical Genetics* (2001), vol. 60, pp. 107–116.

31 K. S. Blair et al., 'The Role of 5-HTTLPR in Choosing the Lesser of Two Evils, the Better of Two Goods: Examining the Impact of 5-HTTLPR Genotype and Tryptophan Depletion in Object Choice', *Psychopharmacology* (2008), vol. 196, pp. 29–38.

32 L. Clark et al., 'Differential Effects of Insular and Ventromedial Prefrontal Cortex Lesions on Risky Decision-Making', *Brain* (2008), vol. 131, pp. 1311–22.

33 Martin P. Paulus and Murray B. Stein, 'An Insular View of Anxiety', *Biological Psychiatry* (2006), vol. 60, pp. 383–7.

34 J. M. Coates and J. Herbert, 'Endogenous Steroids and Financial Risk Taking on a London Trading Floor', *Proceedings of the National Academy of Sciences*, 22 April 2008.

market. These results suggested that higher testosterone may contribute to economic return, whereas cortisol production is increased by risk. The authors went on to postulate that since testosterone and cortisol are known to have cognitive and also behavioural effects, if the acutely elevated steroids they observed were to persist or increase as volatility rose they might shift risk preferences and even affect a trader's ability to engage in rational choice.[35]

These findings and others seem relevant to the neurobiology of hubris syndrome as a condition in which undue confidence leads to (a) impaired risk appraisal, (b) inability to foresee undesirable outcomes and (c) dangerous decision-making and much harm to others. They also suggest that forms of narcissistic personality disorder can remit, as well as arise *de novo* in adult life. It is not far-fetched, therefore, to postulate that hubris syndrome is both acquired and likely to abate once the context of power has changed. This is discussed in relation to George W. Bush in Chapter 7. The neuroscientific explanations are but one factor in a complex area of human behaviour. We are learning more all the time but in the absence of any magic cure it is imprudent to say the least to put all our research eggs in the neurobiological basket. There is considerable overlap. The sort of evidence that is currently available points to a multifactorial basis being behind hubris syndrome and therefore it is wise to keep different approaches drawing knowledge from many different disciplines.

An exceptional book is *A First Rate Madness*[36] by Nassir Ghaemi,

35 Sarah C. Lidstone PhD, Michael Schulzer MD PhD, Katherine Dinelle MSc, Edwin Mak BSc, Vesna Sossi PhD, Thomas J. Ruth PhD, Raul de la Fuente-Fernández MD, Anthony G. Phillips PhD and A. Jon Stoessl MD, 'Effects of Expectation on Placebo-Induced Dopamine Release in Parkinson's Disease', *Archives of General Psychiatry* (2010), vol. 67(8), pp. 857–65.
36 Nassir Ghaemi, *A First Rate Madness. Uncovering the links between Leadership and Mental Illness* (Penguin Press, reprint edition 2013). Nassir Ghaemi, Christos Liapis and David Owen, 'The Psychopathology of Power', Chapter 2, *The Intoxication of Power*, ed. Peter Garrard and Graham Robinson (Palgrave Macmillan, 2016).

Professor of Psychiatry at Tuft's University School of Medicine and Director of the Moods Disorder Programme at Tufts Medical Center in Boston, in which he argues the very qualities that mark those with mood disorders – realism, empathy, resilience and creativity, also make for the best leaders in times of crisis. With Nassir Ghaemi's encouragement I was involved a little with a literature review of the psychological traits that might be associated with hubris syndrome, characterised by unrealistic judgements made by leaders which cause mistaken and harmful decisions. A large amount of experimental psychological research has shown that normal individuals (that is, people with no depressive symptoms or other psychopathology) tend to be more optimistic than circumstances warrant, and often have an excessively unrealistic sense of control over their environment. This normal tendency has been termed 'positive illusion', as opposed to 'depressive realism'.

The role of positive illusion, which occurs with normality and mental health, is intriguing. If this review is correct, a central risk factor for hubris syndrome could be normal mental health, which is associated with mild positive illusion. In the context of power, this mild positive illusion expands into full-blown hubris. The mechanism of this process needs to be further explored. It could be that the real world tends to correct normal individuals with negative feedback if they start to become too illusionary. But in the setting of power, such external influences may be diminished, and the process of being in power itself may magnify positive illusion into hubris syndrome. In other words, the circumstances of power may act as an effect modifier, allowing for normal positive illusion to become hubristic behaviour.

The Greeks were clear that hubris was a word describing a very unattractive feature in a person's behaviour, often expressed in contempt for others. Contempt, when present in a person of power, is almost always a confirmation of hubris syndrome.

The Somatic Marker Hypothesis (SMH) (Bechara and Damasio,

2005; Damasio, 1994) and the associated program of research (Dunn et al., 2006) provides some physiological evidence for the visceral ('gut feel') affective responses in decision making under uncertainty and risk.[37] Another very interesting piece of research is a paper on the 'Effects of expectation on placebo induced dopamine release in Parkinson's Disease' (Lidstone et al, 2010)[38] and an article by Erik Vance (2014)[39] in *Discover* magazine makes things clearer in layman's language about what Sarah Lidstone, who had led the brain-imaging experiment, had done and I describe this in some detail in the Foreword to *The Intoxication of Power. Interdisciplinary Insights.*[40]

Parkinson's patients are especially susceptible to the placebo effect — the phenomenon by which a condition improves solely because the patient believes treatment *has* occurred. When Lidstone's team analysed their patients' brain activity, they found the PET images showed dopamine, in Vance's words, 'flooding the synapses in the crucial motor control region of their brains, just as surely as from a dose of medication. It was the first time placebo responses in Parkinson's disease had been definitively linked to a natural burst of dopamine.'

Is this cementing of gut feelings and expectations an explanation for how hubris syndrome appears to stay for months and years in someone who has acquired it but may recede when power is no

37 Bechara, A. and Damasio, A. R. (2005). The somatic marker: A neural theory of economic decision. *Games and Economic Behaviour,* 52: 336-372. Damasio, A. R. (1994). *Descartes' Error: Emotion, Reason, and the Human Brain.* New York: G. P. Putnam and Sons. Dunn, B.D., Dalgleish, T. and Lawrence, A.D. (2006). The somatic marker hypothesis: A critical evaluation. *Neuroscience and Behavioural Reviews,* 30: 239-271.
38 Lidstone, S.C., Schulzer, M., Dinell, K., Mak, E., Sossi, V., Ruth, T.J., de la Fuente-Fernandez, R., Phillips, A.G and Stoessl, A.J. (2010). Effects of expectation on placebo-induced dopamine release in Parkinson disease. *Archives of General Psychiatry,* 67(8), 857-865.
39 Vance, E. (2014). Power of the placebo. *Discover* Magazine, 7 July 2014.
40 Ed., Peter Garrard, Graham Robinson, *The Intoxication of Power. Interdisciplinary Insights* (Palgrave Macmillan, 2016). Foreword by David Owen.

longer being exercised? Hopefully in a decade we will have learnt much more about an in built brain mechanism that allows some of the powerful to acquire hubris syndrome but not others. I suspect that there is more than one mechanism that triggers hubris syndrome inside the brain.

In a public lecture entitled the 'Neurobiology of decision making: gender and the exercise of power', as part of a seminar at the Royal Society of Medicine on 9 May 2017, Professor Trevor Robbins of the University of Cambridge focused on confidence in judgements, excessive confidence, restlessness, recklessness and impulsiveness.[41] We can all agree that important brain aspects of decision-making resides in the frontal lobes of the brain. It is what goes on there which is becoming better understood.

Robbins characterises decision-making as an effortful and stressful activity and that holding power involves intense decision-making. He goes on to argue that chronic stress depletes serotonin in the brain, and studies show that under conditions of serotonin depletion 'reversal learning' gets impaired (ie the ability to reverse on winning strategies when the strategy starts delivering losses). He cites the fact that 'If you deplete serotonin in the monkey brain . . . you have colossal deficits in reversal learning. So the monkey will continue to take the previously-rewarded option, which is now punished. They're rigid in their decision-making behaviour.' He says, 'Serotonin has something to do with the flexibility of your decision-making, and it's responsive to stress.'

He then states that 'The Hubris Syndrome could be an inevitable consequence of chronic risky decision-making under stress.' As well as this focus on serotonin and stress he also covers the general role of the frontal lobes. 'Frontal lobes are the organ of uncertainty

---

41 Robbins, T., W. Neurobiology of decision making, gender and the exercise of power', RSM, 9 May 2017. https://videos.rsm.ac.uk/video/neurobiology-of-decision-making-gender-and-the-exercise-of-power

and doubt. They are the organs which are cutting back on your tendency to be too confident.' He says of dopamine and reward and social dominance, 'there is something about dopamine and power, if you like or social influence, at least in monkeys.'

What Robbins is indicating is a stress model for hubris syndrome. Serotonin pathways originate in the mid brain in the raphe nuclei and innervate widespread regions of the cortex. The frontal cortex in rats has, what Robbins describes as, 'the executive power from its back projections to control the level of activity in the serotonergic neurones.' Robbins concludes with the hypothesis 'that the Hubris Syndrome could be a consequence of deficient decision-making under chronic stress.' 'A little bit of stress' he says, 'is good, probably improves decision-making, but too much will deplete the system.'

I have no doubt that stress is *the* factor most commonly found in all people in power and in particular those acquiring hubris syndrome. If we can do more research into its linkage to hubris it offers a very real opportunity for improving decision-making. Those close to people in power, their wives or husbands or other family members, can go direct to these individuals and urge them to reduce stress. Professional advisers can explain in scientific terms when excessive hours of working, travelling, particularly across time zones, and the exclusion of hobbies, sporting activities and leisure, can do to their decision-making. Destressing these individuals' lives will not be easy but it is achievable. In our paper in *Brain* Jonathan Davidson and I drew up two tables. Table 1 showed some US Presidents who could be said to have had hubris syndrome but all but President George W. Bush had had other mental illnesses which disqualified them from the diagnosis of hubris syndrome.

Another table amongst British Prime Ministers judged four had developed hubris syndrome while in office: Lloyd George, Chamberlain, Thatcher and Blair.

21

Table 1 Hubris syndrome amongst the 18 US Presidents in office since 1908

Presidents	Related illnesses to hubris	Impairment evident to others or sought treatment	Hubristic traits	Hubris syndrome
Theodore Roosevelt 1901–09	Bipolar disorder	Yes	Yes	No
Woodrow Wilson 1913–21	Anxiety disorder Major depressive disorder Personality change due to stroke	Yes	Yes	?
Franklin D Roosevelt 1933–45	None	No	Yes	No
John F. Kennedy 1961–63	Addison's disease Amphetamine abuse	Yes	Yes	No
Lyndon B. Johnson 1963–69	Bipolar 1 disorder	Yes	Yes	No
Richard Nixon 1969–74	Alcoholic abuse	Yes	Yes	?
George W. Bush 2001–09	History of alcohol-related problems	Yes	Yes	Yes

? uncertain – probable.

Table 2 Hubris syndrome amongst the 26 UK Prime Ministers in office since 1908

Prime Ministers	Related illnesses to hubris	Impairment evident to others or sought treatment	Hubristic traits	Hubris syndrome
Herbert Asquith 1908–16	Alcohol abuse	Yes	Yes	No
David Lloyd George 1916–22	None	Yes	Yes	Yes
Neville Chamberlain 1937–40	None	Yes	Yes	Yes
Winston Churchill 1940–45. 1951–55	Major depressive disorder cyclothymic features	Yes	Yes	No
Anthony Eden 1955–57	Amphetamine abuse	Yes	Yes	No
Margaret Thatcher 1979–90	None	Yes	Yes	Yes
Tony Blair 1997–2007	None	Yes	Yes	Yes

In short, hubris syndrome is an identifiable change in personality, a trait rather than a disorder, occurring in individuals who occupy positions of power and influence. It is a syndrome of people who are not diagnosed as having any identifiable psychiatric condition such as depression. Before they become powerful they can and often are described as 'normal' and may have been chosen for their position of power by well-designed selection procedures, or democratic elections. The onset of the syndrome bears some relationship to the time they have exercised power and in some cases the diagnostic signs and symptoms seem to ease with the passing of power.

Lloyd George is discussed in Chapter 2, George W. Bush and Tony Blair in Chapter 7, and Neville Chamberlain, Margaret Thatcher and Emmanuel Macron in Chapter 10.

In 2006 *The Journal of Nervous and Mental Disease* published a paper entitled 'Mental Illness in US Presidents between 1776 and 1974'.[42] It concluded the likelihood with varying degrees of confidence that 49 per cent of Presidents had major mental illnesses and 27 per cent of these suffered such disorders during their term of office.

The ten Presidents who exhibited psychopathology during their Presidential terms, which, in a number of instances, produced untoward or unexpected changes evident to others. In some cases (eg Pierce), associates commented that he was not the person who had victoriously campaigned for office. Other notable examples in this category are Taft, Wilson, Coolidge, and Hoover.

Two Presidents, Pierce and Coolidge, tragically and unexpectedly lost favourite sons either immediately before (Pierce) or during office (Coolidge). Pierce may have suffered from post traumatic stress disorder and he and his wife saw their son decapitated in front of their eyes in a railway accident. Adams lost a son towards the end of his term in office and Lincoln lost his favourite son. Kennedy

---

42 'Mental Illness in US Presidents (1776-1974)', *The Journal of Nervous and Mental Disease,* vol. 194, Number 1, January 2006.

Table 3 Psychiatric Disorders in US Presidents (1776–1974)

President	Diagnosis (Identified by Raters)*	Confidence Level	Evident in Office	Persistent or Recurrent	Impaired, Evident to Others or Sought Treatment	DSM-IV Criteria
J. Adams (1797-1801)	Bipolar II disorder (296.89)	1	Y	Y	Y	Y
Jefferson (1801-1809)	Social phobia (non-generalized) (300.23)	2	N	Y	Y	N
Madison (1809-1817)	Major depressive disorder (296.2)	1	N	Y	Y	Y
J. Q. Adams (1825-1829)	Major depressive disorder (296.2)	1	Y	Y	Y	Y
Pierce (1853-1857)	Alcohol dependence (303.9)	1	Y	Y	Y	Y
Lincoln (1861-1865)	Major depressive disorder (296.2)	1	Y	Y	Y	Y
	Major depressive disorder, recurrent, with psychotic features (296.34)					
Grant (1869-1877)	Alcohol dependence (305.9)	1	N	Y	Y	Y
	Social phobia (300.23)	1	N	Y	?	Y
Hayes(1877-1881)	Specific phobia (blood) (300.29)	2	N	Y	Y	Y
	Major depressive disorder (296.2)	1	N	Y	?	Y
Garfield (1881)	Depressive disorder NOS (311)	1	Y	Y	Y	Y
T. Roosevelt (1901-1909)	Bipolar 1 disorder (296.44)	1	Y	*Y	Y	Y
Taft (1909-1913)	Breathing-related sleep disorder (780.59)	1	Y	Y	Y	Y
Wilson (1913-1921)*	Anxiety disorder NOS (300.0)	1	N	Y	Y	Y
	Generalized anxiety disorder (300.02)	1	Y	Y	Y	Y
	Major depressive disorder (296.3)	1	Y	Y	Y	Y
	Personality change due to stroke (310.1)	1	Y	Y	Y	Y
Harding (1921-1923)	Somatoform disorder NOS (300 81)	1	N	Y	Y	Y
Coolidge (1923-1929)	Social phobia (300.23)	1	N	Y	Y	Y
	Major depressive disorder (296.2)	1	Y	Y	Y	Y
	Hypochondriasis (300.7) (2)	2	Y	Y	N	Y
Hoover (1929-1933)	Major depressive disorder (296.2)	1	Y	Y	Y	Y
Eisenhower (1953-1961)	Major depressive disorder (296 2)	1	N	Y	Y	Y
L.B. Johnson (1963-1969)	Bipolar 1 disorder (296.5)	1	Y	Y	Y	Y
Nixon (1969-1974)	Alcohol abuse (305.00)	1	Y	Y	Y	Y

*Diagnoses given were anxiety disorder NOS (300.0) (K. C.) generalized anxiety disorder (300.2) (J. D.), and major depressive disorder (296.3) (M. S.)

24

suffered a stillborn child. His drug abuse is not included, surprisingly, in this list, but it is dealt with in Chapter 5. Jackson entered the White House distraught over the loss of his wife and Presidents Tyler and Wilson both lost wives while in office. Three Presidents had the diagnosis of social phobia.

There have been many attempts to prove that President Trump suffers from a mental illness sufficient to find its place in the classification of mental illness as in Jonathan Davidson's Table 3 above from *Psychiatric Disorders in US Presidents 1776-1974* to which I have previously referred. I can find no evidence for Trump fitting into any categorisation. He does not appear to have bipolar disorder or Narcissistic Personality Disorder. Three Presidents in the above table are cited with having social phobia. Trump himself makes frequent references to his being a 'germophobe' but to be a psychiatric illness it would need to be far more disabling than it appears to be, but it is a sign he may have more anxiety than he allows to surface.

About five in one hundred people have some degree of social phobia with women two or three times more likely to be affected. A phobia is also a fear. Many people have fears about flying (aerophobia); a fear of heights (acrophobia); fear of storms, lightning and thunder (astrophobia). A fear of dogs (cynophobia), is allegedly something from which the German Chancellor Angela Merkel suffers and that was exploited by President Putin who brought his dog into the room when they were talking. There is also quite commonly a fear of snakes (ophidophobia); a fear of spiders (arachnophobia); open spaces, sometimes confining people to staying in their own homes (agoraphobia). Less common is mysophobia surrounding a fear when seeing holes clustered together in the form of sponges or a honeycomb (trypophobia). All of these fears are normally managed by people and reflect an underlying anxiety that often does not interfere markedly with a person's life. For example a germophobe can make special arrangements in the way their food is prepared or the frequency in which they wash their hands. It is when their fear becomes overwhelming and disabling that social phobia is diagnosed and that is not Trump's situation.

A study of mental illness in British Prime Ministers was also undertaken by Jonathan Davidson. He trained as a doctor in the UK before moving to the US. His book *Downing Street Blues*[43] studied 51 Prime Ministers of which 37 appear to have experienced mental disorders or significant symptoms. Table 4 below draws extensively on his original table but has been adapted and does not go back quite so far in history but commences at the same time as in Table 3 and cuts off as in that Table in 1974.

Where medical professionals diagnose political leaders, retrospectively, as having suffered from a mental illness and they are also national heroes, the public is often less willing to accept the diagnosis. Bipolar disorder is a case in point, and some psychiatrists have ascribed the condition to Prime Minister Winston Churchill. Bipolar disorder in Churchill's day was called manic depression. Someone had to have had a history of at least one clear-cut manic episode and at least one episode of an affective disorder, usually presenting as depression but which could also present as anxiety. In the past the manic episode often had to be very florid for the diagnosis to be made and the reluctance to diagnose was, in part, because there was no treatment. The term hypomania was used for patients with a mild mood change. Once lithium was found to be a successful treatment the term 'bipolar disorder' began to be used more often. Doctors were more ready to make the diagnosis as it became progressively easier to treat and bipolar disorder began to be seen as a spectrum illness. In this process the sharp edges of manic depression have become more blurred. Hypomania leads into bipolar-II disorder, milder than the depression and the mania of bipolar-I, both of which in the past would have been seen together as manic depression.

---

43 Jonathan Davidson, *Downing Street Blues. A History of Depression and other Mental Afflictions in British Prime Ministers* (McFarland & Company, 2011).

Table 4. Psychiatric Disorders in UK Prime Ministers 1793–1974

Prime Minister	Years in office	Type of problem	Treatment Received	Impaired as Prime Minister
William Pitt the Younger	1783 – 1801 and 1804 – 1806	Alcohol abuse; social anxiety	Yes	Yes
Henry Addington	1801 – 1804	Social anxiety	No	No
William Grenville	1806 – 1807	Dementia; insomnia	No	No
Duke of Portland	1807 – 1809 (2ⁿᵈ time)	Social anxiety	No	No
Earl of Liverpool	1812 – 1827	Generalized anxiety	No	No
Viscount Goderich	1827 – 1828	Anxiety	No	Yes
Duke of Wellington	1828 – 1830 and 1834	Asperger's disorder; depression	No	No
Viscount Melbourne	1834 and 1835-41	Depression; sleep apnea; tic disorder	No	Yes
Sir Robert Peel	1834 – 1835 and 1841-46	Social anxiety	No	No
Lord John Russell	1846 – 1852 and 1865-66	Depression (grief); social anxiety	No	Yes
The Earl of Derby	1852; 1858-59 1866-68	Depression (?seasonal); opioid misuse	No	Yes
Earl of Aberdeen	1852 – 1855	Depression (grief)	No	Yes
Benjamin Disraeli	1868; 1874-80;	Depression (?seasonal)	Yes	No
William Ewart Gladstone	1868 –74; 1880–5; 1886; 1892-4 11892-94	Bipolar; paraphilia	Yes	Yes
Lord Salisbury	1885-6; 1886-92; 1895-1902	Depression	Yes	No
Earl of Rosebery	1894 – 1895	Depression (grief); insomnia; drug use disorder	Yes	Yes
Arthur Balfour	1902 – 1905	Depression (grief)	No	No
Henry Campbell–Bannerman	1905 – 1908	Adjustment, grief; marital	No	Yes
Herbert Asquith	1908 – 1916	Alcohol abuse; grief	No	Yes
David Lloyd George	1916 – 1922	Depression; somatoform	Yes	Yes
Andrew Bonar Law	1922 – 1923	Depression (grief)	No	Yes
Stanley Baldwin	1923-24; 1924-29 and 1935-37	Generalised anxiety; social anxiety; depression; tic disorder	Yes	Yes
Ramsay MacDonald	1924; 1929-35	Depression; dementia	Yes	Yes
Neville Chamberlain	1937 – 1940	Depression	Yes	No
Winston Churchill	1940-45; 1951 -1955	Depression; dementia	Yes	Yes
Anthony Eden	1955 – 1957	Anxiety; amphetamine and barbiturate misuse	Yes	Yes
Harold Macmillan	1957 – 1963	Depression (?seasonal); social anxiety	Yes	No
Harold Wilson	1964-70; 1974-76	Dementia	No	No
Edward Heath	1970 – 1974	Hypothyroidism; social anxiety	Yes	Yes

Hypomania is an exhilaration when one becomes enthused, full of energy and bounding self-confidence. Estimates vary but more than fourteen million people in the United States suffer from mood disorders, depression or anxiety and of these more than two million are likely to suffer from bipolar disorder, to distinguish it from the unipolar disorder of depression alone. There have been many genetic and biochemical studies of bipolar disorder but the biological underpinning remains uncertain.

The following signs and symptoms could all play a role in diagnosing the manic phase of bipolar disorder:

1. Increased energy, activity and restlessness
2. Excessively 'high', euphoric mood
3. Extreme irritability
4. Racing thoughts and talking very fast, jumping from one idea to another
5. Distractability, inability to concentrate well
6. Little sleep needed
7. Unrealistic beliefs in one's abilities and powers
8. Poor judgement
9. A lasting period of behaviour that is different from usual
10. Increased sexual drive
11. Abuse of drugs, particularly cocaine, alcohol and sleeping medications
12. Provocative, intrusive or aggressive behaviour
13. Denial that anything is wrong
14. Spending sprees.[44]

The public seem ready to accept that their heroes suffered from bouts of depression but are less willing to acknowledge manic behaviour. This definitely applies to Winston Churchill and much the same reservations are heard over Theodore Roosevelt. No one

---

44 Source: MedicineNet website.

denies that Churchill was frequently cast into deep sloughs of depression, which he himself called his 'Black Dog' moods. But there is considerable resistance to the diagnosis of mania – either because of a feeling that he never had obvious clinical episodes or because, even if they might have occurred, there was little pathological about them, overall people prefer to see Churchill as a unique figure.

The same sense of uniqueness many ascribe to Franklin Roosevelt. It looked as if he might have been taken over by hubris when, in 1937, he fought and lost a battle with Congress over the Judicial Branch Reorganization Plan, affecting the nomination of justices to the Supreme Court. In the words of Jeff Shesol in his book *Supreme Power*, after the second inauguration, the United States 'was now closer to one-party rule than it had been since Reconstruction'.[45] In early February 1937 Roosevelt announced publicly that he planned to pack the Supreme Court and was asking Congress, where the Senate contained seventy-six Democrats, to enlarge the court from nine to fifteen. He had every intention of adding six liberals to the bench to stop in one fell swoop the Court's majority obstructing his New Deal. Yet on 22 July the Senate rejected the Court Bill by seventy votes to twenty. Roosevelt's defeat, so went the perceived wisdom and newspaper comment, was easy to explain. 'Why would Roosevelt embrace an idea as preposterous as packing the Court? Hubris. What made him think he could get away with it? Hubris. Why did he refuse to listen to reason? Hubris.[46]

Shesol persuasively argues that hubris 'alone is an insufficient answer to the question of what went wrong' in 1937 for Franklin Roosevelt. He writes:

---

45 Jeff Shesol, *Supreme Power: Franklin Roosevelt vs the Supreme Court* (New York: W. W. Norton, 2010), p. 239.
46 Ibid., p. 507.

It was not a choice that Roosevelt made impulsively. It may have been driven – to a dangerous degree – by ego and emotion, but it was also the product of reason. It may have been wrong, but it was not rash. Neither was it made in a vacuum. By the time of Roosevelt's second inauguration, there was a growing national consensus that something had to be done about the Court – that either Congress or, more likely, the President would have to end the impasse.[47]

Roosevelt's temperament was assessed by his wife, Eleanor, a formidable individual in her own right, a moral force behind the President's New Deal, forthright in giving her views and ready to criticise the President. 'You made up your mind to do a thing and you did it to the best of your ability. If it went sour then you started it all over again and did something else but you never spent time refining.' In all these senses President Roosevelt was no more narcissistic than most politicians. He cheerily said to the Cabinet, while mixing cocktails, immediately after the Senate defeat that he intended to have a great deal of fun in the months ahead and it was time for the country to laugh again. In August he 'cocked a snook' at the Senate by nominating for a vacancy amongst the nine members of the Supreme Court one of their own, Senator Black, safe in the knowledge that they would feel unable to reject a colleague at the hearings even though he had been an ardent supporter of packing the Court. Roosevelt was correct and the Senate ratified his appointment.

Yet why did Roosevelt essentially make a major misjudgement of the Senate's readiness to support packing the Court? The answer, in as much as there can be any one explanation, probably lies in the death in April 1936 of Louis Howe who was his first very close associate and a 'toe-holder', a term coined by Louis Howe himself.

---

47 Ibid., p. 249–50.

He and the President's wife, Eleanor Roosevelt, along with Missy LeHand, his secretary, and Harry Hopkins who filled the gap left by Howe, and Judge Rosenman from New York, were all 'toe-holders'. All helped at various times to constrain Franklin Roosevelt so that he did not develop hubris syndrome and that his mood was tempered by debate and controversy eased by humour.

What are the wider lessons from Roosevelt's toe-holders? Of course, his was a special arrangement. These people were ready to provide the extra legs because the President no longer had the use of his own. They were ready, with the exception of Eleanor, to dedicate a large part of their own private life to be with him in varying degrees, providing constant attendance way beyond office hours. There was too the further complexity of love for the man, which in the case of LeHand was clearly sensual; whether sexual or not it involved intimacy and physical contact between the two of them. When she had to leave the White House in March 1942 after a stroke, as level-headed a man as Rosenman told his friend, Justine Felix Frankfurter, it was 'a calamity of world dimension' and she was 'one of the very few people who was not a yes man.'

But there was something more and of critical importance. The President *wanted* criticism. He knew that he was by temperament hubristic and that he was more likely to make wiser decisions if those in his immediate circle felt free to criticise. Even in his appointments such as that of George Marshall, his chief of defence, he sought out independent-minded people. Like most confident people he thrived on argument, indeed on conflict in arguments.

One of the great skills of Harry Hopkins, Roosevelt's replacement for Howe, was that he 'ventured on no ground that Roosevelt had not charted'. In July 1941 in Moscow he carried out his first meeting with Stalin, who at that stage Roosevelt had not met, with 'no written instructions whatsoever from Roosevelt as to what he should say or do. The President could and did trust him fully.' In Hopkins's *White House Papers* there is a fascinating report on Stalin. 'He's built close to the ground like a football coach's dream of a small tackle. He's about five feet six, about a hundred and ninety pounds. His hands are huge as hard as his mind. His voice is harsh but ever under control.'

By the start of the Second World War, in May 1940, Hopkins, to some, was a Svengali, a Rasputin, a Machiavelli. But not to the men who mattered. According to General Marshall, Hopkins 'rendered a service to his country which will never be even vaguely appreciated.' Henry Stimson, Roosevelt's Secretary for War and no New Dealer, said: 'The more I think of it, the more I think it is a God Send that he should be at the White House.' Churchill loved Hopkins's readiness to get down to brass tacks, quoting him as typically saying: '"Surely Mr President, here is the point we have got to settle. Are we going to face it or not." Faced it always was, and being faced, was conquered.'[48] Churchill once joked that after the war was over he would make Hopkins a British Peer and he had the exact title, 'Lord Root of the Matter'.

Churchill was an exuberant personality like Roosevelt. His exuberance was contained by many factors, respect for parliamentary democracy, a sense of humour and of history, and he had a toe-holder in the person of his wife Clementine. She wrote to him in a loving, frank letter to warn him at a moment of national peril on 27 June 1940 of being thought to be 'contemptuous', a classical sign of starting to develop hubris syndrome, which fortunately did not develop. Wives are often crucial toe-holders for husbands in power, certainly my wife was. Another famous toe-holder was Bonar Law for Lloyd George (See p.57).

---

48 Sherwood, *The White House Papers of Harry L. Hopkins, vol. 1*, pp. 344–5, 6–7, 3, 13.

10 Downing Street,
Whitehall
27 June 1940

My Darling,

I hope you will forgive me if I tell you something I feel you ought to know.

One of the men in your entourage (a devoted friend) has been to me & told me that there is a danger of your being generally disliked by your colleagues and subordinates because of your rough sarcastic & overbearing manner – It seems your Private Secretaries have agreed to behave like school boys & 'take what's coming to them' & then escape out of your presence shrugging their shoulders – Higher up, if an idea is suggested (say at a conference) you are supposed to be so contemptuous that presently no ideas, good or bad, will be forthcoming. I was astonished and upset because in all these years I have been accustomed to all those who have worked with & under you, loving you – I said this, & I was told 'No doubt it's the strain' –

Winston. I must confess that I have noticed a deterioration in your manner; & you are not as kind as you used to be.

It is for you to give the Orders & if they are bungled – except for the King, the Archbishop of Canterbury & the Speaker, you can sack anyone & everyone. Therefore with this terrific power you must combine urbanity, kindness and if possible Olympic calm. You used to quote:– 'On ne règne sur les âmes que par le calme –' I cannot bear that those who serve the Country & yourself should not love you as well as admire and respect you –

Besides you won't get the best results by irascibility & rudeness. They *will* breed either dislike or a slave mentality. (Rebellion in War time being out of the question!)

Please forgive your loving devoted & watchful

Clemmie (drawing of cat)

PS I wrote this at Chequers last Sunday, tore it up but here it is now.[49]

---

49 Soames, *Clementine Churchill by Her Daughter*, p. 291.

What Clementine Churchill, watching her husband, carefully describes in her letter is not the manic phase of bipolar disorder, but a description of gathering hubris, incipient always within Churchill but never progressed into full-blown hubris syndrome.

The conclusive evidence that the behaviour in Winston that worried Clementine during May and June was not manic in form comes from John Colville in his diary entry for 25 June 1940, after dining with Eric Seal, Churchill's principal private secretary since September 1939. He writes about Seal's views on Churchill, 'explaining how much he had changed since becoming Prime Minister. He had sobered down, becoming less violent, less wild, less impetuous.'[50] No one had lived constantly so close to Churchill, able to watch every change in attitude, every aspect of his temperament, as Seal during these months. A careful reading of all *The Churchill War Papers*[51] during this period also shows no hint of manic behaviour.

Revealing of the exceptional character of the man is the picture painted by General Hastings Ismay, Churchill's military chief of staff, in a letter written on 3 April 1942 to General Claude Auchinleck, in the desert of north Africa. 'The Auk', as he was called, had recently been on the receiving end of Churchill's volatile mood:

> You cannot judge the P.M. by ordinary standards: he is not in the least like anyone that you or I have ever met. He is a mass of contradictions. He is either on the crest of the wave, or in the trough: either highly laudatory, or bitterly condemnatory: either in an angelic temper, or a hell of a rage: when he isn't fast asleep he's a volcano. There are no half-measures in his make-up. He is a child

50 Martin Gilbert, *The Churchill War Papers, vol. 2: Never Surrender, May 1940– December 1940* (London: Heinemann, 1994) p. 420.
51 Martin Gilbert, *The Churchill War Papers*, 3 vols (London: Heinemann, 1993– 2000).

of nature with moods as variable as an April day, and he apparently sees no difference between harsh words spoken to a friend, and forgotten within the hour under the influence of friendly argument, and the same harsh words telegraphed to a friend thousands of miles away – with no opportunity for 'making it up'... I think I can lay claim to having been called every name under the sun during the last six months – except perhaps a coward; but I know perfectly well in the midst of these storms that they mean exactly nothing, and that before the sun goes down, I shall be summoned to an intimate and delightfully friendly talk – to 'make it up'.[52]

Whether accounts of his 'crazy state of exultation', of his being either 'on the crest of a wave or in a trough', of there being 'no half measures in his make-up' and of 'bursts of energy and brilliance of performance' coexisting with 'lassitude and gloom' provide enough evidence for a settled diagnosis of bipolar will long be debated; in my view it does not. There is no evidence that Churchill led the War Cabinet into irrational decision-making. It could be said on the contrary that it gave him the inspirational quality to lead the country which in 1940 proved so vital. He was never diagnosed as suffering from manic depression but was diagnosed as having a cyclothymic personality by the distinguished neurologist, Russell Brain, after the war was over in the late 1940s when Churchill was Leader of the Opposition. He did have depression and all his life he was hubristic, but he cannot be said to have acquired hubris syndrome, a diagnosis for which he is anyhow excluded by definition because of his pre-existing depression.

---

52 John Connell, *Auchinleck* (London, Cassell, 1959).

Chapter 1

The Emerging US Presidency: Jefferson, Jackson, Theodore Roosevelt

The American founding fathers designed the Constitution in ways that they thought would not create dominant national political parties. Madison writing in the 15th edition of the *Federalist* wrote 'In the extended republic of United States and among the great variety of interests, parties and sects which it embraces, a coalition of a majority of the whole society could seldom take place on any other principles than those of justice and the general good.' There were many checks and balances that contributed to Madison's view contained within the Constitution of relevance but undoubtedly one of them was the electoral college, a term which never appears in the Constitution, which has as the winner of the presidency the candidate who has the majority of the electoral college votes.

In 1787 the American Constitutional Convention considered using the same system as in the then House of Commons where the members of Parliament chose the Prime Minister, but Madison believed in separating power wherever possible and wanted the electors not to be in the Congress. The US Constitution says that each state shall appoint a number of 'electors' which had to be equal to its representation in Congress including the two senators who represent every state to then formally elect the President of the United States of America.

The Convention initially did a dirty deal in the name of a compromise. The Southern States fearing that slavery would be abolished by a federal government, where the Northern States had not only more people but more electoral votes ensured that the counting system for the 'electors would reflect not only the 'free persons' able to vote but also 'three-fifths of all other persons', which favoured the Southern States. For example, under this arrangement whereas Philadelphia had more 'free persons' eligible to vote than Virginia, Virginia – the largest Southern State – was able to have more electors. After the Civil War with the abolition of slavery and the extension of the franchise to women and all citizens of all colours the electoral college system continues to this day.

Yet while no national political parties might have been the dream, a group combination emerged, and though initially it was not called a party, a Federalist Party soon emerged. Alexander Hamilton, the practical politician is now well known because of the highly successful rap musical that bears his name. He was the co-author of the *Federalist Papers* with Madison, as Secretary to the Treasury, but through his funding measures, certainly had a powerful centralising effect while George Washington was still President. His financially related measures challenged the federalist constitutional purity and continued under subsequent Presidents. The Federalists elected their second and last President, John Adams (1797-1801). Thereafter it was Thomas Jefferson who welded together a National Republican Party. This was still in its infancy in the election of 1801 and Federalists and Republicans were often not on speaking terms. Nevertheless, sensing the danger of a split Jefferson, in his inaugural address, claimed a somewhat spurious unity saying, 'We are all Republicans, we are all Federalists.' But in office he had to swallow much of his federalist rhetoric, particularly over bringing into the Union the state of Louisiana. Even so, he had judged the mood correctly and only 14 electoral votes were cast against him for a second term. Jefferson's shaping of democracy continued after 1809, when out of office and continued to acquire a meaning under President James Madison (1809-1817).

'Jeffersonian democracy', in contrast to 'Jacksonian democracy' stressed the importance of leadership by those of the greatest ability and according to the *Dictionary of American History* it pledged that the central government would withdraw between the boundaries established when the Constitution had been adopted. The federal government would cultivate 'peace, commerce and honest friendship with all nations, entangling alliances with none.' It was also committed to establish 'Equal and exact justice to all men, of whatever state or persuasion, religious or political.'

It was the start of the War of 1812 against Britain that gave a huge boost to the morale of the American people. The perception remaining, when the war was over, was 'according to tradition, proud Britain had been humbled by the irrepressible Republic of the Western World. A transient conviction of intense nationalism took possession of the American people such as was not to be seen again in many a decade.'[53]

The war of 1812 suddenly reemerged in a conversation between President Trump and Canadian Prime Minister Justin Trudeau. In a testy telephone conversation in 2018 after Trump had slapped tariffs on aluminum and steel products and was claiming national security as justification. Trudeau challenged Trump's use of national security and Trump needled him with the remark 'didn't you guys burn down the White House?' In fact it was English marines who did this under the command of Rear Admiral Sir George Cockburn who occupied and destroyed parts of Washington. The President's wife Dolly Madison only just managed to escape with the Presidential silverware and a rolled up portrait of George

---

53 Wilfred E. Brinkley. *American Political Parties. Their Natural History* (Alfred A. Knopf 4th Edition, 1962) p. 97.

Washington hastily cut out from its frame before Cockburn sat down and ate the supper intended for the President. The British forces were retaliating following the American attacks on York, Ontario then part of a British Colony.

The Battle of New Orleans on 8 January 1815 fought so skilfully by Andrew Jackson was a decisive victory for the Americans; fortunately it was overtaken by the signing of the Treaty of Ghent on 24 December 1814 with the British abandoning their absurd demand for, in effect, a buffer zone south of the Great Lakes to separate the US from what became Canada. Then the border settlement of 1846 followed when British Colombia and Oregon settled on the 49th parallel.

In 1816 President James Monroe, standing as a Republican, defeated the Federalist candidate King by 183 electoral votes to 34 and having been elected but before his inauguration in 1817, was given a powerful message by General Andrew Jackson, the hero of the 1815 Battle of New Orleans against the English, at this time someone who few thought a likely candidate for President. 'Now is the time to exterminate the monster called party spirit,' argued Jackson. 'By selecting characters most conspicuous for their probity, virtue, capacity and firmness, without any regard to party, you will go far to, if not entirely, eradicate those feelings, which, on former occasions, threw so many obstacles in the way of government: and perhaps have the pleasure of uniting a people heretofore divided . . .' In fact Aaron Burr, who shot and killed Hamilton in a duel on 11 July 1804, had written to his son-in-law Joseph Alston as early as 1815 suggesting Jackson might be a candidate who could overthrow the Virginia 'oligarchy' of Presidents. By contrast, Jackson was saying as late as 1821, when for the first time he saw himself mentioned as a Democratic candidate, 'Do they think I am such a damned fool as to think myself fit for the presidency . . . I can command a body of men in a rough way, but I am not fit to be President.' [54]

---

54 Ibid Brinkley. p. 107.

Notwithstanding this, Andrew Jackson, commonly called 'Old Hickory', did stand in 1824 against John Quincy Adams, the Secretary of State, and got 90 electoral votes, Adams had only 84 and Crawford 41. In a situation where no candidate had an overall majority the House of Representatives was called on to choose from the top three and they chose Adams.

John Quincy Adams was a stopgap President for four years during which the path was prepared for Jackson to achieve an overwhelming victory by persuading his only realistic rival, John C. Calhoun from the Democratic Party, to become Vice President running on the same ticket. Jackson was America's first populist President. A key element in Jacksonian democracy was to introduce the popular vote as the deciding factor. Jackson was determined to win two terms, and every year in his eight annual messages to Congress he recommended the popular election of the President. For the first time in 1824 estimates of the total popular vote for each candidate were published and Jackson won with 42% of that vote. Jackson voters, thereafter, argued the House of Representatives had flouted the popular vote.

The Democratic Party embraced anti-clericalism, and anti-religious crusades which developed under Jackson's close adviser and his successor as President, Martin Van Buren (1837-1841). The nucleus of Jacksonian support were people of Scottish-Irish stock, proud of their kinsman chieftain, an intense minority with an inflexible tenacity of purpose.[55] They were well-organized, anti-English, anti-monopoly. Nullifying the Tariff Act of 1832 Lincoln drew on Jackson's Proclamation against Nullification for his inaugural election despite being a Republican President. The essence of Jacksonian democracy, by the end of the 1830s, was simple, frugal and unintrusive government according to the *Dictionary of American History* 2003. It has been called *laissez-faire*.

55 Ibid, Brinkley, p. 121.

Opposed to tariffs and this was marked by two Presidential vetoes, Maysville Road in 1830 and the Bank of the United States 1832. In Jackson's own words he saw himself as the protector of 'the humbler members of society – the farmers, mechanics, and laborers.' He was against moneyed, privileged interests seeking to turn the public powers of government to unfair private advantage. He saw tariffs, public works and corporate charters as devices to siphon wealth from the poor to the rich and to steal money from the many to benefit the few.

It is probable today that the American Presidential system is still more likely to throw up a populist President than the British Prime Ministerial system is likely to produce a populist Prime Minister. The last three conservative Prime Ministers have emerged under a system whereby members of the party and the party's MPs, elected on a constituency basis, can determine the choice but with a parliamentary filter set at a percentage level. In the last leadership contest they chose a populist in Johnson.

The definition of a populist used in this book is not as dismissive a term as in some people's vocabulary, particularly among elites in Europe in 2018 where populism is said often with a curled lip and a derogatory meaning. A populist I believe is better defined as someone who wants to make decisions on the basis of the people's wishes but does not exclude acting against the popular will. Yet is someone who wants to give a very high priority to following popular opinion. That less censorious definition fits with Presidents Jackson, Theodore Roosevelt, Woodrow Wilson, Franklin Roosevelt, Truman, Reagan, Clinton, Trump and Boris Johnson.

There have only been four occasions in US history when a US President has been elected without winning in both the electoral college and in the popular vote. The first was in 1876 when Samuel Tilden beat Rutherford D. Hayes in the popular vote, but after a deal called the 'Compromise' in 1879 Hayes became President. The second in 1888 when Benjamin Harrison was elected President while the popular vote was won by Grover Cleveland. The third was the Supreme Court decision settling a recount dispute in the state of Florida, which gave George W. Bush the presidency, though Al Gore won 539,000 more votes in the country as a whole. The fourth and the most recent was the Presidential election in 2016 when Donald Trump won 304 electoral college votes while Hillary Clinton only won 227 but Hillary Clinton surpassed Donald Trump in the popular vote by nearly 2.9 million votes. Trump was sworn in as President on 20 January 2017. Such a result if repeated in 2020 could surely lead to a reassessment of the electoral college system and whether a mature democracy like the USA should consider constitutional change. Trump tweeted on 6 November 2012 at 11.45 am, 'The electoral college is a disaster for a democracy.' On 15 November 2016 at 8.40 am, he tweeted 'The electoral college is actually genius in that it brings all states, including the smaller ones into play.' Winning changed his twitter criticism of the electoral college when he wrongly thought that was where the 2012 election was lost.

Looking across the Atlantic from the UK at the American presidency for a post World War Two generation it is easy to see the dominance of the two party system of Republicans and Democrats as a settled reflection of the American system. Only in 1992 did the intervention of a third party candidate have the potential to have an effect on the result with Ross Perot getting 19% to Bill Clinton's 43% and President George H. W. Bush's 37.4 %. Perot's was the biggest third-party candidate vote since former President Teddy Roosevelt polled 27% with his Bull Moose Party in 1912. But that two party political dominance was itself challenged in the 1930s when the Republican party reached the nadir of its fortunes in the Presidential election of 1936 winning a mere eight votes in the electoral college out of 531. In 1938 the Republicans had only 16 out of 96 Senators, 90 out of 425 Representatives and only five of the 48 state Governors and yet by the 1940s the Republicans bounced back as effective challengers though not winning the presidency until 1952 with Dwight Eisenhower, most frequently referred to as 'Ike'.

Some of the faults of Andrew Jackson can be easily enumerated and not a bad place to start is the fact that Jackson 'had been "married" to another man's wife for several years' though there were some extenuating circumstances.[56] He also 'could, and did, kill in cold blood', in a duel on 30 May 1806 which involved a dispute over a horse race and apparently a slur against his wife by a person called Dickinson. Dickinson shot first and hit Jackson but Jackson cocked his gun again after the trigger caught half way, and killed Dickinson.[57] Jackson was also, as were many at the time, a land speculator and a periodic slave trader with at least 16 slaves being bought between 1790 and 1794.[58] Of course, all this was a long time ago and one must be careful in judging his behaviour now when many things are very different. Jackson also demanded 'full government participation (if not leadership) in eliminating the Indian presence.' In the Burr conspiracy, designed for expelling Spaniards, Jackson learnt by its failure, but only that expulsion should be undertaken by the United States Government not frontiersmen. The Creek War was arguably set off by the Creek Indians who massacred white settlers at Fort Mims, Alabama, but Jackson retaliated and in November 1813 over 300 Red Stick Indians were killed. Jackson had only 15 dead and 85 wounded. He subsequently conducted a raid deep into Indian territory. He also insisted on the execution of one of his soldiers charged with mutiny as an example to discipline his men.

By now he was commanding regular troops as well as militiamen from Tennessee making up some 4,000 men. At a battle on Horseshoe Bend, 557 Indians were counted dead on the ground

---

56 Jon Meacham, *American Lion* (Random House, 2008) p. 22.
57 Ibid, pp. 25-6.
58 Ibid, pp. 56-7, 77.

and an estimated 300 Creeks were dead in the river. His own casualties were 47 dead and 159 wounded. This was presented as a great military victory by Jackson and extravagantly praised but he had defeated not trained soldiers but an undersized 'savage' force fighting mostly without muskets.[59] His reputation as a General was now made, but his health was wrecked and yet his 'willpower had grown to monumental proportions.' He later wrote to the Spanish Governor as a regular army major-general a provocative and insulting letter. 'Be warned of my creed', he wrote, 'An Eye for an Eye, Toothe for Toothe and Scalp for Scalp.'[60]

In a review of Jon Meacham's biography of Jackson, *USA Today* wrote how it 'brings alive a profoundly flawed but dazzlingly charismatic American original'. Meacham writes that Jackson, 'proved the principle that the character of the President matters enormously. Politics is about more than personality; the affairs of a great people are shaped by complex and messy forces that transcend the purely party viewpoint. Those affairs, however, are also fundamentally affected by the complex and messy individuals who wield Presidential power. Jackson was a transformative President in part because he had a transcendent personality.'

Theodore Roosevelt said, 'Jackson had many faults but he was devotedly attached to the Union, and he had no thought of fear when it came to defending his country . . . With the exception of Washington and Lincoln, no man has left a deeper mark on American history; and though there is much in his career to condemn, yet all true lovers of America can unite in paying hearty respect to the memory of a man who was emphatically a true American.'

Unsurprisingly Meacham records that Theodore Roosevelt, despite saying Jackson had many faults, approved of Jackson's 'instinct for the jugular' and capacity to 'recognise his real foe and

---

59 Robert V. Remini, *Andrew Jackson and the Course of American Empire 1767-1821* (Harper & Row, 1977), p. 223.
60 Ibid, p. 233.

strike savagely at the point where danger threatens.' Franklin Roosevelt was also fascinated by Jackson, visiting his house, the Hermitage, on 17 November 1934. He made a point of standing painfully on his leg braces as a matter of honour. In 1941 he invoked Jackson's honoured memory and his 'rugged courageous spirit'. Another Democratic President who honoured the first Democrat President was Harry Truman who had a small bronze of a statue he commissioned a decade earlier outside Kansas City Courthouse for a table in the Oval office. He said of Jackson, 'He wanted sincerely to look after the little fellow' adding 'that's what a President is supposed to do.' It is worth recording at this stage that President Trump also made an early visit to Jackson's home. (See Chapter 11.)

In 1884 Grover Cleveland became President having just beaten the Democrats after the intervention of a party called the Mugwumps. Somewhat surprisingly a major row started over the actions of the British government in regard to the disputed boundary line between British Guinea and Venezuela. The US Secretary of State Richard Olney took a very aggressive line in defining the Monroe Doctrine. 'Today the United States is practically sovereign on this Continent.' To which Lord Salisbury replied 'no nation however powerful are competent to insert into the code of international law, a novel principle which was never recognised before, and which has not since been accepted by the Government.'

In 1889, President Cleveland sent a special message to Congress saying the US regarded British action very seriously as an infringement of the Monroe Doctrine and Congress appropriated funds for a Commission to be established. Fortunately the British had agreed to arbitration in 1896 before the Commission reported and the possibility of war between Britain and the US which had seemed possible in a wave of bellicose feeling was never again to raise its head. But what had raised its head became an American view of sovereignty that persists to this day, namely extraterritorial jurisdiction. Criminal law is accepted by most countries as territorial, not so in the US. The US claims extraterritorial rights in a large number of cases and sometimes, challenges for world order, as in the case of Iran, where they are able to enforce them.

There is an important political link between President Andrew Jackson and President Theodore Roosevelt and it lies in the emergence of respectable populism in the farming communities of the West and the Midwest of America. I owe this insight to Doris Kearns Goodwin's book *The Bully Pulpit*.[61] The farmers found themselves under the not very tender mercies of the grain elevator company that stored their crops and the railroad company that carried their crops to markets. A Nebraska newspaper summed it up, 'We have three crops, corn, freight rates and interest. The farmers farm the land, and the businessmen farm the farmers.' A movement called the Grangers fought for state legislative curbs and when they were introduced corporate interests challenged them in the courts and usually won. The Grangers in 1877 won a famous case *Munn v Illinois* in the Supreme Court but nine years later the Supreme Court in effect reversed its decision by claiming only Congress had the right to dictate commerce between states.

In 1890 the Farmers Alliance, which succeeded the Grangers, was successful in putting up candidates and an activist called Mary Lease who travelled around Kansas speaking for Alliance candidates made the charge which had a somewhat similar resonance 127 years later, in the rust belt states, rather than agricultural states, in the Presidential election of 2016. She charged 'Wall Street owns the country. It is no longer a government of the people, by the people and for the people, but a government of Wall Street, by Wall Street and for Wall Street.' When told the explanation was a surfeit of agricultural production she hit back, 'Overproduction!

---

61 Doris Kearns Goodwin, *The Bully Pulpit. Theodore Roosevelt, William Howard Taft, and the golden age of journalism* (Simon & Schuster, 2013), pp. 191-195.

– when 10,000 little children, so statistics tell us, starve to death every year in the United States.'

In 1892 the Populist Party was formed and though their Presidential candidate that year failed to make his mark, through him the working poor were making their case. The journalist William White was one who heard the Alliance message and who from 1892 to 1895 was writing for Kansas City newspapers ridiculing them for 'demagogy'. His effigy was burned in retaliation. He later changed his mind and had a profound influence on Theodore Roosevelt and White explained his then attitude as stemming from being 'A child of the governing classes, I was blinded by my birthright.' Roosevelt too was no better describing the Alliance as 'pinheaded, anarchistic crank(s).' But he also changed his mind.

William White married in 1895 and soon cut his ties to Kansas and purchased the *Emporia Gazette,* a small town newspaper with a circulation of less than 500 copies. He resolutely stayed there while becoming one of America's best known and frequently quoted journalists. This was possible because of the link he established with McClure's magazine in New York and its young founder editor Sam McClure. They both, with a small group of talented progressive thinkers, developed detailed ideas and strategies for challenging corporate power and were in large part the inspiration for the trust busting legislation associated with President Roosevelt's Administration. At Roosevelt's request the first of many meetings with White took place in 1897 in Washington when Roosevelt was Assistant Secretary of the Navy and doing all he could to prepare the US Navy for war with Spain, which he believed was inevitable. In addition to meetings with White, Roosevelt had a lengthy correspondence with him, during the course of which he exchanged more than 300 letters.

It was as Colonel Teddy Roosevelt, leading his men in a cavalry charge to victory at the battle of San Juan Hill on 1 July 1898, in Cuba in the Spanish–American War, that Roosevelt made his mark with the public. He thereafter stormed his way to the governorship of New York on a popular tide of approval.

After a period of wooing the party machine Roosevelt decided as Governor as a matter of 'plain decency' that the large corporations who had been granted lucrative franchises for such public services as telephone and telegraph lines as well as street railways should pay for their franchises. Not unsurprisingly, Senator Thomas Collier Platt, head of the State Republican machine, an old party boss, was appalled by the legislation because it attacked his longstanding financial supporters and their money which he used not for himself but for ensuring a guaranteed voting majority, part of what Roosevelt called the 'invisible empire'.[62]

Platt wrote to Theodore Roosevelt, 'to my very great surprise, you did a thing which has caused the business community of New York to wonder how far the notions of Populism, as laid down in Kansas and Nebraska, have taken hold upon the Republican Party of the State of New York.' To which Roosevelt in his reply spelt out his definition of populism and the philosophy that he carried into the White House:

> "It seems to me that our attitude should be one of correcting the evils and thereby showing that, whereas the populists, socialists, and others really do not correct the evils at all, or only do so at the expense of producing others in aggravated form, that we Republicans hold the just balance and set our faces as resolutely against improper corporate influence on the one hand as against demagogy and mob rule as the other."

With a little amendment the policy he advocated passed through with Platt's people supporting. The New York State Governorship was, however, never going to hold his ambition. He was chosen as

---

62 Ibid, Goodwin, pp. 246-249.

Vice President to William McKinley who was assassinated on 6 September 1901 and Roosevelt, 43 years old, was inaugurated as President on 14 September.

Theodore Roosevelt, as President, was too pragmatic to be a pure populist but he was sensitive to populist thinking while he kept his own style and standards of good governance. He thought it would be a dreadful calamity if the Republican Party ever became 'subservient to the so-called Wall Street men – to the men of mere wealth, the plutocracy.'

Elected President in 1904 for a second term Roosevelt had, to his credit, stepped down in 1909, as he had rather unwisely promised to do, aged fifty-one, rather than stand again as he was entitled to do under the then Constitution. He was for many Americans a great President to be measured against the administrations of Washington, Lincoln and Franklin Roosevelt. Edmund Morris, Pulitzer Prize-winning biographer of Roosevelt, explains his febrile character by citing the short but perceptive essay of a French writer, Léon Bazalgette, who wrote 'that these floods of apparent aggression, half fierce, half humorous, were more indicative of energy than of serious thought. They were part of the excess that was part of Roosevelt's nature. The weir had constantly to spill, to keep the deep water behind clear and calm.'[63] To the layman words such as 'megalomania' and 'hubris' do not go amiss when attached to Roosevelt. He suffered from periodic depressions, however, throughout his life. Three leading American psychiatrists in their paper published in 2006 claim that it was highly likely that Roosevelt, while President, had suffered from bipolar-I disorder.[64] Nevertheless they concluded that his symptoms had not interfered with his effectiveness or performance in office.

---

63 Edmund Morris, *Theodore Rex* (New York: Random House, 2001), pp. 425-6.
64 Jonathan R.T. Davidson, Kathryn M. Connor and Marvin Swartz, 'Mental Illness in US Presidents between 1776 and 1974: A Review of Biographical Sources', *Journal of Nervous and Mental Disease* (2006), vol. 194, pp. 47–51.

On 31 January 1908 Roosevelt wrote a special message to Congress, audacious and controversial and aligning himself with the progressive left. The *New York Times* wrote of his tendency towards 'delusion', especially with regard to conspiracies against himself. The *New York Sun* called it a 'pretentious diatribe' better referred to psychologists.

There is no clear-cut case of an incontrovertibly manic episode in Roosevelt's life. But there is some evidence of manic tendency. Roosevelt 'slept erratically, but after his 18-hour work day the little sleep he had was sound and refreshing – a *sine qua non* of the hypomanic state'.[65] Yet the distinction between lay people describing Roosevelt as showing signs of megalomania and doctors diagnosing him with hypomania is a fine one. It is claimed that he was in a manic rage when he attacked the *New York World* and the *Indianapolis News* for criminal libel associated with the Panama Canal in 1908, and in a fiery message to Congress on 15 December, he replied to assertions that there was some corrupt action saying: 'The stories were scurrilous and libelous in character and false in every essential particular.' He went on to attack Joseph Pulitzer, the proprietor of the *New York World*, who wrote to the *New York Times* saying he objected strongly to Roosevelt's policy of

> imperialism, militarism, and jingoism; his general lawless and autocratic temper, his contempt of Congress, and his abuse of the courts. I am really sorry that he should be so angry, but the *World* will continue to criticize him without a shadow of fear, even if he should succeed in compelling me to edit the paper from jail.[66]

Internationally he secured peace in 1905 between Japan and Russia, for which he received the Nobel Prize but neither he nor

---

65 Ronald R. Fieve, *Moodswing: Dr Fieve on Depression*, rev. ed. (New York: William Morrow, 1989), pp. 132–3.

66 'Mr Pulitzer's reply', *New York Times*, 16 December 1908.

America were much involved in European politics. At home his clean up of politics was accompanied by a fall in the lynch rate. His trust busting established rules for a market economy. Over the handling of black soldiers in the Brownsville incident in August 1906 Roosevelt made and acknowledged serious mistakes. Roosevelt left office as the first great political environmentalist, having created five national parks and eighteen national monuments. He achieved this by cajoling authority out of Congress or by making executive orders. He had a fierce temper, was domineering, impatient and at times bellicose, but he was also much loved.

Roosevelt deeply regretted stepping down for Taft. The two men were friends. Hubris, bipolar disorder or both may explain why he decided, most unwisely, to fight both Taft and Woodrow Wilson, the Democrat nominee, as a third-party candidate in the Presidential election in 1912. He was shot at in November during the campaign, but was saved by a steel spectacles case he kept in his breast pocket. He went on speaking despite a blood-stained shirt, with a bullet lodged in his chest, proclaiming: 'It takes more than that to kill a Bull Moose!' His intervention, as a third party Progressive candidate, meant a split Republican Party, and so the Democrat, Woodrow Wilson won the election. Thayer wrote of this ill-fated electoral challenge: 'If he could not rule he would ruin. The old allegation that he must be crazy was of course revived.'[67] 'For the first time, a retired President returned to the electoral battlefield, challenging a sitting President from his former party, no less. And for the first time since 1860 there was a serious fourth-party candidate in the race who had no chance of winning but who was a veritable lightning rod.'[68] Eugene V. Debs, founding father of the Socialist Democratic Party, fought five Presidential elections starting in 1900; attracting 3 per cent of the vote in 1904 and 1908 and 6 per cent in 1912.

---

67 Candice Millard, *The River of Doubt: Into the Unknown Amazon* (London: Little, Brown, 2005), p. 13.
68 A. Scott Berg, *Wilson* (Simon & Schuster, 2013), p. 236.

As the election developed it became a tussle between Roosevelt and Wilson in which Roosevelt figuratively was throwing political eggs which Wilson sensibly ignored. Roosevelt spoke of the New Nationalism. Wilson was the Jeffersonian proponent of less government. Roosevelt was by now an overt populist.

After Roosevelt fought and lost – though he beat the incumbent, President Taft – he 'suffered from what his family delicately referred to as a "bruised spirit"'; so concerned were they about his state of mind that they discreetly asked his doctor to come for a visit. Roosevelt, who had become a political pariah, confessed to him, 'I have been unspeakably lonely. You don't know how lonely it is for a man to be rejected by his own kind.'[69]

On 6 January 1919 Theodore Roosevelt died aged sixty. His friend and fellow naturalist, John Burroughs, with whom he had done so much for the environment, creating the National Park system, said of this quite remarkable man: 'The world is bleaker and colder for his absence from it. We shall not look upon his like again.'[70]

---

69 Ibid., p. 14
70 Ibid., pp. 335–6.

Chapter 2

Moralism v. Opportunism: Woodrow Wilson and Lloyd George

The first unequivocally international US President was Woodrow Wilson and while that was his academic speciality even he was primarily domestic in his first term. When the Germans ignored Britain's demand that Belgium's neutrality be respected, at 11.00 pm on 4 August 1914 London time, Britain was at war with Germany. Yet over eight million of the US population had been born in Germany or had at least one German parent. There were also some 4.5 million Irish Americans, many with no love for the British. Wilson had written on 4 August to the heads of the warring states in Europe saying he would welcome an opportunity to act for peace. Wilson's call for a neutrality of spirit merely triggered a propaganda war in Washington with Britain, France and Germany opening information bureaux. Wilson said, 'We must be impartial in thoughts as well as actions.' Nothing would happen at least until he was re-elected in November 1916.

There was one exception to this which came following the attack on the US ship *Lusitania*. In March 1916 the British Foreign Secretary, Edward Grey, with Colonel House in London had provisionally agreed what was called the House-Grey Memorandum. 'Colonel House told me that President Wilson was ready, on hearing from France and England that the moment was opportune to propose that a conference should be summoned to put an end to the war. Should the Allies accept this proposal and should Germany refuse it, the United States would enter the war against Germany.'[71] Wilson made at that point in the Memorandum one change putting the word 'probably' before the word 'enter'. The next sentence referring to if the conference met said, 'it would secure peace on terms not unfavourable to the Allies'.

Wilson was content to be depicted in his second term election as the international peace candidate and a Senator for Oklahoma spelt out in the West of the USA to all his campaign meetings in October and early November 1916 that 'A vote for Hughes (the Republican candidate) is a vote for war. A vote for Wilson is a vote for peace.' Wilson was also the first Presidential candidate to benefit from votes for women. Eleven of the twelve states where women were allowed to vote were in the West and ten of these were won by Wilson demonstrating 'women had become an electoral constituency in the United States'.[72] And perhaps for the first time potentially a constituency for peace. Wilson won both the electoral vote and the popular vote and in his inaugural speech on 5 March 1917, unlike in 1913 when he had spoken not a word on foreign affairs, in a clear reference to Germany, he referred to how 'the tragical events of the thirty months of vital turmoil . . . had made us citizens of the world'.

When he addressed both Houses of Congress at the end of that month his ten Cabinet members were united over a declaration of war and, as Wilson put it, the present German submarine war against commerce was a war against all nations and a challenge to all mankind. He then famously justified the war on the basis 'The world must be made safe for democracy.'

It was not, however, until 28 May 1918 that the American

---

71 Patricia O'Toole, *The Moralist,* (Simon & Schuster, 2018), pp. 194-5.
72 A. Scott Berg, *Wilson* (Simon & Schuster, 2013), p. 41.

Expeditionary Force, eventually claiming two million men in the field and two million in training, started to take offensive action in the small French town of Cantigny, 75 miles north of Paris. By the end of the war in 1918 on the 11th day of the 11th month, American troops had seized 485,000 square miles of enemy held territory and captured 63,000 prisoners, 1,300 artillery pieces and 10,000 mortars and machine guns.[73] No fair-minded European could deny the Americans had been crucial in bringing the First World War to an end.

President Wilson sailed for France on 4 December 1918 with a Presidential party of 113 members, ready to negotiate the peace. He committed to his Fourteen Points announced from Washington on 8 January 1918. His Points were summarised as having 'remapped the world, proposed a world order that rested on the equality of all nations rather than the power of a few, committed the United States to the preservation of peace and presented America's war aims'.[74]

Wilson first visited Paris and was then the first sitting President ever to visit London. The public reception in both countries was overwhelming. In Manchester he said the US will 'join no combination of power which is not the combination of all of us'. The US 'is not interested merely in the peace of Europe, but in the peace of the world'. Yet President Wilson was at this stage, though appearing triumphant before the crowds in Europe, but a shadow of his former self. His brain was deteriorating and showing many of the signs of longstanding high blood pressure and associated cerebrovascular disease, with a rigidity in his thinking and an inner hubris that brooked no difference of opinion.

He seemed oblivious to the fact that he no longer controlled Congress. This was because on 5 November the Democrats had lost their majorities in both Houses to the Republican Party in the

---

73 Ibid, *Wilson*, p. 480.
74 Patricia O'Toole, *The Moralist* (Simon & Schuster, 2018), p.307.

mid-term elections. This was, in part, because of his foolish last minute appeal 'to continue to be your unembarrassed spokesman in affairs at home and abroad'. A wiser, healthier Wilson would have acted differently, but as his most recent biographer, Patricia O'Toole, writes 'Wilson expressed no apprehension. Even before meeting Clemenceau, he had written him off (privately) as "an old man, too old to comprehend new ideas". Lloyd George, he regarded as "a second-rate politician". When Colonel House gently pointed out the political realities, Wilson smiled and told him, "Men die, but ideas live."'[75]

Whatever David Lloyd George was, he was not 'a second rate politician' and Wilson's comment showed how little he knew of what had happened in not just Britain, but also in France and Europe as a whole since 6 December 1916, when the Welshman, David Lloyd George, became British Prime Minister. In a complicated manoeuvre he and a significant number of Conservative members of the wartime coalition had pressurised Herbert Asquith to accept a revised form of War Cabinet, which Asquith did on 3 December but then rejected the next day, creating a schism within the Liberal Party the residues of which can still be detected today in British politics.

It was a grim time in the war and Lloyd George's elevation to head of government came as a tonic for public opinion. Fatefully, none of Asquith's supporters were ready to serve under Lloyd George and many Conservatives had qualms, to say the least, about the steadiness of the mercurial new Prime Minister. Lloyd George's coalition was dependent on Conservative MPs' support and he could not rely on half of his own Liberal MPs nor on the Irish National Party. Lloyd George, however, proceeded to make a virtue of this weakness: he introduced what the Conservatives wanted, a small War Cabinet of five members. Lloyd George was the only Liberal. Andrew Bonar Law, the Conservative leader, became Chancellor of the Exchequer and Leader of the House;

---

75 Ibid, *The Moralist*, p.343.

Arthur Henderson, the leader of the Labour Party, continued in office; two Conservative peers, Earl Curzon and Viscount Milner, proconsuls and proven administrators of the Empire, were brought in as ministers without portfolio. The Prime Minister, in effect, contained his own personality by this arrangement. It worked because every day after breakfast Lloyd George would walk along the connecting passage from 10 to 11 Downing Street and spend around an hour with Bonar Law reviewing the day's business and submitting his own imaginative ideas to Bonar Law's practical, critical mind.[76] In this way potentially the most hubristic British Prime Minister in the last century constrained his charismatic and creative personality during the war with a 'toe-holder' from another party. It was a Cabinet structure that contributed massively to his wartime success over the next two years. Lloyd George's biographer, John Grigg, wrote that his power over the War Cabinet 'was due to force of talent and personality rather than to the inherent strength of position' and that while he was bold, positive and decisive he was not autocratic and 'set much store by conciliation and liked, if possible, to carry people with him'.

So it was in 1919 that these two remarkable men, Woodrow Wilson and Lloyd George, met in Paris and in large part deeply influenced the future of the world we live in today. The seeds of the four Balkan wars from 1991-95 were sown in Paris and many of the tensions remain between Serbia, Bosnia, Herzegovina and Croatia. The Kurdish problem and the Shia/Sunni clash in Iraq has its roots in Sunni minority rule from 1919 to 2003, spilling over into Turkey and Syria. The Arab/Israeli conflict after the British gave up the Palestinian Mandate in 1947 to this day continues with fighting in Gaza. Yet before coming to learn the US/UK lessons from Paris 1919 let us examine the two men's personalities, starting with Lloyd George.

---

76 John Grigg, *Lloyd George:War Leader 1916–1918* (London:Allen Lane, 2002), pp. 11–13.

Lloyd George retained good physical health throughout his period in No. 10; there was no history of depression. When at eleven o'clock on the eleventh day of the eleventh month in 1918 the war ended, with the announcement of the armistice terms, it was appropriate that Lloyd George was widely acclaimed as 'The Man Who Won the War.'

On 14 November 1918 a general election was announced to take place in a month's time with votes to be counted after Christmas on 28 December. The coalition planned to continue in office and fought on a joint Lloyd George – Bonar Law manifesto. For the first time women over 30 could vote and in the 'khaki election' the coalition won 473 of the 707 seats in the House of Commons.

The most perceptive commentator on Lloyd George's controversial personality and the hubris which later gripped him was the newspaper proprietor Lord Beaverbrook. He was a Canadian but also Unionist MP for Ashton-under-Lyne from 1910 until 1916. He served with the Canadian forces in France and joined Lloyd George's government as Chancellor of the Duchy of Lancaster in 1918. He generously wrote of Lloyd George's period as wartime Prime Minister in his book, published in 1963, about Lloyd George's decline and fall:

> Here was a man who had done battle with the most dreadful foe his country had ever faced. Great fleets and grand armies had moved at his command. The utmost perils had left him undaunted. He was ever fertile in inspiration and resource. He subdued not only the enemy without, but also the enemy within. He had to contend with recalcitrant colleagues, stubborn Admirals, treacherous Generals, who were quite ready to conspire behind his back, and even to involve the King himself in their intrigues. He looked on tempests and he was not shaken.[77]

---

77 Lord Beaverbrook, *The Decline and Fall of Lloyd George: And Great Was the Fall Thereof* (London: Collins, 1963), p. 141.

It is amazing that President Wilson should have arrived in London after having first visited Paris at the moment of Lloyd George's greatest electoral victory with such a low view of the Prime Minister's political skills.

Yet it was Beaverbrook who also wrote about what happened afterwards, '1921 ushered in two cruel years which were to rip away all the gold brocade and the tinsel too' surrounding Lloyd George's Prime Ministership after the war, when he felt that hubris was at the root of his problems:

> The Greeks told us of a man in high position, self-confident, so successful as to be overpowering to all others. Then his virtues turned to failings. He committed the crime of arrogance. His structure of self-confidence and success came tumbling down. He struggled against fate, but he was doomed. So it was with Lloyd George in the year 1921 and into 1922. Then all was over. His plans good and bad came to nothing. He fell and never rose again ... To keep the seat of power, the place of patronage, he was prepared to stand out as the leader of Empire-minded men – or appear as the Liberal Apostle of Free Trade: as the Man of Peace in Europe – or the Man of War against Turkey and France: as the hammer of the Russian Bolsheviks – or their noble conciliator: as the Tribune of the British working classes – or the Champion of the Tory Landlords against Labour: stern enemy of the Irish – or their tender friend spreading his covering wings about another Celtic race ground under the heel of the oppressor. He took up each position in turn during those tragic years of 1921 and 1922 ... Sometimes and simultaneously he took up contradictory standings. His daring was wonderful to look upon. But to those who never forgot his greatness in his great days, the spectacle wore thin and ere long became pathetic.[78]

---

78 Ibid., pp. 10–11.

A more balanced view of this postwar period, chronicling some of its undoubted achievements, comes from the historian Kenneth O. Morgan: 'For all its failures, the Lloyd George Coalition of 1918–22, alone of peacetime British governments this century, tried to harness political consensus for positive ends.'[79] Morgan, in contrast to Beaverbrook, gives credit to Lloyd George for social reforms that far surpassed those of 1909–13, with the implementation of universal state unemployment insurance, the new expenditure on pensions and social security, the creation of the Ministry of Health, a measure of justice for agricultural workers and education reforms. These measures stalled on Treasury demands for retrenchment. But already the seeds of destruction were traceable in Lloyd George's style, 'the dangers of Caesarism . . . intuitive, erratic diplomacy and confused, ill-prepared encounters'.[80] Morgan goes on to describe how by June 1921 Lloyd George seemed 'a desperate man' and that this underlaid his 'temporary physical breakdown'. 'With the stamp of personal authority so emphatic on the government's programme on all fronts, the press naturally used the Prime Minister as its essential target' and this was symbolised by him summoning the Cabinet to Inverness, near where he was convalescing, highlighting the image of a 'one-man band, goaded into unnatural harmony by a frenetic conductor of aberrant genius'.[81]

While he was selling honours, manipulating friends and enemies and bestriding the world stage, nemesis struck Lloyd George at a famous meeting of Conservative MPs at the Carlton Club, and he was forced to resign that same day, 19 October 1922.

Tracing Lloyd George's downfall one can see that the mistakes and errors he made were born out of hubristic actions. Firstly, he

---

79 Kenneth O. Morgan, *Consensus and Disunity: The Lloyd George Coalition Government 1918–1922* (Oxford: Clarendon Press, 1979), p. 375.
80 Ibid., p. 147.
81 Ibid., pp. 259–60.

was mesmerised by the world stage and the negotiations in Paris which started in January 1919 and ended with the signing of the Treaty of Versailles on 28 June 1919. Having negotiated it for months in Paris, he continued to spend an inordinate amount of time hammering out difficult issues in special conferences, of which he attended no fewer than thirty-three between 1919 and 1922.[82] The 'conference habit' was summed up in a *Punch* cartoon of that name. Secondly, he came to believe he was indispensable. By 1920 Churchill, still a Liberal, was complaining as War Secretary that the Prime Minister had virtually taken over the running of the Foreign Office and historians have written about these years as the start of a form of Presidential government.[83]

Lord Curzon, the Foreign Secretary, wrote to his wife on 21 April 1921 that, 'He wants his Foreign Secretary to be a valet, almost a drudge, and has no regards for the civilities of life.' In March 1922 Lloyd George sacked his Secretary of State for India, Edwin Montagu; speaking at the Cambridge Liberal Club, Montagu said: 'The head of our government is a Prime Minister of great but eccentric genius. He has demanded the price which it is within the power of every genius to demand – the complete disappearance of the doctrine of Cabinet responsibility. He is a great genius – but a dictator.'[84] Lloyd George was now an autocrat, not a democrat.

One reason for the transformation was that Bonar Law stepped down from the Cabinet in March 1921 because of ill health – he had developed pneumonia and his doctors insisted on him taking a six-month rest – this removed the last check on Lloyd George's Presidential style. The two men remained friends. With some hesitation, Bonar Law attended the meeting in 1922 and voted against the coalition with the vote being 185 to 88 against. Bonar

---

82 MacMillan, *Paris 1919*, p. 188.
83 Robert Lloyd George, *David and Winston* (London: John Murray, 2005), p. 164.
84 Purcell, *Lloyd George*, pp. 94, 93.

Law, who hardly knew what ambition was, became Prime Minister. An explanation of his conduct came from a close confidant, J. C. C. Davidson: 'It wasn't the power . . . it was that he would like people to feel that he was fit for it.'[85] In reality Bonar Law already knew that he had laryngeal cancer. By April 1923 he could no longer speak in the House of Commons. He resigned in May and died in October.

Lloyd George, 'the Welsh Wizard', or 'the Big Beast of the Forest' or 'the Goat', as he was called by some, was the most multi-skilled politician of the twentieth century. He had an eloquence unmatched and a rare negotiating genius. He was the most radical Chancellor of the Exchequer and for his first three years, the best Prime Minister. Yet he was also the first British Prime Minister voted out by MPs after acquiring hubris syndrome. Unconstrained from 1920 onwards, his admiration for Presidential governments, which had begun with Theodore Roosevelt and then extended to Franklin, developed apace. Later he even admired Hitler too much for his own good. His hubristic temperament was always there but ran in democratic harness until 1921. Thereafter he paid everyone less and less regard and even lost his respect for Parliament. He died on 26 March 1945. Churchill said, in a most remarkable eulogy in the House of Commons two days later: 'As a man of action, resource and creative energy, he stood, when at his zenith, without a rival.'

Woodrow Wilson, according to David Runciman in *The Confidence Trap* 'had retained a core political philosophy which had been with him since his days in student politics. Wilson had never believed in sudden moments of democratic transformation. Instead he thought democracy needed time to establish itself and take advantage of its underlying strengths. He felt that Americans instinctively recognized this.'[86]

---

85 Andrew Taylor, *Bonar Law* (Haus, 2006), p.109.
86 David Runciman, *The Confidence Trap* (Princeton University Press, 2013) p. 46.

Wilson had suffered from hypertension, or raised blood pressure, for many years before he became President in 1913 and had many neurological incidents from 1889 onwards, which were probably vascular in origin. A normal person's blood pressure is around 120 millimetres of mercury systolic and 80 millimetres diastolic, expressed as 120/80. In hypertension, the systolic blood pressure in the arteries is high and the more troublesomely diastolic usually also rises, reflecting the pumping of the heart and the force exerted on the arteries. Hypertension over time produces changes in the artery walls and predisposes them to clot formation or thrombosis. Retinal artery changes had been recorded as early as 1906 by Wilson's doctors. In 1919, while attending the Paris Peace Conference, Wilson's judgement was not only impaired but 'he was prone to do things which were "unnatural" for him'. Others said that he had developed a one-track mind.[87] By May of that year he was unable to shift his political positions reflectively and had become prejudiced and intransigent.[88] Clearly his capacity to negotiate effectively had a pathological basis in the brain and he was showing signs of dementia. Dementia is a deterioration in mental function occurring in around 10 per cent of people over the age of sixty-five and 20 per cent over the age of seventy-five. It is caused by progressive brain disease, which can be vascular, the result of repeated small strokes. The frontal lobe of the brain contains the motor cortex and those parts of the brain which are concerned with behaviour, personality and learning. A fascinating article has been written by Dr Peter Garrard, 'Frontotemporal Dementia: A clue to the Biological Basis of Hubris Syndrome?'[89] It never mentions

87 'The Impact of Wilson's Neurologic Disease During the Paris Peace Conference', in Arthur S. Link (ed.), *The Papers of Woodrow Wilson, vol. 58: April 23–May 9, 1919* (Princeton, NJ: Princeton University Press, 1988), pp. 612–13.
88 Ibid., pp. 629–63.
89 Ed. Peter Garrard, *The Leadership Hubris Epidemic. Biological Roots and Strategies for Prevention* (Palgrave Macmillan, 2018), 'Frontotemporal Dementia: A clue to the Biological Basis of Hubris Syndrome?' pp. 3-23.

President Wilson but it is highly relevant since hubris became a major aspect of Wilson's behaviour. Garrard points out that 'many of the neural structures that undergo progressive erosion in the context of Frontotemporal Dementia, FTD, are implicated in dysfunction within the dopamine-mediated reward pathways'. (See Introduction). Wilson was described as being 'increasingly egocentric, suspicious and secretive and less discreet in references to people'.[90] It was whispered that Wilson talked to the conference like Jesus Christ, and the French Prime Minister, Georges Clemenceau, called him mentally afflicted, a sufferer from 'religious neurosis'.[91] He was very hubristic but his brain damage precludes him from being classified as having hubris syndrome.

Having returned to the US and his struggle to get Congress to agree to the Treaty wording on the League of Nations in the last week of September 1919, Wilson suffered a progressive thrombosis of a major artery in the right hemisphere of his brain, in other words a stroke.[92] His consciousness became impaired on 2 October, by which time he had developed massive damage to the brain with the loss of the left half of his visual field a complete paralysis of the left side of his body – indeed, he ignored that side of his body entirely, developing what is called 'neglect syndrome'. Wilson explained away the existence of his left-sided paralysis by referring to himself as being 'lame'. This inattention to and disregard of paralysis is well recognised in major strokes of the right cerebral hemisphere of the brain and can lead to a complete unawareness of illness or anosognosia. Very bizarre forms of denial or rationalisations can result. In addition his speech was weak and slurred.

---

90 Edwin A Weinstein, 'Woodrow Wilson's Neuropsychological Impairment and the Paris Peace Conference', in Link, *Papers of Woodrow Wilson, vol. 58*, pp. 630–1.
91 George Walden, *God Won't Save America: Psychosis of a Nation* (London: Gibson Square, 2007), p. 226.
92 Bert E. Park, *The Impact of Illness on World Leaders* (Philadelphia: University of Pennsylvania Press, 1986), pp. 3–73.

President Wilson was in a state of denial about his condition, a state that was medical in origin, but no such excuse can be called in aid to explain the denial by his wife and by his personal physician, Admiral Cary Grayson. They quite simply lied. Grayson had been appointed Wilson's physician when he was a mere junior officer in 1913 because, by chance, he had sewn up a cut on the President's sister. They became friends and Grayson lost all objectivity in his care of the patient.

On 6 October 1919, at the first Cabinet meeting without Wilson, the Secretary of State, Robert Lansing, asked Grayson to inform the Cabinet about the President's illness. Grayson told them that Wilson was suffering only from a 'nervous breakdown, indigestion and a depleted nervous system'. When Lansing mentioned that part of the constitution which provided for the Vice President to assume the office of President during any period of incapacity, Grayson made it clear he would not sign any certificate of disability and repeated thereafter that the President's intellect was unimpaired. In fact, Wilson could neither read nor dictate and lay in a darkened room dealing with no government business for weeks. He was unable to hold a Cabinet meeting until 13 April 1920, nearly seven months after the stroke and lying about Wilson's health was made easier because Grayson was a serving naval officer treating his patient as his Commander-in-Chief and following the wishes of a superior officer. There were real policy consequences of Wilson's failure to step down. For instance, had Wilson been succeeded by the Vice President, Thomas Marshall, Congress might have been persuaded to ratify the treaty establishing the League of Nations. What was needed was for two key people in the debate on the League, Senator Henry Cabot Lodge opposing and Senator Gilbert M. Hitchcock supporting, to be helped to reach a compromise. If that had been done, the League, with the United States the leading nation within it, would have been a far more effective organisation and might have helped prevent the Italian and German march in the 1930s towards the Second World War.

As part of his denial of his medical condition, and to demonstrate who was in control, Wilson petulantly sacked Lansing because Cabinet meetings had been held in his absence and without his permission. In the meantime, Wilson's wife, Edith, was dealing with his workload and for some months, she and Grayson between them gave the false image of a working President. Later, Edith Wilson began to be spoken of as America's first woman President. Woodrow Wilson was not contemplating resignation and even in September 1923, oblivious to the true state of his health, told George Bronnan, an Illinois politician, he was thinking of being drafted for a third term. Fortunately this option became manifestly absurd and Warren Harding succeeded him as President.

Lloyd George visited Wilson on 25 October 1923 when in America and was told to keep his visit short. 'Physically he was a wreck', Lloyd George wrote how he found him still angry about the deviousness of certain French officials in Paris at the conference. 'The old Wilson with his personal hatreds unquenched . . . this extraordinary mixture of real greatness thwarted by much littleness.'[93]

Wilson died on 3 February 1924, the cause of death according to Grayson was arteriosclerosis and the stroke coupled with exhaustion induced by a serious digestive disturbance.

Some of Woodrow Wilson's managing of the Paris Peace Conference related to US domestic politics and as such not an area in which the British or French government had much influence and certainly no control. Self discipline is a requisite for handling international negotiations which have a big US domestic input. There is a long historical learning curve associated with them which started in a major way under Wilson. It continues today under President Trump. Just as President Macron should be looking at Clemenceau's relationship with Wilson so Prime Minister Theresa

---

93 Ibid, Patricia O'Toole, p. 483

May might have considered Lloyd George's relations with Wilson during their meetings in Paris, but Wilson was an intellectual and very different in almost every respect from Trump and a practitioner of moralism in foreign policy.

An interesting insight into Woodrow Wilson's record comes from Richard Holbrooke's own Foreword to Margaret Macmillan's book, *Paris 1919. Six Months that Changed The World*.[94] Holbrooke points out that Wilson's reputation has risen and fallen regularly in the US and 'his supporters from Herbert Hoover to Robert McNamara, have argued that his enemies in both Paris and the United States Senate were responsible for the undoing of one of history's noblest dreams'. Whereas his critics like Senator Henry Cabot Lodge charged Wilson with seeking to undermine the American constitution; whereas another school of thought George F. Kennan and Henry Kissinger accuse Wilson of 'extraordinary conceit' even while conceding that he 'originated what would become the dominant intellectual school of American foreign policy'. Holbrooke adds that Kissinger was horrified when President Richard Nixon put 'Wilson's portrait in the place of honour in the Cabinet Room'.

American moralism in foreign policy is not dead, but it has not under a number of Presidents always been welcomed in Europe. Strikingly in the anger of President Giscard d'Estaing and the German Chancellor Helmut Schmidt over President Carter's criticism of fast breeder nuclear reactors before the G7 meeting in London on 7-8 May 1977 which the UK did not share.[95] Carter was a moralist in the Woodrow Wilson tradition but far more pragmatic as I discovered in dealing with him over Southern Africa from 1977 to 1979. He was nevertheless ready to exert Presidential power and his distinctive positions are well described in Nancy

---

94 Margaret Macmillan, *Paris 1919. Six Months that Changed The World* (Random House, 2002), p. vii
95 David Owen, *Time To Declare* (Michael Joseph, 1991(pp. 319-321.

Mitchell's book *Jimmy Carter in Africa*.[96] That book describes one area of tension between the US and the UK, namely attitudes to Robert Mugabe who I, as Foreign Secretary, believed was by 1978, showing dangerous signs of becoming a zealot conflicted between his Maoism and Jesuitical Catholicism. The UK encouraged a clandestine meeting brokered by President Kaunda and the Nigerian government of General Obasanjo between Joshua Nkomo and Ian Smith late at night in August 1978 in Lusaka. Cyrus Vance was kept in the picture but I was never sure who else he told apart from the US President. The meeting failed, the war continued, but there was no duplicity or double-dealing by the UK towards the US, as alleged in this otherwise excellent book. The UK had no involvement in the premature meeting of 1977 between Nkomo and Smith in Lusaka, brokered by the businessman and friend of Kaunda, Tiny Rowland who was at loggerheads with the UK government. Mugabe's personal zealotry did not surface when elected Prime Minister in 1980, during the amazing initial reconciliation. But by 1982 he embraced the genocide of his own people with North Korean's training a special force in what was by then an independent Zimbabwe. This was followed by economic collapse, massive inflation over the years, grotesque corruption and huge abuses of human rights until a military coup in November 2017 ousted Mugabe.[97] The new President, Emmerson Mnangagwa, who had latterly fallen out with Mugabe was elected in 2018 but he was closely involved with Mugabe in the 1982 genocide. Hopefully he will live up to his new commitment to a truly democratic Zimbabwe. Other examples of US policies conflicting with Europe and the UK were over the Balkans in 1993-95, described in Chapter 6.

---

96 Nancy Mitchell, *Jimmy Carter in Africa. Race and the Cold* (Stanford University Press, 2016).

97 David Owen, 'Mugabe a 'deeply conflicted zealot' who should never have ruled Zimbabwe', *Daily Maverick*, 26 March 2018.

Woodrow Wilson's moralism cannot be separated out from his mental state and one of the most serious problems is how easily foreign affairs analysts skate over his health problems well before, but particularly during the Paris meetings. It is not just that he frequently lost his temper during the Paris Conference,[98] but there was truth in Lloyd George's comment that he came like a missionary to rescue the heathen Europeans with 'little sermonettes'. Lloyd George argued over what Germany should pay for reparations and tried to blur the line between reparations and indemnities. However Wilson held firm on reparations. Lloyd George who had promised in the very recent election to squeeze Germany hard 'until the pips squeaked' did win Wilson over to including pensions in reparations, but Lloyd George was also ambivalent and did not want to destroy Germany economically. Roy Hattersley, in his biography of Lloyd George, brings a politician's realism in describing Lloyd George's difficulties. In conversation with Colonel House he 'had to have a plausible reason for having fooled (the British people) about the questions of war costs, reparations and what not . . . Germany could not pay anything like the indemnity which the French demanded.'[99] Lloyd George was more concerned about money than boundaries. Hattersley describes his Fontainebleau Memorandum as a 'Prediction of brilliant prescience, followed by a forecast which whatever its validity at the time now seems fatuous.' Wilson endorsed Lloyd George's proposed revisions with virtually no reservations. Lloyd George wanted a peace which, while just, would be preferable to all sensible men to Bolshevism. Lloyd George's criticism of Churchill was 'He wants to conduct a war against the Bolsheviks.' (The Russians as we now refer to them.) Woodrow Wilson viewed Lloyd George, somewhat unfairly, as having no principles.

---

98 Ibid, Margaret Macmillan, p. 7.
99 Roy Hattersley, *David Lloyd George. The Great Outsider* (Little Brown, 2012) p. 496, Marconi Scandal, pp. 318–329.

The biggest scandal in Lloyd George's public life occurred when he was Chancellor of the Exchequer and bought a thousand shares in the Marconi Company of America at a cost of £2. His biographer summed up his behaviour as 'disreputable though not dishonest.'

No one was any the wiser after the Paris Conference about what Wilson really meant by his words about self determination. In an extraordinary statement he admitted that he had said the words 'without the knowledge that nationalities existed'. 'Does he mean a race, a territorial area, or a community?' asked his own Secretary of State, Robert Lansing.[100] Yet Wilson let Japan take the Shantung peninsula in China. To Theodore Roosevelt, Wilson was 'an insincere and cold blooded an opportunist as we have ever had in the presidency'. For Lloyd George, who never got his measure, he was 'kindly, sincere, straightforward' but went on to say in the next breath, 'tactless, obstinate and vain'.[101] Harold Nicolson's diary has Arthur Balfour's more generous assessment of Wilson. 'He is charming as usual . . .' and found him 'as good round a table as he was on paper. His attitude on the meetings of the Big Four is firm, modest, restrained, eloquent, well informed and convincing.'[102]

Margaret Macmillan is interestingly the great-granddaughter of Lloyd George yet scrupulously fair in her summary. 'The peacemakers of 1919 made mistakes of course. By their offhand treatment of the non-European world, they stirred up resentments for which the West is still paying . . . They tried, even cynical old Clemenceau, to build a better order. They could not foresee the future and they certainly could not control it; that was up to their successors. When war came in 1939, it was a result of twenty years of decisions taken or not taken, not arrangements made in 1919.'[103]

---

100 Ibid, Margaret Macmillan, p. viii.
101 Ibid, Margaret Macmillan, pp. 6-7.
102 The Harold Nicolson Diaries 1907-1964, edited by Nigel Nicolson (Phoenix paperback edition 2005), p. 19.
103 Ibid, Margaret Macmillan, pp. 493-4.

Chapter 3

The Atlantic Charter: Imperialism Disowned: Franklin Roosevelt and Winston Churchill

I have covered Churchill's relationship as Prime Minister with President Franklin Roosevelt in considerable detail, particularly focusing on May 1940, in *Cabinet's Finest Hour*.[104] This was a moment of dire crisis, for that reason it is very revealing of how these two personalities worked together, first by letter and telephone calls, then off Newfoundland together face-to-face on warships. Churchill has gone down in history for quoted words which he never said, 'Jaw, jaw is better than war, war.' What Churchill actually said is, 'Meeting jaw to jaw is better than war', a much tougher formulation.

Churchill and Roosevelt understood the different political structures in their two countries, the tolerances between their two systems. They did not cross the line into domestic political differences. That distinction between domestic and international is still very relevant as we look at how a British Prime Minister should deal with President Donald Trump. It is not the role of the British government to enter into the US domestic debate today any more than it was in

---

104 David Owen, *Cabinet's Finest Hour. The Hidden Agenda of May 1940* (Haus Publishing, paperback edition 2016).

the delicate time in 1940-41 when America was in an isolationist mood not dissimilar to 1915 described in the preceding chapter.

Respect for the office of a US President is essential to maintain for any British Prime Minister whatever the provocation and vice versa. Criticism 'yes', denigration 'no'. Personalities differ, times change but we can always learn from the past and how different UK Prime Ministers and US Presidents handled their relationships and their controversies. The mood between Churchill and Roosevelt was still tense. Roosevelt's problem was Wendel Wilkie, his Republican opponent for the presidency who started this exchange by saying, 'President Roosevelt is planning to send our boys to England.' In October 1940 when Roosevelt said to American mothers and fathers, 'Your boys are not going to be sent into any foreign wars.' Wilkie then realised his 'fox' had been shot by Roosevelt and exclaimed, 'That hypocritical son of a bitch. This is going to beat me.'

Fortunately, Churchill's relationship with Roosevelt as the President of the United States had started a year earlier. On 3 October 1939 Churchill, then First Lord of the Admiralty, told the War Cabinet that he had received a personal message of a very friendly character from the President, who had stated that he would be glad to receive any personal message which Churchill wished to bring to his notice. Churchill had already told Chamberlain, the Prime Minister, who approved. Their exchanges of correspondence were placed in sealed envelopes and conveyed by diplomatic bag. The constitutional position is that the US President is Commander-in-Chief of the United States Navy. Chamberlain was wise to agree they should correspond in what is first called the 'Naval Person' correspondence and later relabelled the 'Former Naval Person' correspondence when Churchill became Prime Minister.

When the war broke out in 1939 Roosevelt said, 'This nation will remain a neutral nation, but I cannot ask that every American remain neutral in thought as well. Even a neutral has the right to take account of facts. Even a neutral cannot be asked to close his mind or his conscience . . . I hope the United States will keep out of this war. I believe that it will. And I give you assurance and reassurance that every effort of your Government will be directed toward that end.'[105]

On the night that Germany attacked the Low Countries on 10 May, Churchill and the President had a brief phone call but as far as is known no matters of substance were discussed. On 15 May Churchill wrote a very important letter to President Roosevelt:

Although I have changed my office, I am sure you would not wish me to discontinue our intimate, private correspondence. As you are no doubt aware, the scene has darkened swiftly. The enemy have a marked preponderance in the air, and their new technique is making a deep impression upon the French. I think myself the battle on land has only just begun, and I should like to see the masses engage. Up to the present, Hitler is working with specialized units in tanks and air. The small countries are simply smashed up, one by one, like matchwood. We must expect, though it is not yet certain, that Mussolini will hurry in to share the loot of civilisation. We expect to be attacked here ourselves, both from the air and by parachute and airborne troops in the near future, and are getting ready for them. If necessary, we shall continue the war alone, and we are not afraid of that. But I trust you realize, Mr President, that the voice and force of the United States may count for nothing if they are withheld too long. You may have a completely subjugated Nazified Europe established with astonishing swiftness, and the weight may be more than we can bear. All I ask now is that you should proclaim non-belligerency, which would mean that you would help us with everything short of actually engaging armed forces. Immediate needs are: First of all, the loan of 40 or 50 of your

---

105 Franklin d. Roosevelt, *Public Papers of the Presidents of the United States: F. D. Roosevelt, 1939* (Best Books, 1941), p 463.

older destroyers to bridge gap between what we have now and the large new construction we put in hand at the beginning of the war. This time next year we shall have plenty. But if in the interval Italy comes in against us with another 100 submarines, we may be strained to breaking-point. Secondly, we want several hundred of the latest types of aircraft, of which you are now getting delivery. These can be repaid by those now being constructed in the United States for us. Thirdly, anti-aircraft equipment and ammunition, of which again there will be plenty next year, if we are alive to see it. Fourthly, the fact that our ore supply is being compromised from Sweden, from north Africa, and perhaps from northern Spain makes it necessary to purchase steel in the United States. This also applies to other materials. We shall go on paying dollars for as long as we can, but I should like to feel reasonably sure that when we can pay no more, you will give us the stuff all the same. Fifthly, we have many reports of possible German parachute or airborne descents in Ireland. The visit of a United States Squadron to Irish ports, which might well be prolonged, would be invaluable. Sixthly, I am looking to you to keep that Japanese dog quiet in the Pacific, using Singapore in any way convenient. The details of the material which we have in hand will be communicated to you separately.

With all good wishes and respect.

Churchill was well aware of the complex US Constitutional issues over what was and what was not war. He was skating on thin ice with his requests, particularly 'the loan of 40 or 50 of your older destroyers'. Yet Churchill felt Britain had to have more destroyers, several hundred warplanes, anti-aircraft guns and steel to survive. An assessment from Robert Sherwood, a close friend of both Harry Hopkins and Franklin Roosevelt, was that: 'Roosevelt did not discount these requests and subsequent cabled reports from Churchill were not dismissed as exaggerations. During these weeks when horror was piled upon horror, Roosevelt believed that if

Churchill erred at all in his estimates he erred on the side of optimism; but Roosevelt rarely objected to that kind of error.'[106] Yet Sherwood was at pains to declare, 'no one will ever know just what finally went on in Roosevelt's complex mind to determine his decisions.'[107] All Churchill could and did do was to grab his attention by writing private and riveting letters. They were even more important than War Cabinet decisions in producing and increasing US assistance in 1940 and 1941.

Roosevelt repeated not once, but several times to Churchill that, for constitutional reasons, he could not give any assurance that the United States would declare war no matter what the provocation, short of direct attack upon the United States itself.

On 17 May Churchill received a reply from Roosevelt which he read out to the War Cabinet at 10.00 am, the Prime Minister having flown back from France that morning:

> I have just received your message and I am sure it is unnecessary for me to say that I am most happy to continue our private correspondence as we have in the past. I am of course giving every possible consideration to the suggestions made in your message. I shall take up your specific proposals one by one.

Which he did in detail in the rest of the letter.[108] Roosevelt ended 'The best of luck to you.' Churchill certainly needed luck, indeed a lot of luck. But he also needed weapons of war.

Churchill replied to President Roosevelt on 20 May mentioning that the British Ambassador, Lord Lothian, had reported his conversation with Roosevelt.

---

106 Robert E Sherwood, *The White House Papers of Harry L Hopkins: An Intimate History*, p 143.
107 Ibid, p xii.
108 Ibid, *Cabinet's Finest Hour*, pp. 124-5.

I understand your difficulties, but I am very sorry about the destroyers. If they were here in six weeks they would play an invaluable part. The battle in France is full of danger to both sides. Though we have taken heavy toll of enemy in the air and are clawing down two or three to one of their planes, they have still a formidable numerical superiority. Our most vital need is, therefore, the delivery at the earliest possible date of the largest possible number of Curtiss P-40 fighters now in course of delivery to your Army.

With regard to the closing part of your talk with Lothian, our intention is, whatever happens, to fight on to the end in this island, and, provided we can get the help for which we ask, we hope to run them very close in the air battles in view of individual superiority. Members of the present Administration would likely go down during this process should it result adversely, but in no conceivable circumstances will we consent to surrender. If members of the present Administration were finished and others came in to parley amid the ruins, you must not be blind to the fact that the sole remaining bargaining counter with Germany would be the Fleet, and, if this country was left by the United States to its fate, no one would have the right to blame those then responsible if they made the best terms they could for the surviving inhabitants. Excuse me, Mr President, putting this nightmare bluntly. Evidently I could not answer for my successors, who in utter despair and helplessness might well have to accommodate themselves to the German will. However, there is happily no need at present to dwell upon such ideas. Once more thanking you for your goodwill.

On 1 June, Churchill wrote to Roosevelt again on the question of aircraft asking for the release of 200 Curtiss P-40 Warhawk fighters, saying at the present rate of comparative losses, they would account for something like 800 German machines. It was Roosevelt who decided under the Neutrality Act they could not be shipped uncrated and ready to fly but the Act could be circumvented if a British aircraft called at Newfoundland and the aircraft were flown to the Canadian border where they would be *pushed* across the border and then flown to Newfoundland.[109]

Churchill's speech to Parliament on 4 June had an electric effect on Roosevelt and American public opinion. 'We shall fight on the beaches, we shall fight on the landing grounds, we shall fight in the fields and in the streets, we shall fight in the hills, we shall never surrender . . .' The broadcast was actually an impersonation by Norman Shelley, of Churchill's voice as proceedings in the House of Commons were not broadcast. According to Conrad Black's account: 'Roosevelt's response was dramatic. He ordered a reluctant War Department (where stubborn officials managed to delay implementation for three weeks) until overwhelmed by direct presidential instruction to fill British requests for, and to despatch at once, 500,000 Enfield rifles, 900 75mm artillery pieces, 50,000 machine guns, 130 million rounds of ammunition, a million artillery shells, and large quantities of high explosives and bombs. The neutrality legislation was circumvented by selling this equipment and ordnance to private corporations, which sold it on at once to the British. Except for tanks, the British Army would be substantially rearmed, albeit with twenty-year-old rifles and field pieces, within six weeks of returning, shorn and waterlogged, from Dunkirk.'[110]

On 5 June Churchill sent a Most Secret Message to the Canadian Prime Minister Mackenzie King in which his anxiety about President Roosevelt's view that the British Fleet might need to go to Canada is revealed in stark language: 'We must be careful not to let Americans view too complacently prospect of British collapse,

109 Robin Renwick, *Fighting with Allies. America and Britain in Peace and War* (Biteback Publishing, 2016), p. 25.

110 Conrad Black, *Franklin Delano Roosevelt: Champion of Freedom* (Weidenfeld & Nicolson, 2003), pp. 554–555.

out of which they would get the British Fleet and the guardianship of the British Empire, minus Great Britain. If United States were in the war and England conquered locally, it would be natural that events should follow line you describe. But if America continued neutral, and we were overpowered, I cannot tell what policy might be adopted by a pro-German administration such as would undoubtedly be set up. Although President is our best friend, no practical help has been forthcoming from the Unites States as yet. We have not expected them to send military aid, but they have not even sent any worthy contribution in destroyers or planes, or by a visit of a squadron of their Fleet to Southern Irish ports. Any pressure that you can supply in this direction would be invaluable.'[111] Churchill ends by showing his disappointment with America, thanking King 'for destroyers which have already gone into action against a U-Boat' and also demonstrating his Minister of Defence role, aware of every development and engagement of the forces in effect under his direct command.

On 9 June Churchill wrote to Lord Lothian, Ambassador in Washington, to guide him for a conversation he was due to have with the President:

> If Great Britain broke under invasion, a pro-German Government might obtain far easier terms from Germany by surrendering the Fleet, thus making Germany and Japan masters of the new world. This dastard deed would not be done by his Majesty's present advisors, but, if Mosley[112] were Prime Minister or some other

---

111 Martin Gilbert, *The Churchill War Papers, Volume II: Never Surrender* (Heinemann, 1994), p 255.

112 Sir Oswald Mosley, principally known as the founder of the British Union of Fascists (BUF). MP for Harrow 1918–24 and Smethwick 1926–31. Chancellor of the Duchy of Lancaster in the Labour Government of 1929–31. Formed the new Party which merged with the BUF (which included the Blackshirts) in 1932. Interned in 1940, released in 1943.

Quisling[113] government set up, it is exactly what they would do, and perhaps the only thing they could do, and the President should bear this very clearly in mind. You should talk to him in this sense and thus discourage any complacent assumption on United States part that they will pick up the debris of the British Empire by their present policy. On the contrary, they run the terrible risk that their sea power will be completely over-matched. Moreover, islands and naval bases to hold the United States in awe would certainly be claimed by the Nazis. If we go down, Hitler has a very good chance of conquering the world.

No tougher message could have been sent and Churchill must have calculated that when read out in the Oval Office it would have a significant impact.

On 11 June Churchill wrote to Roosevelt having heard Roosevelt's speech the night before in which he had attacked the Italian Declaration of War saying 'The hand that held the dagger has struck it into the back of his neighbour.' Churchill said: 'I have already cabled you about airplanes, including flying boats, which are so needful to us in the impending struggle for the life of Great Britain. But even more pressing is the need for destroyers. The Italian outrage makes it necessary for us to cope with a much larger number of submarines which may come out into the Atlantic and perhaps be based on Spanish ports. To this the only counters are destroyers.'

On 12 June Churchill wrote once again to Roosevelt: 'I spent last night and this morning at the French GQG where the situation was explained to me in the gravest terms . . . The aged Marshall

---

113 Vidkun Quisling was a Norwegian military officer and politician who became nominal head of government of Norway after the Nazi occupation. The puppet government, known as the Quisling regime, was dominated by ministers from Nasjonal Samling, the party he founded in 1933. After WW2, he was put on trial for high treason and executed in October 1945.

Pétain, who was none too good in April and July 1918, is I fear ready to lend his name and prestige to a treaty of peace for France. Reynaud on the other hand is for fighting on, and he has a young General de Gaulle who believes much can be done. Admiral Darlan declares he will send the French Fleet to Canada. It would be disastrous if the two big modern ships fell into bad hands.'

On 14 June German forces entered Paris and two further messages were sent in 24 hours to Roosevelt about France. On 15 June in yet another message Churchill asks: 'Have you considered what offers Hitler may choose to make to France? He may say, "surrender the Fleet intact and I will leave you Alsace-Lorraine", or alternatively, "if you do not give me your ships I will destroy your towns." I am personally convinced that America will in the end go to all lengths, but this moment is supremely critical for France.' He went on to indicate the possibility of a declaration that the United States would if necessary go to war.

At 10.45 Churchill sent another letter as he realised he had gone too far, 'I am of course not thinking in terms of an expeditionary force, which I know is out of the question. What I have in mind is the tremendous moral effect such an American decision would produce, not merely in France, but also in all democratic countries in the world, and, in the opposite sense, on the German and Italian people.'

Churchill followed up his message of 5 June to the Canadian Prime Minister on 24 June saying: 'I see no reason to make preparations for or give any countenance to the transfer of the British Fleet. I shall myself never enter into any peace negotiations with Hitler but obviously I cannot bind a future Government which if we were deserted by the United States and beaten down here might very easily be a kind of Quisling affair ready to accept German overlordship and protection. It would be a help if you would impress this danger upon the President as I have done in my telegrams to him. All good wishes and we are very glad your grand Canadian division is with us in our fight for Britain.'

No decision was more important in setting the tone of Churchill's defiance than on 2 July 1940 when the First Sea Lord, Sir Dudley Pound, sent a signal to Admiral Somerville which had been drafted by Churchill: 'You are charged with one of the most disagreeable and difficult tasks that a British Admiral has ever been faced with, but we have complete confidence in you and rely on you to carry it out relentlessly.' At 2 am on 3 July, Somerville's ships began shelling the French naval vessels at Mers-el-Kébir while aircraft from HMS *Ark Royal* dropped torpedoes. The French Navy lost 1,297. Churchill on this issue had stamped his authority ruthlessly and could allow no doubt anywhere in the world that the British Empire would fight on alone. Ruthlessness is a quality Boris Johnson admires in Churchill.

On 4 July just prior to a Secret Session, Churchill made a statement to the House of Commons on the War Situation and the French Fleet.

> It is with sincere sorrow that I must now announce to the House the measures which we have felt bound to take in order to prevent the French Fleet from falling into German hands. When two nations are fighting together under long and solemn alliance against a common foe, one of them may be stricken down and overwhelmed, and may be forced to ask its Ally to release it from its obligations. But the least that could be expected was that the French Government, in abandoning the conflict and leaving its whole weight to fall upon Great Britain and the British Empire, would have been careful not to inflict needless injury upon their faithful comrade, in whose final victory the sole chance of French freedom lay, and lies.

The House of Commons is a hugely sentimental place. Some MPs had tears in their eyes as had Churchill. Here he was, a Francophile to his core, (twice First Lord of the Admiralty in two

World Wars), who everyone knew had friends in the French Navy and had done everything in his power to avoid sinking the French Fleet: yet he had done his duty. That same recognition touched people worldwide. The former naval person in the White House understood its significance more than anyone – the British were going to be resolute and utterly ruthless. General de Gaulle, in what was a difficult and courageous broadcast for him to the French people on 8 July 1940, said of the French Fleet, 'There cannot be the slightest doubt that, on principle and of necessity, the enemy would have used them either against Britain or against our own Empire. I therefore have no hesitation in saying that they are better destroyed.'[114] On 14 August Roosevelt told Churchill he would supply the destroyers but it was a *quid pro quo* agreement. Britain agreed to 99 years leases on eight British possessions in the Americas on which the US could build air and naval bases to strengthen its own defences.[115]

These vignettes from 1940 vividly demonstrate the relationship between President and Prime Minister. No two people could go through those two months without being as Shakespeare wrote on friendship. Grappled 'to thy soul with hoops of steel.'[116]

Roosevelt was elected for a third term on 5 November 1940. In the electoral vote he had 449 while his opponent Wendell Willkie had 82. In the popular vote Roosevelt polled 27 million votes to Willkie's 22 million. Roosevelt was inaugurated on 20 January 1941 and signed the famous Lend-Lease Act on 11 March 1941.

Still Roosevelt was holding back from declaring war on Germany. It was agreed, however, he would meet soon with Churchill. On 11 July 1941 in Washington, President Roosevelt drew a line on a small map of the Atlantic Ocean that he had torn

---

114 General de Gaulle, *War Memoirs: The Call to Honour 1940–1942*, trans. Jonathan Griffin (Collins, 1955), p 20.

115 Ibid, Robin Renwick, p. 31.

116 David Owen, *Time to Declare* (Penguin paperback, 1992), p.285.

out of the *National Geographic* Magazine and gave it to Harry Hopkins. On Sunday, Hopkins flew from Gander, Newfoundland to Prestwick, Scotland and went straight to see Churchill and showed him the map. The war in Russia with the invading Germans was in its fourth week. No one knew how long it would last, whether the Russians could defend Moscow or even avoid defeat. Roosevelt's map was deeply personal and demonstrated his knowledge of maritime strategy and a readiness to assist militarily. He was suggesting the US should be policing a much greater Atlantic sea area than hitherto and for which the US Navy would assume responsibility. It was designed to free up British escort ships for service elsewhere, particularly the Murmansk sea route to get supplies to the Russians. It was a profound shift of the President's position about getting closer to declaring war and a brilliant strategic move within the constitutional constraints.[117]

Hopkins was now in London and Roosevelt decided that since every key decision on American production and Lend Lease depended on what was happening in Russia and information was sketchy, Hopkins should make a quick trip to Moscow before Churchill and Roosevelt and their respective Chiefs met as planned at the Atlantic Conference. This he did in a new flying boat link from Invergorden to Archangel. He spoke to Stalin on arrival at some length who said, 'You are our guest; you have but to command' and that 'he would be at his disposal every day'. Hopkins ended two days in Moscow with a four hour second visit with Stalin and gained far more information than had ever been given to any outsider. He made three reports. Part III was 'For the President Only.' Stalin said, 'it would be very difficult for Britain and Russia combined to crush the German military machine. The one thing that could defeat Hitler, and perhaps without ever firing a shot,

---

117 David Owen, Foreword to H V Morton's book *Atlantic Meeting* (Methuen, 1943 & 2016).

would be the announcement that the United States was going to war with Germany.'

Stalin wanted Hopkins to tell the President that he would welcome the American troops on any part of the Russian front under the complete command of the American Army. Hopkins told Stalin that his 'mission related entirely to matters of supply and that the matter of our joining in the war would be decided largely by Hitler himself and his encroachment upon our fundamental interests.' But of course the mission served to start Roosevelt's relationship with Stalin that complimented the one he had with Churchill, buttressed by meetings in Tehran and Yalta.

Hopkins then flew back to Scotland and Scapa Flow to board HMS *The Prince of Wales* with Churchill. The Prime Minister had kept all the Allied Heads of Government informed of his travel arrangements to the extent of saying that this would be his first meeting with the President. He tended to forget that he had met Roosevelt when he was Assistant Secretary of the Navy in the First World War at a banquet in London and it was something of a sore point with Roosevelt that he had apparently failed to notice the young American who remembered their meeting clearly. When on 10 August Churchill and Roosevelt met Hopkins told friends 'You'd have thought Winston was being carried up into the heavens to meet God!'

Roosevelt was determined to use the Atlantic Charter to reign in Churchill's hopes for a continuation of the British Empire after eventual victory. On the wording of the Charter Churchill did not get his own way. This is yet another example that all was not just 'sweetness and light' in their personal relationship. Over Japan Churchill hoped for a 'mailed fist' threat and the US instead reasserted its power as a sovereign nation looking after its own interests which meant nothing changed. Churchill had himself drafted Point Three of the Charter. 'They respect the right of all peoples to choose the form of Government under which they will live.' But against his wishes Point Four referred to 'all States, great or small' and Point Five to 'all nations.' Not surprisingly, people in India, Burma, Malaya and Indonesia soon began to realise this applied to them. Roosevelt had, in effect, separated the US from Churchill's post-war Imperial dreams and left the way open for Prime Minister Attlee's commitment to independence for India when Labour won their massive electoral victory in 1945. Churchill told Parliament that the sensitive rewording was intended to apply to the countries subjugated by the Axis, 'a quite separate problem from the progressive evolution of self-governing institutions.' Yet within a few months Roosevelt was asserting the Charter applied 'to the whole world'.

In Conrad Black's words, 'Roosevelt had learned from Wilson's debacle in 1919 to concert war aims with his principal ally in advance, and so to avoid, or at least reduce, post war squabbling.'[118]

For Churchill, the big news reporting to his government was that off Newfoundland in Canada he had established 'warm and deep personal relations with our great friend.' In Britain, there was a slight sense of anti-climax with still no sign of a great American armada coming across the Atlantic when Roosevelt said, 'an interchange of views that's all . . . no closer to war.' The all-important threshold had, however, been passed at the meetings in the one place that mattered: Roosevelt's mind.

Though Roosevelt insisted to the US press, party leaders and members of his Cabinet that nothing had changed, in fact, everything had changed. This was confirmed to John Colville, Churchill's Private Secretary, on 19 August – who was not there in Newfoundland – by John Martin who was and had heard Roosevelt say that 'he did not intend to declare war: he intended to wage it.'[119]

---

118 Conrad Black, *Franklin Delano Roosevelt. Champion of Freedom* (Weidenfeld & Nicolson, 2003), pp. 654-656.
119 *The Fringes of Power. Downing Street Diaries 1939-1955).*

It took Pearl Harbor, on 7 December, in what Roosevelt described to Congress as 'a date which will live in infamy', when Japanese aircraft attacked and sank US Naval ships in Pearl Harbor before the US was formally at war with Japan. On 11 December 1941 Hitler also declared war on the US.

Now the British and the Americans were at war together and with the might of Russia's land army there was a real sense that victory over the Nazis would eventually come. On the shape of that victory, by 1943 it was Roosevelt's decisions that were more important than Churchill's. A mutual respect at a very deep level between London and Washington was building between the two leaders and their military that would last. So much so that the switch to Truman and Attlee in 1945 was seamless and yet it was different from 1945 to 1951.

Argument, sometimes heated, had been present throughout between Churchill and Roosevelt. Of course war concentrates the mind and makes it imperative that differences are overcome and some of these are discussed in the chapter on the Military Mind. Nevertheless, the frankness and the openness in private at a time of great danger between President and Prime Minister demonstrates that as we face problems over NATO in 2020, Prime Minister Johnson must be ready to engage with President Trump. Totally private exchanges of views hold the key. We live in an age of Twitter and social media. But Downing Street must stop letting the press know about every exchange of view with President Trump as from that knowledge flow leaks of the contents. We must never forget in London and not let our European friends forget either, that the US only came very late into the two World Wars and was in the process of 'bringing the boys home' in 1946 when President Truman had the considerable courage to go back on his promise and keep US troops in Europe. NATO is the mechanism for their troops remaining. NATO can and must remain the core – not EU defence – of UK and US defence policy.

Chapter 4

Suez: Lying to America. Anthony Eden and Dwight Eisenhower

Britain had ruled Egypt from 1882 until 1922 and had strongly influenced its monarchy right up to King Farouk's overthrow by Gamal Abdel Nasser in 1952. Free passage along the Suez Canal was regarded by Churchill, Eden and their generation as Britain's lifeline. Eden had negotiated the Suez Canal Base Agreement, involving British troops withdrawing in 1954, which Winston Churchill had disliked and which had been strongly criticised by a section of the Conservative Party. Under it the last British troops left Port Said on 13 June 1956.

As Prime Minister since 1955, Eden was involved in the US–UK discussions over the financing of Egypt's Aswan High Dam on the Nile, an important project for Egypt. President Eisenhower was recovering from ileitis and his Secretary of State, John Foster Dulles, concerned about growing Soviet influence on Egypt, was hardening against supporting the dam. On 17 July 1956 the British Ambassador was told to say in Washington that the UK was not in favour of withdrawing from the project. However Dulles concluded, rightly, that the British were speaking for the record and did not feel strongly. Under pressure from Congress, Dulles announced US withdrawal on 19 July from the Nile project. In London, the President of the Board of Trade, Peter Thorneycroft, went to see Eden to argue for the High Dam project continuing and bore the brunt of one of Eden's famous rages. Eden resented Thorneycroft's intrusion, saying that after the American decision the project was dead and that a suggestion to rescue it was monstrous. This example of a UK Prime Minister's respect for US Presidential decisions, even when wrong, is part and parcel of realpolitik. Churchill's doctor, Lord Moran, in his diary entry for 21 July wrote: 'The political world is full of Eden's moods at No. 10.' It was a tragedy for Eden, that what should have been a routine surgical operation, a cholecystectomy, the surgical removal of the gall bladder, went wrong on 12 April 1953 and Eden's biliary duct was cut. Repair operations followed but he was left with periodic fevers, pain and psychological changes affecting his personality and decision making largely because of the drugs he was taking by the late summer of 1956.

Cabinet had agreed that the UK would withdraw financial support for the dam and then, six days later on 26 July, the anniversary of King Farouk's abdication, in a passionate speech in Manshiya Square in Alexandria, Nasser announced the nationalisation of the Suez Canal Company. It was in part retaliation for the decision over the Aswan High Dam. By chance, when news of Nasser's speech came through, Eden happened to be hosting a dinner in 10 Downing Street for King Faisal of Iraq and his Prime Minister, Nuri al-Said. The Iraqi advice was to hit Nasser hard and fast. After dinner Eden called in the US chargé d'affaires, so seeking – ironically, in the light of subsequent events – to involve the Americans from the start. He also called in the French Ambassador to join the discussion of Nasser's action, along with four Cabinet ministers and two chiefs of staff, Field Marshal Sir Gerald Templer and Admiral Earl Mountbatten. The meeting lasted until 4.00 a.m.

Nationalisation, to Eden, was a direct threat to British interests and he began to see Nasser in 1956 like Mussolini in the 1930s. Publicly Eden declared that Nasser should not be allowed 'to have his thumb on our windpipe' and he made it clear he was ready to use British armed forces to lift the threat of Egyptian interference with the flow of ships along the Suez Canal.

In fact, though, Nasser was keen to show that Egypt had no intention of interfering with any nation's shipping and in the event few other nations, apart from Israel, feared this. The threat to world shipping was an issue on which Britain never really managed to mobilise international opinion. Furthermore, in the way he nationalised the company, Nasser cleverly tried to demonstrate that he was not acting illegally. Shareholders were bought out at the price prevailing on the Paris Bourse at the time Nasser's announcement was made. Nor was international opinion much concerned about Egypt's growing links with the Soviet Union. Most importantly, Eisenhower was not prepared to link the seizure of the canal with the danger from the Soviet Union, and he would turn out to be the single most important person in determining the outcome of the Suez crisis.

Eden's immediate decisions after Nasser's speech on 26 July – to prepare for but postpone immediate military action – were understandable given the attitude of the chiefs of staff, who had no enthusiasm for military action. Indeed it can be argued that, if anything, Eden's decisions at this time were too cautious. This contrasts dramatically with the recklessness of his decision-making from 14 October, when his health had become a key factor. The day after Nasser's speech Eden did not immediately embrace Lord Chancellor Kilmuir's legal view that Britain could base its case to intervene militarily over Suez solely on the claim that Nasser's action was illegal. Nor did Eden take the view of one of his old and close friends, Viscount Cilcennin, then the First Lord of the Admiralty, that if force was to be used, it should be soon, during the summer. Delay was to prove fateful. Later in the autumn, according to Cilcennin, 'Nasser had covered many of his tracks.'[120] Nevertheless, the Cabinet subcommittee established for

---

120 D. R. Thorpe, *Eden: The Life and Times of Anthony Eden, First Earl of Avon 1897–1977* (London: Chatto & Windus, 2003), pp. 475-81.

dealing with Suez minuted on 30 July that the immediate aim 'was to bring down the present Egyptian government'. So regime change was present from the start. Cilcennin also believed that Eden, who had never worked in America, did not understand the effect that the imminence of a presidential election, due in November, would have on the American response to any British action taken against Egypt.

It is not clear when Eden ruled out involving British troops already in Libya, for fear of an Arab backlash. Using these forces in Libya was something which he was still contemplating when Churchill went to see him very privately on 6 August. Churchill left behind a memo which he had dictated in the car and had had typed in a lay-by as he waited *en route* to Chequers, the Prime Minister's country home. Churchill warned Eden with great perceptiveness about just taking over the canal when Nasser's real power base was Cairo; and it is clear he believed that to threaten Cairo and other large towns the British armoured division in Libya would and should be used. The memo from Churchill said:

'The more one thinks of taking over the Canal, the less one likes it. The long causeway could be easily obstructed by a succession of mines. We should get much of the blame of stopping work, if it is to be up to the moment of our attack a smooth-running show. Cairo is Nasser's centre of power. I was very glad to hear that there would be no weakening about Libya on account of the ( )[121] Prime Minister etc., but that the armoured divisions, properly supported by air, with any additional forces that may be needed, would be used. On the other side, a volte face should certainly free our hands about Israel. We should want them to menace and hold the Egyptians and not be drawn off against Jordan.'[122]

---

121 This depicts an illegible word in Churchill's memo, written in the car in which he was travelling.
122 Memorandum from Sir W. Churchill, 6 August 1956. Avon Papers, PM

Churchill saw that toppling Nasser would involve attacking Cairo. But the Cabinet believed that with three divisions on the canal it would not be long before Nasser fell from loss of face. Their plan was that British bombing would be designed for purely military purposes along the Suez Canal and would not extend to Cairo with the political purpose of toppling Nasser. Yet this underestimated the forces of nationalism that Nasser had unleashed. He would still control the country from Cairo and would be able to mount attacks on the invading forces. So there was a central weakness in the plan.

On 7 August Harold Macmillan as Chancellor of the Exchequer circulated a 'little note' to the Egypt Committee about his ideas for an invasion which reflected Churchill's views, told to Eden the day before. Eden criticised Macmillan saying he had no business circulating papers without consulting him as Prime Minister – a sign of the tension that had developed between the two men and which was to become very serious.[123] The British chiefs of staff did not emerge well from the whole crisis, showing neither cohesion nor decisiveness. Throughout they feared a prolonged occupation of Egypt.

On 17 August Eden wrote to Churchill: 'I am sorry to have been away on Monday, but I needed a few hours off. I am very fit now.' He also said: 'Most important of all, the Americans seem very firmly lined up with us on inter-nationalisation' of the Suez Canal. Yet Eisenhower never hid from Eden his opposition to the use of force. On 3 September he wrote to Eden: 'I must tell you frankly that American public opinion flatly rejects the use of force. I really do not see how a successful result could be achieved by forceable (*sic*) means.'

Personal Correspondence, ref. AP20/33/24, Special Collections, University of Birmingham. Also quoted in Martin Gilbert, *Winston S. Churchill, vol. 8: 'Never Despair' 1945–1965* (Oxford: Heinemann, 1988), pp. 1203–4.

123 Clarissa Eden, *Clarissa Eden: A Memoir – From Churchill to Eden*, ed. Cate Haste (London: Weidenfeld & Nicolson, 2007), p. 237.

There was a clear divergence of interest between Britain and the United States throughout the crisis. Britain was concerned not solely with the safety of vessels going through the Suez Canal; the British government wanted to control the canal. Considerations of prestige were also of major importance for Eden, and the government was not able to draw a clear distinction between the question of the canal and that of Nasser's regime. In retrospect, Guy Millard, Eden's private secretary, wrote in 1957 a most detailed private history of this period for the Foreign Office,[124] and came to the conclusion that it had been a mistake for Britain to try to solve the two problems simultaneously. This was a criticism of British policy made by the Americans during the crisis. Eden was not just interested in an arrangement to protect those whose ships used the canal, as envisaged in John Foster Dulles's Suez Canal Users Association initiative, he also wanted a new and different Egyptian government. But, as with the invasion of Iraq in 2003 under Tony Blair, Eden was not prepared openly to champion regime change; he used the threat to shipping as the excuse, rather as Blair used weapons of mass destruction as an excuse later.

On 3 October Eden told the Cabinet that there was 'a risk that the Soviet Union might conclude a pact of mutual assistance with Egypt; if that happened it would become much more hazardous to attempt a settlement of this dispute by force'. He knew too that as the British troop build-up continued in Cyprus and elsewhere there would come a moment when he could no longer hold them in a state of military readiness. On 4 October Dulles said in confidence, 'I know that the British and the French want us to

---

124 Guy Millard, 'Memorandum on Relations between the United Kingdom, the United States and France in the Months Following Egyptian Nationalisation of the Suez Canal Company in 1956.' (Paper written in August 1957 and published by the Cabinet Office for UK Eyes Only on 21 October 1957). National Archives CAB 21/3314. This document does not spell out the detail of the collusion between France, Israel and the UK but is not exactly as originally written by Millard; that original version has disappeared.

stand with them, but we do not know where they stand, nor are we consulted . . .'[125] On 5 October in the United Nations Security Council, Egypt complained about both British and French troop movements. That same day Eden developed cholangitis affecting the liver he had a rigor with a temperature of 106°F. We also know Eden took pethidine and was self medicating including injections.

On Monday 8 October, the day Eden came out of hospital, Rab Butler had to chair the Egypt Committee in the Prime Minister's absence. But by Saturday of that week Eden was well enough to speak in the traditional leader's slot on the last day of the Conservative Party conference at Llandudno. The party faithful loved the passage in which he said: 'We have always said that with us force is the last resort, but cannot be excluded. We have refused to say that in no circumstances would we ever use force. No responsible government could ever give such a pledge.'

On the day of his speech he was informed by Anthony Nutting that the French Prime Minister, Guy Mollet, had requested that Eden urgently agree to see emissaries whom he wanted to send over from Paris. On the evening of 13 October, after he had returned to Chequers from the conference, he was told on the telephone about the visit to London by Sir Gladwyn Jebb, the British Ambassador in Paris who had revealed that the French had delivered seventy-five of the latest Mystère fighter aircraft to Israel without obtaining British and American clearance, as the procedures of the tripartite agreement required. Eden asked Nutting whether the French were putting up the Israelis to attack Jordan, a major British anxiety at the time.

On Sunday 14 October Eden held what turned out to be a fateful meeting with Mollet's emissaries, General Maurice Challe, a deputy chief of staff of the French Air Force, and Albert Gazier,

125 Keith Kyle, *Suez* (Weidenfeld & Nicolson, 1991).

France's acting Foreign Minister. Nutting was also present. The Challe plan was based on a conspiracy with Israel and was ruinously to become the central policy instrument in Eden's handling of the Suez crisis.

Until this meeting Eden had had no inkling that the French were already deep in collusion with the Israelis over Egypt. Two weeks earlier, on 30 September, an Israeli delegation had secretly suggested to the French their concept of a bogus *casus belli*. The plan was that Israel would invade the Suez Canal Zone, on the agreed understanding that British and French forces would then intervene to separate Israeli and Egyptian forces, posing to the world as peacekeepers between the combatants. The RAF would destroy Egyptian planes which might otherwise threaten Israeli territory.

The French had been in close contact with Israel ever since the Suez Canal Base Agreement two years before. Israel felt that the British troop withdrawal from Egypt had made it more vulnerable while France feared Egyptian interference in its massive military and political challenge in Algeria. The French had some 400,000 troops in Algeria and as President Nasser was supporting the insurgents, Paris had a clear incentive for getting rid of him. French arms sales to Israel were already stretching the balance of arms provision in the tripartite agreement.

To any Prime Minister, let alone Eden with his vast experience as Foreign Secretary, Challe's suggestion of collusion with Israel would have seemed contentious and a plan that was bound to be fraught with political dangers at home and abroad. Eden knew that Israel was the only nation whose ships were not allowed by Egypt to use the Suez Canal, and which therefore had a direct interest in who controlled it. Eden should have known that if Britain were to invade it would be better done with the French alone and after the US elections.

Eden did not formally commit himself to the plan but his questions left the French in little doubt that he was on board for the concept. Challe sensed that Eden was thrilled, Millard felt he was merely 'intrigued'. Nutting, previously very close to Eden, asked in his book: 'How and why was this mortal decision arrived at? And how and why did the man, whose whole political career had been founded on his genius for negotiation, act so wildly out of character?'[126] A war started in dishonour ended, not altogether surprisingly, in disaster and the man responsible, Eden, was in no fit medical condition to make such a decision. His high fever and his dependence on amphetamine were affecting his judgement. This is why hubris is such a complex area to describe; the normal mind can become intoxicated in many ways. Sometimes by the body producing its own neuro transmitters and sometimes by the drugs physicians prescribe for patients or which patients take unknown to their physicians. The effects of the drug take time to develop and a convincing diagnosis means analysing in some detail the manner in which decisions are taken. This is not history in the purely historical tradition but medical history too, and how the brain is functioning differently and why. Any study also moves on with more medical and scientific knowledge.

It was over the next few days that Eden decided that he would proceed on the basis of not informing the Americans of his intentions. He foolishly believed he could keep the Israeli connection within the plan secret from the Americans. In all respects that was a massive misjudgement for a man who knew the penetrative quality of the CIA created in 1947. America's reaction was the fateful consequence of Britain's collusion with Israel and France, and if Eden had been fit and well he would have realised that such a course contained the seeds of its own destruction. Bizarrely, the permanent under-secretary at the Foreign Office, Sir Ivone Kirkpatrick, one of the very few senior diplomats who

---

126 Anthony Nutting, *No End of a Lesson: The Story of Suez* (London: Constable, 1967).

favoured military intervention, believed that the Americans would prefer not to know about British plans to use force.

Eden had hoped that a readiness by Britain to proceed with the United States' Suez Canal Users Association initiative to put the canal under international supervision – something he called 'a cock-eyed idea, but if it brings the Americans in, I can go along with it' – would lead to economic sanctions and then John Foster Dulles would eventually reluctantly support military action.[127] But this, by October, looked extremely unlikely.

Only two senior Foreign Office diplomats knew what the French were proposing and Eden specifically excluded the Foreign Office legal adviser, who he knew would say that what Eden was contemplating could not be justified in international law. Instead Eden was now relying on advice from the Lord Chancellor, Lord Kilmuir, who maintained that intervention could be legally justified.[128] But constitutionally the Lord Chancellor is not the legal adviser to the Cabinet – the Attorney General is.

Eden swept his Foreign Secretary, who had flown in from New York, off to Paris within hours of his having landed without either man having had, as far as one can determine, any formal professional input from the Foreign Office, though Eden could rely on Kirkpatrick's support. This failure to consult was an action quite out of character for Eden. He was easily irritated but he was not normally impetuous. It was but one of many examples of how personalised and unstructured Eden's decision-making had become in 10 Downing Street. Under Churchill during the Second World War the machinery of the War Cabinet had functioned fully, and different departments of state had had their

---

127 William Roger Louis, *Ends of British Imperialism: The Scramble for Empire, Suez and Decolonisation* (London: I. B. Tauris, 2006), pp. 653–6.
128 Geoffrey Marston, 'Armed Intervention in the 1956 Suez Canal Crisis: The Legal Advice Tendered to the British Government', *International and Comparative Law Quarterly* (1988), vol. 37, pp. 773–817.

input. Eden himself had always been a stickler for following due procedure.

Eden was by now in very poor physical shape beside the earlier incident of a very high fever. He was taking Drinamyl or Dexamyl often referred to as 'purple hearts', a stimulant dextro-amphetamine.[129] A detailed account of Eden's illness is given in Chapter 3 of *In Sickness and In Power*.[130] Now with amphetamines his behaviour changed.

In a memo signed on 18 October by Selwyn Lloyd, the Foreign Secretary, recording the meeting in Paris on 16 October between Eden and himself, Mollet and Christian Pineau, the French Foreign Minister, and without officials, it is clear that the issue of how the United States would respond if Israel attacked Egypt was discussed and assessed:

---

129 Amphetamine and its dextro-isomer, dextro-amphetamine, together with methyl amphetamine (methedrine) comprise a group of drugs which act by releasing monoamines from nerve terminals in the brain, noradrenaline and dopamine being the most important mediators in this connection (H. P. Rang, M. M. Dale and R. M. Ritter, *Pharmacology*, 3rd ed. (Edinburgh: Churchill Livingstone, 1995), p. 637). They are stimulants which produce a feeling of energy, overconfidence and euphoria. First synthesised in 1887, they were introduced into clinical practice in 1932 and marketed under the name of Benzedrine. This was used in tablet form during the Second World War for military personnel who had to stay awake and amphetamine then became very widely used in the 1950s and 1960s. In 1964, following a press outcry in the UK about their misuse, the unlawful possession of amphetamines was made an offence and doctors began to use them much less. Amphetamines act not only on the brain but also on the lungs, heart and other parts of the body after releasing noradrenaline from binding sites. The effect depends upon the amounts used but even moderate doses often produce insomnia, restlessness, anxiety, irritability, overstimulation and overconfidence. Amphetamines do not create energy, they simply use it up. Prolonged use of even a moderate dose is invariably followed by fatigue; this 'come-down' effect is also often accompanied by difficulty with sleeping. Another sequel described after amphetamine use is called the 'crash' (Martin A. Plant, *Drugs in Perspective* (Sevenoaks: Hodder & Stoughton, 1981), pp. 37–40). These after-effects may be the result of depletion of the normal stores of noradrenaline and dopamine in the brain. These drugs can only be prescribed in the UK now under legislative authority. Amphetamine plays an important role in the next chapter on the health of John F. Kennedy.
130 David Owen, *In Sickness and In Power* (Methuen revised edition 2016).

'The Prime Minister (Eden) thought that the United States Government would be no more anxious than the French or British Governments to take action under the Tripartite Declaration. The Prime Minister said that during our visit to Washington in the early part of the year, the United States had made it quite clear that they would have to get authority from Congress before the United States forces would take any part. It was agreed that if Israel were to act before the end of the American election campaign it was most improbable that Congress could be re-summoned or if re-summoned, would give this authority. It was not thought likely that the Security Council would reach agreement on any action to be taken. In any case the Security Council could only pass resolutions and M. Mollet said that so far as the French Government was concerned, they would not be prepared to have Israel condemned as an aggressor for an attack upon Egypt after the way the Egyptians had behaved. The idea was then put forward by M. Mollet that it might be possible for the western powers to intervene to stop fighting in the area of the Canal. It was thought improbable that the United States would be willing to join such action, particularly during the course of the election campaign.'[131]

On 24 October Selwyn Lloyd noted that the previous day, in a meeting in London with Pineau which Eden joined,

the question of discussions with the Americans was raised. It was not thought that any useful purpose would be served by talking to them as the French and ourselves had talked, owing to their pre-occupation with the election campaign, and the generally unsatisfactory nature of our exchanges with Mr Dulles about US action of any character.[132]

---

131 Selwyn Lloyd personal papers, National Archives, ref. FO800/728, 52–3.
132 Ibid., 58.

The permanent secretary at the Ministry of Defence, Sir Richard Powell, whom Eden continually rang up, described him as 'very jumpy, very nervy, very wrought'. He also described Eden as having 'developed what one might call a pathological feeling about Nasser' and as being 'in a state of what you might call exaltation . . . He wasn't really 100 per cent in control of himself. Extraordinary, strange things happened.'[133] Air Chief Marshal Sir William Dickson, chairman of the Chiefs of Staff Committee, speaking in April 1957 to John Colville, used the same word, 'exaltation', saying that Eden 'during the final days was like a prophet inspired, and he swept the Cabinet and the Chiefs of Staff along with him, brushing aside any counter arguments and carrying all by his exaltation.' Exaltation is defined as 'a marked or excessive intensification of one's mental state or a delusive euphoria'. Dickson added that he 'had never been spoken to in his life in the way the PM several times spoke to him during those tempestuous days'.[134] The Chiefs of Staff were very reluctant to have the Israelis as allies.[135]

A Foreign Office diplomat's diary entry of 1 November 1956 on Eden's state of mind in October reads: 'Guy Millard says he is not mad, but merely exhausted.'[136] Eden was certainly not mad, nor so drugged that he could not carry out his day-to-day duties as Prime Minister. His stamina was in many ways remarkable, particularly after his October fever. But there are many other observations from people involved at the time confirming Eden's

---

133 Transcript of interview with Sir Richard Powell, papers of the Suez Oral History Project 1989–91, Liddell Hart Centre for Military Archives, King's College, London, ref. SUEZOHP 16.

134 John Colville, *Fringes of Power: Downing Street Diaries 1939–1955*, rev. ed. (London: Weidenfeld & Nicolson, 2004), pp. 671–2.

135 Eden, *Clarissa Eden*, p. 250.

136 Diary of Sir Evelyn Shuckburgh, Shuckburgh papers, ref. MS 191, Special Collections, University of Birmingham. Also published in edited form as Evelyn Shuckburgh, *Descent to Suez: Diaries 1951–56*, ed. John Charmley (London: Weidenfeld & Nicolson, 1986).

volatile behaviour and judgement during the Suez crisis. These accounts are fully compatible with what would be expected of someone taking the stimulant Drinamyl.

In his book *Anthony Eden: A Life and Reputation*, the historical analyst Professor David Dutton concluded that 'it is difficult to understand why Eden believed that he would get away with the Franco/Israeli plan and conceal it from the United States unless you believe that his judgement was not what it was at its peak'. He also went on to say that 'all the evidence is that he (Eden) was seriously ill by that stage . . . In the beginning of October he was weak and tired and desperately in need of a rest and probably on the verge of a nervous breakdown.'[137]

The strain on Eden was immense. His Minister of Defence, Walter Monckton, the only senior government figure to come out against the use of force, had remained in that office until 18 October, before being moved sideways. The absence of dissent may explain the fact that the Egypt Committee met thirty-five times between 27 July and 17 October but did not reconvene for its next meeting until 1 November, the day after the RAF started bombing Egyptian airfields.[138]

The situation in Hungary might have turned out very differently if there had been no October invasion of the Suez Canal. By the time of the Israeli attack on Egypt on 29 October, the Hungarian revolution, which had started on the 23rd, was experiencing a ceasefire and Soviet troops, having been repelled, were withdrawing. But on 2 November Nikita Khrushchev flew to see the Yugoslav leader, Marshal Josip Broz Tito, and in the early hours of 3 November Tito agreed it was reasonable for the Soviets to invade Hungary. Khrushchev said to Tito that Suez provided a

---

137 Professor David Dutton, speaking on *Case History: Anthony Eden.*
138 Peter Hennessy, *The Prime Minister: The Office and Its Holders since 1945* (London: Allen Lane, 2000), p. 235.

favourable moment . . . This will help us. There will be confusion and uproar in the West and in the United Nations, but much less than there would have been because Britain, France and Israel are waging a war against Egypt. They are bogged down there and we are stuck in Hungary.[139]

Shortly after midnight on Sunday 4 November Soviet tanks penetrated Budapest's outer defence ring. Next day, Ambassador Pierson Dixon sent a telegram to the Foreign Secretary from the UN: 'We are inevitably being placed in the same low category as the Russians in their bombing of Budapest. I do not see how we can carry much conviction in our protests against the Russian bombing of Budapest if we ourselves are bombing Cairo.' (This was a reference to an earlier bomb which had exploded near Cairo's central railway station.)

The Suez debacle had the most profound long-term effect on British and French foreign policy. The French angrily moved towards challenging US hegemony, the British, after their humiliation, towards rebuilding and relying on the special relationship with the United States. In the words of his *Times* obituary in 1977, Eden 'was the last Prime Minister to believe Britain was a great power and the first to confront a crisis which proved she was not'. A salutary warning for all of us as in 2020 outside the EU we design new foreign and defence policies.[140] Realpolitik is essential.

On 29 October Israeli paratroopers, led by the then unknown commander Ariel Sharon, were dropped into Sinai. The following day the British and French, as agreed with the Israelis, issued their ultimatum demanding a ceasefire and threatening to intervene if this were not agreed. Gamal Abdel Nasser rejected

---

139 Victor Sebestyen, *Twelve Days: Revolution 1956 – How the Hungarians Tried to Topple Their Soviet Masters* (London: Weidenfeld & Nicolson, 2006), p. 251.
140 David Owen & David Ludlow, *British Foreign Policy after Brexit. An Independent Voice* (London: Biteback, 2017), pp 53–86.

the ultimatum and on 31 October, Anglo-French military action began.

By the time of the invasion Eden and Selwyn Lloyd were not alone amongst British ministers in being party to the collusion. It has been clear since January 1987, when, under the thirty-year rule, the Eden Cabinet papers were first made public, that the Cabinet was told about the collusion with France and Israel on 23 October. This was the moment for the Cabinet collectively to have challenged that collusion and Eden's judgement. So why didn't they? Why, despite some initial dissent, did they go along with the policy?

The short answer again is realpolitik. A Prime Minister, supported by the Foreign Secretary, has great influence on a Cabinet decision on international affairs. It is similar to but even greater than the power of a Prime Minister, when supported by the Chancellor of the Exchequer, on domestic affairs. In addition, personal ambition and party manoeuvring played a part, especially for Harold Macmillan, the Chancellor. Harold Wilson later described Macmillan's position as being that of 'first in, first out' and it worked. He became Prime Minister replacing Eden.

Macmillan was on the face of it fully committed to Eden's policy.[141] He advised Eden after privately seeing Eisenhower at the White House on 25 September that 'Ike is really determined, somehow or other, to bring Nasser down. I explained to him our economic difficulties in playing the long hand and he seemed to understand.' The British Ambassador, who had accompanied Macmillan and did not see his note to Eden at the time, later commented that he could see 'no basis at all for Harold's optimism' about Eisenhower's support. But Macmillan did also send Eden a report of his meeting with John Foster Dulles. He told Eden that

---

141 Alistair Horne, *Macmillan 1894–1956: Volume I of the Official Biography* (London: Macmillan, 1998), pp. 420–3.

Dulles had said that while Suez was not playing much part in the election at present,

> if anything happened it might have a disastrous effect. He reminded me of how he and the President had helped us in May 1955 by agreeing to the Four-Power meeting at top level, which had undoubtedly been of great benefit to us in our electoral troubles. Could we not try and do something in return and try to hold things off until after 6 November?

This was much more than a hint from Dulles to delay any action until after the US elections and Eden was also made directly aware of the sensitivity of the US elections in correspondence with Eisenhower. Eisenhower had received a 'Dear Friend' letter from Eden on 5 October requesting some public announcement in general terms to the effect that the United States Air Force would provide technical information to modify aircraft and would train RAF air crews to carry certain types of US atomic weapons. He had answered on 12 October requesting any announcement be held 'in abeyance', referring to 'a number of sensitive issues, both in our domestic political situation and in our relations with our other allies'. The domestic situation was a clear reference to the elections on 6 November. Eden, after a revealing silence, formally accepted delay on 28 October. On 30 October in a 'Dear Anthony' letter Eisenhower calls Eden 'my longtime friend' but is clearly warning him about Anglo-Franco-Israeli military action and ends: 'It seems to me of first importance that the UK and US quickly and clearly lay out their present views and intentions before each other, and that, come what may, we find some way of concerting our ideas and plans so that we may not, in any real crisis, be powerless to act in concert because of misunderstanding of each other.' Eden wrote that same day promising a further letter but the Anglo-French ultimatum was announced in the media before the arrival of Eden's second letter to Eisenhower. Eisenhower wrote back formally on 30 October 'Dear Mr Prime Minister' and an identical message was sent to the French Prime Minister, Guy Mollet.[142]

But as October went on neither Macmillan nor Eden ever seemed to weigh the effect on Eisenhower of invading Egypt on the eve of his presidential election. This is very strange since, as democratic politicians themselves, they must have known that almost all political leaders fear losing elections even when they have commanding leads in the opinion polls and they hate any uncertainty in the last few days before polling. Margaret Thatcher would pack her bags in Downing Street before the elections of 1983 and 1987 'just in case' despite being well ahead in the polls.

For Eden and Macmillan not to have taken the pending US elections into account was folly. Macmillan at least grudgingly acknowledged later in his memoirs: 'Perhaps I should have attached greater weight to the date of the presidential election.'

It was Macmillan, as Chancellor, who, on receiving messages from Washington on the night of 5–6 November, was the first to realise the error of his judgement about Eisenhower's reaction. The crisis had put huge pressure on sterling and was costing Britain's foreign exchange reserves dearly. Macmillan needed to be able to rely on standby credit from the International Monetary Fund. That necessitated the United States helping, but he was told that US support for sterling depended on a ceasefire by midnight. This information, along with news of the US Sixth Fleet harassing Royal Navy vessels off Port Said, was conveyed to Macmillan and he at once changed his position on supporting military action.[143]

Eden's authority, never more brittle than on 6 November, could have been overtly challenged by Macmillan, the one man who could have swayed a Cabinet that had already lost its nerve to

---

142 Peter G. Boyle (ed.), *The Eden–Eisenhower Correspondence 1955–1957* (Chapel Hill: University of North Carolina Press, 2005).
143 Dutton, *Anthony Eden*, p. 442.

disown Eden. But Eden moved first. He summoned the Cabinet to meet in his room in the House of Commons at 9.45 a.m., knowing that he could not expect to maintain a majority in the Cabinet for carrying on with the policy. He said that with the Americans likely to support economic sanctions in the Security Council later that day there was no alternative but to announce a ceasefire. Macmillan, according to one Cabinet member, 'was very strong in his warning of what the US would do . . . he put the fear of God into the Cabinet on finances, as Chancellor'.[144] Without consulting the French the Cabinet abandoned the military campaign. Mollet was furious when told of the Cabinet's decision by Eden on the telephone.

It was a diplomatic debacle; in Eisenhower's words, 'I've just never seen great powers make such a complete mess and botch of things.' It was a humiliating about-turn caused by France and Britain having run out of friends; this was more fundamental than US pressure on the pound and the threatening letter over Suez from Russia (who at dawn on 4 November had moved 200,000 Soviet troops and 4,000 tanks into Budapest). The UK and France faced total isolation in the Security Council. Churchill is reputed to have said, 'I am not sure if I would have had the courage to invade but I am sure I would not have had the courage to stop.'

It would have been better from Eden's personal point of view, and for British and French prestige in the Middle East, to have pushed ahead and taken the whole canal while using with the French, our two vetoes on any UN sanctions resolution. There was no question that this is what Guy Mollet, the French Prime Minister, and David Ben-Gurion, the Israeli Prime Minister, would have much preferred. But domestic British politics intervened. The Cabinet panicked. Eden felt he had to act quickly and pre-empt Harold Macmillan upstaging him in the Cabinet and himself advocated acceptance of Eisenhower's position.

---

144 Horne, *Macmillan 1894–1956*, p. 447.

Later Mollet, meeting on 6 November with Konrad Adenauer, the German Chancellor, was told: 'France and England will never be powers comparable to the United States . . . Not Germany either. There remains to them only one way of playing a decisive role in the world: that is to unite Europe . . . We have no time to waste; Europe will be your revenge.' The Treaty of Rome, the first step to creating the European Union, was signed by the original six continental European countries, with Britain remaining outside, the very next year, 1957.

No hint of collusion with Israel was given to the House of Commons during the actual military operation and that was justifiable. What was bizarre and an indication that Eden believed the cover-up could be made to hold for much longer was his decision to send two diplomats back to Paris in an attempt to gather up and to destroy all the copies of what was later called the Protocol of Sèvres,[145] after the suburb of Paris where the meetings had taken place. Selwyn Lloyd had attended the initial meeting at Sèvres but the second meeting had involved a senior diplomat, Patrick Dean, and Lloyd's private secretary, Donald Logan, whose account is in the Bodleian Library, Oxford. Guy Mollet, and David Ben-Gurion, who had attended both meetings, agreed to total secrecy.[146] Eden should have known, however, that in democracies there can never be perpetual secrecy. The French and the Israeli leaders, who resented the British Cabinet's decision to halt the advancing troops down the canal, and had no guilty consciences about the military operation, were never going to keep it secret.

It was also a wholly unrealistic view of Eden's that any cover-up could be kept from American intelligence for much longer than a few weeks at best, more likely a few hours. In fact the CIA claimed to have known about the operation at all stages, though there is

---

145 Robert Rhodes James, *Anthony Eden* (London: Weidenfeld & Nicolson, 1986), p.331.
146 Thorpe, *Eden*, pp. 515–19.

some evidence to doubt this. On 29 October, when it is alleged John Foster Dulles first heard about the Israeli attack, he suspected French, but not British, involvement. It was only after the announcement of the French and British ultimatum that Dulles saw through the veil of camouflaged intent[147] and asked John Coulson, the British chargé d'affaires, next day how the Egyptians could be expected to give up their own territory and submit again to occupation. Coulson cabled Selwyn Lloyd, saying: 'What rankles the most is what they believe to be deliberate concealment on our part, if not an actual plot with the French and Israelis.'[148] More realistic than Eden, Christian Pineau, the French Foreign Minister told the United States about the facts of their collusion while Eden was still pretending to the Americans that no collusion had taken place, compounding US anger.

Given that Eden had known Dwight Eisenhower for over a decade, it was a major misjudgement of Eisenhower's character to believe that he would not react to being misled on such a vital issue by someone he had previously trusted. Eisenhower, not unreasonably, felt betrayed by Eden's behaviour. And the truth, as the then British Ambassador later said,[149] was that Eisenhower, not Dulles, made the major choices in US foreign policy. Lord Home criticised Eisenhower for demonstrating his hostility by sailing the US Sixth Fleet alongside the British invasion force,[150] but like many he was underrating the toughness that underlay 'Ike's' friendly personality. On 2 November, regarding Eden, Eisenhower concluded: 'It was undoubtedly because of his knowledge of our bitter opposition to using force in the matter that when he finally decided to undertake the plan he

---

147 William Roger Louis, *Ends of British Imperialism: The Scramble for Empire, Suez and Decolonisation* (London: I. B. Tauris, 2006), p.658.
148 Coulson to Lloyd, 30 October 1956, FO 800/741.
149 Lord Sherfield, speaking on *A Canal Too Far*, BBC Radio 3, 31 January 1987.
150 Lord Home, speaking on *A Canal Too Far*.

just went completely silent.'[151] Eisenhower emerges from this two-year correspondence with Eden extremely well and his public image as a semi-detached, golf-obsessed President is very wide of the mark. Eden, who had every reason to know this from personal contact, was foolhardy to ignore Eisenhower's view and from the tone of the earlier letters would never have done so before October 1956, by which time he was on mind changing drugs and had become beguiled by the Israeli option. Eisenhower gave Eden no reason to deceive himself into believing that he, Eisenhower, could afford on the eve of the presidential election to show the Americans how the British were so openly flouting his global authority.

Yet, just after being elected for a second term, Eisenhower was more generous to Eden in defeat than Dulles ever was. He offered to see Eden and it was only Dulles, while in hospital, who persuaded him not to see Eden and Mollet so soon after the ceasefire. In the light of this, if the invasion of the Suez Canal had been launched some weeks later, Eisenhower's reaction might have been more muted. Eden, for his part, reserved his venom for Dulles, referring to him as 'tortuous as a wounded snake, with much less excuse'.[152] But Dulles was being used as a scapegoat: the US viewpoint was a united one and explicit throughout.

The lesson for all future UK Prime Ministers – do not seriously mislead an American President. Doing so was a massive blow to Anglo-American relations and all that had been built up by Roosevelt and Truman. Eisenhower was graceful and did his best with the new Prime Minister, Harold Macmillan, to restore relations.

Eden's continued attempt to cover up diminished his standing, and when he said in the House of Commons on 20 December that 'there was not fore-knowledge that Israel would attack Egypt' it

---

151 Dwight D. Eisenhower, *Ike's Letters to a Friend 1941–1958*, ed. Robert Griffith (Lawrence: University Press of Kansas, 1984), p. 176.
152 James, *Anthony Eden*, p. 617.

was a lie.[153] Lying to the House of Commons was something which Eden had never done in more than thirty-two years as an MP. It was totally out of character and it hastened his resignation on 10 January having written to the Queen the night before.

To lie to the House of Commons, even after the invasion – meant Eden's judgement was seriously impaired and his illness and treatment made the major contribution to that impairment. He was suffering from amphetamine induced hypomania. Somewhat similar to that of Kennedy over the Bay of Pigs described in the next chapter. Lying to the House of Commons on 20 December 1956 by saying 'there was not fore-knowledge that Israel would attack Egypt' was a fatal error for Eden. MPs on hearing those words knew he would have to resign. This he did, claiming health reasons, but health was not the main reason for him resigning. He could not face the House of Commons in January when his lie would very soon have been exposed. To lie on an issue of this importance is a contempt of Parliament which should be as serious as lying to a court of law. The fact that there was never any parliamentary or public inquiry into the Suez crisis was an error for many reasons, but above all because Parliamentarians never exposed the truth that they had been lied to. Eden was allowed to escape any censure. Selwyn Lloyd who knew Eden was lying, went on to become Speaker of the House of Commons. The British establishment closed ranks.

The seeds were laid in 1956, however, for lying to Parliament over going to war in Iraq in 2002 and 2003. In the Iraq war we shared the defeat with the Americans and they helped shield the UK from much of the global legacy of defeat. Over Suez the legacy of defeat was shared between Israel, France and the UK. Nevertheless Suez was less damaging in 1956 to Britain's reputation and standing than the war in Iraq in 2003.

---

153 Hansard, HC Deb, 20 December 1956, vol. 562, col. 1518.

Chapter 5

John F. Kennedy's Drug Abuse in 1961

John F. Kennedy was elected President of the United States in November 1960 with 303 electoral college votes to Richard Nixon's 219, but only a slim majority of the popular vote – 118,574 out of a total of 68,837,000 cast. At forty-three, the new President appeared full of 'vigah' – a much-used Kennedy word – vitality, charm and humour. He was the first Roman Catholic President, the first holder of the office to be awarded a Purple Heart and the youngest President ever elected. Tragically, he was also the youngest President to die in office and the fourth US President to be assassinated.

Few people arrive at positions of authority without some secrets. As he was sworn into office, Kennedy was living with one very big secret: he had deliberately misled the American people about his health, which was far worse than the public had reason to suspect. He had Addison's disease, which left him dependent on hormone replacement therapy to live and, he believed, dependent on secrecy first to win and then to hold the presidency. Addison's disease is also called chronic adrenal insufficiency and hypocortisonism. It is a partial or complete failure of the adrenal glands, which rest on the top of both kidneys, first described by Thomas Addison in 1855. Most doctors nowadays take Addison's disease to mean the auto-immune failure of the adrenal cortex.

Yet the stark difference between Kennedy's inept handling of the Bay of Pigs and the consummate way he handled the Cuban missile crisis eighteen months later can be fully understood only by taking into account his very different states of health during the Bay of Pigs invasion of Cuba and the Cuban missile crisis. We now know there were Soviet missiles in Cuba with nuclear weapons attached to them capable of being fired by Soviet military on the ground without authorization from the Kremlin though Kremlin authority was soon imposed by Kruschev in October 1962.

In 1955 an article called 'Management of Adrenocortical Insufficiency During Surgery' was published in a surgical journal.[154] Case 3, we now know, referred to Kennedy. In the report Kennedy is described as an anonymous 37-year-old patient requiring elective surgery for a back injury on a programme of desoxycorticosterone acetate pellets of 150 milligrams implanted every three months and cortisone in doses of 25 milligrams daily given orally. Knowing that in 1954 Kennedy was already on such large doses of steroids calls into question the later claim in the 1960 report of his doctors, on the eve of the presidential vote, that his ACTH stimulation tests were considered normal in 1958. For such a test to be meaningful his doctors would have had to stop his steroids for some time beforehand. To do so, given the dosage and the fact that he had been on them for more than twenty years, would have been a brave step to take for a small diagnostic return. At Kennedy's post mortem, examination of serial sections of perirenal fat pads revealed no gross evidence of any adrenal cortex or medulla, just a few individual adrenal cortical cells diagnostic of severe Addison's disease, probably starting early in his life. Certainly not caused by tuberculosis which was deliberately put out to the public on the eve of the presidential election, when denying he had the disease.

---

154 James A. Nicholas MD, Charles L. Burstein MD, Charles J. Umberger PhD and Philip D. Wilson MD, 'Management of Adrenocortical Insufficiency During Surgery', *AMA Archives of Surgery* (1955), vol. 71, pp. 737–42.

The article stimulated some enquiries into whether this might be Kennedy as was actually alleged in one press report. A strong denial was issued that the article referred to him but it would not have been hard to demonstrate that in fact it did so. In some ways it was strange, given Kennedy's worries of any publicity about his Addison's disease, that he presumably gave his consent to publish. If he had he would no doubt have been given an assurance that it could not be traced back to him, but the article stated that 'this patient had marked adrenocortical insufficiency'. This demonstrated how inaccurate it was to refer to his illness as mild during the 1960 election campaign. Kennedy received the last rites in October 1947 on the sea voyage back to America having been first diagnosed in London as having Addison's disease. He received them again in 1954 when he had a serious post-operative infection.

The two back operations in 1954 and 1955 were a considerable test of Kennedy's courage and patience and he used the experience to write a book about historical figures who had demonstrated outstanding courage.[155] The more one knows about Kennedy's health problems the more one admires his physical fortitude.

In 1955 Kennedy had thyroid insufficiency with a low basal metabolic rate of -20, high cholesterol of about 350 and borderline protein-bound iodine. He was given a new thyroid preparation, tri-iodothyronine, eventually settling on 50 micrograms a day. Also in 1957 Kennedy had a post-operative abscess on his back, possibly a stitch abscess, infected with a virulent coagulase positive *Staphylococcus aureus*. He was very ill but fortunately the abscess was drained and responded well to streptomycin.

Two days before polling day against Richard Nixon, a statement from Dr Travell, Kennedy's personal doctor, who was an expert in dealing with the pain in his back, was issued by Robert Kennedy:

---

155 John F. Kennedy, *Profiles in Courage* (New York: Harper, 1956)

John F. Kennedy has not, nor has he ever, had an ailment described classically as Addison's disease, which is tuberculous destruction of the adrenal gland. Any statement to the contrary is malicious and false ... In the post-war period he had some mild adrenal insufficiency and this is not in any way a dangerous condition. And it is possible that even this might be corrected over the years since ACTH stimulation tests for adrenal function was (sic) considered normal in 1958. Doctors have stated that this condition might have arisen out of his wartime experiences of shock and malaria.

By using a very narrow definition of Addison's disease, namely, an insufficiency of the adrenal glands caused by tuberculosis, this campaign medical statement was creating a calculated and knowingly misleading diversionary tactic. It was, as one writer described it, undoubtedly one of the most cleverly laid smokescreens ever put down around a politician and a travesty of the truth to say that Kennedy's post-war adrenal insufficiency had been 'mild'.

Americans had to wait over four decades for the truth to slowly emerge about Kennedy's health. Honesty and responsibility in government requires public awareness of when the medical conditions or the treatments given to any head of government have the potential to impair judgement. For that we need, at the very least, a disclosure of medical illnesses, something we clearly did not have with Kennedy. The history of this cover up is in the more detailed account in Chapter 4 of *In Sickness and In Power*.

But it was not only the American people who were kept in the dark about the health of their President. Given the tight secrecy surrounding Kennedy's medical condition, none of even his closest aides knew how ill he really was nor the extent or type of his medication. Had they known they might have been more questioning of his judgement in the early part of his presidency. A privileged few – his wife, his brother Robert and his father – knew most of what his doctors knew. In her memoirs, Travell, who followed Kennedy after his election victory to become his first White House personal physician, mentioned the President once saying to her that in case she could not contact him, 'Ted Sorensen, (Kennedy's close adviser and speechwriter) is the only person here who is fully informed about my health. Discuss it with no-one else.' Restricting all information to only a few continued after the President's death. In the Kennedy Library there is a file dated 6 December 1963 recording the 'ruling' by the Attorney General, Robert Kennedy, who continued in that post under President Johnson, that all correspondence which dealt with personal medical matters should be regarded as a 'privileged communication' and should not go to the central files in the federal archives.

Dr Travell's expertise was in treating Kennedy's back and her particular technique involved flooding procaine or novocaine,[156] through a syringe, into his lumbar muscles. If procaine was used, even when diluted, some was bound to be absorbed into Kennedy's central nervous system. Its effects on the central nervous system include lack of concentration, inattention, tiredness, mood changes and a mixture of indecisiveness and impetuosity, anxiety and restlessness, all noticeable at times early in Kennedy's presidency.[157]

To ease his back pain, the President sometimes took five hot showers a day in the White House, swam in a warm swimming pool and used a rocking chair. Controversially, Travell used these

---

156 Procaine is a synthetic substitute for cocaine which was discovered in 1905. Cocaine was isolated from the leaves of coca, a South American shrub, in 1860; as a local anaesthetic it is mainly confined today to ophthalmology and minor nose and throat surgery. The tendency of procaine to produce unwanted central nervous system effects is one reason for its replacement in clinical use today by agents such as lidocaine and prilocaine, whose central system effects are much less pronounced.

157 In the Kennedy Library there is a file dated 6 December 1963 recording the 'ruling' by the Attorney General, Robert Kennedy, who continued in that post under President Johnson, that all correspondence which dealt with personal medical matters should be regarded as a 'privileged communication' and should not go to the central files in the federal archives.

injections as often as three times a day and sometimes even more frequently – five or six times has been mentioned. Some of Kennedy's other doctors became increasingly worried by the summer of 1961 about her repeated use of procaine injections, and in her clinical notes there is evidence of progressively greater use from July until October.

In the White House, however, she was never given the trust or the authority by the President to get on top of all the different types of recreational medication (including self-medication) that were accumulating in his body, having been prescribed by different doctors or just given to him by friends or acquaintances.

The Bay of Pigs fiasco on 17 April 1971, a few months after Kennedy became President when 1,500 anti-Castro Cubans attacked Cuba with American support, was, in the words of the historian Theodore Draper, 'one of those rare events in history – a perfect failure'. The Vienna summit with Khrushchev, which followed, was arguably an even more serious debacle, for which Kennedy alone was responsible. The simple and assiduously advanced explanation for this series of failures is inexperience on the part of Kennedy and his team. But that was a cover story and does not explain the reality.

The early plans President Eisenhower had seen for the invasion of Cuba were different in important respects from the one Kennedy eventually approved. The first CIA plan presented to Kennedy was a naval landing at the coastal town of Trinidad under the hopes that the population of the town would join the US-trained Cuban forces. Feeling this 'too spectacular' and too much like a Second World War invasion, Kennedy wanted to land at a different place and project the appearance of an infiltration by guerrillas in support of an internal revolution. Yet his rejection of heavily populated Trinidad in favour of the remote Bay of Pigs made a mass uprising much less likely. And it was the view of the Joint Chiefs of Staff that the absence of a Cuban uprising would make it unlikely that the invasion would succeed. This was something which Kennedy felt, afterwards, should have been made clearer to him. He had perhaps unwittingly also effectively ruled out the option of guerrilla fighting in the mountains, which were now some 80 miles away across swamps and jungle.

At the end of March, Kennedy consulted the former Secretary of State Dean Acheson about the plan. Acheson did not think highly of Kennedy and asked: 'Are you serious?' When Kennedy admitted that he was supporting 1,500 invaders against Castro's likely deployment of 25,000 defenders, Acheson retorted: 'It doesn't take Price Waterhouse to figure out that fifteen hundred aren't as good as twenty-five thousand.'[158] Senator J. William Fulbright, the powerful Democratic chairman of the Foreign Relations Committee, was also briefed and strongly criticised the whole concept.

Yet Kennedy went ahead. Why? The attack meant lying to the world about what was a naked act of aggression against another country in pursuit of the Monroe Doctrine, which was a strange way of starting the presidency of a young 'New Frontier' age. Kennedy was driven in part by a determination to demonstrate his toughness and not to be seen as a weakling in comparison to Eisenhower. But it is questionable whether Eisenhower would have authorised the invasion. Kennedy's brother Robert was also urging him to act decisively, brutally and savagely against Cuba. As the Attorney General he was well placed to influence his brother but he was also motivated by a deep hostility to Castro and he later became involved in plotting to assassinate him. Richard Goodwin, a close young aide, described the atmosphere at the meetings on whether to invade Cuba: 'Beneath the uninformed acquiescence, there was also arrogance – the unacknowledged, unspoken belief that we could understand,

---

158 Richard Reeves, *President Kennedy: Profile of Power* (New York: Simon & Schuster, 1993), p. 77.

even predict, the elusive, often surprising, always conjectural course of historical change.'[159] Furthermore, in the early months of 1961 the election campaign was still very fresh in the minds of both the President and his brother. Everything seemed to be going their way. The President's style and mood was cavalier and clearly hubristic and much of this was due to the drugs he was taking.

During the first six months of his presidency in 1961 Dr Travell's written records show that 'stomach/colon and prostate problems, high fevers, occasional dehydration, abscesses, sleeplessness and high cholesterol accompanied Kennedy's back and adrenal ailments'. Doses of so many drugs were being administered that an ongoing medicine administration record was kept,

> cataloging injected and oral corticosteroids for his adrenal insufficiency; procaine shots to painful 'trigger points', ultrasound treatments, and hot packs for his back; Lomotil, Metamucil, paregoric, Phenobarbital, testosterone, and Transentine to control his diarrhea, abdominal discomfort, and weight loss; penicillin and other antibiotics for his urinary infections and abscesses; and Tuinal to help him sleep.[160]

On 19 March Travell refers to a Demerol derivative being given as treatment, it appears, for his irritable colon, presumably in small oral doses. Demerol is a synthetic morphine-like drug.

As part of his necessary replacement therapy for Addison's disease Kennedy had to have testosterone. We know in patients then this produced varying blood testosterone levels. With high blood testosterone levels there follow mood changes.

As the Bay of Pigs invasion date approached it was a time of great stress for Kennedy, when the replacement drug therapy of

---

159 Richard N Goodwin, *Remembering America: A Voice from the Sixties* (Boston: Little, Brown, 1988), p. 173.
160 Dallek, *An Unfinished Life*, p. 398.

anyone with Addison's disease would automatically be tested. Additional stress means it is not easy for a doctor to judge at all times the appropriate replacement dose of steroids and testosterone. This was particularly so when the President was also being treated for two spells of urethritis in the month before the invasion, since infections often need higher dosages of replacement steroids. Dr William Herbst, a urologist based in Washington, saw Kennedy on 14 April 1961 and started treatment with an anti-spasmodic, Transentine.

What was the effect of all this treatment at the time when decisions over the Bay of Pigs were being taken and during the actual Bay of Pigs invasion on 17–18 April? The answer is that he had constant and acute diarrhoea and a recurrence of his urinary tract infection. Undoubtedly this was part of the reason he appeared totally demoralised in defeat. The President was given 600,000 units of procaine penicillin intramuscularly for his urinary infection on 17 April, the day of the Bay of Pigs invasion. He had had a similar flare-up in his chronic urethritis three weeks earlier, for which he was also treated. For anyone in good health, this infection and treatment would have left them feeling below par but for Kennedy, having Addison's disease, the effect was likely to be much greater.

On Saturday morning, 15 April, eight US B-26s flying from Nicaragua bombed three Cuban airfields, but destroyed only five of Cuba's thirty-six combat aircraft. An aircraft with Cuban markings also flew from Nicaragua to Miami, to give the appearance of being a defector. It landed in Miami with bullet holes in its fuselage and it was claimed that it had flown in from Cuba. In the UN that same day Adlai Stevenson, twice the Democrats' presidential candidate and appointed Permanent Representative to the UN by Kennedy, derided allegations that the United States was involved as being 'without foundation' and said the planes that had bombed the airfields were Castro's.

Stevenson was furious when he discovered he had deliberately not been informed of the true position. Had he known the truth he would have chosen more diplomatic words to avoid an outright lie. After treating Stevenson with such contempt, a clear sign of hubris, Kennedy had to personally pacify him to stop him from resigning.

A second B-26 air strike was planned for the morning of 17 April, the day the American-trained Cuban exiles stormed the beaches. This air strike did not take place, since Kennedy grounded the aircraft even though the CIA warned him that a failure to hit the beachhead from the air would be disastrous. Later, on 3 May, in giving evidence on the operational plan to General Maxwell Taylor's committee, which had been established by Kennedy to find out what had gone wrong, Robert McNamara, the Secretary for Defense said: 'There was one important modification that the chiefs never knew about and one about which they all felt strongly. This was the decision to cancel some of the D-Day air strikes. This decision was made at the only meeting which neither I nor the chiefs participated.'[161] McNamara's evidence was a damning indictment of the manner in which decisions were then being made in Kennedy's White House.

By Tuesday 18 April, there was no evidence of an internal uprising in Cuba and the Cuban government's air force had sunk the exiles' principal supply ship. Kennedy was not sure what to do. At a meeting from midnight until 3.00 a.m. on 19 April, he authorised a message to Admiral Dennison that six unmarked US jets should fly over the beaches to defend Cuban expeditionary forces from air attack. But they were not to hit any Cuban targets on the ground or to go looking for a fight. Kennedy must have known that this would have been an ineffectual limited

---

161 *Operation Zapata: The 'Ultrasensitive' Report and Testimony of the Board of Inquiry on the Bay of Pigs* (Washington, DC: Aletheia, 1981), p. 202.

intervention. It was meant to coincide with a Cuban émigré air drop, which due to a timing error never took place. By 1.00 p.m. on 19 April the Joint Chiefs of Staff concluded that there was nothing left to do but evacuate. Only fourteen anti-Castro troops were rescued and 1,189 surrendered.

The Bay of Pigs episode was more than a failure, it was a total disaster. Afterwards, US public opinion was somewhat assuaged by Kennedy's acceptance, as President, of sole responsibility. The Kennedy team's masterful manipulation of the short-term media reaction triumphed, and the President's wit was well tuned with attractive self-deprecation, as he told reporters: 'There's an old saying, victory has a hundred fathers, and defeat is an orphan.'

On the evening of 18 April Kennedy got so overwrought that he stopped mid-sentence and went out in the dark by himself for almost an hour, walking in the Rose Garden. The following morning Pierre Salinger found him crying in his bedroom. Jackie Kennedy told her mother-in-law that he had been practically in tears and that she had never seen him so depressed except after the operation on his back in 1955. Kenneth O'Donnell thought he was as close to weeping as he had ever seen.

Chester Bowles described Kennedy at a Cabinet meeting on 20 April as 'quite shattered' and talking to himself and interrupting conversations with an out-of-context remark: 'How could I have been so stupid?'[162] He could not sleep and described the whole episode as the worst experience of his life. He was constantly on the telephone to his father. This was not the behaviour of a fit, resilient Commander-in-Chief, nor that of a man suffering from depression. It was instead the behaviour of a man physically unwell, buoyed up by a variety of drugs, some replacement, some recreational, but then brought to a low ebb by failure which Kennedy was not used to.

---

162 *Foreign Relations of the United States 1961–1963, vol. 10: Cuba 1961–1962* (Washington, DC: Department of State, 1997), p. 305.

It is also worth noting that on 29 April 1961, as the Pentagon Papers show, President Kennedy agreed at a National Security Council meeting that clandestine actions should be taken in Vietnam. Army special forces left a few weeks later for South Vietnam. Some believe this was the critical moment in the escalation of the Vietnam War. The day before he had had sex with a mobster's mistress in Chicago. Kennedy was certainly not well placed physically or emotionally to make such a far-reaching decision.

Within weeks of the Bay of Pigs fiasco, President Kennedy faced his first summit meeting with the Soviet leader, Nikita Khrushchev, in Vienna. On 16 May, two weeks before the meeting, McGeorge Bundy, the National Security Advisor, wrote a very revealing memorandum to Kennedy which is sometimes referred to as the 'I hope you'll be in a good mood when you read this' memo. It was about how he should have been preparing to meet Khrushchev.

> We can't get you to sit still . . . The National Security Council, for example, really cannot work for you unless you authorise work schedules that do not get upset from day to day. Calling these meetings in five days is foolish and putting them off for six weeks at a time is just as bad . . . Truman and Eisenhower did their daily dozens in foreign affairs the first thing in the morning and a couple of weeks ago you asked me to begin to meet you on this basis. I have succeeded in catching you on three mornings for a total of about 8 minutes, and I conclude that this is not how you like to begin the day. Moreover, 6 of the 8 minutes were given not to what I had for you but what you had for me from (Bundy went on to list queries from journalists and others) . . . Right now it is so hard to get to you with anything not urgent and immediate that about half of the papers and reports you personally ask for are never shown to you because by the time you are available you clearly have lost interest in them.[163]

163 McGeorge Bundy, memo to Kennedy, 16 May 1961, National Security Files, John F. Kennedy Library, boxes 287–90.

This is an indication of how restless and hyperactive, to little purpose, Kennedy had become. It was during this period that he resumed taking medical treatment from Max Jacobson, a doctor nicknamed 'Dr Feelgood' by his New York patients, who he had seen during the presidential election campaign. Jacobson was certainly no ordinary doctor, but someone who had built up a reputation amongst a particular type of ambitious, often rich, achiever who can be found in most of the big prosperous cities of the world and who want doctors to give them extra energy. Some want improved sexual performance and general help to pursue a lifestyle that requires them to be pepped up. Jacobson earned his 'Dr Feelgood' reputation by dispensing amphetamines, as 'pep' pills and in vials for intramuscular injection. He is known to have injected between 30 and 50 milligrams of amphetamine intramuscularly into his patients, and sometimes to have given even larger doses. Selected patients were also taught to inject intravenously amphetamine in liquid form, more often at that time referred to as 'speed'. He would also commonly supply his patients with injectable vials to be self-administered.

Jacobson's licence to practise as a medical doctor was revoked in New York in April 1975 and an application for it to be restored rejected in 1979 on evidence taken from him starting around February 1966. We know a lot about how two patients in particular were treated between 1961 and 1968 from a 1975 report. The report, which I have read in full, shows that self-administration of injectable amphetamine supplied by Jacobson was commonplace and the description of the effect of those injections is 'elation' or 'euphoria'.

During an interview with Jacobson in 1969 agents from the Bureau of Narcotics and Dangerous Drugs had 'noticed he had needle tracks on his hands. He admitted that he injected himself with 25 grams of methamphetamine (speed) every two or three days.' Presumably the bureau meant milligrams, not grams, injected intravenously. Jacobson died in 1979.

The first report of Jacobson treating President Kennedy came in the *New York Times* only in 1972,[164] though the reporters felt they had to put in a rider that it could not be said with certainty that Kennedy had received amphetamines. Slowly, despite denials from Kennedy supporters, more and more information has emerged. Eventually Robert Dallek's biography of Kennedy, published in 2003, confirmed that Kennedy 'had injections of painkillers and amphetamines' from Jacobson.[165]

Kennedy had first been introduced to Jacobson shortly before the televised election debate with Richard Nixon in 1960 by Charles Spalding, a close friend from the early 1940s.

A revealing chapter on Kennedy's condition is included in Jacobson's unpublished memoirs, from which his medical claims can be analysed. The treatment of stress was one of Jacobson's specialities. After his first consultation, in September 1960, Kennedy is described as saying that his muscle weakness had completely disappeared and he felt cool, calm and very alert. Jacobson did not describe the treatment he gave but it was probably the intramuscular injection Jacobson most often used on patients, called XAM, a compound he himself made up containing amphetamine and steroids. Jacobson did not mention giving Kennedy any vials for self-medication to take away with him although that was his normal practice.

Several weeks after the presidential inauguration Jacobson had a phone call from Janet Travell enquiring about his treatment of stress. She confirmed his question that this referred to the President and he claims he gave her detailed information over the phone but that she bluntly refused his offer to send the same information in writing and a sample of his XAM formula.

---

164 *New York Times*, Monday 4 December 1972, based on reporting by Boyce Reusberger and the paper's medical correspondent, Lawrence K. Altman, amongst others.

165 Dallek, *Unfinished Life*, p. 398.

The next contact Jacobson described with the White House was three months later, on 12 May 1961. He was telephoned and asked to fly down to West Palm Beach to see the President. No mention is made of Jacobson treating the President on this occasion or giving him any vials for self-medication.

Kennedy visited Canada from 16 to 18 May. The President seriously hurt his back while digging to plant a small oak tree and began to be photographed actually using crutches. On 25 May, Dr Travell undertook two infiltration treatments with intramuscular procaine at 8.30 a.m. in three sites and at 8.00 p.m. in two sites and a further entry on 28 May noted that she carried out the same treatment at Kennedy's summer home, Hyannis Port. She had in her medical papers a chart outlining a male torso front and back. The sites were marked where she had infiltrated muscles in four places.

Jacobson described his receptionist telling him of a call from a Mrs Dunn in Washington on 23 May. 'Dunn', he claimed, was their code name for a call from the President's office. This clearly implies that a close arrangement for liaising between his office and the President's secretary in the White House had already been established. Jacobson flew to Washington. Almost certainly he gave the President an intramuscular injection of amphetamine with steroids. 'It has been observed that Addisonian patients are unusually sensitive to the mood-elevating effects of steroids.'[166] Nevertheless, Jacobson often supplemented the amphetamine he gave with heavy doses of steroids, garnished with vitamins, even at times adding ground-up bone marrow, placenta, electric eels and whatever other solubilised particles he perceived to be beneficial.[167] The steroids Jacobson gave would therefore have been in addition

166 William Alwyn Lishman, *Organic Psychiatry: The Psychological Consequences of Cerebral Disorder* 3rd ed. (Oxford Blackwell Science, 1998), p. 519.
167 Reports of the Committee on Discipline, Regents of the University of the State of New York, 22 March 1973–25 February 1975.

to the doses already being given as part of the President's replacement therapy. It has been alleged, but not proven, that the FBI uncovered five vials left by Jacobson at the White House, which on analysis revealed high concentrations of amphetamines and steroids.

The President was able to walk more easily after this treatment in May 1961 and Jacobson claimed he told him that he felt very much better and asked if he would come with him to Europe the following week. Kennedy also commented that his secretary had had no bill for his visit to Jacobson's office in New York earlier in September. This account suggests that the last time Jacobson had treated him had been in September 1960, but it does not rule out the possibility that Kennedy had been self-administering drugs supplied by Jacobson on that occasion in the interim. Yet to be sure it is best to assume that Jacobson had not treated Kennedy with amphetamines or given him self-administering vials during the Bay of Pigs crisis. But in the run-up to and during the meeting with Khrushchev in Vienna, Jacobson was in constant attendance on Kennedy and definitely gave him frequent injections.

None of Jacobson's therapy was ever coordinated with any of the President's doctors who were giving him normal replacement therapy for Addison's disease. Jacobson's treatment meant at least double dosages of drugs such as steroids and this certainly did matter and did have damaging consequences. Jacobson's amphetamine and steroids injected intramuscularly made Kennedy feel better for a time but, as is well known, neither cocaine derivatives nor amphetamines create energy; they give a temporary boost followed by a feeling of let-down. The 'speed' effect produced by amphetamines given intravenously was by then, also becoming well known in America. Selling injectable amphetamines without a prescription or on the basis of a forged or telephone prescription from a user posing as a physician was increasing. In 1962 federal, state and local law enforcement agencies were trying to stop such practices. When the injectable amphetamine scandal broke, Abbott

Laboratories in 1962 withdrew Desoxyn ampoules from the market and in July 1963 Burroughs Wellcome similarly withdrew Methedrine ampoules from distribution through retail pharmacists. Amphetamines were kept only for hospitals. But illicit factories called 'speed labs' took the place of pharmacies (Brecher, *Licit and Illicit Drugs*, pp. 282–3).

A senior Secret Service agent, according to Larry Newman, an agent who joined the presidential detail in the autumn of 1961, 'knew what the guy (Jacobson) was doing and tried to keep him away' from the President and the First Lady. 'We didn't see them (shots) administered or know the schedule of when Kennedy gave himself other shots', said the agent, 'but I was aware that during the waking hours . . . it was every six hours.'[168] Though the use of amphetamines in the early 1960s was not as strongly controlled as it is now, no serious doctor would have given anything like these sizes of dose to a patient with Kennedy's medical history.

We know that by the summer of 1962 Robert Kennedy was very worried about Jacobson's relationship with his brother and had the FBI analyse the substance Jacobson was injecting. 'Inconclusive lab tests, however, allowed Jacobson to continue treating Kennedy through at least the fall of 1962.'[169] From at least 24 May 1961, Jacobson was intensively treating Kennedy in the White House, in Paris and then in Vienna and London, in all of which places he gave Kennedy injections of amphetamine and steroids. It would no doubt have appalled Kennedy's White House doctors that such injections should have been given to the President at all, let alone in the run-up to a vitally important two-day meeting with Khrushchev, scheduled to start on 3 June in Vienna. Kennedy dismissed criticism of the treatment Jacobson was giving him by saying: 'I don't care if it's horse piss. It works.'[170]

---

168 Hersh, *The Dark Side of Camelot*, pp. 234–5.
169 Dallek, *An Unfinished Life*, p. 582.
170 Reeves, *President Kennedy*, p. 147.

But did it work? The cumulative evidence points to the repeated amphetamine injections from 24 May as having had very damaging consequences for President Kennedy's performance in Vienna. We know that no single doctor 'was in overall charge'[171] and the claim that 'Kennedy was more promiscuous with physicians and drugs than he was with women'[172] was probably true and not indicative of moderation.

Jacobson claimed that when he saw Jacqueline Kennedy on the morning after his visit on 24 May, she showed him a vial of Demerol or meperidine hydrochloride painkiller she had found in her husband's bathroom, presumably for self-injection. To Jacobson's credit he strongly objected to the President taking this, saying that it was highly addictive – which it was – and would interfere with his own medication. Jacobson was making a distinction between drugs that cause physical withdrawal symptoms and addictive dependency and amphetamines, whose users 'only in about 5 per cent' of cases move on to full-blown dependency.[173] No one apart from the President knew how long he had been taking Demerol, apart from its oral use for an irritable colon in March referred to earlier. It is not unreasonable to believe that he had been having injections during the Bay of Pigs crisis. Mrs Kennedy asked Jacobson if he would try and stop the President from using it. He claimed he raised the issue directly with Kennedy, concerned that it would affect the President's thinking.[174] Later that day Mrs Kennedy told Jacobson that a Secret Service agent had given Kennedy the drug and had since been dismissed. It was one more revelation of the strange cocktail of drugs which were being taken

171 Dallek, *An Unfinished Life*, pp. 369–70.
172 Michael Beschloss, *The Crisis Years: Kennedy and Khrushchev 1960–1963* (New York: Edward Burlingame, 1991), pp. 189–91.
173 H. P. Rang, M. M. Dale and R. M. Ritter, *Pharmacology*, 3rd ed. (Edinburgh: Churchill Livingstone, 1995), p. 639.
174 Reeves, *President Kennedy*, p. 147.

by the President, not known about by any of his White House doctors and definitely amounting to drug abuse.

Jacobson, not Travell, became in effect the President's personal physician for the next few weeks. Indeed Travell did not know that Jacobson was travelling to Paris. After four days of treating Kennedy in Washington, Jacobson returned to New York and then flew with his wife to Paris, but not before he gave the President another treatment on Air Force One at what was then called Idlewild airport in New York, later to be renamed after Kennedy. In Paris, Jacobson claimed he saw the President every day at the Palais d'Orsay, reserved for visiting dignitaries. Kennedy's visit to Paris was the prelude to meeting Khrushchev in Vienna. President de Gaulle thought it was foolish of Kennedy to be meeting Khrushchev but said: '*Tenir bon, tenir le coup.*' Hold on, be firm, be strong. Wait them out. One day, communism will fall of its own weight. De Gaulle wrote privately of his visitor: 'Enjoying the advantages of youth, but suffering the drawbacks of a novice.'[175]

Kennedy was keen to know more about Nikita Khrushchev and he was presented with a 'personality sketch' before he arrived in Vienna, prepared by the CIA. They noted Khrushchev's 'depressions and vulnerability to alcohol' but focused on his 'hypomanic' character.[176] Taubman cites a psychoanalyst's listing of hypomanic characteristics as almost perfectly describing Khrushchev:

> Elated, energetic, self-promoting, witty and grandiose ... overtly cheerful, highly social, given to idealisation of others, work addicted, flirtatious and articulate while covertly ... guilty about aggression toward others, incapable of being alone ... corruptible and lacking a systematic approach in cognitive style ... Grand

---

175 Ibid., pp. 149, 154.
176 Dr Bryant Wedge, 'Khrushchev at a Distance: A Study of Public Personality', *Trans-Action*, October 1968, pp. 24–8.

schemes, racing thoughts, extended freedom from ordinary physical requirements such as food and sleep ... constantly 'up' – until exhaustion eventually sets in.[177]

Khrushchev's wife Nina said of him: 'He's either all the way up or all the way down.'

Max Jacobson claimed that he flew in Air Force One to Vienna while Janet Travell was in Air Force Two. He went immediately to the US Ambassador's private residence, where the summit was due to take place. It is possible from Jacobson's description that an injection of amphetamine and steroids was given intravenously there since he stressed that the atmosphere was tense and that he was called to see Kennedy immediately. He claimed that Kennedy said to him: 'Khrushchev will arrive momentarily. The meeting may last for hours. I can't afford any complications with my back.' An injection containing amphetamine was then administered to the President. We do not know for sure whether it was given with steroids into his muscle as usual or whether methyl amphetamine was given into a vein. Jacobson recalled treating Kennedy in the White House in November 1961, when the cellist Pablo Casals gave a concert, and that Kennedy had asked for a repeat of the 'Vienna treatment'. This clearly implies that the Vienna treatment was different and probably an intravenous injection of amphetamine, an indefensible abuse.

Kennedy, however, was misinformed on the timing and Nikita Khrushchev did not arrive until forty-five minutes later. Kennedy ran down the steps to meet Khrushchev as if to demonstrate his vigour and health, in contrast to the rather portly 67-year-old Soviet leader. Jacobson almost certainly gave the amphetamine intravenously in order for it to act quickly and, if so, it would have

---

177 Nancy McWilliams, *Psychoanalytic Diagnosis: Understanding Personality Structure in the Clinical Process* (New York: Guilford Press, 1994), p. 248.

had a greater impact on Kennedy in the sense of a 'high' coming early and a low coming before the end of the meeting.[178]

Robert Dallek wrote, 'As the day wore on and an injection Jacobson had given him just before he met Khrushchev in the early afternoon wore off, Kennedy may have lost the emotional and physical edge initially provided by the shot.'

The first meeting with Khrushchev, on 3 June, went badly wrong and even Kennedy blamed himself for its failure. He acted totally out of character and the experienced Sovietologist Llewellyn 'Tommy' Thompson, then Ambassador to Moscow, seated behind Kennedy, told his State Department colleagues that he was shocked that Kennedy just sat there taking one shot after another from the Russian.[179] After that first meeting Kennedy raged that Khrushchev had treated him like a little boy and one of his own note takers at the meeting, Charles Bohlen, said of his President: 'He's a little bit out of his depth, isn't he.'[180] George Kennan, one of the great post-war American diplomats, thought the President had seemed tongue tied and totally unsure of himself. Criticism of this kind was

---

178 Quite apart from the combination of amphetamines and steroids, injections of steroids alone can produce behavioural effects, with very high doses producing manic or psychotic symptoms. High doses can give a feeling of energy and well-being and increased physical and sexual appetite. Even with all the recent advances, doctors treating Addison's disease have difficulty in setting the right doses of steroids. Eugene Cohen, Kennedy's endocrinologist, at this stage in all likelihood knew nothing about Jacobson's arrival on the scene, and was therefore completely in the dark as to the dosage of steroids he was giving the President. Most endocrinologists at the start of the twenty-first century believe that in the past patients were given too high a dosage. The most widely accepted regime now would be 10 milligrams of hydrocortisone in the morning followed by 5 milligrams at lunchtime and 5 in the evening. Some would choose to give prednisolone or cortisone. What is clear is that Kennedy, when Jacobson was treating him in addition to Cohen, was receiving much more. This is demonstrated by photographs of Kennedy during his presidency showing some fullness and puffiness in the face; this is associated with Cushing's disease, where there is overproduction of cortisol.

179 Reeves, *President Kennedy*, p. 162.

180 Reeves, *President Kennedy*, p. 172.

JOHN F. KENNEDY'S DRUG ABUSE

unusual, for Kennedy did not normally come across in this way. It was almost certainly brought on by the after effect of the drugs Jacobson had given him.

Next day, the conversation on West Berlin became ugly when Khrushchev said: 'The USSR will sign a peace treaty with the German Democratic Republic.' Kennedy asked if this peace treaty would block access to Berlin, and Khrushchev said yes. The gauntlet had been thrown down. 'Force would be met by force,' Khrushchev said. 'If the US wants war that's its problem.' Ending the meeting Kennedy said: 'Then, Mr Chairman, there will be war. It will be a cold winter.'

Kennedy knew he had not handled the meeting well. This is the view of David Reynolds in an assessment of this and other summits, who picks out Kennedy's failure 'to change tack and get out of the ideological argument on that long first afternoon'.[181] When James Reston, the Washington bureau chief of the *New York Times* and an experienced journalist, asked Kennedy ten minutes after the finish in a personal meeting how it had gone, Kennedy replied: 'Roughest thing in my life,' and said: 'He savaged me.' He went on: 'I think I know why he treated me like this. He thinks because of the Bay of Pigs that I'm inexperienced. Probably thinks I'm stupid. Maybe most important, he thinks that I had no guts.' Reston thought that Kennedy was practically in shock, repeating himself, blurting out things he would never say in other circumstances.[182] But little of this appeared in the *New York Times*. Reynolds describes the summit as a 'surreal meeting'.[183] It is impossible to escape the conclusion that Jacobson's injection had played a substantial part in Kennedy's performance and that this had a profound effect on Khrushchev and Soviet policy leading up to the Cuban missile crisis.

181 David Reynolds, *Summits: Six Meetings That Shaped the Twentieth Century* (London: Allen Lane, 2007), p. 204.
182 Reeves, *President Kennedy*, p. 172.
183 Reynolds, *Summits*, p. 202.

The President and his party left Vienna for London to meet Prime Minister Harold Macmillan. Max Jacobson claims he treated Kennedy that evening in the home of Prince Stanisław Radziwiłł, the husband of Jackie Kennedy's sister, Lee. He also claims he saw him the next day and flew back to the United States with him in Air Force One the following day, treating him on the plane.

At their first working session in London on 5 June it was obvious to Macmillan that Kennedy was in pain from his back, tense and fatigued; rather than have the scheduled formal session, he took him to his own room to have an informal chat – just the two of them – from 11.30 a.m. to 3.00 p.m. over sandwiches and whisky. Kennedy told Macmillan how surprised he had been by the brutal frankness of the Soviet leader.

Macmillan described Kennedy's reaction to Khrushchev as being 'rather stunned – baffled would perhaps be fairer' and 'impressed and shocked'.[184] Kennedy, he felt, saw Khrushchev as a 'barbarian'.

Kennedy went on to complain about the way the press had treated him and Jackie in Vienna and said to Macmillan: 'How would you react if somebody should say "Lady Dorothy is a drunk!"?' Kennedy laughed when Macmillan cracked back: 'I would reply "You should have seen her mother!"' Kennedy enjoyed his relationship with Macmillan and vice versa, despite their different ages and attitudes to many things, not least women. Macmillan on another occasion had no such quick rejoinder when, after talking about nuclear questions, Kennedy casually said: 'I wonder how it is with you, Harold? If I don't have a woman for three days, I get a terrible headache.'

In his brutal, belligerent way, Khrushchev later declared that Berlin was like 'the testicles of the West: every time I want to make

---

184 Alistair Horne, *Macmillan 1957–1986: Volume II of the Official Biography* (London: Macmillan, 1989), pp. 290, 303–4.

the West scream, I squeeze on Berlin'. Yet we now know from the archives that Khrushchev did not want war, but stability and recognition for Walter Ulbricht's East Germany. Kennedy for his part knew after this meeting that he would face a challenge from Khrushchev. Vienna was perhaps the turning point for Kennedy personally. After the Bay of Pigs he was privately blaming the failure on others; after meeting Khrushchev he knew the failure was his and his alone. On the flight back to Washington he apparently found solace in a quotation from Abraham Lincoln:

I know there is a God – and I see a storm coming;
If He has a place for me, I believe I am ready.

Yet the Kennedy that arrived back in Washington on 6 June was certainly not ready mentally or physically to face any such storm in that summer of 1961. He was becoming reliant on Jacobson's amphetamine injections. He had also refused Jacobson's offer to step aside made, Jacobson claims, because he had sensed Dr Travell's hostility to his presence as one of Kennedy's doctors. The severity of the President's back trouble was admitted to the press on 8 June, who were told he was on crutches and was going to Palm Beach to rest.

Meanwhile, on 10 June Khrushchev released to the world the aide-memoire he had given Kennedy and on 12 June in Geneva the nuclear test ban talks were effectively killed off by the Soviet delegation. Back in Washington on 16 June, the President, unable to walk up the stairs, had been lifted onto Air Force One by an airport cherry picker, normally used for work on aircraft engines.[185]

On 20 June the President had a sore throat, and by 22 June Travell describes the President as having his sickest day in the White House with a fever spiking at 105°F, thought to be because

---

185 Reeves, *President Kennedy*, p. 181.

of a streptococcus infection. Only after the urine culture was the cause of the infection certain – enterobacter cloacae – which is fatal in 20-40 per cent of cases; a sexually transmitted disease mainly affecting those immuno compromised, in layman's terms, a considerably increased susceptibility to infection. There are detailed chronological notes, probably made by a nurse during this period, from which it is clear that the President was seriously ill and he was treated with 'large doses of penicillin' and cold sponge baths. Yet the press corps at the White House was only told of a temperature of 101° by Travell, whose bland statement said: 'There is no serious concern about the President's health.'

On 28 June, Kennedy, now much better, spoke to the press, charging the Soviets with wanting 'to make permanent the partition of Germany' and adding: 'No one can fail to appreciate the gravity of this threat.' The political pressures on post-Vienna Kennedy were still considerable and generally he rose to the challenge but in dealing with Berlin he was handling a crisis area that had been long planned for and the President could rely on the extensive contingency planning. On the night of 12–13 August East German security forces put up barbed wire barriers to block people fleeing to West Berlin as a prelude to building the Wall. Kennedy's view was that 'a wall is a hell of a lot better than a war'. Having spoken out firmly, he called up reserves, rushed additional forces to Europe, made clear a firm intention to defend West Berlin and sent his Vice President, Lyndon Johnson, to the city. Kennedy also asked Congress for an extra $3.25 billion for the defence budget. The crisis froze that autumn but dangers lurked in East Germany and in other countries behind the Iron Curtain. Not until 1989, when the wall was eventually knocked down and Soviet communism itself began to crumble, did the Berlin situation cease to be a persistent cause for concern, fully justifying the Quadripartite mechanism between the four Foreign Ministers of France, Germany, UK and the US, having regular informal meetings.

The 'storm' came for Kennedy, after his prediction in June 1961, in the shape of Soviet missiles photographed in Cuba on 16 October 1962. Fortunately the President's back condition had improved substantially by then, as had his whole medical treatment. The detailed story of how he was medically transformed and ready for the challenge is told in the chapter on Kennedy in my book *In Sickness and In Power*, which details the thirteen days' handling of the Cuban missile crisis. On 22 October 1962 Kennedy went on TV to openly challenge the Soviet Union. Militarily, diplomatically, politically and psychologically I believe he managed the crisis brilliantly.

While Kennedy can be acquitted of recklessness overall in his political life it is not so easy to do so in his private life, with regard to recreational drugs and certain politically exposed women. When allegations were first made about his use of powerful recreational drugs, they were easily brushed aside by the President's former aides. But today the evidence, exposed particularly in 2005 in a book on Frank Sinatra, shows that Kennedy was a recreational user of mood-changing drugs, both before and during his presidency. The allegations include 'a claim that he used cocaine during a visit to Las Vegas in early 1960, experimented with marijuana and LSD with a lover in the White House, and – with his brother-in-law Peter Lawford – gave amyl nitrate to a woman to see how it affected her sexual experience'.[186] This represents a degree of total irresponsibility.

Womanising is not a disqualification for being President; nor is lying about it, as President Bill Clinton's failed impeachment proceedings over his affair with Monica Lewinsky show. But Kennedy's sexual recklessness with two particular women cannot be ignored. Most Americans would not have been too censorious

---

186 Anthony Summers and Robbyn Swann, *Sinatra: The Life* (New York: Alfred A. Knopf, 2005), p. 476.

about Kennedy's affair with Marilyn Monroe had it leaked out while he was alive. Yet conducting an affair with Judith Campbell, when Kennedy was well aware that she was the girlfriend of the infamous Mafia figure Sam Giancana, was political foolhardiness. Kennedy was the head of an administration pledged to clamp down on organised crime. At a one-to-one lunch with the head of the FBI, J. Edgar Hoover, on 22 March 1962 Kennedy was warned off seeing Campbell but did not stop telephoning her until August 1962.

On 3 July 1963 Hoover again tried to restrain President Kennedy, this time from seeing Ellen Rometsch. The problem with Rometsch was that she had grown up in East Germany and was believed to be a spy, having allegedly worked as a secretary for Walter Ulbricht, the head of government. She had made repeated visits to the White House, where she attended naked pool parties and had sex with Kennedy. She had been introduced to the President by Bobby Baker, secretary to the majority in the Senate, who was well known for making call girls available for Senators.

Both the Rometsch and Campbell affairs raise questions not about Kennedy's womanising but about his risk-taking with national security during his presidency. Hoover told Robert Kennedy about his brother's affair with Rometsch and Robert arranged to have her deported on 21 August to West Germany. Hoover told senior senators that an FBI investigation had shown no evidence that Rometsch was a spy or a visitor to the White House, a blatant lie and an example of the way in which Hoover ingratiated himself with President Kennedy and later President Johnson in order to stay head of the FBI.[187]

The key question is: to what extent was Kennedy's personal sexual risk-taking, even to the point of endangering national security, due to a propensity for reckless behaviour inbuilt into his

---

187 Dallek, *An Unfinished Life*, pp. 636–8.

character? Or was it driven by taking testosterone and steroids, part of his replacement therapy, or by recreational drugs such as amphetamines, Demerol or other drugs? The answer is probably a combination at various times of all of these.

As the world saw with President Clinton, sexual risk-taking or hubris does often fall into a separate compartment. A majority of the public sensibly understand this, judge their leader's competence and claims to stay in office, and decide how to vote as a separate issue. To some extent the public accept the sexual activity of a President as a private matter, even going as far as tolerating Clinton's false responses in his deposition, for which he accepted a two-year suspension of his law licence in Arkansas and a $25,000 fine.[188] There was little public pressure to move to formally impeach Clinton. The same tolerance may be extended by the public as distinct from the elite to allegations of Donald Trump's sexual activities before he was elected President and financial activities as a real estate dealer in New York. The fact that he does not drink alcohol makes it less likely that he was involved in New York's drug culture though it does not exclude it.

The vital lesson to learn from Kennedy's drug abuse is that he handled domestic political issues, not just foreign policy, with more composure and skill as his mental health improved and he became less dependent on drugs. By 1962 he was exercising regularly and began playing golf frequently by 1963, and his back had never felt better. The fact that he did not need or depend any longer on recreational drugs and they were taken less frequently owes a lot to Dr Kraus, a rock climber and trainer of the Austrian Olympic ski team, who did so much to transform Kennedy's health. When Kennedy last saw him in October 1963, he believed he would throw away his back corset in the New Year.[189] Tragically, that was

---

188 Sidney Blumenthal, *The Clinton Wars* (New York: Farrar, Straus & Giroux, 2003), p. 786.
189 Schwartz, *Into the Unknown*, p. 204.

a promise he was never able to fulfil and his assassination in Dallas on 22 November 1963 brought to an end a presidency which promised much but had yet so much to deliver.

After Robert Dallek's account of President Kennedy's health was written up in 2002 in *Atlantic Monthly*, a *New York Times* editorial concluded: 'It's hard to read the list of ailments and medications without wondering whether there were times when he may have been too impaired to do the job he was elected to do.'[190] This was not Dallek's view. He wrote that Kennedy's 'medical difficulties did not significantly undermine his performance as President on any major question'.[191] This is a view I do not share and I think it is very important that this complacent interpretation is challenged, and future politicians, Presidents and Prime Ministers learn the lessons from the two distinct phases of Kennedy's presidency very well described by Nassir Ghaemi in his book *A First Rate Madness* as recently as 2013. He diagnoses Kennedy as a hyperthymic cyclothymic personality who abused testosterone-based anabolic steroids. They were 'changing his moods, probably causing manic and depressive symptoms, in a way that for a while harmed his ability to lead'.[192]

In my judgement, when Kennedy met Khrushchev in Vienna in June 1961, his presidential performance was seriously impaired. A combination of back pain and Dr Max Jacobson's unregulated injections of amphetamines and steroids interacted with his replacement drug therapy of testosterone and steroids for his Addison's disease to cause a state of exhaustion, restlessness and fluctuations of mood that considerably reduced his ability to do the job of President. Kruschev sensed political weakness and risked testing Kennedy first over Berlin and then over Cuba.

As to the invasion of the Bay of Pigs, Kennedy's drug abuse is less clear and any conclusions more speculative. It is unlikely that

---

190 'The J.F.K. file', *New York Times*, 19 November 2002.
191 Dallek, *An Unfinished Life*, p. 705.
192 Nassir Ghaemi, *A First Rate Madness*, pp. 164-169.

Kennedy was taking Jacobson's amphetamine and steroid injections but he was taking many other drugs including morphine derivatives. I believe that the balance of probability is that Kennedy's decisions over the Bay of Pigs were significantly undermined by his medical condition, treatment and drug abuse. On well-controlled medication President Kennedy might have confidently dismissed the CIA and military advice in 1961 to give US backing for the Cuban exiles' invasion as not befitting a great nation. In doing so, he would have been fully supported by Senator J. William Fulbright, Dean Acheson and many other significant figures and experts in international affairs.

There is no denying that an emotionally steadier and better prepared Kennedy, positioned to handle more skilfully his Vienna meeting with a belligerent Khrushchev in June 1961 would have ensured that Khrushchev did not leave Vienna underestimating Kennedy's resolution and his authority. Khrushchev did decide to place nuclear-tipped missiles in Cuba on 21 May 1962. It is ironic that the sequence of events – Kennedy's bad decisions over the Bay of Pigs, his weak handling of the Vienna meeting with Khrushchev and his subsequent anti-Castro and anti-Russian stance – provoked the very Cuban missile crisis which he then so ably resolved in October 1962. Kennedy thereby with his health transformed laid the foundation for holding firm during the Cold War, despite the building of the Berlin Wall, until 1989. Tolerating the wall was part of the containment strategy of Soviet communism for it highlighted the fact that East Germans were opting with their feet for Western standards of living and the freedoms of democratic societies. President Reagan's public demand to 'tear down this wall' was the end point of a sustained process of détente and *Ostpolitik* agreed with the UK, France and Germany and held to by Presidents Johnson, Nixon, Ford, Carter, Reagan, George H. W. Bush. We should never forget this. It is why we must persuade President Trump about the benefits of NATO. But also Kennedy's flexibility and determination in handling Kruschev with the maritime block-ade can guide President Trump as to how best to deal with President Putin's Russia. The key is to establish principles before starting to negotiate, while accepting the value of dialogue through meetings with President Putin.

In September 2009 in the *Annals of Internal Medicine* an endo-crinologist, Dr Lee Mandel, after seeing all Kennedy's records gave what is likely to be the definitive diagnosis of his Addison's disease, namely that Kennedy had a rare auto-immune disease known as auto-immune polyendocrine syndrome type 2, or APS 2.[193] Patients with APS 2, also known as Schmidt's syndrome, have Addison's dis-ease along with auto-immune thyroid disease and/or type 1 diabetes, but do not have hypoparathyroidism or candidiasis (John Lackie, *A Dictionary of Biomedicine* (Oxford: Oxford University Press, 2010)).

Well controlled Addison's disease should not disqualify anyone from running for the highest office anywhere in the world. After having decided to run for Congress with a view to later running for President, Kennedy should have had the wisdom to start a different, more open and indeed more democratic relationship with the public after he had been diagnosed with Addison's in 1947. It would have been understandable and reasonable politically to link it to his war service and veteran status even if that, we now know, had little if anything to do with it. He would have enhanced his presidency if he had chosen to be more open about his Addison's disease. President Eisenhower had been very open over his illnesses and Kennedy could have started a greater openness in 1956 when he was setting up a marker as a possible Vice President for Adlai Stevenson. What was required was gradually to shift, in the light of medical advances, and the shift in public attitude to illness, to end his denial, so dangerous to himself and the country.

---

193 Lee R. Mandel MD MPH, 'Endocrine and Autoimmune Aspects of the Health History of John F. Kennedy', *Annals of Internal Medicine* (2009), vol. 151, pp. 350–4.

This short encapsulation of Kennedy's history of drug abuse is a warning notice of how easy it is for the rich and powerful to take mind changing drugs. 'Dr Feelgood' is not a one-off phenomenon and decision making amongst leaders in many walks of life but particularly political and business life, are still being affected by the taking of drugs. The older generation are more likely to be using amphetamines, one whose brand name is commonly used is Adderall. Also widely used today is methylphenidate (MPH), a psychostimulant prescribed to treat attention deficit/hyperactive disorder (ADHD), commonly called Ritalin. Psychotropic effects and pharmacological pathways evoked by MPH are similar, but not identical, to those produced by amphetamines and cocaine. Use without any medical or psychiatric diagnosis is increasing and claims of usage among college students indicate that it is far higher than has been assumed and is growing. Society as a whole should view this pattern of drug taking far more seriously.

Another scandal involves the privately-owned US company, Purdue Pharma, that made OxyContin, released for patients in 1995 as a breakthrough long-lasting narcotic. It was promoted for less acute conditions: arthritis, back pain, sports injuries and fibromyalgia, despite its addictive nature which led to an "opioid epidemic". "Its sole active ingredient is oxycodone, a chemical cousin of heroin which is up to twice as powerful as morphine . . ." The company funded research and paid doctors to make the case that concerns about opioid addiction were overblown."[194] In 2007 the company paid out the largest ever fine levied against a pharmaceutical firm for mislabelling its product. It is estimated that more than 2.5 million Americans have an opioid-use disorder. The company filed for Chapter 11 bankruptcy in September 2019.

---

194 Patrick Radden Keefe, 'The Family That Built An Empire of Pain', *The New Yorker*, 23 October 2017.

Chapter 6

Vietnam: How Harold Wilson Resisted Lyndon Johnson's Demands for UK Military Involvement

It is one of the strangest coincidences in relationships between US Presidents and UK Prime Ministers that when Kennedy was assassinated, waiting in the wings as Vice President was Lyndon Johnson and soon to become Prime Minister was Harold Wilson. Two figures with a lot more in common that either would have wished to be acknowledged. Johnson in early 1960 asked his staff how many Vice Presidents had succeeded to the Presidency. The answer was ten. John Adams, Thomas Jefferson, Martin Van Buren, John Tyler, Millard Fillmore, Andrew Jackson, Chester A. Arthur, Theodore Roosevelt, Calvin Coolidge and Harry Truman. He then asked his staff for another figure. How many Presidents of the US had died in office. The answer was seven. At that stage there had been 37 Presidents, these were good odds on a Vice President succeeding to the presidency. At John F. Kennedy's inaugural ball, Clare Booth Luce, a former Congresswoman and wife of the *Time Inc* publisher asked Lyndon Johnson why he had agreed to accept the nomination as Vice President. He replied, exaggerating the figures, 'Clare, I looked it up. One out of every four Presidents has died in office! I'm a gamblin' man, darling! And this is the only chance I got.'[195] Cynical? Hard-headed? Calculating? All of these but also highly manipulative.

Harold Wilson took a gamble also on the best route for him to become, first, leader of the Labour Party and then Prime Minister. He calculated that he had to be seen to be a man on the left of the party. On 24 April 1951 he resigned as the youngest member of the Cabinet and as President of the Board of Trade under Prime Minister Attlee who was in hospital at the time. He chose to support Aneurin Bevan who was a powerful figure, senior to him in the Cabinet as Minister of Health. The issue was of prescription charges for medicines on the NHS. Though Wilson claimed it was for him the rise in the defence budget and not health charges. John Freeman, later editor of the *New Statesman* who resigned as a Minister with Wilson, knew Wilson well. He saw Wilson was not keen to be labelled a Bevanite, and described how 'He wore the label, like a poppy on Remembrance Day – for form's sake.'

When three years later on 13 April 1954 Bevan stormed out from the shadow Cabinet leaving a vacancy the next in line of succession was Wilson. Bevan said if Wilson took his place he would regard it as black treachery and likened Wilson to Ramsay MacDonald, the Labour Prime Minister who formed a national government in 1931 and is always regarded as a betrayer of the Labour Party. Wilson cannily read the mood of the party far better than Bevan and accepted the vacancy. His reward was that he topped the poll in the constituency section for the National Executive Committee later that same year.

Both Wilson and Johnson were supreme political calculators and well matched over the vexed question of how to handle the war in Vietnam. When Wilson visited Johnson in the White House in December 1964 he found a larger-than-life Texan, hugely

195 Robert A. Caro, *The Years of Lyndon Johnson. Vol 4: The Passage of Power* (The Bodley Head, 2012), pp. 114-5.

enjoying being President from 1963 after Kennedy's assassination. What is more he was considered then a great success and his gamble had paid off. Never happy as a mere Vice President appendage to Kennedy, Johnson was intent on using his great office to bring in the civil rights reform legislation that was long overdue.

Johnson had been the very successful Senate majority leader. Yet on Saturday 2 July 1955 he had a serious heart attack and was given a 50:50 chance of survival. He was prescribed complete rest. At the age of forty-six he found himself written off from ever being able to challenge for the presidency. There was even some doubt whether he would be able to stay as leader of the Senate. Johnson fell into a deep depression, a common side effect following heart attacks, although violent mood swings, with clear-cut depressive episodes, had always been part of Johnson's character. He left the hospital on 7 August. On doctors' orders he had to stop smoking and drinking coffee. He had also been told to lose weight so without nicotine, caffeine, calories, sex or the Senate, he had nothing to satisfy himself. Suddenly, he started to read books and to tell people, somewhat unconvincingly, that it was wonderful to 'have time just to sit and think'. According to his biographer, Robert A. Caro, when Johnson went back to his ranch in Texas, he 'fell into a despair deeper even than his despair in hospital', sitting for hours, 'staring at nothing, and saying nothing'.[196] Eventually we may learn more about what, if any, drug treatment for depression Johnson was given then and during the years he was President. Many years later he was diagnosed as having bipolar disease in the study of mental illness amongst Presidents.[197] (Table 3, Introduction.)

---

196 Robert A. Caro, *The Years of Lyndon Johnson, vol. 3: Master of the Senate* (London:Vintage, 2003), pp. 620–36.
197 Jonathan R.T. Davidson, Kathryn M. Connor and Marvin Swartz,'Mental Illness in US Presidents between 1776 and 1974: A Review of Biographical Sources', *Journal of Nervous and Mental Disease* (2006), vol. 194.

Johnson was intensely ambitious and unscrupulous. Clark Clifford, who knew well all the US Democrat Presidents from Truman to Carter, described Johnson as 'the most complex man I ever met; he also may have been the most difficult'; he could be 'astonishingly devious' and 'a terrible bully'.[198] But he understood political power. Dean Acheson, formerly Truman's Secretary of State, wrote to Clifford that Johnson presented 'an unbelievable combination of sensitivity and coarseness, of understanding and obtuseness'. Yet Clifford believed that, had it not been for Vietnam, Johnson 'would have been one of our most illustrious Presidents'.

Johnson had tried to stop the momentum for Senator Kennedy to become President at the July Democratic convention in 1960. He described him to the *Chicago Daily News* as a 'little scrawny fellow with rickets'. India Edwards, who was very close to Johnson politically, claimed at a press conference at the convention that Kennedy had Addison's disease. A 'reliable' source had apparently told her that he had been present at a governor's mansion during a Kennedy campaign stopover and that Kennedy, as a result of forgetting his cortisone, had lapsed into a coma until a state trooper had been able to get some to his bedside that night.[199] This claim was widely seen as a dirty trick from the Johnson camp but according to India Edwards, Johnson himself lashed out at her for implicating him in the allegation. While Jack Kennedy appeared not to blame Johnson for this attack on his health, his brother Robert did blame him and never forgave Johnson. From the start Robert Kennedy resented his brother having offered the role of Vice President to Johnson and found it difficult to accept Johnson as President after his brother's assassination.[200] It was probably old

---

198 Clark Clifford and Richard Holbrooke, *Counsel to the President: A Memoir* (New York: Random House, 1991), pp. 385–6.

199 Jeff Shesol, *Mutual Contempt: Lyndon Johnson, Robert Kennedy, and the Feud that Defined a Decade* (New York: W.W. Norton, 1997), p. 35.

200 Ibid., p. 361.

Joe Kennedy who persuaded Jack to offer Johnson the Vice Presidential position on his ticket and they both told no one about their decision.

There are many stories of Johnson's wheeling and dealing nature; one involves Kennedy's father, Joe, saying to him that if Johnson put his son Jack, on being newly elected to the Senate, on the Foreign Relations Committee, Joe would never forget the favour for the rest of his life. Revealingly Johnson recalled his reaction and why he put him on the Committee:

> Now I knew Kefauver (Estes Kefauver, a Tennessee senator) wanted the seat bad and I knew he had four years seniority on Kennedy. And I would have preferred showing preference for Tennessee over Massachusetts. But I kept picturing old Joe sitting there with all that power and wealth feeling indebted to me for the rest of his life and I sure liked that picture.[201]

Joe Kennedy was a powerful influence on his son Jack, far more so than Robert. Joe Kennedy would have been attracted to having Johnson on the ticket, calculating that Texas was a state that had to be won; and he would not have worried about alienating those Democrats who disliked Johnson. In the 1960 presidential election John F. Kennedy beat Richard Nixon by 303 electoral votes to 219 but virtually tied in the popular vote with 34,226,731 votes to Nixon's 34,108,157. After his inaugural speech his popularity and style had the effect of making Johnson appear as a dimmed and diminishing figure until everything dramatically changed on 22 November 1963 when Kennedy was assassinated.

The Gulf of Tonkin incident[202] in August 1964 gave rise to the

---

201 Robert Dallek, *Lone Star Rising: Lyndon Johnson and His Times 1908–1960* (Oxford: Oxford University Press, 1991), p. 556.
202 David Owen, *The Politics of Defence* (London: Jonathan Cape, 1972), Chapter 4 pp. 52-63.

famous wide-ranging Congressional resolution of 7 August 1964, which President Johnson made the 'functional equivalent' of a declaration of war. The resolution was itself frequently cited by President Johnson as his authority from Congress to conduct war operations against North Vietnam, though on 5 August, appearing before the Security Council of the United Nations, Adlai Stevenson declared that American reprisals were 'limited in intention'. The resolution was not terminated until 12 January 1971, when President Nixon signed an Act formally repealing the resolution which had given virtually unlimited authority to an American President to intervene in South-East Asia for six years.

The facts on which the Senate decided to pass the resolution were hotly disputed, not least by Senator Fulbright, who had played such a crucial role in persuading his fellow Senators to pass it. He later believed that he had been misled by the Administration into believing the hurried initial presentations that this was a deliberate and unprovoked attack on American ships on the high seas.

Even from the start there was doubt whether the North Vietnamese had attacked the destroyers *Maddox* and *Turner C. Joy* on 4 August.

Many people believed that Johnson was at the time desperately searching for a pretext for escalation of the war into North Vietnam. The detailed Pentagon study published in the *New York Times* on 12 June 1971[203] revealed that a Congressional resolution was discussed in the State Department in mid-February 1964 and prepared on 25 May. This only confirmed the suspicions of Congressional dissenters who had at the time alleged that the Tonkin Gulf incident was merely the pretext to push a ready-made resolution through a compliant Congress.

Appeals in July by President de Gaulle, UN Secretary General U Thant and even from North Vietnam for the reconvening of the

---

203 *The Pentagon Papers* (New York, 1971), p. 245.

Geneva Conference had been summarily dismissed both in Washington and Saigon. Lyndon Johnson, in a presidential election year, was clearly wary of taking a posture which might support the Republican charge that he was 'soft on Communism'. Meanwhile the faltering regime in South Vietnam was clamouring for a step-up of the war.

It is worth noting not only that the CIA had frequently challenged the domino theory as applied to the possible fall of South Vietnam, but that it had also advised that the bombing of North Vietnam would not cause Hanoi to stop supporting the insurgency in the South. Yet the Joint Chiefs of Staff and the politicians ignored this advice.

It is an interesting fact that, all along, Hanoi never denied the first attack on the *Maddox* on 2 August. It was, they said, a reprisal for the amphibious raid on the North Vietnamese islands that had taken place on 30 July, which we know now was part of a series of clandestine operations carried out by the South Vietnamese but under the control of the United States Military Assistance Command.

We know too that McNamara's claim in his 1964 testimony that the United States Navy had played no part in the attack was dangerously misleading.[204] On 3 August, President Johnson himself had ordered that the *Maddox* and *Turner C. Joy* should return to the Tonkin Gulf and the Commander-in-Chief Pacific (CINCPAC) Fleet had sent a message suggesting that the *Maddox* and *Turner C. Joy* should draw the North Vietnamese patrol boats away from the islands. The task group commander had also already warned that the North Vietnamese considered the American ships as enemies because of their involvement. It is clear from the Pentagon study that McNamara had received reports on the clandestine attacks and that Dean Rusk had also been kept informed.

---

204 *Pentagon Papers*, p. 265.

The Tonkin incident has one clear message. No democratic government should attempt to involve its nation in a major war on the basis of lies, half-truths and deliberate deception. A message that was forgotten by the time of the invasion of Iraq in 2003 when this time, not just the US, but the UK too, went to war on the very same basis of lies, half truths and deliberate deceptions.

Across the Atlantic at the time of Kennedy's inauguration Harold Wilson, out of office since his resignation in 1951 was, like Lyndon Johnson, a much diminished figure since his rival Hugh Gaitskell, Leader of the Labour Party since 1956 was now in the ascendant despite losing the 1959 General Election to Prime Minister Harold Macmillan. Macmillan no longer looked a powerful Prime Minister and few doubted that Gaitskell would soon become Prime Minister.

Suddenly in January 1963 Gaitskell died and Harold Wilson became leader of the Labour Party. Wilson saw Kennedy alone for an hour in the White House. Kennedy had been impressed by Wilson's knowledge but according to Henry Brandon, the *Sunday Times* correspondent in Washington, 'did not take to him as a person'. After the assassination 'Lyndon Johnson was an unknown quantity.'[205] Wilson first visited Lyndon Johnson early in 1964 as leader of the Opposition, not yet in government and there was little serious discussion of South East Asia.

Harold Wilson won back power for Labour in October 1964 with the slimmest majority of four. As in 1945 some expected a 'socialist' foreign policy where the left dominated by socialists wanted an anti-imperialist international policy. Labour's 1964 election manifesto promised 'an end to colonialism', wanted to relax Cold War tensions, planned new initiatives on disarmament and chose the United Nations as the main forum. Wilson appointed

---

205 Philip Zeigler, *Wilson: The Authorised Life* (Weidenfeld & Nicolson, 1993), pp. 148, 151, 221.

as a political permanent representative, Lord Caradon, a career colonial servant and brother of Michael Foot MP, who following Aneurin Bevan's death took over as the titular leader of the left. The manifesto called for a 'move away from the anarchy of power politics toward the creation of a genuine world community and the rule of law'.[206]

An excellent account by Rhiannon Vickers, 'Harold Wilson, the British Labour Party and the War in Vietnam' published by the *Journal of Cold War Studies* covers many aspects of policy towards Vietnam from a British perspective and on which I have drawn extensively.[207] This was a time when the United Kingdom was still East of Suez and was fully occupied all through 1964 in what was called the Indonesian Confrontation. By the start of 1965 the UK had deployed its largest force since the Korean war in the Far East. Some 80 Royal Navy vessels, 6 infantry battalions and a force of V-bombers all aimed at deterring the Indonesian President, Sukarno, from mounting a full scale invasion of Malaysian territory. It was a triumph for the controlled use of deterrence and ended with a new government in October 1965 and the official end of confrontation on 11 August 1966. There is no way in 2020 that a UK return East of Suez even with our two new aircraft carriers will be able to mirror the scale of our engagement in the 1960s and we should not pretend otherwise.

An illegal declaration of independence from Southern Rhodesia in 1965 was an added constraint economically on British armed forces undertaking what the US Administration wanted, UK military support in Vietnam. The US Ambassador in London, David Bruce, fortunately was an astute judge of the domestic political pressures and was understanding of Wilson's problem. But

206 'Labour Manifesto 1964' in F.W. S. Craig, ed., *British General Election Manifestos, 1900-1974*, rev. and enlarged ed. (London: Macmillan, 1975), pp. 267-270.
207 Rhiannon Vickers, 'Harold Wilson, the British Labour Party, and the War in Vietnam, *Journal of Cold War Studies,* Vol. 10, No 2, Spring 2008, pp. 41-70.

tension between Johnson and Wilson began to mount when in December 1964 during a visit to Washington in the Rose Garden of the White House, Wilson was pressed by Johnson 'to send the Black Watch to Vietnam, even a few pipers would be better than nothing', a request to which Wilson did not directly respond.[208] It was Foreign Secretary Gordon Walker, however, who told US Secretary of State Dean Rusk that the UK already had troops in Malaysia and 'was emphatic that the UK could not have troops on the ground in Vietnam'. Britain was ready, however, to train men in jungle warfare, to dispatch more police advisers to Saigon, and support greater cooperation in the medical field.[209]

Wilson surreptitiously provided a little more than just moral support. Britain sold arms to the United States for use in Vietnam, with clandestine deliveries of weapons, including napalm and 500-pound bombs, from Hong Kong.[210] In the House of Commons, Wilson artfully denied that such deliveries were taking place, claiming that 'no licences have been granted for the export of arms to Vietnam' and that 'we are not supplying arms directly or indirectly for the fighting in Vietnam'.[211] From 1968 to 1971, Britain supplied economic aid to South Vietnam valued at $2.4 million.[212] The SAS also provided some training for US Special Forces personnel in Borneo.

Wilson's refusal to commit British troops stemmed not just from military and economic overstretch but from the fact that it

208 Philip Zeigler, *Wilson. The Authorised Life of Lord Wilson of Rievaulx* (London: Weidenfeld & Nicholson, 1993), p.222.

209 'The Prime Minister's Visit to the United States and Canada,' 6–10 December 1964, p. 31, in PREM 13/104, TNAUK. See also 'Memorandum of Conversation,' 8 December 1964, in *FRUS, 1964–1968*, Vol. I, p. 985.

210 Stephen Dorril, *MI6: Fifty Years of Special Operations* (London: Harper Collins, 2000), p. 718– 719; and Sylvia Ellis, 'British Opposition to the Vietnam War, 1964–68,' in Kristaan Versluys, ed., *The Insular Dream: Obsession and Resistance* (Amsterdam: VU University Press, 1995), pp. 173– 174.

211 Harold Wilson, Speech to the House of Commons, 17 May 1966, *H.C. Deb.*, 5th Ser., Vol. 728, Col. 1119.

212 Stanley Robert Larsen and James Lawton Collins, *Allied Participation in Vietnam* (Washington, DC: Department of the Army, 1975), pp. 166–167.

would have caused outrage within the Labour Party and the government. Some government ministers would likely have resigned, and some left-wing Labour MPs might have refused the Labour Party whip in protest. With only a majority of four MPs this would have risked a General Election. Yet Wilson courageously, in the sense he judged it in the national interest, continued to offer strong public moral support for the US intervention in Vietnam and this is the crucial lesson for handling the Trump Administration. Wilson never shifted from believing that you treat allies as friends. An attitude that Boris Johnson shares.

On 7 February 1965 Wilson, worried about the escalation, telephoned President Johnson and an acrimonious conversation ensued. Wilson admitted, 'To my surprise, he let fly in an outburst of Texan temper', saying that there was no point 'jumping across the Atlantic' every time a critical situation arose. 'I won't tell you how to run Malaysia' Johnson said, 'and you don't tell me how to run Vietnam . . . If you want to help us some in Vietnam send us some men.'[213]

Wilson knew in the House of Commons the next day, he would face criticism from his own backbenchers over support for US policy and said to Johnson that if he could say he was going to visit the President immediately to discuss the situation, it might help. Johnson's reply was that 'it would be a mistake for the Prime Minister to try to use the President as an instrument in the House of Commons' and that Wilson 'would have to decide what side he was on'.[214] In a memorandum to Johnson, National Security Adviser McGeorge Bundy spoke of 'the very great damage which Wilson did to himself by his outrageous phone call to you'.[215] Yet

213 Harold Wilson, *The Labour Government 1964–1970: A Personal Record* (London: Weidenfeld and Nicolson and Michael Joseph, 1971), p. 80.
214 'Memorandum of Telephone Conversation between President Johnson and Prime Minister Wilson,' 10 February 1965, in *FRUS*, 1964–68, Vol. II, p. 230.
215 McGeorge Bundy to Johnson, 22 March 1965, in Vol. 4, Memoranda to the President, NSF, LBJL.

Secretary of State Rusk urged Johnson to meet with the new British Foreign Secretary, Michael Stewart, and reminded the President that 'the British Government has, despite pressures from the left wing of the Labor (sic) party, maintained solid support for United States policy in Vietnam'.[216]

There was a professional realism in the UK about the Vietnam war of which Wilson was well aware. Sir Robert Thompson, the head of the British Advisory Mission to South Vietnam, had sent a memorandum to the Foreign Office in August 1964 reporting that the situation in South Vietnam was hopeless, that defeat of the South by the Viet Cong was 'inevitable', and that the Americans should negotiate with the North while they still could.[217]

According to the US embassy in London, the British reaction to US policy resulted primarily from three factors: first, an underlying fear that the conflict might lead to a Third World War; second, a widespread sense that 'it is high time for vigorous expressions (of) criticism (of) U.S. policy in order to influence it'; and third, the 'persistence of (a) relatively small but well-organized and vociferous group (of) left-wingers and pacifists who (are) adept at exacerbating these fears and frustrations'.[218]

Another Wilson line of defence to his critics was that the UK was co-chairman of the Geneva Conference, and was pressing its co-chairman in Moscow for action leading to a conference.[219] Wilson's various initiatives to bring peace over Vietnam are not worth describing for they never had a chance of success. It was clear to the Vietnamese and governments sympathetic to them, that Wilson did not have the confidence of Washington. He was a realist

---

216 Memorandum from Dean Rusk to President Johnson, 10 March 1965, in Box 2778, POL 7, 1964–66, Record Group (RG) 59, U.S. National Archives and Records Administration II (NARA).

217 Thompson to FO, 13 August 1964, in FO 371/175501, TNAUK.

218 Telegram, U.S. Embassy in London to Secretary of State in Washington, 16 December 1965, in Box 2786, POL 1 UK-US, 1964–66, RG 59, NARA.

219 Wilson, *Government*, p. 84.

but he had to pretend to an influence which he did not have. His initiatives were only important in keeping the peace inside the Labour Party and showing that he was listening to genuine concerns.

Wilson's position had not been helped by Labour's defeat at the Leyton by-election held on 21 January 1965 where the candidate had been Patrick Gordon Walker, Wilson's Foreign Secretary, who had lost his seat in Smethwick in the October 1964 election. Wilson had insisted on appointing him while knowing it would be hard to win any by-election. The swing against Labour in Leyton had been 8.7 per cent. Another General Election was even more necessary.

In meetings with Secretary of State Rusk on 23 March 1965 in Washington, Michael Stewart, the new Foreign Secretary 'emphasised the extremely strong feelings that had been aroused by the use of gas and napalm bombs which inflicted undue suffering and were of limited military value'. Rusk responded that Britain itself had used such weapons before and that 'this Viet-Namese war was not a Sunday-school party. It was a rough business'.[220] In a speech to the National Press Club that day in Washington, Stewart said that 'in the choice of measures everyone responsible should consider not only what is militarily appropriate for the job in hand but the effect on people around the world'. Wilson wrote that Stewart's 'uncompromising approach won the approval of Labour MPs'.[221]

In the General Election held on 31 March 1966 Labour was returned to power with a large majority ending up with 363 seats, the Conservatives 253, and Liberals 12.[222] I was one of the new Labour intake of MPs and watched very closely how Wilson handled relations with Washington.

---

220 Record of a Conversation between the Foreign Secretary and Dean Rusk, 23 March 1965, in PREM 13/693 DV 103145/60, TNAUK.
221 Wilson, *Labour Government*, pp. 85–86.
222 David Butler and Gareth Butler, *British Political Facts 1900–1985*, 6th ed. (London: Macmillan, 1986), p. 227.

In May 1966 the bombing of Hanoi and Haiphong in North Vietnam caused outrage and widespread anger among Labour MPs, in particular among a new and younger group. In response to earlier complaints from the Parliamentary Labour Party (PLP), Wilson had repeatedly told the Commons that 'we could not support any extension of the bombing against North Vietnam by stages to Hanoi and Haiphong'.[223] On 29 June, in a carefully worded statement, Wilson in part did criticise the specific action and told the House of Commons that the government 'noted with regret' the bombing of Hanoi and Haiphong and dissociated itself from that action. But he also stressed 'that the United States are right to continue to assist the ... South Vietnamese', that 'the North Vietnamese refusal alone' was preventing peace negotiations, and that 'we deplore Hanoi's constant rejection of the path of peace'.[224]

At the 1966 annual conference, a resolution from the Fire Brigades Union was passed calling on the government 'to bring all pressures on the United States of America to end the war in Vietnam'. At the 1967 annual conference a resolution was narrowly adopted calling on the government to 'dissociate itself completely' from US policy in Vietnam, to persuade the United States to end its bombing of North Vietnam 'immediately, permanently and unconditionally', and to strive for a peace settlement based on the 1954 Geneva Agreement. The Foreign Secretary by then was George Brown who urged the conference not to support the resolution, but it passed by 2,752,000 votes to 2,633,000 – a rejection of the government's policy by the party's membership.[225] This defeat called in to question relations between the PLP and the

223 See, for example, Harold Wilson, Speech to House of Commons, 21 December 1965, in *H.C. Deb.*, 5th Ser., Vol. 722, Col. 1909; and Harold Wilson, Speech to House of Commons, 8 February 1966, *H.C. Deb.*, 5th Ser., Vol. 724, Col. 259.
224 Harold Wilson, Speech to House of Commons, 29 June 1966, *H.C. Deb*, Vol. 730, Cols. 1796–1797.
225 *LPACR,* 1967, pp. 235-236.

party in the country. As far back as 1907 Keir Hardie, then leader, suggested that the party conference could not bind the PLP:

> Resolutions instructing the Parliamentary Party as to their action in the House of Commons be taken as the opinions of the conference, on the understanding that the time and method of giving effect to these instructions be left to the party in the House, in conjunction with the National Executive.[226]

Wilson used that interpretation to assert MPs' rights and rejected the conference's resolution.

A review carried out in 1970 for the National Executive Committee by Tom McNally, now Lord McNally and a Liberal Democrat, said that Vietnam had been 'the issue which caused most disillusionment within the Party' and that 'leaving foreign policy to the foreign policy pundits' was dangerous, 'especially since the Labour Party has always had among its rank a higher percentage of people deeply concerned about foreign policy issues than can be found among the electorate as a whole'. McNally concluded:

> The lesson to be learnt from this is that a wrong foreign policy decision may lose us only a minute percentage of votes; but it can lose us a much higher percentage of party activists. Foreign policy has, for this reason, a much greater importance for the Labour Party than crude statistics of voting motivations would suggest. For many thousands of our activists their socialism only has meaning if a socialist domestic policy is also reflected in our foreign policy.[227]

---

226 *Keesing's Contemporary Archives,* Vol. 12, *1959–60* (London: Keesings Worldwide, 1960), p. 17,744. See also Kenneth O. Morgan, *Keir Hardie: Radical and Socialist* (London: Weidenfeld and Nicolson, 1975), p. 168.
227 Tom McNally, 'Foreign Policy Formation,' June 1970, in International Department, ID/1970-71/65, Box LI, 23 June 1971, NEC Mins, LPA.

That is where Jeremy Corbyn, the leader of the Labour Party, comes from. Some of his controversial stands over Venezuela, Palestine and nuclear deterrence are deeply rooted in the Trotskyist left of the Labour Party. Ernest Bevin as Foreign Secretary was given a very rough ride from Labour MPs over Palestine. But that was not connected to anti-Semitism, perhaps because memories of the Holocaust were so strong. Exactly how that anti-Semitism grew in the Labour Party is now the subject of a major inquiry by the Equality and Human Rights Commission. Although anti-Semitism was probably a factor in turning Labour activists away from the party, it was not such a large element in the voters' choice to explain Labour's heavy defeat in the 2019 General Election.

Wilson handled Johnson, no easy task, extremely well. There was at that stage much less of the press paranoia that bedevilled his second period in office from 1974 to 1976. He was cool, rational and careful in his handling of both Johnson and American public opinion. He instinctively liked America and Americans yet was careful to distance himself from the protesters in Washington and elsewhere, who singled out President Johnson for personal attacks.

There is a choice to be made in close UK diplomatic and political links with America, summed up in the words, 'in for a penny, in for a pound'. There is only rarely a halfway house. US foreign policy is determined by the President; it is not a collective decision making process with Congress, let alone with friendly foreign governments. US policy can be influenced and will be influenced even under President Trump but it is subject to personal presidential decisions to use another aphorism, 'you have to take the rough with the smooth'. Harold Wilson understood this. It is clear that Boris Johnson as Prime Minister does also. However President Trump is proving harder to handle than President Johnson.

In 1965, when Johnson had an attack of acute cholecystitis, affecting the gall bladder, he consulted Dwight Eisenhower about his illness and Eisenhower recommended openness and pointed out the advantages of candour. Johnson, normally obsessed by secrecy, took his advice, told the Vice President Hubert Humphrey and then the Cabinet, and went into Bethesda Naval Hospital for the removal of his gallstones and gall bladder. Then twelve days after the operation, on 20 October, he had a famous photograph taken for the press showing a long scar over his stomach. Very interestingly after that operation Johnson experienced post-operative depression bad enough that he wanted to draw up papers to resign from the presidency.[228] This story has never had much publicity but its source was very close to the Johnson family. He was dissuaded from resigning by the few people who knew and even today, nearly fifty years later, this dramatic episode is shrouded in mystery. There were other episodes of paranoid instability and irrationality but this is the only known report of him wanting to step down before he finally announced he was doing so in 1968. Johnson also had a family history of alcoholism, debt and hypersexuality, which strengthens the suspicions that he had bipolar disorder, which is an inheritable illness.

The assassination of President Kennedy reignited interest in a constitutional amendment covering illness in a President. It was realised that Kennedy might have survived but been seriously disabled, and there were worries about Johnson's own health, after his serious heart attack eight years earlier. The Twenty-Fifth Amendment was therefore agreed in July 1965 and ratified by the necessary thirty-eight states on 10 February 1967. That mechanism some have argued should be used to terminate President Trump's presidency. The UK government as in 1967 and now in 2020 must stay well away from making judgements on this issue, which is a matter of US domestic politics only.

Yet in the late spring of 1965, after Johnson's staggeringly successful presidential election when he won 486 electoral votes

---

228 Liz Carpenter, *Ruffles and Flourishes: The Warm and Tender Story of a Simple Girl Who Found Adventure in the White House* (New York: Pocket, 1971), p. 261.

and had 43,127,041 popular voters, Richard Goodwin was alarmed at what he perceived to be the President's 'increasingly irrational behaviour'.[229] Goodwin, his principal speech writer and someone who had been in constant touch with the President for three years, began to study medical textbooks and talk confidentially with professional psychiatrists. Unbeknownst to Goodwin, his friend Bill Moyers, perhaps the President's closest young confidant, took the same course and talked independently to two psychiatrists.

> In all cases the diagnosis was the same: we were describing a textbook case of paranoid disintegration, the eruption of long-suppressed irrationalities. As for the future, it was uncertain. The disintegration could continue, remain constant, or recede, depending on the strength of Johnson's resistance, and, more significantly, on the direction of those external events – the war, the crumbling public support – whose pressures were dissolving Johnson's confidence in his ability to control events, that confidence which was his protection both against the buried cauldron of non-rational suspicions, and his fear of being left alone and helpless in a hostile world.[230]

Nearly forty years later on the Bill Moyers Interview of 14 September 2017, these very same issues about the alleged disintegration of a sitting US President were being discussed in relation to President Trump. Moyers was interviewing America's leading psychohistorian Robert Jay Lifton renowned for his studies of people under stress. This included survivors of the nuclear explosion at Hiroshima, Vietnam veterans and Nazi doctors. This was therefore a discussion between two experts as distinct from elitists. Lifton argued that he and others who were publishing a new book *The Dangerous Case of Donald Trump* by St Martins Press and had a duty to warn if we think we have learned something about

229 Richard N. Goodwin, *Remembering America: A Voice from the Sixties* (Boston: Little, Brown, 1988), p. 398.
230 Ibid., p. 403.

Donald Trump that is dangerous to our country. Moyers countered that some 'argue that our political system sets no intellectual or cognitive standards for being President' and 'it's not normal people who always make it to the White House'. Lifton defines 'solipistic reality' in relation to Trump as meaning 'that the only reality he's capable of embracing has to do with his own self', but goes on to say 'He's not psychotic.' Moyers asks about a 'delusional disorder', to which Lifton replies 'I'm not sure it qualifies as a bona fide delusion. He needs things to be certain, to be a certain way even though they aren't, and that's one reason he lies.' Moyers asks about 'When the Democrats make a deal with him, as they did recently are they edging him a little closer to being accepted despite this record of bizarre behaviour?' Lifton replies 'We are normalising him when the Democrats make a deal with him. But there is a profound critical issue here and it's not easily answered.' Later Lifton says 'something has gone wrong with our democratic system in electing a man with all these characteristics . . .' Moyers concludes the interview with these words 'I think quite a few more things than our "democratic system" have gone wrong for us to elect a person like Trump as our President. We have allowed the creation of an effective oligarchy, which leads to neglect and resentment.'

A small group of people have controlled the US and the UK for many decades now and Moyers with all his experience is correct to identify neglect and resentment. The result is a people's revolt in the rust belt states of the US and outside London in the UK.

In 2006, the review of biographical sources of American Presidents that diagnosed Theodore Roosevelt as suffering from bipolar-I disorder classified Johnson likewise during his presidency, with a high likelihood of the diagnosis being correct. It is not surprising, given Johnson's suspicious character, that any information about his mental condition is hard to find. He would probably have instructed his doctors not to leave any paper trail because, being paranoid, he would have feared any revelation about his health. There is little doubt that Johnson had clinically significant depressions throughout his life. The review of the available literature led these psychiatrists to interpret Johnson's coarse and volatile behaviour as reflecting the opposite pole, mania, to that of his depression. Johnson had a habit of speaking of 'my air force' and had an unshakeable belief in his entitlement as President to lie.

President Johnson's early time in the White House was, in terms of legislative social reforms, particularly on civil rights, outstanding. He used all his formidable skills honed in Congress to assemble majorities which no President before or since has been able to achieve. As his presidency continued it became ever more dominated and indeed haunted by the war in Vietnam. Goodwin explained:

> The results of this narrowed focus were devastating. Within government reasoned argument, the exchange of divergent views, critical appraisal of fundamental policy, came to a halt ... power alone can check power, and if the restraints, not of men but institutions, are dismantled, then democracy is in mortal danger. I have worked with many powerful men. They were all convinced that their goals were righteous, that their sole objective was the public good; and they all resented obstacles to their will.[231]

The strains and anguish over Vietnam meant Johnson went through long periods of stress and during the years 1965–7 his conduct clearly changed. One of his biographers wrote that Johnson's 'paranoia raises questions about his judgement and capacity to make rational life and death decisions'. Also he admitted that 'determining psychological incapacity may be impossible'. He then went on to question: 'Who then is to say when a President has passed the bounds of rational good sense?' Nevertheless, his biographer Dallek concluded: 'Certainly in Johnson's case, for all the cranky nonsense he espoused about his enemies, he remained largely in control of his

---

231 Ibid., p. 390.

faculties and more than capable of functioning as President.'[232] It is true that the war in Vietnam would have been an extremely testing challenge for any President. What was required was the capacity at least to consider rationally and calmly the withdrawal of US troops; this was something that Johnson, with all his self-doubt and paranoia about being thought to be weak, was incapable of doing. He chose instead incremental increases in troop levels and bombing activity, less than the generals wanted, more than his critics could support. He announced he would not run for President in 1968. Robert Caro's last and fifth volume of his exceptional biography so far will be important in making any judgement as to what extent any mental illness affected his abilities to function as President.

The deep-seated controversy over American handling of the Vietnam war from the viewpoint of the Labour Party and the Left in Europe ensured an indelible mark for a generation and more. Rhiannon Vickers was generous to Wilson in the concluding section of her paper:

> On balance, Wilson's approach to the Vietnam War can be deemed relatively successful in view of the contradictory domestic and international pressures he was facing. He resisted U.S. demands for British troops but preserved close Anglo-American relations that were crucial to Britain. Wilson's dual policy of dissociating Britain from the U.S. bombing of North Vietnam while upholding Britain's support for the overall U.S. action in Vietnam repeatedly won support in the House of Commons. Similarly, his peace diplomacy was just enough to placate a party that contained activists who to a large extent viewed Vietnam as a war of liberation rather than a Cold War struggle.[233]

---

232 Robert Dallek, *Lyndon B. Johnson: Portrait of a President* (London: Penguin, 2005), pp. 376–7.

233 Rhiannon Vickers 'Harold Wilson, the British Labour Party, and the War in Vietnam', *Journal of Cold War Studies*, Vol. 10, No. 2, Spring 2008, pp. 41–70

Chapter 7

Iraq: Hubris of George W. Bush and Tony Blair

George W. Bush became President in January 2001 and started by saying he would appoint good people, delegate authority and hold them accountable for results – and promised when running for office that America's stance in the world would be 'strong but humble'.

On 16 February 2001 George W. Bush agreed that US and UK bombers, as part of the ongoing policy inherited from President Clinton's eight years, should hit Iraqi radar and command centres and on 10 August the United States and Britain bombed three Iraqi defence sites. Press comment was low key and it did not seem to betoken any major change in policy towards Iraq.

Whether or not Bush really did intend to be 'humble abroad' and not 'engage in nation-building' as well as being a delegating, hands-off leader will remain one of the unknowns of history. But it is clear that after 9/11 that would have been an impossible stance for any American President to maintain. Bush was understandably deeply shocked, as his face showed when, in a school in Florida, he was told the news of first one and then a second plane hitting the World Trade Center in New York. The 9/11 Report from the National Commission on Terrorist Attacks Upon the United States was told by the head of the CIA George Tenet, 'the system was blinking red' during the summer of 2001. The Commission reported 'Officials were alerted across the world. Many were doing everything they possibly could to respond to the threats. Yet no one working on these late leads in the summer of 2001 connected the case in his or her in-box to the threat reports agitating senior officials and being briefed to the President. Thus these individual cases did not become national priorities. As the CIA supervisor "John" told us, no one looked at the bigger picture; no analytic work foresaw the lightning that could connect the thundercloud to the ground.'

No longer was America going to be governed by the long-standing philosophical guidelines set down by John Quincy Adams when he was Secretary of State in 1821. America 'goes not abroad in search of monsters to destroy. She is the well wisher to the freedom and independence of all. She is the champion and vindicator only of her own.' Bush changed too, from the moment he seized the bullhorn or portable loudhailer in the devastation and rubble in New York on 15 September 2001, saying: 'The people who knocked these buildings down will hear all of us soon.' He began to refer to himself as the 'decider', and signs of a developing hubris within Bush began to be visible as the military planning developed to deal with Al-Qaeda in Afghanistan and then over Iraq.

Tony Blair had been at the Labour Party conference in Brighton on 9/11 and we now know, from an article published in the *Sunday Times* on 28 August 2011, nearly ten years after the event, having rushed back to Downing Street he was met by John Scarlett from MI6 and Stephen Lander, head of MI5.

'Who's done this?' asked Blair.

'The most likely is Osama Bin Laden's organisation,' Lander replied, adding that he felt Bin Laden was most probably linked to Afghanistan's Taleban.

Blair was apparently taken aback. 'If it's coming from Afghanistan did I know about this?'

The spies coughed a little. 'Well,' said Lander, 'if you'd read the JIC material fully you would have come across some of this stuff.'

A JIC report from 16 July sent to Blair had warned that Al-Qaeda, operating from bases in Afghanistan, was in the 'final stages' of preparing an attack on the West, with UK interests 'at risk, including from collateral damage in attacks on US targets'. A sufficient warning one would have thought to be remembered if indeed Tony Blair had read it, which seems unlikely.

This ambivalence about Saddam Hussein being involved in 9/11 was a very destructive feature of the early handling of the crisis. The motivation for it was mixed. To mobilise US opinion to action having the two villains, Osama Bin Laden and Saddam Hussein, in the sights of American armed forces had an obvious added appeal. Yet it stopped the sole focus being on Afghanistan and it started a corruption of the evidence against Saddam Hussein. It began an assumption that Iraq had retained its weapons of mass destruction despite their removal in 1991 and a refusal to recognise that Saddam Hussein would nevertheless have good reasons not to admit having done so.

Confirmation of the ignorance in No 10 came in a revealing interview with Jonathan Powell, Blair's chief of staff at the time, for a BBC2 documentary shown in September 2011:

> In the aftermath it occurred to me how little we knew about the Taleban at all. 9/11 had happened and we had not really had the Taleban on our radar screen at all. So I walked down Whitehall to Waterstone's at Trafalgar Square and bought a copy of all the books I could find on the Taleban and the only one that was of any use was by Ahmed Rashid, which is a very good book on the Taleban and the fight with the warlords. And I sat at my desk and read this for the next twelve hours – read the whole book – and Alastair and Tony were getting very jealous and wanted to have my copy and had to wait. Alastair got to read it first and then Tony after that and then we were all experts on the Taleban.

Alastair Campbell, Tony Blair's spokesman, and his boss were now 'experts'! Fortunately the British government did have within it considerable expertise. In the garden of the British embassy in Washington on the day after 9/11 the heads of MI6, MI5 and GCHQ gathered and, in the words of Eliza Manningham-Buller in her Reith Lecture in 2011, discussed:

> the near-certainty of a war in Afghanistan to destroy Al-Qaeda bases there and drive out the terrorists and their sponsors, the Taleban. We all saw that war in Afghanistan as necessary. And in Afghanistan documents and rudimentary laboratories were discovered showing the terrorists' keen interest in fulfilling Bin Laden's stricture to acquire and use nuclear material. What none of us anticipated was that this unity of purpose would be tested by the decision of the US, supported by the UK, and others, after the rout of the Taleban, to invade Iraq. Saddam Hussein was a ruthless dictator and the world is better off without him. But his regime had nothing to do with 9/11 and despite an extensive search for links, none but the most trivial was found.

At this time the historian of Labour Party history, Lord Morgan, wrote:

> Blair seemed a political colossus, half-Caesar, half-Messiah. Equally, as times became tough following the Iraq *imbroglio*, he became an exposed solitary victim, personally stigmatised as in the 'cash for peerages' affair. Blair discovered, like Lloyd George and Thatcher before him, that British politics do not take easily to the Napoleonic style.[234]

---

234 Lord Morgan, 'The Judgement of History', *Parliamentary Monitor* (2007), vol. 149, pp. 16–17.

The conduct of President Bush and the British Prime Minister Tony Blair, in deciding to go to war in Iraq must be judged against that historic background. They were taken completely by surprise personally despite being warned by their officials.

On 20 September 2001, Blair and Bush met in America and 'when Blair asked about Iraq, the President replied that Iraq was not the immediate problem. Some members of his administration, he commented, had expressed a different view, but he was the one responsible for making the decisions.'[235] The Bush administration nevertheless began publicly and deliberately to link Iraq to Al-Qaeda. It also started to convey to the world an image of the United States as a country that would do as it liked and did not need to take other countries into account. International law was treated with contempt. This was Bush's policy every bit as much as that of Donald Rumsfeld and Dick Cheney, who some still believe bear the major responsibility. Bush personally could, and should, as President have constrained them. There is not much evidence to show at this stage he wanted to. He personally began to show a brash readiness over Iraq to break out of all international restraints with scant regard for the consequences.

Officials responded to the lead of the President and on 9 January 2002 the lawyer John Yoo went as far as to send a memo to the Pentagon declaring that the laws of war including the Geneva Conventions no longer applied to the conflict in Afghanistan. William Taft IV, the State Department's chief legal adviser, replied to Yoo: 'Your position is, at this point, erroneous in its substance and intolerable in practice.' By the 25th of the same month, White House Counsel Alberto Gonzales had weighed in on Yoo's side: 'This new paradigm renders obsolete Geneva's strict

---

235 Thomas E. Ricks, *Fiasco: The American Military Adventure in Iraq* (London: Allen Lane, 2006), p. 31, quoting the National Security Council summary of the conversation reported by the 9/11 Commission.

limitations on questioning of enemy prisoners and renders quaint some of its provisions.'

There were to be no limits of law on rendition, the returning of suspects for interrogation to their country of origin, there would be fewer restraints on interrogation, though access would still be granted to the findings gained from this process. Waterboarding and a tolerance of behaviour by the intelligence services and even the armed forces that was previously clearly banned became acceptable. Rendition, we now know some 19 years later, also came to be accepted within the British government.

Bush and Blair, professed Christians, were the heads of governments that acquiesced in torture and their overall fervour blinded them to the fact that torture is illegal. To scapegoat the CIA and MI6 for using or acquiescing, as happened later, is to miss the truth – the tone in the deepest sense, the morality of a government, stems from the top. In the UK successive Cabinet Secretaries have disgracefully blocked a proper acknowledgement of what happened. Despite huge sums of money being paid out to people who suffered there has been no legal action against the senior decision makers. Despite apologies by the UK government we have stopped short of exposing individual accountability. Will Boris Johnson do the same?

The 'victory' that Bush had in mind was the quick one he was certain would come in Iraq. It was a dangerous assumption but one to which Blair also began to subscribe. They both came to believe that ousting Saddam Hussein would frighten or impress extremists so much that they would abandon jihad.[236]

It was to become a feature of both Bush and Blair during the Iraq war that neither showed much attention to process or detail, nor were they great respecters of the facts. The combination was, of course, massively unequal in terms of power, but Blair made up

---

236 Mark Danner, 'Cheney:"The More Ruthless the Better"', *New York Review of Books*, 8 May 2014, p. 56.

for what he lacked in power in the relationship by his far greater verbal fluency and passionate language. Blair's political importance was that he reinforced Bush's beliefs and prejudices in the period after the invasion of Afghanistan and in the run-up to the invasion of Iraq. It was a form of what psychiatrists see in family relationships as a *folie à deux*. Blair's links with Clinton also became useful to Bush in helping to keep the Democrats 'on board' for war on terror.

On taking office Blair was the most inexperienced British Prime Minister since Ramsay MacDonald in 1924, neither having held any ministerial office before entering No. 10. That lack of experience, in retrospect, was to prove very damaging to Blair's record. According to an article in *Management Today*, Blair wanted to act like a chief executive: 'fast on his feet, flexible in his thinking and able to make quick decisions, often taken on the hoof, in shirtsleeves, on the sofa, coffee latte in one hand, mobile phone in the other, running Great Britain plc as if it were a City investment company'.[237] But the role of Prime Minister is not that of a chief executive and the UK government is not a company making profits for shareholders.

In 2001, in the flush of victory after winning a second general election, Blair, with no prior parliamentary examination or scrutiny, changed the whole basis of Cabinet government as it had related to foreign and defence matters. A system which had evolved during the First World War was swept aside without a single serious objective study. This was not modernisation but hubristic vandalism, for which, as Prime Minister, Blair alone bore responsibility. Shockingly there was little public or parliamentary recognition of the importance and significance of these changes, for Cabinet government and democracy as a whole.[238]

---

237 Francis Beckett, 'Blair's Way', *Management Today*, 1 March 2005.
238 Lord Owen 'The Ever-Growing Dominance of No. 10 in British Diplomacy since 5 April 1982', in Graham Ziegner (ed.), *British Diplomacy. Foreign Secretaries Reflect* (London: Politico's, 2007) pp. 19–42.

The new structure was deliberately designed by Blair to ensure he could exercise over international policy much the same powers as a US President. The Cabinet Office method of handling foreign and security matters had, until then, been designed to service the Cabinet as a whole. From the summer of 2001 onwards, the key officials and their staff on foreign affairs, defence and the European Union were brought into the political hothouse atmosphere of 10 Downing Street in two new secretariats, answerable to the Prime Minister.[239] These No. 10 secretariats were designed to service the Prime Minister alone, politically and strategically. Blair was to do much the same to the Joint Intelligence Committee, in terms of its working arrangements in No. 10 if not of its formal structure. The new foreign and defence organisation in No. 10 was conceived to cause the progressive downgrading of the Foreign Office and the Ministry of Defence and their respective secretaries of state. Inexplicably, it was virtually ignored by the press, who had become enamoured of the aura which Blair had begun to project of a successful Prime Minister, his charisma and decisiveness served the interests of the parliamentary press lobby. Defence and diplomatic correspondents were downgraded.

A few months after the two secretariats were in place in No. 10 the new structure provided the means to project Blair's very personalised response to the 9/11 attacks in New York and Washington and led eventually to the disastrous handling of the invasions of Afghanistan and Iraq.

The undoubted novelty of a terrorist organisation being able to extend its reach to create such devastation in the two most important American cities led Bush, and Blair too, to claim that this meant that the challenges they now faced were unparalleled in human history. It soon became a feature of the way Bush and Blair

---

239 David Owen, 'Two-Man Government', *Prospect*, December 2003; Owen, 'The Ever-Growing Dominance of No. 10 in British Foreign Policy since 5 April 1982'.

spoke after 9/11 that the world they lived in had, almost by definition, to be different from the world past leaders had lived in. Their problems had to be somehow greater and more challenging than those of other leaders – a ludicrous claim when one considers the challenges that the Second World War and the ensuing nuclear weapons stand-off in the Cold War posed for the post-war generation of leaders.

A warning sign of Blair's developing hubris was the astonishing speech that he gave to the Labour Party conference immediately after 9/11, when he promised the American people: 'We were with you at the first, we will stay with you to the last.' The consequence of Blair's exclusive dependence on his new No. 10 secretariats was to be the lack of objectivity, probity and collectivity which became the hallmarks of his misjudgements and incompetence in handling the aftermaths of the 2001 invasion of Afghanistan and the 2003 invasion of Iraq.

There have, of course, been incompetent Presidents and Prime Ministers before but Blair's incompetence during the war was to be of a very particular sort, and it was largely shared by Bush. It was triggered by three characteristic symptoms of hubris: excessive self-confidence, restlessness and inattention to detail. A self-confidence that exclusively reserves decision-making to itself, does not seek advice and fails to listen to or is contemptuous of the wisdom of others, particularly if it conflicts with the leader's own viewpoint, is hubristic. If this is combined with an energy that is restless for action and is ready to intervene on the basis of a loose sense of the broader picture rather than the detailed study of all the relevant information, then serious mistakes are almost inevitable. Such was to be the case in Bush and Blair's handling of affairs after 9/11: the misjudgements were those of hubristic incompetence.

Bush and Blair began to pride themselves on being 'big picture' politicians following 9/11. They both felt they had the insight to realise that the whole world, not just Afghanistan and Iraq, must now be seen anew and in fundamentally different terms after 2001. In this dangerously flawed vision they reinforced each other. Blair was a nation builder already. Bush took longer to embrace the same vision. In fact, the world, as looked at from the perspective of many centuries, did not change fundamentally on 9/11. There was, admittedly, more irrationality and less predictability. Islamic fundamentalists were more obviously ready to sacrifice their lives as part of committing acts of terrorism, which made bomb-carrying more deadly and a primitive nuclear device in a suitcase conceivable. But this was not new. It took some years for Bush's visionary and religious rhetoric to cool; with Blair it still has not cooled in 2020. He strives for an influence which is dwindling.

Blair, who had appeared to have an excellent relationship with Clinton when President, later said to one of his aides: 'Clinton messes you around but when Bush promises something, he means it.'[240] Experienced officials began to question whether Blair was deluding himself about his relationship with Bush. They worried about the lack of substance that arose from the Bush–Blair dialogue and about the extent of the mutual posturing. They noted how Margaret Thatcher had nailed Ronald Reagan down in a way that Blair never did with Bush, or how John Major, though only having a short time before the 1991 Gulf War, started nevertheless to build a relationship of some depth with Bush's father.

Blair's own particular form of hubris was his obsession with presentation and his need to put himself visibly at the centre of events. This had already become evident when a private memo he wrote to his staff in 2000 was leaked. In it he urged them to search around for 'two or three eye-catching initiatives . . . I should be personally associated with as much of this as possible'.[241] The

---

240 John Kampfner, *Blair's Wars* (London: Free Press, 2003), p. 263.
241 Leaked memorandum of 29 April 2000 from Tony Blair to staff, reported in *The Times*, 18 July 2000.

biographer of another inexperienced Labour Prime Minister, Ramsay MacDonald, wrote of Blair's ten years in office:

> The true origin of his tragedy lies in an intellectual deformation that is becoming more and more prevalent in our increasingly paltry public culture. The best word for it is 'presentism'... His fascination with fashionable glitz, his crass talk of a 'New Britain' and a 'Young Country' and his disdain for the wisdom of experts who had learned the lessons of the past better than he had were all part of the deadly syndrome.[242]

The world after 9/11 provided Blair with endless opportunities for such eye-catching initiatives and he indulged in considerable posturing. Following 9/11 he pursued a frenetic schedule. He held fifty-four meetings with foreign leaders, and travelled more than 40,000 miles on some thirty-one separate flights.

Bush, by contrast, was more disciplined than Blair in how he handled his schedule, insisting on having enough time to sleep, and appeared less frenzied and more controlled. The British press were encouraged by No. 10, with its new foreign affairs and defence secretariats, to exaggerate to the British people the extent of the UK's early involvement in Afghanistan. The UK launched a few cruise missiles and made a contribution from its SAS. The attack was, however, first and foremost an American operation. In all its major parameters it was led by the CIA, who cleverly used dollars to build up its relationship with the Northern Alliance of Afghan fighters. The Pentagon used its special forces and air power to tilt the balance of fighting in favour of those Northern Alliance leaders ready to take on the Taleban, which they did on the ground with considerable success.

---

242 David Marquand, 'A man without history', *New Statesman*, 7 May 2007
.

To reinforce the impression of his own central role, Blair flew into Kabul in early January 2002, just eight weeks after the Taleban-controlled capital had fallen to the Northern Alliance. He was chronically short of sleep and despite a recent holiday in Egypt was exhausted, mentally and physically.[243]

Blair tried to keep up the same pace through 2002 and much of 2003. His determination to be at the centre of everything was designed for and highlighted by the British press. US public opinion, however, liked Blair's easy style, and admired his verbal felicity and presentational skills. It thus suited Bush to build up Blair's importance over Iraq.

Blair summed up his strategy in March 2002 in a letter to the Archbishop of Canterbury, Dr George Carey; vainglorious but with some truths.

> Bluntly, I am the one Western leader the US will really listen to on these issues. That carries a price. It means that I don't grandstand; I don't negotiate publicly; I don't list demands. It is a v. difficult and delicate line to tread. Of course if I disagreed fundamentally with their objectives, I wd have to say so and wd ... My objectives must be to pull the Americans towards a strategy that is sensible in Iraq, contemplate military action only in the right circumstances, and broaden strategy so that it is about the wider world, including the Middle East peace process, Africa, staying and seeing it through in Afghanistan.[244]

By now there was little disguising that British foreign policy was being run from 10 Downing Street, with the Foreign Office being

---

243 Paul Scott, *Tony & Cherie: A Special Relationship* (London: Sidgwick & Jackson, 2005).

244 Quoted in Anthony Seldon, *Blair Unbound* (London: Simon & Schuster, 2007), p. 87.

increasingly sidelined. The British Ambassador in Washington recorded that: 'Between 9/11 and the day I retired at the end of February 2003, I had not a single substantive policy discussion on the secure phone with the Foreign Office. This was in contrast to many contacts and discussion with No. 10.'[245]

On the afternoon of 5 August 2002 at a meeting Bush held with Cheney, Powell, Rumsfeld, Rice and her National Security team, General Franks presented his plan for a light-footprint invasion of Iraq using far fewer troops than in the 1991 Gulf War. According to Peter Baker in his 2013 account *Days of Fire*,[246] Bush turned to George Tenet and asked how the Iraqi people would react to an American invasion. 'Most Iraqis will rejoice when Saddam is gone,' Tenet replied. This was Cheney's account of what Tenet said, which he later made clear was his own view, publicly. It was 'a forecast that would become a symbol of hubris'.

It was probably the defining moment of the Bush presidency and not one of the presidential advisers challenged the judgement. This was the moment when a collective hubris gripped the Bush administration and was not to be shifted until well after the Iraqi planned insurgency had taken hold following the invasion in 2003. Colin Powell can perhaps be excused for not expressing any disagreement given that immediately after the meeting he had dinner with the President without Cheney or Rumsfeld, as he put it 'without all the warlords in the room'.

Bush's own hubris up until then was intermittent and not of itself qualifying for a diagnosis of hubris syndrome. From then on, however, the inattention to detail in the aftermath planning and his contempt for the Iraqis supportive of Saddam Hussein grew.

---

245 Christopher Meyer, *DC Confidential: The Controversial Memoirs of Britain's Ambassador to the US at the Time of 9/11 and the Iraq War* (London: Weidenfeld & Nicolson, 2006), p. 190.

246 Peter Baker, *Days of Fire: Bush and Cheney in the White House* (New York: Doubleday, 2013), pp. 207–8.

Collective hubris in a democracy is more dangerous than individual hubris. Even when every member of the presidential cabinet and all the advisers that should have been present it was symptomatic that no dissenting voice was heard. The fatal flaw was hubris reinforced collectively by 'groupthink'.

Discussions were held in Washington and London on whether Iraqi WMD might be passed on to other Muslim countries, although most experts felt this was unlikely given Saddam's suspicion of and hostility towards all his neighbours. But – and it is a big but – neither Bush nor Blair displayed a sufficient readiness to understand politically why Saddam Hussein might reasonably never admit to his neighbours that he had given up nuclear weapons after UN inspectors in Baghdad on 24 September 1991 had found documentary details of his nuclear programme which was then dismantled. Both men's strategic aim was regime change, and for perfectly valid reasons. Bush was open about this and with the existing congressional decision he was entitled to use US forces. Blair felt he could not be as open, lacking Cabinet and parliamentary authority. George Tenet, then head of the CIA, has confirmed this: 'The United States did not go to war in Iraq solely because of WMD. In my view, I doubt it was even the principal cause. Yet it was the public face that was put on it.' [247]

Bush's overconfidence was fed by the overconfidence of his colleagues, Vice President Cheney and Defense Secretary Rumsfeld. This helped to reinforce his confidence and discount the doubts of his Secretary of State, Colin Powell.

The linkage over Iraq between hubris and incompetence has been repeatedly made by a number of serious commentators.[248]

---

247 Tenet, *At the Center of the Storm*, p. 321.

248 H. D. S. Greenway,'Fatal combination of hubris and incompetence', *Boston Globe*, 11 July 2003; Jonathan Freedland,'The blind prophet', *The Guardian*, 3 September 2003;Arthur Schlesinger Jr, 'Opportunity knocks', *American Prospect*, 21 November 2004; Charles A. Kupchan and Ray Takeyh, 'Middle

But merely asserting the linkage is not sufficient to demonstrate hubris syndrome. There has to be a detailed examination of the nature of the incompetence and of the incoherence which frequently accompanies hubris. As in all wars, many straightforward errors of judgement were made between 2003 and 2006. I do not intend to imply by focusing on hubristic incompetence that this was the only source of error but it was a significant part of the total decision-making.

Colin Powell and Dick Cheney, had been in Bush's father's Cabinet when Saddam Hussein had invaded Kuwait. Against that background, one would have thought that the question of how to handle in detail the aftermath of another invasion twelve years later, this time aimed at deposing Saddam Hussein, would have pre-occupied the President, particularly since he, unlike his father, was intending to occupy Baghdad. Yet he appears to have believed that having toppled Saddam there would be few problems, since the Americans would be seen as liberators. The harsh truth is that he gravely underestimated the aftermath of the invasion.

General Tommy Franks, who missed the signs during the early hours of the invasion that Saddam had planned for an insurgency to strike back, is harder to read on this question of aftermath planning.[249] He personally ensured a quick exit to honourable retirement as soon as Saddam Hussein's forces appeared to have been defeated. On 12 December 2001 before the invasion he had proposed softening up Iraq, telling Rumsfeld, 'I'm thinking in terms of spikes, Mr Secretary. Spurts of activity followed by periods of inactivity.' That strategy seemed to be subsumed by the actual pre-invasion bombing campaign.

The choice for Bush in 2003, intent on invading, was what to do after taking Baghdad. The choices were clear, either a political fix

East: reaping what Bush sowed', *International Herald Tribune*, 19 July 2006; Ricks, *Fiasco*.
249 Gordon and Trainor, *Cobra II*, pp. 500–1.

177

and appointing an Iraqi leader and arranging an early handover to the Iraqis, allowing for a speedy exit; or occupation with a programme of nation-building inside Iraq, with an exit postponed until this had been achieved. Bush should have chosen one or the other of these options well before the invasion and discussed his decision with Blair. This was not a decision for just the US to make, though they were the senior partner; this was a key strategic issue and it should have been jointly made. What happened was that, sensing division amongst his key advisers, Bush postponed any decision until well after the invasion and Blair acquiesced in him doing this.

It was clear in Washington and London from their stance on Afghanistan that Cheney and Rumsfeld, well before the invasion of Iraq, were dismissive of Powell and the State Department's views about the need for nation-building and reluctant to get involved in it. They and the leading neo-conservatives, the deputy Defense Secretary, Paul Wolfowitz, and a colleague at the Department of Defense, Douglas Feith, 'did not believe the US would need to run post-conflict Iraq'. Their aim was to turn the country over very quickly to their favoured Sunni exiles in the Iraqi National Congress (INC) and make a rapid exit. In accordance with that policy Cheney stuck his finger into Powell's chest late in 2003, saying: 'If you hadn't opposed the INC and Chalabi (Ahmed Chalabi, its Shia leader) we wouldn't be in this mess.'[250] Chalabi had links to Iran but he tried with the INC to build links to everyone and prided himself on wanting to end the animosity between Tehran and Baghdad. The State Department, by contrast, under Powell, suspected the bona fides of the INC and favoured nation-building all along. It was a massive error that Bush left this vital issue of aftermath planning seemingly unresolved. But by choosing Rumsfeld to handle the aftermath and not Powell, he set

---

250 George Packer, *The Assassin's Gate: America in Iraq* (New York: Farrar, Straus & Giroux, 2005), p. 147.

a pattern. In part he reversed that when after the invasion, he personally appointed Paul Bremer to be the head of the Coalition Provisional Authority in Baghdad. In an article in the *Guardian* following the Chilcot Report from the Iran/Iraq Enquiry, Bremer defended on 6 July 2016 his de-Ba'athification programme as being 'much narrower than the similar de-Nazification program in 1945' which 'affected only the top one percent of party members and only forbade them from holding government positions'. Bremer wrote that a Rand report he saw just before arriving in Iraq concluded the coalition 'would need some 480,000 troops to provide adequate security'. In the event they had less than half that number, 180,000 US troops and 20,000 British.

Bremer also wrote that he did not share the Chilcot Report's view that in early 2003 the 'strategy of containment' was adequate to the challenges posed by Saddam's Iraq.

Paul Wolfowitz, who told the House Budget Committee that the military were 'wildly off the mark', explaining: 'It's hard to conceive that it would take more forces to provide stability in post-Saddam Iraq than it would take to conduct the war itself and to secure the surrender of Saddam's security forces and his army. Hard to imagine.'[251] For those experienced in post-war conflict it was, on the contrary, all too easy to imagine why more forces would be needed in the aftermath and that was the military consensus but not taken up by Tony Blair.

I first met Tony Blair for a serious conversation on 15 July 1996 at his home, when he was Leader of the Opposition and I had finished being the EU negotiator in the Balkans from 1992-95. The issue was whether I was willing publicly to support New Labour. I declined for a number of reasons, not least because of his passionate belief that Britain should adopt the euro on the basis at that time of what appeared zero knowledge. I first discussed Iraq

---

251 Packer, *The Assassins' Gate*, pp. 114–15.

with him on 2 March 1998 in Downing Street and, as a sign of my depth of feeling about Saddam Hussein's regime, gave him a book about the Kurds written by Jonathan Randal, an experienced war correspondent with the *Washington Post*. It reflected why I believed that the handling of the Kurdish position, so long ignored by the Western democracies, had become so crucial. It discussed how the aftermath of the defeat of the Iraqi forces in 1991 had much to be desired. Trump's handling of the Kurds in Syria in 2019 was no better. Randal wrote:

> The American planning was a hodgepodge of naivety and realpolitik, more tactics than strategy, seemingly consistent only if its peculiar assumptions were correct. No-one should have been surprised by anything that happened from 2 August 1990 when Iraq invaded and occupied Kuwait to the end of the following March, when Saddam Hussein crushed the Shia and Kurdish uprisings.[252]

Following the withdrawal of UN inspectors from Iraq in December 1998 in response to Saddam's non-cooperation, the United States and Britain launched a four-day bombing campaign against Iraqi targets. More than 600 bombs were dropped and 415 cruise missiles launched against Iraqi targets during this action, killing an estimated 1,400 members of Iraq's Republican Guard. It was action aimed at protecting US and UK military aircraft still successfully protecting the Kurds from attack by Saddam Hussein's forces and also at trying to destabilise Saddam Hussein. Not a direct attempt at regime change but hoping for a change nevertheless.

This military operation was undertaken, as in 1993 and 1996, and again in 2002 and 2003, with the US and the UK claiming the

---

252 Jonathan C. Randal, *Kurdistan: After Such Knowledge, What Forgiveness?* (London: Bloomsbury, 1998), p. 73.

authority of continuing UN resolutions passed in 1990 and 1991 and in addition UN Security Council Resolution 1205, passed in 1998.

Tony Blair asked me and my wife to dinner at 10 Downing Street on 18 December 1998, the third evening of the bombing blitz. The main reason for the invitation was Blair's wish to dissuade me from establishing a cross-party organisation later called New Europe, which opposed the UK joining the euro. But we also discussed Iraq at some length.

He had started well as Prime Minister, particularly in handling Northern Ireland, and it looked as if he was set to be a success. There was no undue hyperactivity. He did not excuse himself to get an update on the attacks on the third night that they had been launched and I found him cool, rational and anything but hubristic. He was ready to discuss the complexity of the relations between the Shiite majority and the Kurds and Sunnis in Iraq in some detail but he was not very knowledgeable about them and he had obviously not yet read Randal's book. We agreed that the situation which allowed Saddam to stay in power was totally unsatisfactory and shared the frustration about UN limitations within which he, Blair, felt formally he had to operate unlike Clinton where the Iraq Liberation Act had been passed by an overwhelming Congressional majority.

On 24 July 2002 my wife and I were again asked by Tony and Cherie Blair to dinner at No. 10. It soon became very clear in conversation that Blair was going to commit Britain to Bush's Iraq policy and I agreed with him. Blair's purpose in talking to me about Iraq that July evening was evidently not to consult me but to brief me about what he was going to do and to bring me into the personal 'big tent' of supporters which he liked to create around any controversial new policy.

Of course we again discussed whether Saddam was developing nuclear, biological and chemical weapons. Given my detailed and long-standing involvement writing in books and specialised journals about WMD[253] of course I questioned Blair about a revived programme of WMD following the September 1991 discovery of Saddam's nuclear weapons planning referred to earlier. Blair was very clear that the intelligence showed that Saddam had restarted a nuclear, biological and chemical weapons programme. I now know the intelligence assessments that Blair had available to him and by no stretch of the imagination could they have been used to justify what he said to me about their assessments.

We now know from the Report of the Iraq Inquiry chaired by Sir John Chilcot, eventually published in 2016, that Blair wrote to Bush only a few days after our dinner with him, 'I will be with you, whatever.' The Report went on to say, 'We have concluded that the UK chose to join the invasion of Iraq before the peaceful options for disarmament had been exhausted. Military action at that time was not a last resort' and that 'The judgement about Iraq's capabilities were presented with a certainty that was not justified.' It described the process for deciding that the war was legal as 'perfunctory' and that 'no formal record was made of that decision, and the precise grounds on which it was made remains unclear'. The Report also concludes 'If the UK had refused to join the US in the war it would not have led to a fundamental or lasting damage in the UK's relationship with the US.'

This assessment reinforces Jack Straw's reminder to Blair just before the invasion, when Blair returned from meeting Bush in the Azores on 16 March 2003, that it was possible to do what Wilson did over Vietnam – support the policy but not join the military action. Wars and even the realistic threat of going to war have to be planned for with some secrecy since it takes time, as in the build-up to the Iraq war in 1990–1, to deploy significant armed forces, particularly tanks and heavy weapons. That means that when the preparatory decision points are coming near to action there has to be full

---

253 Ed. David Owen, *Nuclear Papers* (Liverpool University Press, 2009).

justification and disclosure before the Cabinet so that a clear majority are convinced of the need to go to war. Prime Ministers may have the authority to declare war but only in practice when they have carried the majority of the Cabinet with them. Also Parliament must be informed honestly. None of these unwritten constitutional safeguards were put in place by Tony Blair. The Chairman of the Inquiry, Sir John Chilcot, was correct to say that he believed Blair was not 'straight with the nation'. The problem for the members of the Inquiry in drafting their conclusions was that the International Criminal Court was ever present in the background. Anything which implied criminal conduct of the war rather than going to war, opened up the potential for Blair and others to be arraigned before the Court, not a prospect that the vast majority of British people either wanted to see or realised was possible.

My concern about Blair from that meeting on 24 July 2002 was not his support for an invasion, which I shared, nor his wish to get the message out indirectly, which I understood, but the closed nature of his mind. I regret very much that this did not sufficiently alarm me at the dinner. But I was left with the strong impression that Blair was a very different man from the one I had met three and a half years earlier.

I now recognise that several clear symptoms of hubris syndrome were present over that second dinner which became clearer to me as I discussed them afterwards driving home with my wife. First, there was now a new total confidence in himself with a new restless, hyperactive manner, very different to our previous dinner. His brushing aside of the difficulties that circumstance was likely to throw in his way meant to me that the die was cast in his own mind over forcing regime change. As before, WMD were not a major topic in Blair's conversation in responding to my questions. He was focused quite simply on getting rid of Saddam for moral and geopolitical reasons, all of which I supported. But, as my wife said afterwards, he was *messianic* – a word subsequently applied to Blair frequently.

The opportunity to exercise decisive and controversial leadership is one of the strengths of representative democracy and there is a need from time to time for a certain boldness in policies whether domestic or international. But representative democracy also demands under the UK system that leaders' decision-making be open to democratic scrutiny in the Cabinet and where possible in relation to war in Parliament. Prime Ministers' parliamentary colleagues assume that they tell the truth and that after making the key decisions they know they will be held accountable and, if found wanting, resign from office or face a charge of contempt of Parliament. His former Foreign Secretary, Robin Cook, then in the Cabinet as Leader of the House of Commons, did exercise a right to talk to MI6 and was convinced there was not sufficient evidence on weapons of mass destruction being restored to justify an invasion, and resigned, to his great credit. The Leader of the Liberal Democrats, Charles Kennedy, to his credit also opposed the invasion.

That Blair *believed* that gas and chemical weapons were inside Iraq in 2003, and a nuclear weapons programme had been restarted is one thing, *quoting* as evidence without their caveats from intelligence reports is very different. That is to misrepresent their reports, in effect to lie and a contempt of Parliament. Blair should have had to apologise and have been called to the House of Commons to do so standing at the bar before the Speaker, but there was no stomach for it because Parliament had voted for war.

The Whitehall machine was assuming that a protracted and costly nation-building option was likely to be forced on it, but, along with the intelligence services, the military were deeply alarmed by the lack of any positive post-invasion planning in Washington. A senior official recalls that when advising Blair about the difficulties ahead, Blair would say: 'You are Neville Chamberlain, I am Winston Churchill and Saddam is Hitler.' It is very difficult to conduct a serious dialogue with a leader thinking in these emotional terms and giving such a simplistic example.

Charles Tripp, an academic expert on Middle East politics, was called in along with other experts to give advice. He later wrote an account of his meeting:

> At a Downing Street meeting in November 2002 attended by Blair, Straw and six academics familiar with Iraq and the Middle East, two things became clear. The first was that Straw thought post-Saddam Iraq would be much like post-Soviet Russia and could thus be easily pigeon-holed as that strange creature, a 'transitional society'. Either he had been persuaded of this by the recycled Cold Warriors clustering round the Bush administration, or they had failed to inform their 'key ally' of their determination to dismantle Iraq's state and security structures. More ominously, Blair seemed wholly uninterested in Iraq as a complex and puzzling political society, wanting confirmation merely that deposing Saddam would remove 'evil' from the country.[254]

That Blair should be interested only in being reassured that he was fighting evil can be equated with Bush's simple talk of his crusade to rid the world of 'evil doers'.

Apologists for the British policy and for Blair personally over Iraq tend to put all the blame for the admitted incompetence on the Americans. This is to underestimate British knowledge of the region. Britain, unlike America, had been involved in Iraq through most of the twentieth century. By 1918 David Lloyd George had sent more than a million British and Commonwealth troops into Ottoman territory to impose a post-war settlement.[255] Britain had administered Iraq, albeit not very successfully, under a League of Nations mandate from 1920 until 1932, and had remained close to King Faisal and

254 Charles Tripp, 'Militias, vigilantes, death squads', *London Review of Books*, 25 January 2007.
255 David Fromkin, *A Peace to End All Peace: The Fall of the Ottoman Empire and the Creation of the Modern Middle East* (New York: Avon, 1990).

Nuri al-Said, who dominated the country for the next two decades. The British Foreign Office and Ministry of Defence had knowledge and experience and some well-formulated views on the best way of handling the aftermath of any invasion, especially in the light of the mistakes of 1991. But this expertise was never utilised by Blair. A Foreign Office strategy paper, which the State Department was hoping would arrive, their own having been ignored by the Pentagon, never came.[256] The then British Ambassador to Washington has written about the 'titanic struggle' for six months to keep Britain 'onside for war' and how 'there was little energy left in No. 10 to think about the aftermath. Since Downing Street drove Iraq policy, efforts made by the Foreign Office to engage with the Americans on the aftermath came to nothing.'[257]

This was the consequence of Blair handling so much of the preparation for war himself, sidelining the Foreign Office and ignoring warnings from the military and the intelligence services. Even so, it would still be reasonable to expect that in any substantive relationship between two heads of government, there would be detailed discussion on all of the key issues, including dealing with the aftermath. But there is little evidence that Bush and Blair ever did discuss them in detail before the invasion. Rumsfeld was formally put in charge of post-war planning by Bush on 20 January 2003 and planning details thereafter, in as much as they existed at all, were very closely held.

On 31 January 2003 in Washington Blair was told that the US start date pencilled in for bombing Iraq was 10 March 2003. It is clear that neither he nor Bush seemed to think it necessary to plan for the possible consequences of Bush's own expectation, stated at the meeting, that the Iraqi army would 'fold very quickly'. Indeed Bush is reported by Robert Draper, the author of *Dead Certain*, as

---

256 John Newhouse, *Imperial America: The Bush Assault on the World Order* (New York: Alfred A. Knopf, 2003), p. 43
257 Meyer, *DC Confidential*, pp. 8, 223–4.

saying: 'The policy had been to keep the army intact; didn't happen,' but he couldn't remember how he had reacted when he found that the policy had been reversed. I was told by a prominent US neocon at the time that, far from folding, whole divisions of the Iraqi forces would come over to the allies intact and help maintain law and order. Bush and Blair at their meeting seemed to envision a quick victory and swapped ideas about the post-war Iraqi government, with Blair saying: 'People would find it very odd if we handed it over to another dictator.' Indeed they would have. Yet both Bush and Blair knew that handing over to US-selected Iraqis was still central to Cheney/Rumsfeld/ Wolfowitz thinking. When Blair asked about aftermath-planning, 'Condi Rice said that a great deal of work was now in hand.' But Bush still spoke of 'the dilemma' of 'managing the transition to the civil administration', making clear that this issue was still unresolved. Sir Christopher Meyer, the UK Ambassador in Washington, revealed in the BBC television programme *No Plan, No Peace*, shown on 28 and 29 October 2007, the true state of play in Washington. It was a Blair decision not to replace Meyer when he came home before the war, leaving the Ambassador post vacant for far too long over this critical period until Sir David Manning was released from No. 10 to take over in Washington. The evidence points to the fact that 'post-war planning was no more a priority in London than in Washington'.[258] They were locked in another example of dangerous 'groupthink'. A 'personality-determined malaise', the symptoms of this process are well described in the book *On the Psychology of Military Incompetence* and were displayed in President Kennedy's handling of the Bay of Pigs fiasco. (See Chapter 5.) Analysis of past military incompetence produces four most frequently occurring symptoms: 'wastage of

---

258 John Ware, 'Revealed: Blair was warned of looming disaster in Iraq', *Sunday Telegraph*, 28 October 2007.

manpower, over-confidence, underestimation of the enemy and the ignoring of intelligence reports'.[259]

Seven months before the invasion of Iraq the US Secretary of State, Colin Powell, persuaded Bush to go first to the UN before embarking on direct military intervention. Powell warned Bush, over dinner on 5 August 2002, not to add Iraq to Afghanistan as an American unilateral intervention but to seek UN support. Condoleezza Rice was the only other person present. According to the journalist Bob Woodward, Powell said to Bush: 'You can still make a pitch for a coalition or UN action to do what needs to be done,' and he warned of a 'cauldron' in the Arab world that would suck the oxygen out of just about everything else the United States was doing, not only in the war on terrorism, but in all other diplomatic, defence and intelligence relationships.[260]

Revealingly, an American book on the Iraq War was simply called *Hubris*.[261] On 1 May 2003, George W. Bush, dressed like a Hollywood actor in a pilot's flying gear, flew onto the aircraft carrier *Abraham Lincoln* off the coast of California and stood on the flight deck to celebrate victory in Iraq. The ship's control tower was emblazoned with the slogan 'Mission Accomplished'. This was a hubristic act of a very high order. It was also a contemptuous, albeit unintended, insult to the troops in the field, wrestling with a growing insurgency, with more and more losing limbs or their lives. Most of the troops knew all too well by then the slogan's patent absurdity. Even Donald Rumsfeld had the sense to dissuade Bush from actually using the phrase in his speech. Nevertheless Bush did say: 'In the battle for Iraq, the United States and our allies have prevailed.'

259 Norman Dixon, *On the Psychology of Military Incompetence* (London: Jonathan Cape, 1976), pp. 399–400.
260 Bob Woodward, *Bush at War* (New York: Simon & Schuster, 2002), pp. 333, 334.
261 Isikoff and Corn, *Hubris*.

Rumsfeld, for all his faults, was too cynical to suffer from hubris syndrome. In response to the rapid breakdown of law and order in Baghdad and wide-spread looting, most of which was the result of Bush accepting his advice that there was no need to increase troop numbers on the ground to control the occupation, the Defense Secretary simply said: 'Stuff happens.' It took the playwright David Hare to dramatise the deeper significance of this remark.[262]

The scale of the incompetence after the invasion of Iraq will be something over which historians will long puzzle. How could Washington, particularly the Pentagon, be so incompetent on both the political and the military organisational levels? How could the White House not have challenged this? One answer lies in the indifference to detail to which many witnesses of Bush's behaviour testify. A candid assessment of these characteristics in Bush's conduct in office comes from a former Secretary of the Treasury, Paul O'Neill, who served from 2000 until 2002. He comments that from the start Bush was 'clearly signing on to strong ideological positions that had not been fully thought through. But of course, that's the nature of ideology. Thinking it through is the last thing an ideologue wants to do.' O'Neill goes on to describe one meeting as 'like many of the meetings I would go to over the course of two years. The only way I can describe it is that, well, the President is like a blind man in a roomful of deaf people. There is no discernible connection.'[263]

Another early example came from David Kay, the former UN weapons inspector in Iraq, who from 5 June 2003, was responsible for finding WMD. He was at Bush's early morning briefing on 29 July, having flown in from Baghdad the day before to report. He

---

262 David Hare, *Stuff Happens* (London: Faber & Faber, 2004).The play premiered at the National Theatre in London on 1 September 2004.

263 Ron Suskind, *The Price of Loyalty: George W. Bush, The White House, and the Education of Paul O'Neill*, pb ed. (New York: Simon & Schuster, 2004), pp. 127, 149.

told the President: 'The biggest mistake we made was to let looting and lawlessness break out,' and he went on to warn that they had not found any WMD and might not find any. Looters, by then, had taken two tons of 'yellow cake', 194 tons of high-melting-point explosives and 141 tons of rapid detonation explosives.[264] Kay left the meeting almost shocked at Bush's lack of inquisitiveness on WMD, especially when compared with Donald Rumsfeld's detailed probing. In part, of course, this was a reflection of a different knowledge base. At this stage Bush knew little about military matters. Rumsfeld as Secretary of Defense knew a lot. Bush initially, through no fault of his own, was showing the hubris of a novice. Rumsfeld was not hubristic; he knew the problems of taking Baghdad and he wanted out soon, hence his wish to have an early exit and leave the mess for the Iraqis to sort out.

Bush and his war Cabinet discussed 'de-Ba'athification' on 10 March before the invasion but while the conclusions lacked specificity, one person at the meeting has said: 'The thrust was clear: treat these people leniently and try to work with them.'[265] It is claimed that the eventual document forcing de-Ba'athification, issued by Paul Bremer was not shown to Condoleezza Rice or Colin Powell, who believed the policy drafted in Douglas Feith's office did not represent the compromise the War Cabinet had agreed. It was a fateful mistake by Rice, then in charge of the National Security Council, to tolerate procedures that allowed this type of document to go out direct from the Pentagon without being checked by her office. The British Secretary of State for Defence, Geoff Hoon, said in May 2007 that to de-Ba'athify was an error. 'I think we felt that a lot of the Ba'ath people were, first and foremost, local government people and, first and foremost,

---

264 Peter W. Galbraith, *The End of Iraq: How American Incompetence Created a War without End* (New York: Simon & Schuster, 2006), p. 102.
265 Chandrasekaran, *Imperial Life in the Emerald City*, p. 77.

civil servants – they weren't fanatical supporters of Saddam.'[266] The Chilcot Report felt some de-Ba'athification was necessary. But an example of Bremer's vice-regal style was the CPA Order No. 2, which he issued eleven days after arriving in Iraq, in which he dissolved the Iraqi army, air force, navy, ministry of defence and intelligence services. On 12 March, before the war, Bush and his inner circle agreed to disband the Republican Guard but retain the regular army. Bremer apparently did not consult the State Department, the CIA or Rice on the terms of the order, nor did he mention it to, let alone consult with, Iraqi politicians. This is almost impossible to believe – even General MacArthur in Japan did not take such decisions without regard to the Department of Defense and the White House. (See Chapter 8 on Hubris and the Military Mentality.) It was perhaps the fatal mistake of the Iraqi invasion.[267] But it was one which Bremer refused to change when challenged.

Nor were US experts in Baghdad consulted. 'By nightfall, you'll have driven 30,000 to 50,000 Ba'athists underground,' the CIA station chief in Baghdad warned Bremer.[268]

According to Colonel Lawrence Wilkerson, Powell's former Chief of Staff, in dealing with Iraq Bush was 'too aloof, too distant from the details of postwar planning. Underlings exploited Bush's detachment.'[269] But Bush was never a pawn; he made the big moves, but sometimes without knowing all the positions on the chess-board. He took Powell's advice all too rarely, Rumsfeld's and Cheney's all too frequently, but he was still choosing for himself. Bush's problem was that he had created what Rice called in August 2003 'the dysfunctional US government'.[270] As the journalist Bob

266 *The Guardian*, 2 May 2007.
267 Chandrasekaran, *Imperial Life in the Emerald City*, p. 84.
268 Ricks, *Fiasco*, p. 158.
269 Quoted in Joseph S. Nye Jr, 'Transformational Leadership and US Broad Strategy', *Foreign Affairs*, July/August 2006, p. 148.
270 Woodward, *State of Denial*, p. 241.

Woodward concluded, around Bush 'the whole atmosphere too often resembled a royal court, with Cheney and Rice in attendance, some upbeat stories, exaggerated good news, and a good time had by all'.[271] The reality was that it wasn't just Bush's government that was dysfunctional, it was Bush himself as Commander-in-Chief. Shades of Donald Trump.

The figure Bush seems most to have trusted and worked directly with was General Tommy Franks, the regional commander for Afghanistan and Iraq, 'a tall, hot-tempered Texan' who openly disparaged the Joint Chiefs of Staff.[272] In his book *Fiasco*, Thomas Ricks, the former senior Pentagon correspondent at the *Wall Street Journal* and later in the same role for the *Washington Post*, describes Franks 'as a product of his Army and his faults reflected those of that institution. The Army went into Iraq with a considerable amount of hubris.'[273]

Bush imbibed that hubris. Speaking like a cocky sheriff in a cowboy movie, he had promised the American people after the fall of the Taleban government in Afghanistan that Osama Bin Laden would be taken 'dead or alive'. This was something his wife Laura teased him about, which was a good sign that not everyone close to him was going along with everything he said. People close to the Bush marriage say she is a rare critic but a very influential one and like Clementine Churchill qualifies as a 'toe-holder' which I describe in the Introduction.

There was a compelling logic for starting to develop a dialogue with Iran in 2002 before the invasion of Iraq. It is easy to forget that the Iranians had been helpful to the United States over the invasion of Afghanistan, influencing some members of the Northern Alliance, as well as throwing out Al-Qaeda operatives from the holy city of Mashhad when they crossed over into Iran in

---

271 Ibid., p. 226.
272 Ibid., p. 82.
273 Ricks, *Fiasco*, p. 129.

2002. Given that toppling Saddam was bound to bring the Shiite majority to power in Iraq, the potential for mischief-making from Iran was obvious. Yet Bush believed they could deal with Shiites in Iraq while rejecting a wider Iranian dialogue. It is hard to be sure what lay behind Bush's thinking over dealing with Tehran. It probably reflected his use of the term 'axis of evil' and its inclusion of Iran. Overconfidence was certainly a factor. His refusal to have any dialogue with Syria was also damaging, for the Syrians could have influenced the Sunnis in Iraq. The Sunni–Shiite relationship was bound to be fraught at the time of any invasion, with a Sunni minority in any evolving democratic system, having to get used to no longer being the dominant power. By the US and UK going it alone as an occupying force they were laying themselves open to frustrated Sunni insurgents supported and sustained across Iraqi borders by Syria and other Arab states, including Saudi Arabia.

Bush, who started with focused meetings and confidence in the military and the CIA, revealingly, later began to blame them. He said 'Tommy Franks and the generals' had looked him in the eye and had assured him that the Iraq invasion was undertaken with 'the right plan with the right troop levels'. Franks probably believed this when he said it, meaning it covered the invasion. To cover the aftermath it was insufficient and judged so within the Pentagon amongst senior military figures. By the summer of 2003, with the insurgency well underway, it was patently not true. According to Bob Woodward, Bush also claimed that the head of the CIA, George Tenet, had been extremely bullish, recalling his claim over the existence of WMD in Iraq: 'It's a slam dunk case', a basketball term meaning certain success.[274] Yet Tenet in his account, published in 2007, claims he used the phrase 'slam dunk' in relation to strengthening the public presentation, and that it was later taken

---

274 Woodward, *Plan of Attack*, p. 249.

out of context in Woodward's book.[275] The 'blame game' had become a feature of the Iraq fiasco by 2007. In a BBC radio interview Lawrence Wilkerson said that he wished he had resigned in 2004 over Guantánamo and that, reading Tenet's book and hearing Tenet give interviews, he was thinking some people in the CIA had 'lied' to Colin Powell before his Security Council meeting on 5 February 2003.[276]

The second attempt to deal with Fallujah was still underway when Powell saw both Bush and Blair at the White House. Powell said: 'We don't have enough troops . . . We don't control the terrain.'[277] The following month Bush was being cabled by the CIA station chief in Baghdad: 'We face a vicious insurgency, we are going to have 2,000 dead.' A few days later a US military intelligence expert told Bush to his face about the insurgency: 'It's robust, it's well fed, it's diverse. Absent some form of reconciliation it's going to go on and that risks civil war. They have the means to fight this for a long time.'[278]

In a book about Iraq entitled *Imperial Hubris*, Michael Scheuer, the former head of the CIA's Bin Laden Unit, claims: 'Arrogance is not the worst of it for America as she charges forward in the cause of instant democracy. That honor falls to the category of hubris, buttressed by ignorance.'[279]

A characteristic of hubristic leaders is that they do not easily change their positions, because this means they would have to admit error. Blair would boast that he had 'no reverse gear' to the Labour Party conference; a more absurd claim can barely be imagined by any democratic leader. If the facts change you should

---

275 Tenet, *At the Center of the Storm*, p. 362.
276 Lawrence Wilkerson, *PM*, BBC Radio 4, 11 May 2007.
277 Ricks, *Fiasco*, p. 407.
278 Ibid., p. 408.
279 Michael Scheuer, *Imperial Hubris: Why the West Is Losing the War on Terror* (Washington DC: Potomac, 2005), p. 203.

change. If the settled will of the people you lead changes, you at least should as a democrat consider changing policies or direction or both.

In relation to the law, Bush seemed to relish acting unilaterally with little or no consultation with friends or allies. In effect he ripped up long-standing international legal agreements and announced that America would do as it liked. The resulting damage in Britain to Tony Blair's credibility on human rights, let alone America's credibility abroad, can hardly be exaggerated. The treatment of prisoners taken in Afghanistan, prisoners held in Guantánamo, and what happened in Iraq's Abu Ghraib jail, when US and UK personnel taunted and abused Muslim prisoners, shocked people of goodwill in the United States and Britain. When it was confirmed that both their countries had been involved in the shameful policy of secret 'rendition' and flying terrorist suspects to countries whose regimes were prepared to adopt none-too-scrupulous methods of interrogation people were shocked and remain so. Bush's claim that America condemned all torture seemed to many a contemptuous denial of obvious facts. Blair passed the buck in explaining our involvement with rendition to his Foreign Secretary, Jack Straw.

The Times editorial on 29 June 2018 'Complicit in Torture' says it all. 'Five years after the House of Commons Intelligence and Security Committee launched its efforts to get at the truth of British involvement in torture and rendition after 9/11 it has done its best and given up.' The Committee asks if British intelligence agents turned a blind eye to the systematic use of torture and rendition and *The Times* answer was, 'yes, except that the eye seems wide open.' Parliament was again lied to. Straw and Blair are the only two individuals who could and should have stopped it. They both should on this specific issue, be brought to the bar of the House of Commons and apologise for contempt of Parliament and it should happen in 2020.

The sentence of death by the Iraqi Special Tribunal was passed for the crime of using gas against Iraqi Kurdish citizens in 1988 in Halabja, where for two days Iraqi jets dropped a hydrogen cyanide compound and more than 5,000 civilians were killed. Shamefully, the CIA sent out a briefing note to its embassies in 1988 stating that the gas might have been dropped by the Iranians.[280] With this genocide against his fellow countrymen, Saddam was correctly judged guilty of a clear breach of the 1948 UN Convention on Genocide.

The American and British governments' past acquiescence in the Iraqi invasion of Iran and the eight-year Iran–Iraq War followed the practice of a very dubious form of realpolitik, explicable in terms of hoping that by helping to keep the war going that long, Iranian revolutionary zeal would burn itself out. But it was deeply misguided, for the zealotry of Iran's religious leaders and the Republican Guard continued unabated. It would undoubtedly have been in the best interests of the US and the UK to uphold the rule of international law in 1980 and penalise Saddam Hussein for crossing an international boundary into Iran but there was little enthusiasm for UN sanctions at the time.

Blair's hubristic self-confidence over Iraq had begun to desert him by the end of 2003. At the annual diplomatic reception at Buckingham Palace, on 4 November 2003, I had another interesting, but shorter, talk with him about Iraq. He insisted on us sitting down together for a serious discussion in the ballroom and ignoring for a time the foreign diplomats circulating around. This was a very different Tony Blair from the messianic leader I had talked to over dinner in July 2002. He was far less sure of himself and he appeared somewhat chastened by events: the inability to find any WMD in Iraq was clearly troubling him. I felt rather sorry for him and tried to cheer him up though I was, by then, fearful of a debacle and annoyed at his incompetence.

---

280 Robert Fisk, *The Great War for Civilisation: The Conquest of the Middle East* (London: Fourth Estate, 2005), p. 262.

By January 2004 I had become convinced that Blair had permanently lost authority and credibility and should choose an early moment to step down and take another job. I wrote an article in the *Sunday Times* on 4 January entitled 'Self-rule by Blair gives him a Suez crisis.' While I still believed that toppling Saddam Hussein was a legitimate policy I suggested that Blair should step down as Prime Minister no later than the expected 2005 general election. I wrote:

> Blair's authority has been severely, probably irreparably, damaged over Iraq, not just in his party but within the country . . . A well-conducted exit would make it more likely that Blair's Prime Ministership would be well regarded by history. There are other opportunities that lie ahead for Blair, not least perhaps as the next head of the World Bank.

Though subsequently Paul Wolfowitz was appointed to the World Bank, the United States had for some time been interested in the chairmanship of the International Monetary Fund, letting a European run the World Bank. Blair, for the next few years as Prime Minister, never fully recovered the authority and trust of the British people and the House of Commons on a cross-party basis that any Prime Minister requires when soldiers are being killed in battle.

On 14 July 2004 the so-called Butler report, on failures of intelligence prior to the invasion, was published.[281] Blair was apparently surprised that it was not more damaging, as were many other people, but it was he who had deliberately limited its terms of reference and chose the safety of a former Cabinet Secretary, Lord Butler, to chair the inquiry. He also placed on the committee a loyal former Cabinet colleague, ensuring that criticism would be deftly drafted. Nevertheless the Butler report, unusually, went beyond its remit into intelligence failings before the war and

---

281 *Review of Intelligence on Weapons of Mass Destruction*, HC 898, 14 July 2004.

commented on the nature of Blair's decision-making process. It singled out for criticism Blair's personalised sofa-style way of making key decisions: 'We are concerned that the informality and circumscribed character of the government's procedures . . . risks reducing the scope for informed collective political judgement.' The press reporting focused on this but the underpinning Whitehall language was more damaging than at first appeared. True to form, the Blair spin machine defused the potential fallout and the question which Butler claimed he dreaded, 'Should the Prime Minister resign?' was never asked.

I was invited to give evidence to the Butler inquiry. The night before I was to go before the Inquiry I heard on the 10 o'clock BBC News on 6 May 2004, that John Scarlett, head of the Joint Intelligence Committee, was now to become head of MI6. I was outraged by this example of manipulation and felt Butler as a former Cabinet Secretary had to have been told about this and agreed it by the current Cabinet Secretary. I prepared a statement if I was not satisfied by Butler's explanation, for release the next morning.

STATEMENT BY LORD DAVID OWEN TO THE BUTLER ENQUIRY ON FRIDAY, MAY 7th 2004 AT 9 A.M.

Before I give an initial oral statement in support of my written evidence, I would like to comment, if I may, about yesterday's appointment of Sir John Scarlett to be the new head of MI6.

I decided to give written evidence to your Enquiry despite the boycott by the Liberal Democrats and the Conservative Party because I have great respect for the personal integrity of all of you on this Enquiry. I hoped that in the country's interest, you would be able to make positive suggestions to improve our intelligence on weapons of mass destruction. Despite the narrowness of your terms of reference, I believed you could help to restore some of the shattered public confidence in our intelligence services on the assumption that the present situation continues and that no WMD are found in Iraq.

I was amazed to hear yesterday that the Prime Minister had seen fit to announce an appointment of anyone to head up MI6 in advance of hearing your conclusions. It seems to me that whoever was appointed given their likely involvement as senior members of MI6 in advance of the Prime Minister receiving your conclusions at the end of July risks pre-empting your findings. It also in my judgment puts you all in a very difficult position in that if you felt you should criticise the record of anyone appointed as the head of MI6 you would have to weigh against doing so, even further damaging that organisation at a time when the threat of international terrorism is so high.

For me to proceed giving evidence to your Enquiry this morning as if nothing happened yesterday is not credible. I wonder therefore if I could ask before giving oral evidence how your Enquiry intend to respond to this appointment. For instance, would you consider asking the Prime Minister to put this appointment on hold until you have submitted your report in July when Sir Richard Dearlove is due to retire? At the very least, will you publicly announce today that your Enquiry remains completely unfettered in considering any criticisms of Sir John Scarlett's role?

You know and I know that public cynicism of enquiries in this area of intelligence after the Hutton Report is at an all time high. It is widely predicted and not just by the two opposition parties that your Enquiry will be another whitewash. I do not need to tell you of the danger of your being seen to be mere poodles of the government given the controversy over the terms of reference of your Enquiry.

I hope you understand why I feel I must ask you how you intend to proceed. Of course, if you would like time to deliberate on this question, I am fully content to wait outside until you have reached a conclusion.

Having heard Butler's waffle where he neither confirmed nor denied whether he had been consulted, I deeply regret not stepping out of the room and refusing to give evidence and publishing my statement. Why didn't I? Perhaps because I too am part of a British elite that papers over the cracks. Yet I did not do this when an MP over the Westland affair. Old age, the atmosphere of the Lords being a dignified old people's home, somehow means one's instinct for the jugular in politics is not there.

In an intervention in the House of Lords, on 22 February 2007, Butler, as if making up for his pusillanimous handling of the intelligence inquiry, spoke for the first time as an individual, not as the chairman of the inquiry. He accused Blair of being 'disingenuous' about the intelligence, a word that only just avoids the parliamentary ban on saying that someone has lied:

> Here was the rub: neither the United Kingdom nor the United States had the intelligence that proved conclusively that Iraq had those weapons. The Prime Minister was disingenuous about that. The United Kingdom intelligence community told him on 23 August 2002 that we 'know little about Iraq's chemical and biological weapons work since late 1988'. The Prime Minister did not tell us that. Indeed, he told Parliament only just over a month later that the picture painted by our intelligence services was 'extensive, detailed and authoritative'. Those words could simply not have been justified by the material that the intelligence community provided to him.[282]

---

282 Hansard, HL Deb, 22 February 2007, vol. 689, col. 1231.

In the run-up to the 2005 general election, Blair tried initially to campaign on his own, downplaying the electoral role and importance of Gordon Brown. This strategy was clearly failing in terms of public opinion, particularly with Labour Party supporters, and Brown was quickly brought back with a central role in the campaign, which Labour won, albeit with a greatly reduced majority and with only 36 per cent of the vote. Labour was staying in power but with only 9.6 million votes, down from 10.7 million in 2001 and 13.5 million in 1997.

Blair privately recognised that the election was virtually a defeat and said it was his fault because of Iraq. But he still clung on to office and, despite a massive reduction in the number of votes and seats, his supreme self-confidence soon returned and lasted for over 20 years. He never understood why the country would not 'move on' over Iraq. His hubris revived in 2005, though never becoming as marked as in 2001–3. His obsession about his legacy began to dominate decisions over the date of his promise to step down. He conveyed the impression that he and he alone, with a unit in No. 10, could put into effect the programme of change his government had recently embarked upon for education and, most misguidedly, the marketisation of the NHS, but as over military matters his constant intervention and 'presentism' destabilised both these services, demoralised the professional staff and had the effect of reducing the benefits of the substantially increased funds being allocated. 'Deliverology' as developed by Blair[283] had one all-pervasive weakness, the wish to improve his personal image and exercise personal central control from No. 10.

His former Cabinet Secretary articulated the general problem in December 2004:

---

283 Michael Barber, *Instruction to Deliver: Tony Blair, Public Services and the Challenge of Achieving Targets* (London: Politico's, 2007).

There is too much emphasis on selling, there is too much central control and there is too little of what I would describe as reasoned debate in government at all levels ... The Cabinet now – and I don't think there is any secret about this – doesn't make decisions ... All this is part of what is bad government in this country.[284]

His nemesis came because a significant number of Labour MPs demanded he make his last annual Party Conference speech as leader in 2006.

An article in the *Financial Times* on 12 September 2006 wrote of 'the seven habits of a highly ineffective Prime Minister', reckoned to be failure to lead a collegiate administration; failure to manage expectations and follow through on ideas; adoption of the 'heroic CEO' model; top-down autocratic style; failure to listen to constructive, well-intentioned criticism; addiction to arbitrary targets and performance measures; and failure to manage a stable and orderly succession. All these habits are symptomatic of hubris syndrome.

No British Prime Minister in wartime, not Asquith, Lloyd George, Churchill or even Eden over Suez, nor Thatcher during the Falklands war, nor Major on the first invasion of Iraq, have made the strategic decisions over war so personally and without systematically involving senior Cabinet colleagues as Blair did.

There is no single diagnostic test as yet of hubris syndrome which Blair certainly developed. The words that politicians use can, however, provide a rich source of data for historians to study. A paper entitled 'Linguistic Biomarkers of Hubris Syndrome' studied three Prime Ministers, Margaret Thatcher, John Major and Tony Blair, during the period 1989 to 2007.[285] All their answers in

---

284 'How not to run a country', interview with Lord Butler, *The Spectator*, 9 December 2004.
285 Peter Garrard, Vassiliki Rentoumi, Christian Lambert and David Owen, 'Linguistic Biomarkers of Hubris Syndrome', Cortex (2013), http://dx.doi.org/10.1016/j.cortex.2013.08.014

the Hansard official report of Prime Minister's Questions were analysed and the results showed what words and phrases became more frequent with time. Thatcher included the phrase 'we shall' more often while phrases that included the word 'duties' diminished. It was also found that her language became more complex at the end of her term of office and less predictable during hubristic periods.

Somewhat similar results were found for Tony Blair. They found that 'I' and 'me' and the word 'sure' were amongst the strongest positive correlations in Blair's speeches. Also his use of the word 'importance' increased with time. None of these linguistic patterns were reflected in the language of the much less hubristic Major. The Introduction deals with the latest neuroscience of hubris syndrome. All this leads to the question: why does hubris develop in some heads of government and not in others? I think the answer lies both in the particular external circumstances and in the internal personality of each individual.

With George W. Bush his hubris syndrome developed quickly after 9/11 but faded by 2006 as he learnt from his mistake and increased troop numbers.

One of Tony Blair's most consistent journalistic supporters, Philip Stephens, wrote an article in the *Financial Times* on 14 July 2006 entitled 'Hubris is the thread running through Blair's many travails'. My own personal experience of Blair is that his hubris started to develop in 1999 during the Kosovo crisis and built up over Sierra Leone and through the general election in 2001, after which he developed a presidential office in No. 10 and by 9/11, he would and did conduct detailed foreign and defence policy himself.

Blair's hubristic preoccupation with wishing to be seen to be at the centre of events, even if he could achieve nothing of substance, was very apparent by the G8 meeting in St Petersburg in July 2006. Unknown to Bush and Blair, a microphone was left switched on and the world was able to hear how Bush talked to him. 'Yo,

Blair!'[286] But what was much more revealing was Blair's offer to undertake a piece of shuttle diplomacy over the Lebanon crisis. Blair made it clear that what he had in mind was that he could 'go and just talk' and that a failure on his part to achieve anything would not damage the proposed later visit of Condoleezza Rice, by then the US Secretary of State. Blair was happy just to act as her advance man. It is not simply that this was demeaning for a British Prime Minister, as was the way Bush inarticulately brushed Blair's offer aside, but that it vividly illustrated how Blair's primary focus had become himself, his personal position and its presentation through 'eye-catching initiatives'. This was more important to him now than the substance and complexities of the issue.

As regards any personality traits which might incline Blair towards hubris, several stand out. Firstly, as all his biographers make clear, his early passion was not politics but performing: both at school and at Oxford as an actor or a member of a rock band. It appears that he was not led into politics by ideological conviction – he was, at school, a Conservative and he has always struggled to articulate a political philosophy that would root him better in the Labour Party. Politics offered him a very large stage on which to perform. The brilliance and range of Blair's acting repertoire as a politician has been much noted and is rivalled on this aspect only by Prime Minister Harold Macmillan. Politicians, particularly actor-politicians tend to be especially narcissistic – their political vision tends to place themselves at its centre, commanding the stage with all eyes upon them. It is hardly surprising that presentation and spin become so important for such politicians.

A second trait of Blair's personality concerns his view of himself, in that he thinks he is always good. The journalist and author Geoffrey Wheatcroft has argued that this is so strong in Blair that

---

286 Geoffrey Wheatcroft, *Yo, Blair! Tony Blair's Disastrous Premiership* (London: Politico's, 2007).

he is a latter-day antinomian – the name given to the sixteenth century heretics who believed that 'to the pure all things are pure', meaning that whatever they did was, by definition, pure. Someone who believes they cannot act badly lacks the constraint on behaviour which the fear that they might would otherwise impose on them. They believe, particularly, that they cannot lie, so shading the truth can easily become such a habit that they appear as liars. Again, the link to hubris is obvious: to believe that you are always good removes an impediment to behaving hubristically.

Linked to this is the nature of Blair's religious beliefs and the particular way he sees his relationship with God. In a television interview on 4 March 2006, and perhaps because he knew he was committed to stepping down as Prime Minister before another general election, Blair abandoned his reservations in talking about his religion and said, in relation to Iraq: 'If you have faith about these things then you realise that judgement is made by other people. If you believe in God, it's made by God as well.' The implication is that the accountability that really matters to Blair is not to the electorate but to God. If, however, he is already convinced of his own goodness, that accountability is not constraining as it would be to the believer aware of his own capacity to sin. The belief in God became a spur to hubris rather than a constraint.

Blair's post retirement behaviour has shown that unlike Bush, who retired with grace and lost his hubris, he had to continue to prove himself. The quest for money, the endless travel and the dubious sources of some of his money has destroyed his reputation, as shown in public opinion polls but more devastating in a growing indifference to his views. Nemesis came, but slowly and sadly.

In October 2006 Bush reached out to Robert Gates, then President of Texas A&M University and former director of the CIA under President George Bush Sr to see whether he would consider coming into his administration to replace Donald Rumsfeld as Secretary of Defense. On 31 October Gates met Bush on his ranch near Crawford, Texas. Bush made it clear that the current strategy in Iraq was not working and he needed a new initiative. He said he was thinking seriously about a surge in troop levels and was interested in appointing the then Lieutenant General David Petraeus to lead it. At the end Bush said, as if it might be a question for Gates: 'Cheney?' He smiled and continued: 'He is a voice, an important voice, but only one voice.' Vice President Cheney had opposed the President's decision to replace Rumsfeld but his comment to Condoleezza Rice on Gates was revealing: 'a good man'.

Robert Gates, who served Bush between 2006 and 2008 and went on to serve President Obama in the same post, found Bush 'at ease with himself' and 'more intellectually cautious than his public image.' He further described him as 'peppering (interlocutors) with questions', many of them tough and forcefully expressed. Gates identified in Bush 'a very low threshold for boredom and not much patience with structured (or long) briefings'. 'Bush relied a lot on his own instincts. The days of funny little nicknames for people and quizzing people about their exercise routines and so on were mostly long over when I came on board.' For Gates, 'Bush was a mature leader who had walked a supremely difficult path for five years.' This analysis contrasted with that of Secretary of the Treasury, O'Neil, quoted earlier. When two Cabinet ministers, both experienced outside politics, make different judgements of two different phases to the Bush presidency – pre-surge and post-surge in troop levels, I am inclined to think that Bush displayed a gathering hubris in the first phase and a welcome decline in the second.

For Bush by December the crunch moment was coming close and he clashed openly with Rice, who he respected and was now Secretary of State, and 'was supplanting Cheney as his most influential adviser. Rice made the case that any additional commitment by the United States might be pointless unless the

Iraqi leaders stepped up.'[287] 'So what's your plan, Condi?' he snapped. 'We'll just let them kill each other, and we'll stand by and try and pick up the pieces?' 'No, Mr President,' she shot back. 'We just can't win by putting our forces in the middle of their blood feud. If they want to have a civil war we're going to have to let them.' They soon made up and Rice then supported the surge as did Gates, who had now replaced Rumsfeld.

The military surge in 2006 which President Bush embarked on was what his wife called 'the loneliest of George's decisions' but which turned out to be his best. While it laid the basis for eventually ridding ISIS from both Iraq and Syria, they can still be found in the Sinai, Afghanistan and north Africa. Iraq and Baghdad in 2020 are not in good shape.

Gates in his book described the reaction to the new policy:

> All hell broke loose. In a span of forty-five years, serving eight Presidents, I can recall only three instances in which in my opinion a President risked reputation, public esteem, credibility, political ruin and the judgement of history on a single decision he believed was the right thing for our country: Gerald Ford's pardon of Nixon, George H. W. Bush's assent to the 1992 budget deal (against his previous stance, 'Read my lips: no new taxes'), and George W. Bush's decision to surge in Iraq. In the first two cases, I think one can credibly suggest the decisions were good for the country but cost these two Presidents re-election; in the latter case, the decision averted a potentially disastrous military defeat for the United States.[288]

This decision was very personal to Bush. Most senior military leaders and others in government were opposed to the surge right

---

287 Baker, *Days of Fire*, p. 515.
288 Robert M Gates, *Duty: Memoirs of a Secretary at War* (New York: Alfred A Knopf, 2014), p. 48.

up to his announcement. He sent five brigades to Baghdad and two further battalions of marines. It all involved admitting that he had been wrong for nearly four years on the troop levels deployed and on the basic tactical and strategic planning. It came when many polls showed an increased hostility to America even being in Iraq and amidst bad results in the mid-term elections. It was a decision tinged with a certain humility, from a leader ready to admit mistakes. It was not impossible that there was still hubris in his attitude and thinking, but it seemed that the peak of his hubris on the aircraft carrier in May 2003 emblazoned with 'Mission Accomplished' had been curtailed by 2006 and that a more humble, yet more determined, President was in the White House.

The sacking of Donald Rumsfeld and Vice President Cheney becoming less influential, with Condoleezza Rice as Secretary of State more influential lead to other changes. She talked Bush around to accepting a very limited dialogue with Syria and Iran but only in the context of regional conferences called by the elected Iraqi Prime Minister Nouri al-Maliki. By April 2007 Bush increased US troop levels in Baghdad, while the UK was reducing its forces around Basra, where a very serious defeat was inflicted on the British army. With a new, intelligent, US military commander in Iraq, General David Petraeus, a different and better strategy for tackling the insurgency and stiffening the Iraqi army was under-way, much of it recommended in the Baker–Hamilton cross-party report.

The United States was, at last, trying to win around some in the Sunni resistance movement and isolate Al-Qaeda insurgents and others who had come in to exploit the situation and destroy the invading armies.[289] By the autumn of 2007 there were some signs of improvement in Baghdad and as US casualties eased slightly, public opinion inside the US began to shift towards

289 Roger Cohen,'Why Iraq's resistance differs from insurgency', *International Herald Tribune*, 14–15 January 2006.

accepting a slower withdrawal and transfering to Iraqi rule over a period of years.

The surge lasted until September 2007; then until September 2008 the debate was on the pace of troop withdrawal and trying to keep Congress and in particular the Republican element on board for the fight to withdraw slowly. Another sign that Bush was listening and moderating his views. Bush supported Gates and opposed Israel acting unilaterally over bombing Iran, turning down all requests to supply concrete-busting bombs and other equipment. Cheney disagreed deeply and fundamentally with Gates and the Chief of Defense Staff, Admiral Mullen on Iran. Bush not only supported Gates but while Obama was President-elect, very helpfully let it be known that he had rejected the then Israeli Prime Minister Olmert's request for material and political support.

President Obama during his eight year term kept a level of US troops in Iraq which helped slowly to stabilise the country. Meanwhile all through the Obama period President Assad stayed in power in the Syrian civil war. By the start of 2020 no political cooperation had materialised between President Trump and President Putin over the Middle East as a whole despite appearing to do so at their meeting held in Helsinki on 16 July 2018. The Middle East is still deeply affected by the consequences of the 2011 Arab Spring, which started in Tunisia and spread to Egypt and Syria. The US, Russia, France and the UK did coordinate air power over Syria to deal with ISIS but keeping Turkey in NATO has meant damaging relations with the Kurds who did most of the fighting on the ground against ISIS. Realpolitik by Trump was messy but necessary.

Bush's born-again Christianity started with a meeting with the evangelist Billy Graham in 1986, at his family holiday home in Maine, while his father was Vice President. He writes in his book *A Charge to Keep* how that meeting sparked a change in his heart over the course of that weekend: 'Rev. Graham planted a mustard seed in my soul, a seed that grew over the next year. He led me to the path and I began walking. It was the beginning of a change in my life.' Bush sees his God not as a power to keep him in check but as the force that spurs him on. Bush once told the Palestinian Foreign Minister: 'I'm driven with a mission from God. He told me: "George, go and fight those terrorists in Afghanistan." And I did. And he told me: "George, go end the tyranny in Iraq." And I did.'[290] Geoffrey Perret, the biographer of many Presidents – among them Ulysses Grant, Abraham Lincoln and Dwight Eisenhower – wrote: 'This is the language of no other Commander-in-Chief in American history.'[291] From James Madison until George W. Bush, US Presidents issued 322 'signing statements' to ensure presidential power and prerogatives, an average of eight per President. Bush's certainty that his presidency was directed by a higher power meant that in his first six years in office, he produced nearly 800 such statements in defence of his belief in the doctrine of the unitary executive and the claim in an emergency to rule by decree. That provided a dangerous precedent on which President Trump continues in his own way to build. Another dangerous precedent was George W. Bush's endorsement of a policy of pre-emptive action to deter 'potential adversaries from pursuing a military build-up in hopes of surpassing or equalling the power of the United States'. As his narrowly defeated rival in the 2000 presidential election, Al Gore, said:

> President Bush now asserts that he will take pre-emptive action even if the threat we perceive is not imminent . . . An unspoken part of this new doctrine appears to be that we claim this right for ourselves – and only for ourselves . . . What this doctrine does is to destroy the goal of a world in which states consider themselves

---

290 Norma Percy, 'An almighty splash', The Guardian, 24 October 2005
291 Geoffrey Perret, Commander-in-Chief: How Truman, Johnson, and Bush Turned a Presidential Power into a Threat to America's Future (New York: Farrar, Straus & Giroux, 2007), pp. 375, 392.

subject to the law, particularly in the matter of standards for the use of violence against each other. That concept would be replaced by the notion that there is no law but the discretion of the President of the United States.[292]

Hubris syndrome is linked to the possession of power and in the cases of the military, real physical power. Since the syndrome is by definition acquired it is reasonable to look for any diminution in it when power is lost. In Bush's case when he ceased to be President his hubris visibly diminished and may even have disappeared. As an acquired syndrome it should be possible for hubris syndrome to fall away even in power in circumstances where the power base of the individual is being challenged. In Bush's case he lost popularity in office in his second term and the foreign policies that he was pursuing were contested very strongly in public debate. This might also have eroded his hubris and created the mental attitude where he could contemplate surging troop levels. There are interesting signs that in his case both of these developments actually occurred. What the Iraq war and its differing effect on Blair and Bush demonstrates is the interesting interface between the military mind and the political mind. In this chapter we have examined its effect on two politicians, in the next chapter we will examine the military mind more generally.

---

292 Al Gore, speech at the Commonwealth Club of California, San Francisco, 23 September 2002.

Chapter 8

Hubris and the Military Mentality

The ancient Greeks' worries about a leader developing the contempt that often accompanied hubris was reflected in their concerns on what we would call the military class and what they called a 'guardian' class. As Plato put it in *The Republic*, this class comprised 'noble dogs': men who had to combine being 'gentle to their own, to their fellow citizens, and cruel to their enemies'.[293]

Hubris did not occur just in mythology. The Greek historian, Thucydides, in his famous book *The Peloponnesian War* charts what to those who lived then must have appeared like a 'world war'. Contrary to what one might have expected, it was mainly the free-spirited Athenians who failed to see when to call it a victory and make peace. Their hubris led to their downfall. Had they not sailed against Syracuse, but calmly solidified and strengthened their empire, Hellas might have stood stronger against the Macedonians a century later, and perhaps would not have succumbed to Rome so easily in 200 AD when the much-weakened Athenians actually invited the Romans to get rid of the hated Macedonian rulers.

On the translation of Thucydides's book, the writer Finley in Appendix 3 and in the Introduction to the book claims that Thucydides has invented more or less everything in the Melian Dialogue except the fact that negotiations did take place between

---

293 Plato, *The Republic, Book II* (New York: Basic, 1968) 375a–d, pp. 52–3.

the Athenians and the Melians on the island of Melos and that when the negotiations broke down the male population were killed.[294] Yet the importance of the Dialogue is it narrows down to an exposure of hard realism or expediency. You are too weak the Dialogue warns: 'hope is an expensive commodity.' For Thucydides, 'history was in the most fundamental sense a strictly human affair, capable of analysis and understanding entirely in terms of known patterns of human behaviour . . .' Thucydides warned not just about hubris and its accompanying contempt but about the power of the powerful – elitism particularly at times of war. The following extracts are chosen to give a flavour of the 'power to compel' from the Melian Dialogue.

Athenians: we recommend that you should try to get what it is possible for you to get, taking into consideration what we both really do think; since you know as well as we do that, when these matters are discussed by practical people, the standard of justice depends on the equality of power to compel and that in fact the strong do what they have the power to do and the weak accept what they have to accept.

Melians: If we surrender, then all our hope is lost at once, whereas, so long as we remain in action, there is still a bit of hope that we may yet stand upright.

Athenians. Hope, that comforter in danger! If one already has solid advantages to fall back on, one can indulge in hope. It may do harm, but will not destroy one. But hope is by nature an expensive commodity, and those who are risking their all on one cast find out what it means only when they are already ruined . . .

---

294 Thucydides, *The History of the Peloponnesian War,* Penguin Classics Translated by Rex Warner with an Introduction and Appendices by M. I. Finley (Harmsworth English Penguin Books, 1972.) Appendix 3

In the end of the Dialogue the Melians surrendered unconditionally to the Athenian military who put to death all their men of military age and sold their women and children as slaves. The abiding message is human behaviour matters, it is the glue that holds society together and if human respect is eroded or lost then society is weakened progressively to the point it no longer exists.

One of the Athenian claims, 'this is not a law that we made ourselves, nor were we the first to act upon it when it was made.' To underwrite this view is to underwrite the harsh Athenian code that the law of nature has no room for mercy. The advent of Christianity and many other religions and humane non-religious teaching is to treasure a role for mercy and Shakespeare put that into the mouth of Portia as a truth: 'the quality of mercy is not strained, it droppeth as the gentle rain from heaven, upon the place beneath, it is twice blest, it blesseth him that gives and him that takes.' (*The Merchant of Venice*, Act IV, scene I.)

The military are prone to acquiring hubris syndrome with their power increasing as they move up the ranks. But the element of being gentle to their own men is a factor that can work against the development of hubris. Not many of the really great military commanders have risen high without a reputation for worrying about the lives and the conditions of the men that they lead, but some have. We demand of our military the capacity to develop a very broad mindset: what the historian Samuel P. Huntington describes as 'pessimistic, collectivist, historically inclined, power-orientated, nationalistic, militaristic, pacifist and instrumentalist in its view of the military profession. It is, in brief, realistic and conservative.'[295]

The military mind, which is trained to respond instantly to higher commands, is prone to model itself on great military figures

295 Samuel P. Huntington, *The Soldier and the State: The Theory and Politics of Civil–Military Relations* (Cambridge MA: Harvard University Press, 1959), p. 68.

from the past, for whom there is considerable tolerance of vanity, arrogance, pride and egotism. There is also the culture of uniforms, medals, bands, march-pasts, which plays to any narcissistic tendencies. But there is also, as a balancing factor, the military tradition of leaders looking after their subordinates, of caring about their wellbeing and trying to protect their lives and their limbs. Amongst 311 newly-promoted majors in the British Army observed, more than 90% of respondents had observed personnel displaying toxic leadership in one or more rank.[296] A review article entitled 'Toxic Leadership in the Military' by J W Dagless in its conclusion agreed with Major General Craig Orme that 'the risks of poor or toxic leadership are much greater in the military than they are in (many) civilian organisations' and went on to write, 'real change can only be delivered through sustained engagement from the military's trop brass' and 'whether it chooses to continue to appear to turn a blind eye, or be seen to actively enforce its policies.'[297]

The courage, the risk-taking and the resourcefulness of a military leader may stem from a hubristic temperament but that is not the same as acquiring hubris syndrome. Young military leaders can respond to mentoring from their peers but they are also prone to hero worship. A remedy for the propensity for hubris to develop in the higher military command structure is to write and to talk more about it and recognise its signs and symptoms early enough to mentor and moderate its development or ensure that the person never reaches the top echelons of military command.[298]

296 Hart S.J.E. 2015.Army leadership review:Army division response, Shrivenham Defence Academy of the United Kingdom.
297 Ed. Peter Garrard, *The Leadership Hubris Epidemic. Biological Roots and Strategies for Prevention* (Palgrave Macmillan, 2018) pp. 93-135.
298 Lord Owen, 'The Conundrum of Leadership: Leadership in Government, Foreign Affairs, Defence and Society' (2012), COMEC Occasional Paper No. 2, http://www.comec.org.uk/documents/occasional_paper_no_2_122_small_file.pdf (last accessed 15 May 2014).

Another remedy for hubris is to rely on the public's reluctance to go to war which has been an inhibiting factor after two World Wars. Over a million people marched against the Iraq war. Recently much discussion has been on 'Wars of the peoples.' It was written about in the context of the Balkan wars of the 1990s by amongst others, General Rupert Smith.[299] But in fact it was General von Molke the Elder who presided over the German victory over France in 1870 who warned we have moved from 'cabinet wars to peoples wars'. Once you start the wars of the peoples, when the passions of the peoples are involved, it is very hard to stop them.[300]

In seeking examples of hubristic behaviour in wartime military leaders and their decision-making the richest biographical area is provided by the Second World War. In the First World War there are many interesting examples of military leaders clashing with their political leaders, of hubristic leaders, but there is not the same level of disclosure about their personalities that could lead to a judgement on their behaviour or mental state, let alone any mental illness or signs and symptoms of hubris.

While some military matters are too sensitive to bring to Parliament, not bringing them to Cabinet is a very serious matter as was recognised in 1911 when the Cabinet was first told about the Military Conversations with France when they had begun in 1906.[301] By any theory of proper Cabinet government it was a grave mistake by Prime Minister Campbell-Bannerman and Foreign Secretary Grey not to tell the Cabinet, a view held rightly by many who have studied the issue, but theory was overtaken by harsh political realities. They knew the start of conversations would

---

299 Rupert Smith, *The Utility of Force: The Art of War in the Modern World* (Penguin, 2006).

300 Margaret MacMillan, 'War and Humanity', First in series of Reith Lectures June/July 2018.

301 David Owen, *The Hidden Perspective: The Military Conversations 1906-1914* (Haus Publishing, 2014).

divide the Cabinet. At root, what this is all about is parliamentary democracy. Lord Sanderson was the senior Foreign Office diplomat who told the French Ambassador in 1906, copied to Grey, that, 'if the Cabinet were to give a pledge which would morally bind the country to go to war in certain circumstances, and were not to mention this pledge to Parliament, and if at the expiration of some months the country suddenly found itself pledged to war in consequence of this assurance, the case would be one which would justify impeachment'.[302] Asquith did not know about the Military Conversations until a few years after he became Prime Minister.

Lloyd George became War Minister after Kitchener was drowned at sea in 1916, when his ship was sunk by a German submarine. Thereafter he was saddled with General Sir Douglas Haig as his main military adviser, a situation which continued when he became Prime Minister in December 1916 since the Conservatives had made Haig's continuation in office the price for supporting Lloyd George.

In his memoirs, written many years after the war, Lloyd George writes witheringly of Haig's capabilities:

> Haig might have minimised the disastrous effect of his intellectual shortcomings had he called to his aid men who were equipped as advisers if not as leaders, with the qualities in which he was himself deficient. Unfortunately amongst Haig's qualifications, no one has ever attributed to him the capacity for judging men.[303]

Others are not so harsh. Like so many aspects of the 1914–18 war opinions differ about the military. Lloyd George, whose hubris was contained all through the First World War, nevertheless used all his political skills to circumvent Haig. He saw salvation in letting the

---

302 Ibid, pp. 59–60.
303 David Lloyd George, *War Memoirs of David Lloyd George, volume II* (London: Odhams Press, 1938), p. 2016.

French, who had the largest army, provide the overall leader and in this way get around the political block he had circumscribing his undoubted wish to sack Haig. He wrote that the name 'Haig' 'never sent a thrill through the ranks on the eve of battle . . . That was why the appointment of Foch as Generalissimo was hailed with such relief and delight throughout the British Army . . . He did not possess that eye within an eye which is imagination.'[304] In the Second World War Churchill and Roosevelt chose and dismissed their own commanders and their choices did not merely follow the line of seniority.

On matters of peace and war there has to be a recognition that some measure of 'needing to know' and restriction of the number of people who do know is the price of victory, and a smaller War Cabinet is therefore essential. The skill of a good Prime Minister, helped by verbal reports at the top of the agenda routinely made by the Foreign Secretary, is to keep the whole Cabinet well informed and abreast of all the key issues and during long periods of international tension revealing whatever they can to Parliament.

In July 1914 there was no question that the Liberal Cabinet agreed by a large majority reluctantly to go to war. The ultimate authority to declare war lay with Herbert Asquith as Prime Minister. In the US the decision was made by Woodrow Wilson though he did consult his Cabinet and constitutionally went to Congress as did Franklin Roosevelt in 1941. In the Second World War Neville Chamberlain took the decision in 1939, as did Clement Attlee over the Korean War in 1950, under UN authority, and Margaret Thatcher in 1982 over the Falklands. In 1991 John Major could easily have gone to Parliament over the Gulf War, following Iraq's invasion of Kuwait, but judged it more helpful to maintaining cross-party unity with Labour not to put the issue to the vote and have some opposition MPs voting against. With regard to the Iraq

---

304 Ibid, p. 2015.

War, discussed in detail in the earlier chapter on Blair, while throughout 2002 there was too little real information and debate in Cabinet, by 2003 there was a proper Cabinet decision. The best description of that Cabinet decision is in *Blair Unbound*; 'I never saw any doubts from Jack (Straw) nor did he express in my recollection any doubts in Cabinet, Hoon, Defence Secretary, recalled. Straw explained his post-Azores letter to Blair as part of his "duty" as Foreign Secretary. Yet Straw's reservations went far further than that and are a matter of record. To some his failure to speak out in Cabinet was weak; to others it was a fine demonstration of service.'[305]

Clare Short, after thinking hard about it overnight made the vote (for war) unanimous, though Robin Cook had resigned on 17 March before the Cabinet meeting. The Conservative Party supported the government and despite a backbench revolt of 139 Labour MPs there was still a majority of Labour MPs voting for war. There were massive public protests and not since the Poll Tax had there been so strong a dissent. Nor was this the elite versus the rest, many of the elite had great reservations.

The vote in Parliament might well have established a precedent for always having to vote for war. Gordon Brown as Prime Minister was pledged to examine abandoning the Prime Ministerial prerogative to declare war but he found it impossible to devise a sufficiently flexible mechanism. It is hard to see any way that it can be changed, given the necessity in some circumstances for speed and for secrecy of action to be preserved.

The two votes of the House of Commons on 30 August 2013 over Syria were not about a declaration of war. It was a hurriedly called meeting for which Parliament was brought back from holiday to agree to David Cameron lining up with President Obama's possible limited military response to the use of sarin gas.

305 Anthony Seldon, *Blair Unbound* (London: Simon & Schuster, 2007) p. 169.

The debate demonstrated that a significant number of MPs on a cross party basis saw military action targeted from the air on Syria in retaliation for the use of gas as risking enhancing Sunni extremism. This was becoming an ever greater anxiety even before ISIL emerged a little later into public recognition. I was arguing at the time the case for negotiating the removal of all Syrian biological and chemical weapons. David Cameron as Prime Minister was quick to recognise that with the large number of Conservative abstentions he could not go ahead with the Americans but it soon became clear that Congress was not keen either for the US to be involved. The House of Commons vote had important and immediate consequences for it led to President Obama wisely deferring the proposed US action on Syria until Congress gave its approval. He knew they would be hesitant about endorsing such action. This delay gave time for a much-needed diplomatic dialogue between the Foreign Minister of Russia Lavrov and the US Secretary of State Kerry, leading to a unanimous UN resolution for the destruction and removal of sarin gas from Syria under international supervision which was until done in large quantities, the first positive action over Syria in a deadlocked Security Council for more than two years. But Assad cheated by rebuilding supplies and using them.

There was no vote on Syria in the House of Commons, the US Congress or the French Assembly when President Trump decided in 2018 to launch air strikes in response to chemical weapons being used against civilians. Nor was the democratic process damaged by this. The three countries had to coordinate their military response and brief the Russians so that none of them were attacked by accident while operating against ISIS. It allowed Trump to mark the difference between himself and Obama, something that he increasingly liked to do. Damagingly this differentiation policy came into play over the nuclear agreement that the US had been party to with Iran and involved Russia, China, France and the

UK in the 5+1 Security Council members and Germany. As we face up to the challenge of dealing with President Trump over NATO in particular it is worth examining some lessons from the military partnership between the UK and the US in the Second World War.

Winston Churchill was a military man as much as a politician. Carlo D'Este says in *Warlord*: 'Long before he became a statesman, Winston Churchill was first a soldier. The Boer War and soldiering generally were in his blood, inspiring his earliest fantasies as a child and his greatest adventures as a young man.'[306] It was also as Lieutenant Colonel Churchill that on 5 January 1916 he was given command in the field of the 6th Battalion, Royal Scots Fusiliers, having gone to Flanders to fight after resigning from the Cabinet on 11 November 1915 as Chancellor of the Duchy of Lancaster. By then he was greatly diminished in stature following his dismissal from the more important post of First Lord of the Admiralty following the debacle of the Dardanelles and Gallipoli campaign. It was not until July 1917, at which point Churchill had served in the Army for over eighteen months that Lloyd George, as Prime Minister, was able to overcome the resistance of the Conservatives in his coalition, and appoint Churchill, still a fellow Liberal as Minister of Munitions.

Churchill, out of government in the early 1920s until 1939, often referred to as his 'wilderness years', not only constantly warned against appeasement but became the best-informed MP on all matters related to German rearmament and studied Hitler with great attention. This exposure to military matters served him and the country well when on 10 May 1940, aged sixty-five, he took over as Prime Minister and Minister of Defence. It was a moment of national peril and a change of Prime Minister from Chamberlain

---

306 Carlo D'Este, *Warlord. A Life of Churchill at War 1875–1945* (London: Allen Lane, 2009), p. xv.

was inevitable when Labour and Liberal MPs voted against Chamberlain as did some Conservatives and many abstained. The House of Commons removed Chamberlain but many Conservatives were opposed to Churchill. Yet across the political parties a greater number of MPs knew Churchill, his weaknesses as well as his strengths; they had weighed them up, particularly what they all knew of his mood changes or cyclothymic personality, but they saw the warrior the country needed.

The House of Commons is an extremely intimate place and across party lines, amongst MPs, there is often a fair measure of agreement about an individual's overall qualities. By May 1940 most desperately wanted Churchill's inspirational abilities and judged this to be his all-important attribute. The force of his personality was elemental, and that is why they made him war leader and head of government. He was also experienced, having had a direct and personal relationship with the military commanders in the First World War.

Churchill in power as Prime Minister in 1940, loved the whole ambience of war. He intervened over strategy and military appointments, and wore the Chiefs of Staff to a frazzle over long alcoholic dinners that went into the early hours. He was not always right. He clashed with General Wavell in August 1940, accusing him of breaking his pledge to resist the Italian invasion of Somaliland. Wavell, stung by his criticism, wrote back refusing to set up the court martial of Major General Godwin-Austen that was being demanded. Churchill appeared to have forgotten that he had sent an earlier memo to both Eden, then Secretary of State for War, and General Sir John Dill, Chief of the Imperial General Staff, in which he said: 'The evacuation of Somaliland is enforced on us by the enemy, but is nonetheless strategically convenient.' Wavell enraged Churchill with the last sentence of his letter, 'a big butcher's bill was not necessarily evidence of good tactics'. Churchill's mood was dark and he was not ready to accept that his own telegram to

Wavell was couched in terms that were unforgivable. His critical attitude to 'wavering Wavell' became a fixation, and he would eventually deprive him of command in the field – an injustice now widely accepted as such. Wavell was a brilliant brain and as overall commander he laid the foundations for Auchinleck's and later Montgomery's victories in Egypt.

By December 1940 the Foreign Secretary, Lord Halifax, after the clash with Churchill over opening negotiations with Mussolini, was pushed out of the government with an underwhelming offer to go to Washington as Ambassador. It was a position of undoubted importance but somewhat diminished later with Churchill also sending to Washington the former Chief of Defence Staff, Field Marshal Dill. He was called 'Dilly-Dally' by Churchill but with affection, having put him in to replace Ironside, the then Chief of Staff, within a day of taking office. Dill had very soon established relations of respect with the US military, particularly with General George Marshall, and Churchill, seeing this correctly, moved him to Washington to become head of the Joint Staff Mission once he decided General Alan Brooke should take Dill's place as Chief of the Imperial General Staff and principal military adviser to the War Cabinet. Churchill knew that Brooke, a tough-minded Northern Irishman was not going to be a pushover for him, nor was he. Throughout the war, Brooke resisted many of Churchill's ideas. His unexpurgated diaries are the best of all the war diaries. Unvarnished, expressing his often brutal opinions, they have the immediacy and strength of vigorous debate with Churchill. Though there was give and take it was conducted under conditions of great stress but there was underlying respect between politician and military leader. The old adage that war is too important to be left to the generals is very true, but the same would apply to leaving it all to the politicians. Brooke sacrificed a lot when he declined Churchill's offer to take command in the desert, a post which he longed to fill, and suggested Montgomery. Fortunately Brooke knew he was needed at home to curb Churchill's wilder ideas. He was disappointed again when he argued to postpone D-Day when he might have hoped to be the overall Commander. By 1944 the predominance of US forces made it inevitable that an American had to be overall commander, and George Marshall, US Army Chief of Staff chose General Eisenhower.

General Montgomery's arrival in north Africa, pale, having had no exposure to sun, small, slight, wearing a light-coloured pullover, without insignia of rank, over a desert shirt and trousers with a black beret, was a picture of eccentricity and underlying genius. Though hugely vain and conceited, Montgomery had always subjected his hubristic traits to great inner control.

Montgomery's powers to alienate even those who managed to get close to him and liked him were present throughout his life. Yet his legendary insensitivity was a reflection of one of his greatest qualities, a simplicity of thought. He pared down the options before him and in preparing his plan there was a sparseness to his decision-making as in his personal life. In that limited sense, there was little conceptual grandeur and perhaps this spared him from developing hubris syndrome as he rose in rank and status. His certainties grew with power but they were pretty absolute from the start of his career. In that sense what you saw was what you got; he conducted himself in the same way before El Alamein as he did after El Alamein and then in France and Germany. Montgomery always struggled to be granted more military power in the field and was always critical of the broad-front approach of Eisenhower for advancing into Germany. However, when his bids to win control over General Bradley failed, as in December 1944, he accepted it. He could even appear to be contrite after behaving badly, writing to Eisenhower after such an occasion:

> I am sure that there are many factors which have a bearing quite beyond anything I realize. Whatever your decision may be, you can

rely on me one hundred per cent to make it work and I know Brad will do the same. Very distressed that my letter may have upset you, and I would ask you to tear it up. Your very devoted subordinate, Monty.

An excellent description of Montgomery's underlying mentality is in Stephen Bungay's book *Alamein*:

Both Montgomery's successes as a general and his failings as a human being arose from the unusual way in which he thought about the world. He was brought up in a world of strict religiosity, which he accepted, and strict rules, against which he rebelled. Both were equally formative. Things were right or wrong, and there was a right and a wrong way of doing things. He was intelligent, but not an intellectual, as for example Wavell was, which meant that he could analyse situations and understand their essentials, but he was not interested in subtleties and possibilities. He simplified until he arrived at a single course of action: the right one. His "masterplans" were the result of rejecting alternatives. There were no scenarios, or options A, B and C, which is what he found when he arrived at the desert (north Africa). His thinking was designed to result in action. At the end of the day, he had to do one thing, and do it with conviction ... Montgomery's world view was binary. It contained no grey.[307]

Brooke's choice of Montgomery to take over command in France of his corps on 30 May 1940, when he returned to England, was the crucial turning point in Montgomery's career. Such decisions make history and Brooke stuck by Montgomery in good times and bad, making excuses for his manner but keeping any doubts about some odd judgements to himself. The oddest of

---

307 Stephen Bungay, *Alamein* (London: Aurum Press, 2002), p. 225.

which was Arnhem in the autumn of 1944. Though written about extensively and immortalised in a book by Cornelius Ryan and made into a film, 'A Bridge Too Far', Arnhem needed analysis devoid of the Montgomery gloss and it has come from Anthony Beevor in 2018.[308] Montgomery wanted to 'be the first Allied general into Germany'. There were two plans. One involved dropping men and equipment on the bridge at Arnhem – Operation Market. The other Operation Garden meant breaking German lines and forcing through '103 km up a single road to outflank the enemy'. The key was surprise and speed. The fatal flaw in Operation Market, as Beevor points out, was that the drop zones were not near enough to the bridges and there was no surprise which meant that the ground operation, in any case too optimistic over the time it would take, given there was no surprise, could not reach the parachutists holding the bridges. Beevor describes Montgomery as an 'insufferable bore with a highly inflated ego.'

While Winston Churchill led the free world in the fight against Hitler from May 1940 until Pearl Harbor in December 1941, by 1943 the baton had clearly passed to the greatest democratic political leader of the twentieth century, Franklin Roosevelt, proven both in the economic depression of the 1930s and as the leader of the most powerful nation in the world in the Second World War, from December 1941 to May 1945. Roosevelt had great charisma, considerable guile and an undoubted hubristic temperament. On coming into office in 1933 Roosevelt knew in military matters it was wise to be careful in handling promotions and demotions. Somewhat surprisingly, he extended General Douglas MacArthur's term of office as Chief of Staff of the US Army for another year despite serious doubts. Wisely, having waited, it was easier in 1935, without controversy, to get rid of MacArthur by sending him to the Philippines to prepare the

---

308 Anthony Beevor, *Arnhem* (Viking, 2018).

country for independence and to develop their own armed forces on which America could rely. Roosevelt explained to his close adviser Rexford Tugwell his attitude to both MacArthur and Joseph P. Kennedy, another dominating and somewhat eccentric leader, in his case in business: 'We must tame these fellows and make them useful to us.' He wanted them either where he could keep an eye on them or out of the way.[309] He first appointed Joseph Kennedy to regulate the stock market on the basis that it takes a thief to catch a thief, and then as Ambassador to Great Britain in order to keep the isolationists happy in America.

Roosevelt never contemplated recalling MacArthur to Washington in 1939; the reasons had a lot to do with his fundamental assessment of MacArthur's character. He had known MacArthur since he was a military aide to his distant cousin, President Theodore Roosevelt. One biographer of Roosevelt has written about his views of MacArthur that while 'he thought him a brave and capable military commander' he also saw him as 'an American Bonapartist, a vain-glorious man on horseback prone to confuse legitimate democratic public opinion with mob rule'.[310] Roosevelt had strongly opposed the way President Hoover and General MacArthur handled a group of First World War veteran protesters called the Bonus Marchers in July 1932. It is interesting, too, that the then Major Dwight Eisenhower advised his chief, MacArthur, against personally leading the military attack on the marchers. MacArthur far exceeded his orders from Hoover to merely conduct the marchers back to their camp and thereafter Roosevelt knew that MacArthur did not have the qualities to be his top military adviser. Eisenhower was also giving the first indication on a major politico-military matter that the US Army had a potential leader of great quality.

---

309 Conrad Black, *Franklin Delano Roosevelt: Champion of Freedom* (London: Weidenfeld & Nicolson, 2003), p. 320.
310 Ibid., p. 242.

HUBRIS: THE ROAD TO DONALD TRUMP

Yet the impression that Eisenhower disagreed with MacArthur's handling of the Bonus Marchers has been exaggerated over time. In her book on Eisenhower, Jean Edward Smith wrote that except for his long-after-the-fact testimony 'there is no evidence to substantiate any disagreement he might have had with War Department policy, or with what MacArthur did. To the contrary: As Ike saw it, it was not MacArthur but the press who were at fault.'[311]

When asked years later by a woman whether he knew MacArthur, Eisenhower drily replied that he had 'studied dramatics for seven years under General MacArthur'. During those years when Eisenhower was only a major serving the Army Chief of Staff he learned much, not just about all aspects of the US Army but also how to deal with politicians in Washington and how to handle as hubristic a leader as MacArthur.

By 1939 President Roosevelt had settled on General Marshall to succeed MacArthur's replacement, General Malin Craig, as Chief of Staff. In retrospect Marshall was a brilliant appointment. Thirty-two generals outranked Marshall but twenty-eight of them were too old under the unofficial rule that they would turn sixty-five during their normal four-year term of office. Of the remaining four, Marshall was chosen. He had developed a somewhat surprising friendship with Harry Hopkins, the President's closest adviser. His main rival was the better-known General Dunn, who was a friend of another presidential confidant, James A. Farley. Marshall never toadied to the President; when he differed he openly disagreed and he deliberately kept his distance. It was as if he was almost fearful of Roosevelt's seductive powers. Marshall chose not to vote in presidential elections in order to preserve his image of being apolitical. Later President Truman had great difficulty in persuading him to become, in effect, a politician as Secretary of State.

---

311 Jean Edward Smith, *Eisenhower: In War and Peace* (New York: Random House, 2012), p. 115.

Roosevelt did not want or need a pliant military commander. Marshall, for his part, did not suffer fools gladly and was, until he felt he knew and respected a person, somewhat aloof. But he was a man of outstanding integrity and judgement whom Roosevelt soon trusted. Each man came to appreciate the other and it proved to be a winning combination. Roosevelt, while not constantly intervening in Marshall's territory, like Churchill, nevertheless did not hesitate to make clear his views on strategy. When Marshall, on 5 May 1942, asked for another 750,000 men to make a total of 4.35 million under arms by January 1943, Roosevelt sent back a significant memorandum next day to Marshall and his other senior advisers asking that it not be circulated beyond them. 'I always think it well to "outline" in simple terms and from time to time complex problems which call for overall planning,' he began. 'Therefore, I would like you gentlemen to read the following.' Emphasising that his view could only apply to the present, he made clear: 'The whole of the Pacific Theater, calls, at the present time, fundamentally for a holding operation.' This Germany-first strategy was no surprise to Marshall but for Admiral King and the US Navy it went against their wishes and their plans. It is one of many examples where Roosevelt showed a clarity of thinking. On military matters, unlike political matters, where he was more devious, he was neither equivocal or reluctant to state his views. He had thought long on military issues, helped by his earlier involvement as a junior politician in the Navy Department.

The military differ in a number of important ways from other professions. They can never expect to have only one employer: governments change – and the military have to adjust. In the US the President is Commander-in-Chief. In the UK the Prime Minister is not the Commander-in-Chief. The role does not exist. The Monarch has, however, a unique and unquantifiable role in relation to the military. They have open access. Appointments are made in the Monarch's name. The military serve Her or His

Majesty's government as it used to be described by politicians. Now more and more Prime Ministers talk about 'my government'. None as yet have spoken of 'my military'. The military are required to achieve 'political ends designated by statesmen' and 'their political masters find it difficult (or what is worse from their point of view, merely inconvenient) to fully elaborate in advance the purpose for which they have invoked military action, or the conditions under which they intend to limit or terminate it'.[312]

The major strategic difference between the US and the UK in the Second World War was when to cross the Channel. Marshall and Roosevelt wanted to do this in 1942 and Churchill and Brooke were opposed. It was still with some reluctance that the British came on board by 1944 for D-Day and Brooke even wrote in his diary entry before the battle:

> In a few hours the Cross Channel invasion starts. I am very uneasy about the whole operation. At the best it will fall so very far short of the expectations of the bulk of the population meaning all those who know nothing of its difficulties. At the worst it may well be the most ghastly disaster of the whole war.[313]

To the Americans the explanation for the British hesitancy was, in crude terms, that having fought in the Battle of the Somme in the First World War, the British neither forgot the experience nor wanted ever to repeat it. Marshall wanted one main focus for the battle, and believed that should be France. Churchill was always looking to find other pressure points and in this he was often supported by Brooke. Slowly by 1944 the two sides of the Atlantic had come together at the level of the Supreme Commander Eisenhower.

---

312 Eliot A. Cohen, *Supreme Command: Soldiers, Statesmen, and Leadership in Wartime* (New York: Anchor, 2003), p. 257.
313 Field Marshal Lord Alanbrooke, *War Diaries 1939–1945*, ed. Alex Danchev and Daniel Todman (London: Weidenfeld & Nicolson, 2001), p. 554.

The qualities of a supreme military commander are to calculate carefully, keep all options open, but when the die is cast shoulder full responsibility and have alternative strategies to fall back on so that the overall victory can still be delivered. As supreme commander, General Dwight Eisenhower demonstrated all these qualities. He had already postponed D-Day once but after hearing the weather forecast, he gave the order to commence the invasion at 4.15 a.m. on 6 June 1944. He then sat down and wrote out in pencil the words he intended using if he had miscalculated:

> Our landings in the Cherbourg–Havre area have failed to gain a satisfactory foothold. I have withdrawn the troops. My decision to attack at this time and place was based upon the best information available. The troops, the air and the navy did all that bravery and devotion to duty could do. If any blame or fault attaches to the attempt it is mine alone.

As field commanders, neither General Patton nor General Montgomery would ever have written out such a note. A supreme commander, by contrast, has to prepare to handle defeat while embarking on victory. For Patton and Montgomery, there was only Plan A; they had no need to contemplate a Plan B for their self-assurance as field commanders was such that victory was everything and defeat was not to be contemplated. Their battles were on narrow fronts, albeit crucial ones. The supreme commander had to balance many offensives on different fronts; coordinate land, air and sea; establish the logistical support; keep some elements in reserve; and deal with allies, often time consuming and patience stretching. As the war proceeded, the American–British relationship became ever more unequal. It was well expressed by Brooke after his meeting in Malta with Marshall on 1 February 1945, at which Eisenhower was not present. In an assessment from the 1950s he is more reflective but also still critical of Marshall than in his diary entries:

The 'force of circumstances' was that we were dealing with a force that was predominantly American, and it was therefore natural that they should wish to have the major share in its handling. In addition there was the fact that Marshall clearly understood nothing of strategy and could not even argue out the relative merits of various alternatives. Being unable to judge for himself he trusted and backed Ike, and felt it his duty to guard him from interference.[314]

Marshall, unlike Brooke, had in Roosevelt a political Commander-in-Chief who did not interfere anywhere near as often as Churchill did. Marshall also gave Eisenhower, his chosen supreme commander, considerable latitude, which he took particularly on personnel matters in his handling of all field commanders but also, as his authority increased in the later stages of the war, in his readiness to work directly to Stalin, who was the Soviet Union's military commander, not just the political leader and head of the Politburo. The war against Japan was lead to a far greater extent by the Americans. Brooke had to contend with an American leading the invasion of France, which was a theatre in which he had already operated as a field commander in 1939 and to which, he had been led to believe by Churchill, he might return as supreme commander. It was virtually impossible for him to distance himself from what he believed would be the effect of Eisenhower's decisions. Such distancing was much easier for Marshall to do, preoccupied worldwide as he was.

Hubris was not present in the personality of either Marshall or Brooke and for that fortunate fact the overall conduct of the Second World War was greatly enhanced. They were two generals of considerable ability and strength of purpose. Both delegated well and did not have an urge to constantly interfere, and both backed

---

314 Ibid., p. 653.

their immediate subordinate commanders. There were few elements of hubris in the character of Eisenhower, many in his deputy, Montgomery, and many more in Patton. What is fascinating is how Eisenhower handled Patton, and in some ways it is a textbook case of how to live with the hubris of a military commander in the field while curbing that part of his hubris which can impact on his effectiveness and damage the overall strategy.

For anyone of the generation who remembers the film *Patton*, which in 1970 earned George C. Scott an Oscar for Best Actor following his portrayal of General George S. Patton Jr, it is hard to separate myth from reality. Patton was by the end of the war, despite numerous indiscretions and barely forgivable incidents, a conquering hero, appearing at official functions in full-dress uniform, his helmet with its four stars shining, a pistol in his belt and carrying a riding whip.

Throughout his life Patton was an ancestor worshipper 'whose veneration of his forefathers verged on obsession'. In 1912 he represented the United States in the modern pentathlon at the Stockholm Olympics, and he served under General Pershing in Mexico and in World War One. 'He saw himself as the modern embodiment of his heroic Confederate antecedents, and because of the enormously successful façade he created, the tender, even romantic, side of Patton was virtually unknown in his lifetime outside his circle of friends and admirers.'[315] 'Blood and Guts', as he was called, had many detractors. The historian Paul Fussell characterised him as one of the Second World War's 'masters of chicken shit', a headline grabber obsessed about personal glory, arrogant, profane, volatile, someone for whom the lives of his men were expendable.

Patton, like many famous generals before and since, relished being in command from the day he landed in North Africa on 11

---

315 Carlo D'Este, *A Genius for War: A Life of General George S. Patton* (London: HarperCollins, 1995), p. 2.

November 1942, his birthday, as head of the US Expeditionary Force. Soon afterwards he took Casablanca from the recalcitrant French and his career took off. During that period he grew ever more self-confident and contemptuous of others. In Sicily he slapped two soldiers while he was visiting hospitals and publicly abused them. This was a supreme act of contempt and makes it almost certain that he had acquired hubris syndrome. The first occasion was on 3 August 1943. He slapped an infantryman, and even went as far as to kick him in the rear. On 10 August 1943 he struck an artilleryman across the face while continuing to curse him and then strode back and hit him again. The two incidents were followed by a memo from Patton to all commanders in the 7th Army:

> It has come to my attention that a very small number of soldiers are going to the hospital on the pretext that they are nervously incapable of combat. Such men are cowards and bring discredit on the Army and disgrace to their comrades ... those who are not willing to fight will be tried by court-martial for cowardice in the face of the enemy.[316]

The two slappings became common knowledge among American troops in Sicily. General Omar Bradley, who never liked Patton, nevertheless when given a written report on the second incident from a surgeon at the hospital had it locked away, explaining to one of his staff that he felt he could not go over Patton's head to Eisenhower. Three newspaper correspondents, who also knew, instead of sending their story back to the US, arranged to meet with Eisenhower, who already had the facts because of a report sent through medical channels to his chief surgeon, General Frederick A. Blesse. Eisenhower refused to be blackmailed into getting rid of Patton by the three journalists. He

---

316 Ibid., pp. 532–46.

told them he had reprimanded Patton and after explaining his reasons wisely left it to them to use their judgement as to whether to publish, telling them there would be no censorship if they did file reports. The journalists made an agreement amongst themselves not to file reports out of respect for Eisenhower but they still disapproved of Patton's conduct.

Despite this controversy, on 16 August, Patton triumphantly entered Messina, bringing the Sicily campaign to an end. Soon afterwards he was handed an envelope with a letter from Eisenhower in the strongest terms refusing to excuse his 'brutality, abuse of the sick, and exhibition of uncontrollable temper in front of subordinates'. Contrary to popular belief the letter did not call for a personal apology to every soldier and unit in the 7th Army but contained an instruction: 'You make in the form of apology or otherwise such personal amends to the individuals concerned as may be within your power.'

Encapsulated in his decision are many of the unique features of military decision-making. Why did Eisenhower decline to dismiss Patton? Fundamentally, because he was indispensable to the war effort and, Eisenhower believed, one of the guarantors of victory. He had known Patton well at Camp Meade when Patton had just returned a hero wounded and decorated from France in the First World War. But as Michael Korda writes in his thoughtful and penetrating book *Ike*, 'It was to Ike's credit that he somehow saw the serious soldier behind the pose and understood that Patton was a thoughtful and well-read student of war.'

War is about victory and in its pursuit – within the constraints of the Geneva Conventions – almost everything else is dispensable. The supreme military commander has to have a relentless focus on victory and what subordinate commanders can deliver, namely victory in the field. When assessing Eisenhower as a military commander, it is easy to miss the fact that he had in full measure this crucial and even brutal characteristic.

Eisenhower, interestingly, did not write about the Patton incident to his superior, General Marshall in Washington. Only in late November did the story break in Washington when the columnist Drew Pearson sensationalised the story on his weekly radio programme. Yet Marshall, as well as Secretary of Defense Stimson and President Roosevelt, all backed Eisenhower's decision to keep Patton in his command position.

Eisenhower had severely jolted Patton's hubris with the nature of his reprimand, as he intended to do. But he knew he had to go further. He refused to have Patton in a battlefield command in France on D-Day, much to Patton's anger and frustration. Only on 6 July 1944, a month after D-Day, did Patton get to France. Instead he became part of a decoy strategy, appearing overtly in English ports close to the Calais–Boulogne coastal area in the belief that German spies would relay information about his presence and this would increase their conviction that that was the most likely area for the invading forces to strike, not Normandy. Eisenhower never had any illusion about Patton's inner flaws but he never wavered from his overall assessment of him, describing him in 1946 as 'the most brilliant commander of an army in the open field that our or any other service produced'.[317]

Immediately after saving Patton's career in August 1943 Eisenhower talked frankly to Harry Butcher, his wartime naval aide for three years, in a stream-of-consciousness explanation which Butcher wrote down and then, somewhat embarrassingly, published in his diary very soon after the war.

> For half an hour Eisenhower had sat in his room debating the question and with himself. He cited history to show that great military leaders had practically gone crazy on the battlefield in their zeal to win the fight. Yet Ike feels that Patton is motivated by

---

317 Ibid., p. 818.

selfishness. He thinks Patton would prefer to have the war go on if it meant further aggrandisement for him. Neither does he mind sacrificing lives if by so doing he can gain greater fame.[318]

This blunt analysis shows that Eisenhower did not even give Patton the credit of being careful with the lives of the men under him and that he was ready to recognise that some generals in the field were often flawed characters but nevertheless brilliant leaders of men. Eisenhower, nevertheless, saw that Patton had that rare but vital quality – he could summon up from his men a readiness not just to make a supreme effort but to willingly risk making the supreme sacrifice.

When the Germans made their successful offensive through the forests of Ardennes in December 1944, Eisenhower faced a crisis in his overall strategy. Despite having no prior intelligence and with bad weather preventing reconnaissance from the air, Eisenhower never panicked. He expected something like the German initiative and he let the Germans advance. He told his generals: 'The present situation is to be regarded as one of opportunity for us and not of disaster.' Patton saw what Eisenhower was doing, building up forces for a counter-attack and not worrying unduly about the German advance. He said: 'Hell, let's have the guts to let the sons of bitches go all the way to Paris, then we'll really cut 'em off and chew 'em up.'

Patton repaid the belief that Eisenhower had in his military genius when Ike asked him to wheel his advancing tanks through 90 degrees and at a moment's notice head off at breakneck speed to Bastogne to challenge the German Panzers which had broken through using the forests as cover. This was a spectacular feat of repositioning which saved the broad-front strategy which

---

318 Harry C. Butcher, *Three Years with Eisenhower* (London: William Heinemann, 1946), diary entry for 21 August 1943.

Eisenhower was criticised for pursuing. But it was Eisenhower who rallied his commanders, acting quickly to contain the attack. Again he took responsibility, writing in his book *Crusade in Europe*, while his memory was still fresh as Chief of Staff in Washington in 1948, that if historians condemned him for giving Hitler this chance in the Ardennes then their condemnation should be directed at him alone.

Perhaps Eisenhower had in mind General William T. Sherman, when he talked confidentially to Butcher of Patton and other generals going crazy. Sherman had his Union command removed from him in Kentucky in November 1861 when the newspapers labelled him 'insane'. Only recently have historians documented Sherman's four major depressive episodes, which raise questions as to whether he was suffering from bipolar disorder. Yet by 1864 Sherman was literally back in the saddle, having entered Georgia early that year with his troops, giving rise to a song, 'Marching through Georgia'. Little had been heard from him, in part because he was fighting a very different sort of war, avoiding set-piece battles and instead ruthlessly destroying the basis of the South's economy. Suddenly in the summer of that year Sherman captured Atlanta. He had laid waste not just to Georgia but the Carolinas also, splitting the Confederacy and promoting such unaccustomedly good news that it helped Lincoln to be re-elected. Sherman's campaign broke the morale of the civilian population in the South. With their cities and their farms destroyed the Confederate soldiers had nowhere to return to.

Sherman's genius has been described by the Professor of Psychiatry at Tufts University, Nassir Ghaemi, as a 'manic originator' and cited as an example of his thesis how a psychiatric illness can be a positive, not a negative, feature of someone's life.[319] This is

---

319 Nassir Ghaemi, *A First-Rate Madness. Uncovering the Links between Leadership and Mental Illness* (New York: Penguin, 2011) pp. 23–39.

an important concept which is counter-intuitive for most people, but Ghaemi gives many convincing examples.

History teaches us that religion and war are often linked. In the Bible, St Paul captures the spirit of an invocation to battle: 'Put on the whole armour of God, that ye may be able to stand against the wiles of the devil.'[320] Not for nothing do many battlefield leaders feel empowered by God. Certainly Patton did. So did Montgomery.

Eisenhower had been authorised at Yalta, as part of better coordination with the Russians, to communicate directly with the Soviet High Command. On 25 March 1945, when he wrote to Stalin a military letter as one supreme commander to another, he deliberately made no effort to communicate his intentions to the British chiefs of staff or to Churchill, who he had met that same day at Rheinberg. The letter was numbered SCAF 252 and drafted by General Harold Bull. The actual message to Stalin was somewhat obscurely phrased and full of intended military dispositions but the intention behind the letter was clear. Stalin could take Berlin.

Stalin quickly telegraphed back his acceptance of the plan with the assurance that Berlin had lost its 'former strategic importance' and that he would allocate only secondary forces to it in mid-May. Churchill rang Eisenhower to protest and only then did Eisenhower send a message to clear his line with Marshall in Washington, which he did without difficulty. Eisenhower also wrote to Montgomery about blitzed Berlin: 'That place has become, so far as I am concerned, nothing but a geographical location, and I have never been interested in these.'

General Bradley in the field knew Eisenhower's views and agreed with them. 'I think that to capture Berlin might cost us a hundred thousand casualties.' Much of the argument that Eisenhower should have taken Berlin is retrospective wisdom not

---

320 Ephesians 6:11.

reflected in the realities of war, the risking and the saving of soldiers' lives.

General Marshall chose wisely in Eisenhower. While he did not have all the ideal attributes – who has? – Eisenhower had more than any of his rivals. The one exception to this was not a rival, but Marshall himself, a man arguably of all the talents though that was not Alan Brooke's military view. Roosevelt wisely wanted to keep Marshall close to him in Washington. Marshall honourably accepted that as his duty. Eisenhower never developed the tell-tale signs of hubris, which eventually destroyed General MacArthur.

Dwight Eisenhower became US President on 21 January 1953, serving two terms. Many commentators, still to this day, write dismissively and disparagingly about 'Ike' the politician. They fail to understand the depth of his intellect, his overall wisdom and his occasional ruthlessness. It is still, for example, while President Trump deals with North Korea, an issue for debate as to whether in May 1953 Eisenhower was bluffing China over the use of nuclear weapons in Korea. He had been sceptical, probably personally against, using nuclear weapons against Japan when informed about the decision at the time when Truman was at the Potsdam Conference in 1945. So it was highly significant when the Joint Chiefs of Staff on 19 May 1953 definitely recommended their use that President Eisenhower asked John Foster Dulles, the US Secretary of State, when in India to talk to Jawaharlal Nehru and ask him to warn Zhou Enlai that the US would drop atomic bombs north of the Yalu River unless peace was agreed quickly in the talks of Panmunjom between North and South Korea. Fortunately they did make rapid progress but we know Eisenhower had talked of an area of North Korea as suitable for demonstrating American seriousness with a tactical nuclear bomb.[321]

---

321 Max Hastings, *The Korean War* (Michael Joseph, 1987), pp. 393–4.

Many in the US, seventy years later, seemed to forget this political precedent when Trump upped the ante in threatening to use nuclear weapons against North Korea. Although Trump was on record nineteen years earlier saying 'he would negotiate like crazy' before considering any nuclear strike. In May 2016, during his presidential election campaign, Trump said he would sit down and talk to Kim Jong-un and again mentioned that readiness when later threatening to rain 'fire and fury' on him if North Korea targeted America. Following the personal meeting in June 2018 in Singapore between President Trump and the much younger North Korean leader some argue that Trump should never have agreed to meet. But Trump was correct to engage and in choosing to do so in such an unconventional way he is still entitled to claim that all the conventional approaches have failed.

Why did Eisenhower exhibit so few hubristic tendencies, let alone never come close to acquiring hubris syndrome? The best resource for studying this aspect is the biography by Michael Korda. He describes how from humble origins Eisenhower underwent in his own lifetime a rapid transition to world-class, five-star hero and then to being ridiculed as an old fuddy-duddy in the White House. 'Although Eisenhower, with his big grin, looked like a gregarious soul, this was in part a façade or a protective mechanism.' He had a 'stubborn streak'. His 'father had a quick temper (like his son Dwight, whose outbursts of temper in later life often took the unwary, lulled by his big grin, by surprise).' Time and again, that red-necked anger could be seen in the blood vessels in his neck but it was very rarely let loose. This quick temper holds the key to understanding Eisenhower's personality. Though he could be impulsive and blow off steam he learned from his mother the necessity of keeping it under control and to play in a team. He was a considerable scholar too with an amazing memory, leaving him full of facts, particularly about military history, Hannibal, Caesar and Scipio were no strangers to him. His extensive knowledge of ancient warfare was aided and abetted by General Fox Connor, who was an important influence on Eisenhower's character development.

Yet his knowledge too he learned at a very young age to hide, never wanting to appear a know all. His home town was Abilene in the state of Kansas, where most people farmed or in some way served the farming community. His father's family, from long back of German stock, were Mennonites, followers of Menno Simon, a Swiss preacher who took the Bible literally. His mother, Ida, was a pacifist and a Jehovah's Witness who cried her heart out when her son left for the West Point military academy. Ike was influenced by his lifelong close friendship with Swede Haaelt, who a year earlier had left school to join the Annapolis naval academy. Eisenhower did not share his parents' religious commitment, never joining a church or regularly attending Sunday service, but he was respectful of religion.

At West Point, despite the draconian discipline, Eisenhower showed a 'wild streak' and a competitive one, leading to the recommendation that he be assigned to a strict commanding officer. When he was not visiting nearby forts marking battles in the Revolutionary War, as described in class textbooks, he participated in his 'favourite indoor sport' at West Point – poker. This was yet another side of his character, hidden from view.

General Pershing offered Eisenhower the chance to go to Paris in 1928 and it provided the opportunity for him to study all the great battlefields of the First World War, a precious knowledge for his return to France as a warrior sixteen years later. Interestingly, his affection for the French was returned by General de Gaulle, a man despised by Roosevelt, who wrote of Eisenhower in his memoirs: 'He knew how to be adroit and supple, but although he relied on these gifts, he was (also) capable of great daring.' It was in Paris while helping to draft Pershing's war memoirs that Eisenhower first met Colonel Marshall, who marked him down for future promotion.

On D-Day minus 7 in 1945 with the battle plan set, he had been faced by Air Chief Marshal Trafford Leigh-Mallory, his British Commander-in-Chief for Air, questioning the wisdom of dropping the 82nd and 101st Airborne Divisions behind enemy lines on the Cherbourg peninsula. Always sceptical of the plan, Leigh-Mallory had become convinced from aerial photos of German defences that the divisions would lose 70 per cent of their gliders and 50 per cent of their paratroop strength. Eisenhower by himself had to decide whether to disregard the view of his technical expert. He then telephoned him to say the attacks would go ahead and confirmed it in writing. Little wonder that now that all his decisions, including his 24-hour postponement of the invasion against Montgomery's advice, were being put to the test, he was wracked with anxiety. This was no hubristic leader but a supreme commander waiting for the battle. The fact that he deliberately sought calm during that stage of the war, with a woman, Kay Summersby, by his side is understandable. Yet when he returned permanently to America he cut off all contact with her, stayed in the Army and prepared to run for President.

After the war was over Eisenhower became a popular hero on a grand scale. On a tumultuous visit to London thousands lined the streets and *The Times* commented that his speech

> had the moving eloquence which is native to the words of a sincere and modest man ... if history now begins to take a course towards a happier order, in which the curse of war shall at last be exorcised from human relations, no man of our time will have made a nobler contribution to that issue than this great American.

In his book *Ike's Bluff,* Evan Thomas writes Eisenhower 'had the kind of confidence that allowed him to be humble'.[322]

---

322 Evan Thomas, *Ike's Bluff: President Eisenhower's Secret Battle to Save the World* (New York: Little Brown, 2012), p. 415.

A very different man to Eisenhower was General MacArthur, who was chosen by Harry Truman four months into his presidency to be the Supreme Commander for the Allied Powers (SCAP), based in Japan, with a simple directive: 'You will exercise your authority as you deem proper to carry out your mission.' Truman had never met MacArthur and in his personal diary for 17 June 1945 he describes him as 'Mr Prima Donna. Brass Hat, Five Star MacArthur. He's worse than the Cabots and the Lodges – they at least talked with one another before they told God what to do. Mac tells God right off.' Truman went on to describe him as 'a play actor and a bunco man', wondering 'how a country can produce such men as Robert E. Lee, John J. Pershing, and Eisenhower and Bradley and at the same time produce Custers, Pattons and MacArthurs.' Yet he appointed him despite knowing that Admiral Chester Nimitz, whom he respected, wanted the job. Perhaps Truman was influenced by knowing that Roosevelt in 1944 had chosen MacArthur rather than Nimitz to be the key figure in the Pacific area. Both these Presidents had made the key assessment that despite all his vanity MacArthur had not yet been corrupted by power in the sense of Lord Acton's famous dictum, and only when MacArthur crossed that line five years later did Truman sack him.

An assessment of MacArthur is made by Seymour Morris Jr in his perceptive new book, *Supreme Commander*, when he writes that MacArthur 'until Korea was careful not to step on any Washington toes while enjoying the prerogatives of an emperor, a shogun and a President all rolled into one'.[323] MacArthur arrived at the Atsugi airstrip in Japan on 30 August 1945 to preside over the formal surrender. On the face of it his plan, called the Initial Post-Surrender Policy for Japan, was entirely his own; in reality he had received a document on the 29th that had been in development in

---

323 Seymour Morris Jr, *Supreme Commander: MacArthur's Triumph in Japan* (New York: Harper, 2014).

Washington for over a year and adopted its fifth draft, which was released to the press on 23 September. MacArthur personally summarised it and announced the eleven priorities to his staff on the plane.

Before landing MacArthur made another important decision: he and his staff would step down off the plane unarmed – even though there were only 4,000 American troops in the vicinity of the airfield as against 300,000 Japanese and only sixteen days earlier 32 Japanese officers had attacked the Emperor's palace after he conceded defeat. By doing this MacArthur demonstrated his determination to be a transformational leader, which the historian Kazuo Kawai, quoted by Morris, identifies in the following passage:

> One reason for his influence on the Japanese was his dedicated sense of mission. The egoism fringed with mysticism, with which he regarded himself as the chosen instrument for the reformation and the redemption of the Japanese people, might sometimes be ludicrous and sometimes irritating, but there was no mistaking the sincerity and intensity of his idealism ... He lifted the tone of the Occupation from a military operation to a moral crusade.[324]

Nowhere was this more evident than in the delicate way MacArthur handled the Emperor. So it becomes ever more surprising that this five-year occupation, the aftermath of the military defeat of Japan, which was planned for and executed with considerable skill, involving the State Department and the military, was not replicated 63 years later by the Bush administration in Iraq. There the occupation was conducted with no substantive aftermath planning, the casual dismantling of all the structures of government and military command, and in the case of the proconsul-like appointment of Paul Bremer he had neither the prestige nor the

---

324 Ibid., p. 292.

authority of MacArthur. President Bush would have been wiser to have asked Colin Powell to give up being Secretary of State and given him the same crisp instructions after the invasion of Iraq as came from President Truman and let him get on with it.

The first sign that MacArthur was ready to be flexible was when he planned to issue three directives, the first of which was for a military government. The Japanese Foreign Minister, Mamoru Shigemitsu, made the case for putting the Japanese government in a position where they could prove their worth and have these directives kept in reserve. MacArthur saw the case, reversed his position and scrapped the three directives. That was not the action of a man in the grip of hubris syndrome.

America, to this day, is still divided on whether MacArthur was the greatest soldier in American history, the view held by many who fought in the Pacific theatre and by some who watched him as the American 'viceroy' reconstruct Japan. It is hard not to admire either how MacArthur won back the initiative in Korea with his amphibious landing behind enemy lines in Inchon, undertaken in the teeth of opposition from the American Joint Chiefs. Yet to many others MacArthur was an egotistical 'Caesar', a five-star fake, who finally risked World War III with his desire to attack China.

Myths surround MacArthur like all great men, but in the end he has to be judged on the merits of his dismissal by President Truman. It was announced at a hurriedly called press conference in Washington at 1.00 a.m. on 11 April 1951 to demonstrate, once the news of his ousting had leaked out, that he was being fired by the President and giving him no time to resign. MacArthur heard about it on the radio and only on the following day did he actually read Truman's order 'I deeply regret it becomes my duty as President and Commander-in-Chief of the United States military forces to replace you as Supreme Commander Allied Powers, Commander-in-Chief of the United Nations Command, Commander-in-Chief, Far East, Commanding General, US Army, Far East.'

Initially, a wave of public sympathy engulfed MacArthur and it looked as if he might become the next President of the United States as a Republican after Truman stepped down. Always a brilliant speaker, he tore at the heart strings of Americans in his homecoming address to both Houses of Congress, with wild applause and frequent standing ovations. At his final peroration, 'I am closing my fifty-two years of service . . . Old soldiers never die, they just fade away', many wept. But in the subsequent congressional hearings, MacArthur had no answer to the testimony and evidence of the greatly respected George Marshall, by then in the civilian post of Secretary of State. Nor had he any answer to the chairman of the Joint Chiefs of Staff, General Bradley, who said that to involve China as the focus of the struggle 'would involve us in the wrong war, at the wrong place, at the wrong time, and with the wrong enemy'.[325] Thus MacArthur's political bandwagon was effectively overturned, not essentially by Truman but by MacArthur's own military colleagues.

The evidence is that, by 1950, MacArthur, always hubristic, had acquired full-blown hubris syndrome in the all-powerful military position he had assumed in Korea. On 24 December he submitted to Washington a list of retaliation targets in China and North Korea which needed twenty-six atomic bombs. The fact that his chief of intelligence, General Charles Willoughby, subverted the intelligence about China's intention to enter the Korean War as American troops approached China's border is incontrovertible. The massing of Chinese troops above the Yalu River was known to Willoughby but, as is brilliantly described in the late David Halberstam's book on the Korean War, Washington was not kept fully informed.[326] Contempt for Truman and his administration, and contempt for the

325 Geoffrey Perret, *Old Soldiers Never Die: The Life of Douglas MacArthur* (London: André Deutsch, 1996), p. 574.
326 David Halberstam, *The Coldest Winter: American and the Korean War* (New York: Hyperion, 2007), pp. 373–82.

Joint Chiefs of Staff were the hallmark, by then, of MacArthur's frame of mind. What MacArthur wanted Willoughby made true. MacArthur had told Truman that the Chinese were not going to cross the border, therefore none of the intelligence that they *had* crossed, and in substantial numbers, could be accepted. Years earlier General Marshall had spotted MacArthur's weakness. 'My staff—', MacArthur had begun. Marshall interrupted. 'You don't have a staff, General. You have a court.'

The commentator Joseph Alsop likened the situation at MacArthur's headquarters to the court of Louis XIV and held that this sycophancy was what tripped him up in the end. For a man who had, all his life, prided himself on being a disciplined soldier, it was a tragedy as great as any of the great Greek dramas. He had by 1950 or perhaps 1951 acquired hubris syndrome and he met in Truman a modest man but one courageous enough to be his nemesis. All MacArthur was left with, in retirement, was the nostalgia for hearing again the sound of the bugles of his youth.

What of the other military commanders of the twentieth and early part of the twenty-first centuries? Those who fought through the Burma campaign are unstinting in their respect and admiration for Field Marshal Slim. In South East Asia, as a very young commander, Louis Mountbatten, 'Dickie', has always had his admirers reinforced by his short spell as Viceroy of India and his detractors when he brought forward the deadline given him by Clement Attlee and took a deeply divided India to independence. He was undoubtedly vain and full of hubris. He was once told to his face by Field Marshal Gerald Templer, who had earned people's regard particularly in Malaysia, 'Dickie, you're so crooked that if you swallowed a nail you'd shit a corkscrew.' But Mountbatten had the grace to handle coming back to the Admiralty and serving his time as a far more junior Admiral. He rose to be the Chief of the Naval Staff because of his undoubted ability. He opposed the invasion of the Suez Canal and eventually became Chief of Staff. I met him first when a junior Minister for the Navy on the Royal Yacht and I found him a modern man, very well versed in technology and science with deep insights into all questions of military and defence strategy. He also queried the need for a super sophisticated, very costly, nuclear deterrent for the UK and in this he was aided by his wartime adviser and later close friend, Lord Zuckerman, who advised me on nuclear matters when I became Foreign Secretary.

Wars make and break leaders. The Falklands War made Margaret Thatcher for after it she was invincible in the General Election of 1983. On 31 March 1982, there came what Thatcher described as 'the worst moment of my life', brilliantly reconstructed by Charles Moore, her official biographer. John Nott, the Defence Secretary, arrived to see her bearing intelligence about an impending Argentinian invasion of the Falkland Islands. Nott and his permanent under-secretary, Frank Cooper, told her that the recapture of the Falkland Islands was all but impossible, a view shared by the Chief of the General Staff. The Chief of the Defence Staff, Admiral Sir Terence Lewin, was away in New Zealand. In 1977, when Chief of the Naval Staff, he had unsuccessfully opposed the deployment of a nuclear submarine to the Falklands and even denied it had rules of engagement.

Admiral Sir Henry Leach, the First Sea Lord, arrived from Portsmouth in uniform to find a naval staff briefing on the Falklands in the Ministry of Defence that advised: 'Don't touch it.' Fortunately Leach was a man of resolution and intelligence, as I knew from my time as navy minister between 1968 and 1970 when he was head of naval plans.

Leach went down to the House of Commons still in uniform to ask the Prime Minister for political clearance to assemble a task force.

'Can we do it?' she asked.

'We can, Prime Minister.'

HUBRIS: THE ROAD TO DONALD TRUMP

'Why do you say that?'

Leach replied: 'Because if we don't do it, if we pussyfoot . . . we'll be living in a different country whose word will count for little.'

Few British Prime Ministers would have reacted as Thatcher did and send a naval task force, three weeks sailing away, to retrieve a small, distant archipelago of little strategic significance. Yet the decision itself was not hubristic, as I know from my own conversations with her during that war. While utterly determined, she was surprisingly cautious and in private she was more anxious than belligerent. Her 'rejoice, rejoice' statement on the steps of No. 10, following the landing of British troops on South Georgia, is often quoted as an example of hubris, but it was as much relief as exaltation. What was hubristic was to take a march-past of those who had served in the Falklands campaign, arranged by the Lord Mayor in the City of London. That role, Thatcher well knew, was properly one for the Queen.

Margaret Thatcher was, with Clement Attlee, one of the two truly outstanding post-war Prime Ministers, both at one stage war leaders, Attlee over Korea in 1951 and Thatcher over the Falklands in 1983. Her personal grip on power increasingly came to an end from 1988 to 1990 when she began repeatedly to pit herself against her own source of power in Parliament, the bulk of Conservative MPs. She had hitherto always held, despite controversy, the respect – even admiration – of the majority of her MPs but reached a stage where she was not listening to her parliamentary colleagues and appeared to enjoy deriding their views. The Cabinet had been reduced in stature and in quality. Majority opinion in the Conservative parliamentary party was frequently flouted or manipulated. People of substance, who well knew that Cabinet government was a great constitutional safeguard, had allowed this to develop over the years to the detriment of the British democratic system. She developed hubris syndrome described in more detail in

Chapter 10. Margaret Thatcher was removed from office very soon after Kuwait was invaded. President George H. W. Bush had chosen as his Chief of Staff, Colin Powell, the first ever black military leader to hold this office, dipping down into the list of senior officers to do so.

Powell had been a young colonel in the Vietnam war. As Chief of Staff he earned huge respect for his contribution to the removal of Saddam Hussein from Kuwait in 1991. He had learnt from the mistake of the gradual build up of forces in Vietnam over years and in months ensured the multinational coalition went into Kuwait with overwhelming force. Yet the face of the US Army in the field was not Powell but that of General H. Norman Schwarzkopf, a massive man physically, who had as his joint commander General Prince Khaled bin Abdul Aziz, the Saudi Prince. The British wisely chose an Arabic speaker and former SAS officer, General Peter de la Billière, who ensured that British tanks played an integral role and all its ground forces were under the tactical control of the Americans. An irreverent account of this war, which ended very quickly followed by an effective peace settlement can be found in Robert Fisk's monumental but illuminating book, *The Great War for Civilisation. The Conquest of the Middle East.*[327] He was at the time war correspondent for *The Independent* and his publisher describes his book as 'a passionate outcry against the lies and deceit that have sent soldiers to their deaths and killed tens of thousands of men and women Arabs, Christians and Jews over the past century.'

The Middle East has been in a state of war almost continuously since 1990 and the situation 30 years on is worse after conflicts in Iraq, Libya and Syria. There are no great military commanders that have shone through those years because sadly the management of these wars have been dominated by politicians: Bush, Clinton,

---

327 Robert Fisk, *The Great War for Civilisation. The Conquest of the Middle East* (First Estate. 2005), Chapter 15 & 16.

Bush, Blair, Sarkozy and Cameron. The civilian carnage these wars have brought in their wake across Iran, Iraq, Libya, Syria, Lebanon, Gaza and Sinai and the Yemen cannot be stressed enough. During that time there have been four wars in the Balkans, a war in Georgia and the continuing war involving Russia and Ukraine, although in relative terms to the Middle East these wars have resulted in fewer military and civilian casualties.

I spoke to Tony Blair on the telephone when I was in Berlin on 16 April 1999 during the Kosovo war when NATO was engaging in air attacks against Serbia and Serbian forces on the ground in Kosovo. Boris Yeltsin had not been ready to support action at the UN. Yeltsin got on well with Clinton and appeared to be waiting in the wings ready to help. Blair's anxieties over the deteriorating situation was because the Serb military were still largely unaffected by the NATO bombing. He was surprisingly frank and we had an animated discussion. I sensed, however, for the first time a note of exaltation in his voice. Soon afterwards real tension developed between Blair and Clinton about the need for ground forces. Fortunately for NATO, President Yeltsin sent the former Prime Minister and former head of Gazprom, Chernomyrdin, twice to Belgrade to meet with Milosevic, the first occasion alone, and I suspect he threatened to cut off Russian gas supplies to Serbia. On the second visit a few weeks later he was accompanied by Martti Ahtisaari speaking for the EU. Milosevic agreed to order the withdrawal of Serbian troops from Kosovo. This was deeply resented by the troops themselves who believed they were winning the war. In the midst of their phased withdrawal Russian troops arrived unannounced on the main Pristina airfield in Kosovo. The US SACEUR ordered the British General Jackson, a Russian speaker, to abandon the withdrawal plan and to isolate the Russian contingent on the airfield. General Jackson refused and reportedly told his superior commander, 'I'm not going to start the Third World War for you.' He exercised his right to appeal to

London who under the rules of NATO could appeal to the US Chiefs of Staff in Washington. They fortunately upheld Jackson's view that it was wiser to keep to the agreed withdrawal plan with the Serbian military. Jackson thereafter established a working relationship with the Russian general commanding the detachment at Pristina airport, giving him a bottle of whisky on arrival. Later NATO took over the airfield from the Russians with no force being used. This was yet another practical example of how NATO's command and control system has developed with inbuilt procedures for dealing with sensitive differences of opinion in this case between two NATO countries.

One damaging side effect of Kosovo, of the so-called victory, in retrospect, was the mood of self-confidence and personal dominance that began to appear in Blair's handling of foreign affairs. Kosovo was Blair's first test in a big international crisis and unmistakable signs of hubristic attitudes were beginning to emerge. Visiting refugee camps he was hailed as a hero. At one stage, Clinton angrily told Blair to 'pull himself together' and halt 'domestic grandstanding'.[328] He was starting to display excessive pride in his own judgements. Clinton's aides mocked Blair's 'Churchillian tone'.[329] One official who frequently saw him said: 'Tony is doing too much, he's overdoing it and he's overplaying his hand.'[330] One of Clinton's aides suggested Blair 'was sprinkling too much adrenalin on his cornflakes'. Clinton, who has hubris in his make-up, yet was the most empathetic politician after Franklin Roosevelt, more so than President Obama in whom there is an academic reserve, this and the scandal leading to impeachment, stopped Clinton developing hubris syndrome. He was, unlike Bush and Blair, also risk averse and very careful about being involved

328 Kampfner, *Blair's Wars*, p. 57.
329 Andrew Rawnsley, *Servants of the People: The Inside Story of New Labour* (London: Hamish Hamilton, 2000), p. 272.
330 Kampfner, *Blair's Wars*, p. 49.

militarily. In that respect mirroring the reservations of many Americans scarred by fighting in or, in the case of Clinton, watching the Vietnam war unfold.

Yet the slow encirclement of Russia by NATO between 1990 and 2010 was supported by Clinton. It lay at the root of a long drawn out Russian grievance when President Putin seized Crimea. When the Russians under Gorbachev did not use military force to save East Germany in 1989 and the Berlin Wall fell, they were given to understand by the US under George Bush Sr that NATO would not be deployed right up to their borders. The same understandings were given to Boris Yeltsin when the USSR collapsed into the much smaller Russian Federation. Gradually under Presidents Clinton and Bush Jr NATO encroachment grew to the extent that the US made the case for extending membership to Georgia and Ukraine. Fortunately in relation to Georgia, this was blocked by the new German Chancellor, Angela Merkel, prior to the 2008 crisis and there was therefore no obligation on NATO countries to intervene. Nor, in February 2014, was there any obligation on NATO to intervene militarily on Russian forces put into Crimea and Ukraine. This Russian deployment was persistently and vehemently lied about by President Putin. Maintaining Ukraine's pre-existing state boundary is something Britain and the US were pledged to do as two of the four signatories to the 1994 Budapest Memorandum, the others being Russia and Ukraine. This memorandum was signed when Ukraine transferred its nuclear armoury to Russia. It was, however, the EU/Ukraine Association Agreement talking up EU defence in a way that was bound to upset the Kremlin and helped trigger the war. Russia's occupation still continues in 2018 and has already cost 10,000 lives and serious casualties, including the tragic shooting down of the Dutch civilian airliner, by Russian forces firing ground to air missiles. It was a feature of the Ukraine that the UK under David Cameron as Prime Minister was content to stay on the sidelines and it was handled in the Minsk I and II negotiations by Chancellor Merkel and President Hollande.

Cameron masterminded with Osborne the appallingly short-sighted savage defence cutbacks of 2010. He quickly emerged as 'the dominant figure on foreign policy, eclipsing Foreign Secretary Hague, and even on defence, eclipsing Fox'.[331] He soon took 'to the full the opportunities a Prime Minister possesses – trips, speeches, visits and PMQs – to achieve limelight to advance his agenda'. He made it clear he was not interested in maintaining relationships for the sake of relationships – a 'blasphemous concept to the Foreign Office' – nor was he interested in strategy for the sake of having a strategy, 'blasphemous to the MOD'. He established himself 'rapidly as *sans pareil* at establishing one-to-one relationships with overseas leaders'. He was cocky rather than hubristic. A modern 'Flashman', the figure depicted in numerous books by George Macdonald Fraser. Quick, clever, but not wise. Yet Cameron ran a coalition government with the Liberal Democrats for the first full five year fixed-term Parliament. The Conservatives won the general election of 2015 with a working majority of their own MPs only for this to disappear after Theresa May lost Conservative seats in her snap general election in 2017 and was forced to form an arrangement with the Democratic Unionist Party, DUP.

Over Libya, initially under Cameron's chairmanship, the new NSC's machinery met at least once a day and there were sixty-nine meetings eventually of the full NSC or its Libya sub-committee. Significantly, one option was off the table: UK 'boots on the ground'. No one advocated it. An NSC meeting later in March revealed a widening split between John Sawers who, as head of MI6 or SIS, argued that Libya was not a matter of national interest but acceptable for humanitarian reasons. Cameron replied, 'Yes,

331 Anthony Seldon & Peter Snowdon, *Cameron at 10: The Inside Story 2010–2015*, William Collins, 2015, p. 62.

yes, but it is important that we do these things.' It is general answers like this, according to Anthony Seldon, that led many in the intelligence and defence community to worry that the whole situation was 'not clearly thought through'.[332]

Libya in 2020 is a country that has collapsed into chaos and become a major trafficking hub for migrants seeking to cross to Europe. Aerial bombing to enforce a no-fly zone initially led predominantly by the US worked, but no boots on the ground, except for special forces and some well trained troops from Qatar, once again raised questions about whether this type of intervention was justified.[333] The lack of enthusiasm from the US, at the start, for the intervention in principle may have contributed to this outcome. The Obama administration's reluctance certainly dictated the shape of a limited intervention in Libya. Yet without their initial attack on ground-to-air missile emplacements the no-fly zone would have been very difficult militarily to impose relying only on the resources that came from a few other NATO countries, particularly France and the UK. Germany was not militarily involved in Libya as in the Balkan wars from 1991-1995.

Of great importance was the reluctance to involve Russia from the start in continuing discussions begun at the UN Security Council. In the Security Council vote, Russia and China, by abstaining, had let the UN resolution approving action through, but they had been assured throughout that regime change was not the objective. Dmitry Medvedev, who was, at the time, the President of the Russian Federation, was helped in his decision not to use the veto by Obama saying publicly: 'Broadening our military mission to include regime change would be a mistake . . . If we tried to overthrow Gaddafi by force our coalition would splinter.'

---

332 Ibid., p. 103

333 This account of Libya and Syria owes much to the book *British Foreign Policy After Brexit* (Biteback Publishing, 2017), pp. 135-158 co-authored by David Owen and David Ludlow.

Whatever the rights or wrongs of handling Gaddafi, a large section of global opinion believes both France and the UK in particular were intent on removing him, and much of what Sarkozy and Cameron said at the time fed that impression.

In the US and the UK, those of us who advocated a no-fly zone in February 2011 did so to correct the imbalance where only Gaddafi's forces had access to air power,.[334] Senator John Kerry on 3 March used a budget hearing in the Senate to press Hillary Clinton to support a no-fly zone saying: 'The global community cannot be on the side lines while airplanes are allowed to bomb and strafe.' On 6 March, Gaddafi sent in his tanks and artillery against disorganised rebel forces that advanced swiftly along the Libyan coast towards Benghazi. On Monday 7 March, at a Cabinet meeting held in Derby, the British Prime Minister David Cameron told ministers he did not regard UN support as a prerequisite for military intervention in Libya, rather something desirable but not essential; shades of Prime Minister Blair's attitude in 2003 over Iraq.

On 11 March, EU leaders met at an emergency summit in Brussels over a dinner with fellow leaders, at which Sarkozy became so angry with the failure of other leaders to support the emerging Anglo-French initiative that he stormed out. We are led to believe Cameron soothed Sarkozy enough to bring him back to the table, but their fellow EU leaders were still far from convinced of the need for a strong military response. Angela Merkel felt let down and out of the loop, while Obama had an eleventh-hour change of heart, and began to favour a no-fly zone. The Italians were more ready to act, as were some other EU countries, but as an entity, the EU was split.

The transforming decision came on 12 March 2011 when the Arab League called for the UN Security Council to impose a

---

334 Mark Landler, *Alter Egos: Hillary Clinton, Barack Obama, and the Twilight Struggle over American Power*, WH Allen, 2016, p. 169.

no-fly zone over Libya, attacking the Gaddafi government. In the US those in favour of UNSCR 1973 were Secretary of State Hillary Clinton, Vice President Joe Biden and UN Ambassador Susan Rice. In opposition were much of the State Department, Secretary of Defense Robert Gates and National Security Advisor Thomas Donilon. Obama, while his position remained unclear, did not take calls from Downing Street. In the White House late on 15 March President Obama rechristened the 'no-fly zone' as a 'no-drive zone' in relation to Gaddafi's tanks threatening Benghazi. Also, Susan Rice, then the US Ambassador to the UN, having exchanged harsh words with her French counterpart, Gérard Araud, saying: 'You're not going to drag us into your shitty war', to which he retorted France wasn't a 'subsidiary of the United States of America Inc.', had to call back after Obama decided to seek UN authorisation for 'all necessary measures', telling the Frenchman, 'OK, we're a go.' But the US position became somewhat unfairly characterised as 'leading from behind' and France and Britain, now that US power had delivered a situation where their planes could fly virtually anywhere risk-free, began to escalate the conflict. Merkel remained decided that Germany would not participate.

On 17 March, UNSCR 1973 was passed with ten votes in favour and none against. There were five abstentions (Russia, Germany, Brazil, China and India). The Gulf Co-operation Council (GCC) and Arab League ensured regional support from other Arab and Muslim states. On Friday 18 March, Cameron held an emergency Cabinet meeting and later made a statement to the House of Commons. The Libyan Army was now on the outskirts of Benghazi and the expectation was that the city might fall at any moment. Had Gaddafi pulled his forces back, UN Resolution 1973 would not have passed. On Saturday 19 March, Cameron travelled by train to Paris while the NSC met in Whitehall. As the train entered Gare du Nord, Cameron was talking on a mobile phone and took the decision to go to war.

The US Secretary of Defense, Robert Gates, while being opposed to the whole intervention, had control of the means to create an effective no-fly zone. For Gates implementing a no-fly zone is a declaration of war, not a half way house. In many ways he is right and as Chief of the Defence Staff, General Richards was clear from the start that curtailing Gaddafi's air power alone through the imposition of a no-fly zone would be insufficient. He saw that it was essential to target and hit Gaddafi's tanks and artillery from the air in order to create what he called in military parlance a Ground Control Zone. Admiral Mullen agreed the UN Resolution's wording involving the vague 'right to protect' doctrine was sufficient authority to be able to hit targets on the ground, but that was where the strategic vision about how to handle the aftermath of enforcing a no-fly zone in Libya ended. We saw very soon what a misguided decision the coalition government had made to scrap the carrier-based Harrier jump jets. With no UK aircraft carrier carrying fighter planes available, UK Tornado pilots had to fly from the UK, conducting three mid-air refuelling operations on the way out and one more on the flight back home. Later, the RAF flew from southern Italy. Richards had no doubt an aircraft carrier would have made the task a lot easier. Fortunately Qatari trainers were present in Libya, and their chief of staff later acknowledged, 'the numbers of Qataris on the ground were hundreds in every region'.[335] Yet no mechanisms existed to enforce an overall strategy in Libya. Small, ill-disciplined rebel groupings began to spring up and there were no substantial bodies of British or French forces to control them. It is no use blaming the Americans for this, as they had made it clear from the start they would not be providing such forces.

A BBC reporter asked General Richards about Gaddafi as he was leaving No. 10 after a meeting, and Richards said that he

---

335 Ian Black, 'Qatar admits sending hundreds of troops to support Libya rebels', *The Guardian*, 26 October 2011, https://www.theguardian.com/world/2011/oct/26/qatar-troops-libya-rebels-supp

thought he was not a legal target. His more specific view was that under the UN resolution, Gaddafi could be targeted if he was in a military complex or another setting where he was helping to direct the war. Cameron's tart response was to tell Richards: 'You do the fighting, I'll do the talking.'

In the NATO-led campaign, there were NATO lawyers who argued that some actions were inconsistent with the UN Security Council resolutions, and they ruled some out. This rational approach vital for maintaining a tenuous unity in the Security Council, as well as among some NATO countries, provoked Cameron to favour cutting loose from NATO and taking action unilaterally. *Cameron at 10* recalls that:

> Richards' complaints do not let up: he feels Cameron and the NSC are interfering with the military operation and being involved even down to the most tactical level. 'We had really frequent meetings where the Prime Minister felt that the system wasn't really committed or trying its hardest to make this work', recalls one official. 'He wanted to keep checking on all the details.'[336]

It is very hard to decide in a humanitarian military operation whether one is entitled to pursue regime change by targeting a political head of government, when, as in the case of Gaddafi, he was clearly, at times, acting as a military commander. Attacking him in a military command position was therefore judged acceptable; the question which remained was: is the headquarters or the head of government the real target? The same difficulty had not applied to Saddam Hussein for the US in Iraq since Congress had authorised action against him; and the US/UK invasion was never presented primarily as a 'humanitarian operation', but one taken explicitly to remove weapons of mass destruction. In Libya, a

---

336 Anthony Seldon & Peter Snowdon, ibid., pp. 110–11.

further complicating factor was that the head of state Gaddafi, had recently given up the nuclear weapons option as a result of UK and US worthwhile diplomacy under Blair and Bush. No nuclear weapons were found when Gaddafi's government collapsed during the war.

From the start there were real problems therefore of target selection, as Gaddafi continued to operate as the controlling force of the military. There should have been a discussion with the Russians even if there might well have been no agreement in the NATO/Russian Council. Cameron and Sarkozy's goal soon became to capture Gaddafi dead or alive, allowing Putin, then nominally only the Russian Prime Minister, to characterise the Libyan operation as a medieval crusade by the West. The Russian President Medvedev deserved better from the US, UK and France who at that time were colleagues on G8. At no stage were the US, UK or France ready to talk strategy through with the Russians about how to deal with Gaddafi.

The Libyan intervention became bogged down in what, to many, is now perceived as a military failure. With continued support from France, the UK and Qatar, including the intensification of air strikes, the rebels reached Tripoli and captured Gaddafi's compound. The fighting continued in other parts of the country and it was not until Gaddafi was captured and subsequently killed, following an attack on the convoy in which he was travelling that NATO operations ended on 31 October.

On 15 September Cameron and Sarkozy, eager for the publicity, were eventually able to visit, and they were mobbed by the hysterical crowds in Benghazi. Shades of Blair in Kosovo. Cameron was cautiously optimistic – too optimistic, it turned out. Libya was never to be the success that the Falklands War was for Thatcher.[337] Yet Cameron invested much personal and political capital in Libya

---

337 Anthony Seldon & Peter Snowdon, p. 113.

and made many of the same mistakes as Blair had done in Iraq. From 2013 the situation in the country gradually deteriorated before collapsing into increased factional violence in 2014, and it is still chaotic in 2018. It was a disgrace that the handling of this war in Libya never had the benefit of some of the detailed findings of the inquiry into the Iraq war. Had it been published as it should have been much earlier and its lessons absorbed at every level including the military there might have been fewer mistakes.

President Obama, in an interview with the *Atlantic* magazine in March 2016 was critical of the UK and France for failing to stop Libya becoming what he called a 'mess'. He singled out Cameron for allegedly becoming 'distracted by a range of other things'. Not least was announcing on 23 January 2013 his commitment to holding a referendum on the UK's EU membership.

In 2020 the situation over Libya has become very serious with NATO partners on different sides. As part of Turkey's more assertive foreign policy they are supplying armed forces and military equipment to the UN-backed government of national accord in Tripoli, GNA. The Italian government quietly supports this and the UK goes along with the UN. On the other side supporting the forces of General Haftar and his self-styled Libyan national army, LNA, which already control large parts of oilfields, are Russia, France and Egypt and UN experts are in no doubt that the UAE have been flying into eastern Libya weapons on a large scale for the LNA. Attempts to broker a settlement in Germany broke down after a two-week ceasefire. Coupled with this there is growing tension in the east Mediterranean over gas and oil rights between Turkey, Cyprus, Syria, Israel and Egypt. No Middle East conference will want to include these new areas of tension and conflict, but they will impact on Middle East negotiations.

The Syrian civil war started in 2011 as part of the Arab Spring revolts first triggered in Tunisia. What was needed from the start was a containment strategy to prevent the war spreading outside of

Syria while supporting attempts to get rid of Assad using moderate rebel forces though linked to Islamic extremist groups. The US rejection of the Turkish wish, first put forward in the summer of 2015,[338] to establish a 'safe zone' for refugees on Syrian territory near their border and from which to exercise control over a sector of Syria in a quasi-partition, was a significant event which I believed, despite the failure of 'safe areas' in Bosnia, was feasible with US and Turkish planes flying from bases close by in Turkey and which could also have helped ensure Aleppo did not fall to Assad forces.

On Syria General Richards wrote, 'While we – the West – dithered on the side lines, the conflict became ever more complex and fractured with Muslim extremists increasingly taking advantage.'[339] Richards' strategy from 2011 was 'Extract, Equip and Train'. It was a sensible plan, to train a proxy Syrian Army that could provide the land component to be used decisively against the regime alongside air and maritime offensive action by Western powers. Its major problem was it would only take effect in a few years' time. His ambitious idea was to extract tens of thousands of Syrian men and then equip and train them in bordering countries over a twelve month period. It was never tried. Yet in the slow build up of forces in Iraq to take Mosul back, the Americans did take this much longer view and prepared and trained Iraqi forces, taking their time in planning to destroy ISIS in Mosul while limiting civilian casualties. This success points to the feasibility of Richards' strategy.

David Petraeus, as Director of the Central Intelligence Agency (CIA), supported Richards, but President Obama had concerns about vetting and arming rebels of whom so little was known and who might have turned out to be Islamic extremists. Richards

---

338 Erin Cunningham, 'US, Turkey aim to create buffer zone on Syria border. Nobody knows how', *Washington Post,* 13 August, 2015.
339 General Sir David Richards, *Taking Command,* Headline Publishing, 2014, p. 321.

believed, had his strategy been implemented in late 2011, the war could have ended by the autumn of 2012 and certainly in 2013.

The Turkish strategy was for NATO to have accepted President Erdoğan's early wish for a safe zone to be established within Syria but sustained from the Turkish border. But the US saw it as an anti-Syrian Kurd device to stop them, and Kurdish elements in Iraq as well, having a military presence along the entire Syria/Turkish border. This it almost certainly was, but Turkey had the resources and the will close by to make the designated area properly safe. Neither Washington, London nor Paris demonstrated the will to help create it.. Yet it made enormous sense strategically to let the Turkish government control an area inside Syria to include Aleppo at the time the Russians intervened to save Damascus. That was the time for Obama to ratchet up US policy but he was ultra cautious and in his own words intent on not doing anything 'stupid' which could blight his last few years as President.

The truth is – and not just in retrospect – everything changed in Syria in the summer of 2015 when Assad warned the Russians the road link between Damascus and the Mediterranean was in danger of being blocked militarily by rebel forces, and Putin responded swiftly and intelligently. In September 2015, the Russian naval base, which they had occupied since 1971, was quickly reinforced by adapting a nearby Syrian airfield, and Russia began flying their planes on a bombing campaign to tilt the balance back in favour of Assad, while claiming they were going in to attack ISIS. The Russians were obviously now going to control an area of Syria in the west like the Turks had wanted to do in the east. President Obama should have acted at this stage very differently, for the threat to Damascus, to which Putin was responding, was real. Had Damascus been captured by rebels with ISIS already ensconced in the suburbs, it would have been devastating. It would have been a bold policy but Obama should have welcomed Putin focussing on Damascus and the Mediterranean and used their intervention to justify NATO helping to protect Aleppo and create from the air a 'safe zone' for refugees. That would diplomatically and militarily have forced a *de facto* partition, with Russia and the US influencing different parts of Syria. This would have resulted in a far more controllable situation in which Assad could be contained. Neither Assad nor Erdoğan would have had total control respectively of Damascus or Aleppo. The Kurds might have been left in control of a small part of Syria under such an arrangement. Doing nothing made an Assad victory inevitable.

Slowly and brutally, Assad's area of control of Syria increased sufficiently to use gas again in April 2017. This time, it was President Putin who might have acted very differently towards President Trump. It was an opportunity for the US and Russia to have restarted cooperation over Syria in the UN Security Council in much the same way they did in August 2013 when Foreign Minister Lavrov had been authorised by Putin, to negotiate with Kerry over an earlier sarin gas attack. Putin could have said publicly that he was very disturbed to hear of the use of gas – having thought in good faith Assad had removed all gas in 2013 – and added that he was ready to agree to UN inspectors going back into Syria. Russia would have gained respect for such a stance. But Putin was overconfident and instead Trump, to the surprise of many, did act wisely in a limited intervention overseen by Mattis his Secretary for Defense. Perhaps we overestimated Putin's power over Assad in 2018 and underestimated Assad's belief that with Iran's support he is not solely reliant on Russia, an explanation for Assad's use of gas again which certainly embarrassed the Russians. Now in 2020 Putin is in control.

The realpolitik in 2020 is Syria has become a Russian sphere of influence using its new Mediterranean air-base that saved Damascus. Putin's fixed objective is to see Assad in control of the whole of Syria. The one joint activity that has been a success is Russian, US, French and UK cooperation in the use of airpower against ISIS and US special forces cornering Baghdadi and his suicide. Trump abandoning the Syrian Kurds in late 2019 was much criticised but ambivalence about the Kurds is not new. Turkey will never accept a Kurdish State in the east of Syria. Nor in Iraq. Iran will not accept a Kurdish state in their country. President Erdoğan having been re-elected in June 2018 is buying Russian missiles and is playng with Russia. He should restart talks with the rebel Kurdish leader he holds in prison. Meanwhile NATO and EU relations with Turkey are deteriorating and Trump is fed up with being criticised. He and Putin should chair a middle East conference as was done in 1991 in Madrid.

Military intervention from the air without 'boots on the ground' has failed in Libya and Syria, troops were needed on the ground to help restore order. General Richards was never in any doubt that, as a rule, a land component was essential for a successful military campaign. 'You will not win wars by air and sea alone. So if you are not prepared to put boots on the ground yourself, you have to find a substitute.'[340] Qatari ground to air guidance teams were vital in Libya at the start.

Throughout the diplomatic world, there is a reluctance to grapple with a period of partition as a technique for de-escalating conflict. It is feared, not unreasonably given past experience, that any sub-division, however much it may be presented as temporary, will become permanent. But this principled opposition frequently refuses to face up to the casualties and displacement of people on the ground. Such was the case over Syria. The tragedy of the Syrian civil war is that it has continued much longer because of a reluctance to accept temporarily or permanently a geographical division as a result of fighting on the ground and also to face up to the boundary problems created by the 1919 settlement over Syria and wars with Israel.

---

340 General Sir David Richards, *Taking Command*, Headline Publishing, 2014, p. 317.

An eventual evaluation of the Syrian war will have to make retrospective assessments of all these issues. A case can be made that outside intervention in Syria following the Arab Spring from 2011 onwards made the internal situation worse, and that view has been forthrightly expressed by Peter Ford, former UK Ambassador to Syria from 1999 to 2003. 'The British Foreign Office to which I used to belong, I'm sorry to say has gotten Syria wrong every step of the way . . .' The UK, in his view, should either have 'put everything, including our own forces on to the battlefield or if in our judgement – as it would have been my judgement – that was not realistic, refrain from encouraging the opposition to mount a doomed campaign.'[341] On 7 April 2017, Peter Ford went on to criticise the American attack on the Syrian airfield which the US had identified as the location from which planes carrying chemical weapons had flown. The attack on 4 April affected civilians, many of them children, in the town of Khan Sheikhoun in Idlib province. On this Ford was wrong. Chemical weapons are outlawed and their use reprehensible.

No policy is defensible if it ignores the Geneva Protocol signed by the UK in 1925, and which came into force in 1928 with further treaties in 1972 and 1993. They covered the production, storage or transfer of chemical and biological weapons. British, French and US policy is governed by what is universally regarded as international law, and rules out the use of gas in all warfare, in part because of the widespread revulsion to the use of gas in the First World War. Realism is a virtue in diplomacy but principle has its place too. It will never be acceptable for diplomats and/or politicians to treat the use of weapons of mass destruction (WMD) as a fact of life which can be tolerated. That mistake was made, as we turned a blind eye to Saddam Hussein's use of chemicals, as discussed earlier, in the

341 Joe Watts, 'Former UK Ambassador to Syria accuses Foreign Office of lying about the country's civil war', *Independent*, 23 December 2016.

Iraq–Iran War in the 1980s with dreadful consequences for the whole Middle East. We must not make that mistake again. The Ford analysis is not correct. What is justified is his criticism of the way we responded to the Arab Spring in Egypt and in Syria. We should have been more active as political reformists rather than being so relaxed over militant uprisings challenging the existing order.

The analysis by the Algerian diplomat, Lakhdar Brahimi, that it was not the UN that failed over Syria, is worth studying and very persuasive.[342] He served as the UN and Arab League special envoy to Syria from 2012 to 2014. 'A deeper understanding is needed', he argues, 'of why the UN fails when it fails, and why the UN succeeds when it succeeds.'

What failed over Egypt was the way the Muslim Brotherhood was handled. It was unwise to actively favour Moisi, third in the hierarchy; better to have let the Brotherhood choose their own candidate for President. Wiser to have been fully engaged thereafter, in helping to establish good governance and more compromises from the Brotherhood's true leader.

Syria was essentially the failure of the Russian Federation post Libya, to work with the US, France and the UK together in the Security Council. There is a direct linkage with the failure of the UK and France to work with Russia over Libya. Syria has been a horrific human tragedy in which, according to some estimates, as many as 470,000 people may have died, while there are five million refugees and thirteen and a half million people in desperate need of humanitarian assistance. The superficial, distorted analysis that almost every country made in 2011 of the likely balance of any fighting in Syria was quite simply wrong. The regime did not disintegrate. The UK and US should re-evaluate assessments which were made at the time by their intelligence communities. Russia's analysis that Assad's regime

---

342 Lakhdar Brahimi, 'Did the UN fail Syria?', UNA-UK Journal, Vol. 1, 2017.

was stronger than Western governments believed was correct. It was too easy to forget that the Assad family, father and son, had good longstanding relations with revolutionary Iran who throughout supplied money, food, weapons and militia to Syria. UN professionals, by contrast, were right to warn that there was no military solution to the conflict. It took nearly three years before this even began to be recognised. Israel was wise in its handling of Assad, watching, waiting and intervening sparingly until its own interests were being threatened by Iran. Military interventions having failed in Iraq, Afghanistan and Libya, there were good grounds for believing we would fail again in Syria.

What is crystal clear now is that without the political involvement of Russia there will be no end to the long conflict in the Middle East. The main reason for President Trump's limited military action over Assad using gas was the lack of any prior response from Russia to support the UN Resolution calling for credible on-the-ground inspection. This was a mistake by President Putin. It is a sign of hope in 2020 that Presidents Putin and Trump are likely to meet in some way around the G7 meeting at Camp David. Well before that the US and Russia should establish negotiations with all the Middle East countries and include Iran and Israel.

President Obama was right in his article in *The Atlantic* in March 2016 to say:

> The world is a tough, complicated, messy, mean place, and full of hardship and tragedy. And in order to advance both our security interests and those ideals and values that we care about, we've got to be hardheaded at the same time as we are bighearted, and pick and choose our spots, and recognise that there are going to be times where the best that we can do is to shine a spotlight on something that's terrible, but not believe that we can automatically solve it. There are going to be times where our security

interests conflict with our concerns about human rights. There are going to be times where we can do something about innocent people being killed, but there are going to be times where we can't.

Obama was a significant US President, the first black President and also crucially for this reason a two term President. His victories cannot be dismissed as reflecting a transient mood. He did not fulfil all the hopes of the people who voted for him but nor did he fulfil all his own hopes. What he did represent was a different style of leader, thoughtful and neither hubristic nor flash. Patiently his achievement was the JCPOA with Iran on their nuclear programme. Now his successor Trump, is right to insist on curbing Iran's military involvement in Syria and Lebanon. One thing should remain fixed. There should be no encouragement or tolerance for a Sunni/Shia war in the Middle East. If President Trump should fall into that trap, then the UK and the EU should not go there with him. In fairness his inclination is to work with Russia over the Middle East and with Saudi Arabia, Egypt and Israel and this should be encouraged against any domestic resistance in the US concerning involvement with Russia.

After impeachment is over, there will be a six month period before the next Presidential election makes it hard for any major diplomacy to take place. In that period only Putin and Trump working together can instigate the complex series of trade offs that are going to be necessary to bring peace in the Middle East.

The assassination by a drone in Iraq of the Iranian General Soleimani, followed by the accidental shooting down by the Iranian military of the Ukrainian airliner, demonstrated how dangerous the Middle East is and how destabilising the use of proxy powers can be. President Trump did not take the battle to Iran on his own but it was done with the full support of his Secretary of State Mike Pompeo, who as a Congressman and former head of the

CIA, has long studied Iran's Islamic Revolutionary Guard Corps (IRGC). It followed four recent provocative actions by the IRGC and its proxies against shipping in the Gulf and around the Straits of Hormuz, against Saudi Arabian oilfields, and the US Embassy in Baghdad as well as US personnel in Iraq. Their presence is at the request of the Iraqi government for training Iraqi soldiers and for dealing with ISIS over a number of years. Iraq and Iran are both majority Shia countries but there are still tensions between them. Despite the capture and hanging of Saddam Husssein, the eight year Iran/lraqi war has left a legacy. But the number of Iranian manufactured missiles and IRGC trained operatives in bases in the Lebanon on route to Syria are the real danger, with war with Israel looming large once again.

Chapter 9

Hubris and the Character of Business

Politicians in the US using the Federal Reserve, and in the UK using the Bank of England, did attempt in the late 1930s to curb much business excess, personal recklessness and corporate exuberance after the economic troubles of the late 1920s and early 1930s with new regulations. Politicians in the US and the UK, urged by business, casually removed many of these curbs in the 1980s and 1990s. The 2008 massive global financial bubble, from the bursting of which we are still suffering, is a clear case of collective hubris. When I asked a banker friend why no one had been able to blow the whistle on what was going on his answer was simple. He said that anyone in banking who had had the temerity to argue that their bank was following the wrong course would simply have lost their job, and there is some evidence that this did happen to a few critics. What makes that collective hubris so alarming is that it was so blind. Many at high levels in the board-rooms of these banks did not and some still do not seem to understand the nature of the financial bubble they have been feeding. We are asked to believe they simply did not understand the 'game' that their own employees were playing and some still are playing. The Libor (London Interbank Offered Rate) scandal we are asked to believe is an example of this; that the leaders of the banks perverting Libor knew nothing about what was going on.

Hardly credible yet conceivable and described later. The complexity of the securitised financial world – collateral debt obligations, credit default swaps – needed rules and discipline. This was ignored by many banks' senior board members, some of whom had no banking experience whatsoever prior to being appointed.

This question of experience also involves politicians and it is important. Politicians need to have more people in their ranks aware and knowledgeable about business issues. Also the public deserves to know the details of all those politicians. My full declaration of interests are in the House of Lords register. As an MP, I was for two years from 1970 to 1972, Chairman of a small company, Decision Technology International. Its parent company was in Boston linked to MIT building behavioural decision-making computer models. As Navy Minister, with four Naval Dockyards' large industrial workforces, I had earlier experienced the ship repairing industry. Only after being the EU Negotiator in the Balkans in 1995, did I join the Boards of international companies like Coats Viyella and then Abbott Laboratories. As well as being chairman of companies as different as Yukos International in Russia or Middlesex Holdings in the UK. I also worked with Alisher Usmanov, a very rich Russian businessman born in Uzbekistan and who for many years had a 30% holding in Arsenal Football Club. I also served for five years on the advisory board of Terra Firma.

That experience has helped me to study the individual and collective hubris that has gripped the world financial community over two decades – on Wall Street and in the City of London. Those years were dominated by the tenure of Alan Greenspan as chairman of the US Federal Reserve from 1987 until 2006.

Greenspan published his book *The Age of Turbulence* in 2007 a year before the global crash, a turbulence which he described as 'a conceptual framework for understanding the new global economy' and one which he had done much to establish.

273

Three powerful decision-makers in 2008, Bernanke, Geithner and Paulson, comment in vivid terms in their book *Firefighting* in 2019 on the regulatory framework before the crisis. 'The Wild West with better plumbing was still the Wild West.'[343]

The problem is that the financial services industry Greenspan was writing about wanted the law to protect its assets but not its conduct. That continues to this day, with shockingly very few major prosecutions of large companies or their senior executives, just the likes of Bernie Madoff, the New York businessman responsible for a blatant Ponzi-type scheme. Greenspan argues that market failure is the rare exception and its consequences can be assuaged by a flexible economic and financial system. But that is not correct. Twice in a century the world economy has collapsed. After the first collapse recovery came, mainly because of the Second World War. In a fundamental sense, following the second collapse, the economy has still not recovered. No one can be sure in 2020 that they can truthfully claim that the 2008 crisis is behind us. We hope it is, but hope is not enough; we need to continue to tackle outstanding fundamentals in order to be sure and we are not doing so.

But it was left to Martin Sandbu, the *FT's* European economics commentator, to pose the real question in a review of *Firefighting.*

No doubt these policymakers did a solid job in extraordinarily challenging circumstances. Their policies worked, and they worked rather well. But they were not the only policies available, nor do their choices have a strong claim to being the best ones; bank bailouts have after all fuelled populism. What they do not seriously consider is whether their policies to restart credit flows could have worked even with a less bailout-friendly approach,

---

343 Ben Bernanke, Tim Geithner and Henry Paulson, *Firefighting. The Financial Crisis and Its Lessons* (Penguin, 2019).

saving both money and political anger. These are the ideological blind spots revealed by reading *Firefighting* between the lines.[344]

Paul Volcker, Greenspan's distinguished predecessor at the Federal Reserve, expected trouble. In a speech at Stanford University in February 2005 he said, 'Baby boomers are spending like there is no tomorrow . . . and we are buying a lot of houses at rising prices . . . Big adjustments will inevitably come. And as things stand it is more likely than not that it will be a financial crisis rather than policy foresight that will force the change.'[345] Was Greenspan driven by optimism or by his own hubris, and, if the latter, did that grow in office? Did he acquire hubris syndrome in office or was his hubris part of his pre Federal Reserve career and did not change? There are pointers in what Greenspan said and wrote. President Roosevelt in 1933 wisely separated the business of securities underwriting from commercial banking. His legislation was repealed by President Clinton near the end of his term of office. Many times Greenspan testified and argued for the Glass–Steagall Act to be repealed. Was he responding to pressure from the interested parties in Wall Street who the Federal Reserve should control? An attempt to reinstate Sections 20 and 32 of the Act as part of the Dodd-Frank Wall Street Reform and Consumer Protection legislation was rejected by the Senate. The Democrat Senator, Warren argues that the Glass-Steagall Act kept banks from doing 'crazy things' and, as a candidate for the Democrats to challenge Trump, continues to argue for reform. The Volcker Rule became law on 21 July 2010. Some called it Glass-Steagall 'lite', yet companies like J P Morgan continue to object to this Rule and argue that all must go. President Trump appears sympathetic. Lawrence H. Summers, key adviser to Presidents Clinton and Obama continued to argue that the Rule

344 Martin Sandbu, 'Reflections on a crisis', *Financial Times,* 13/14 July, 2019.
345 William L Silber, *Volcker. The Triumph of Persistence* (Bloomsbury Press, 2012).

should go in an article on the Social Europe website September 2018, called 'Setting the record straight on secular stagnation.'

Volcker who perceptively opposed Clinton's decision at the time, tried, with some limited success, to persuade President Obama to reinstate Glass–Steagall in a modified form. While not wholly approving of the form in which Congress has reinstated it, Volcker's concerns are shared by many who argue convincingly the Dodd-Frank Act has yet to be shown to work. Given the strength of the resistance from the financial services industry on both sides of the Atlantic, it is still uncertain as to whether there will ever be a true separation.

Greenspan was not alone in his mistaken optimism. On 20 June 2007 Gordon Brown, after ten years as Chancellor of the Exchequer and seven days away from becoming Prime Minister, made remarks that were very revealing. He and Greenspan were friends; indeed Greenspan wrote that 'Britain's success with the free market thrust of Thatcher and "New Labour" suggests that their GDP enhancing reforms are likely to persevere through the next generation.' Brown certainly thought so.

As Chancellor, Brown talked of 'the beginning of a new golden age for the City of London'. Having boasted for some time of ending 'boom and bust', in this speech he claimed that during the first decade of the twenty-first century, out of 'the greatest restructuring of the global economy, perhaps even greater than the Industrial Revolution, a new world order was created'. Yet within months the world was facing its worst economic crisis for more than 70 years. Soon more than half of British banks were either nationalised or had the government as their largest shareholder. The magnitude of what happened cannot be downplayed, but austerity continuing on from 2010 to 2019 was not the answer for the UK.

In the autumn of 2007 Greenspan said that 'we are fortunate that, thanks to globalisation, policy decisions in the US have been largely replaced by market forces. National security aside, it hardly makes any difference who will be the next President. The world is governed by market forces.' (*Observer*, 20 July 2018, 'Beyond the Crash', Adam Tooze, Professor of History, Colombia University.)

What went wrong? Many things but essentially the answer lies in a failure to understand human nature and human behaviour. We are social animals, and a social rather than a free market was at one stage presented as the model for stabilising raw market forces. The words social market were put in the Lisbon Treaty in 2010, but the very characteristic of the EU's handling of the Eurozone crisis has been the way social has never been interpreted as having an inbuilt commitment to lowering the extraordinarily high unemployment rates for those under 25 years of age in Greece, Spain, Portugal and Ireland; at times as high as 50% and accompanied by emigration. A social market could be part of the 'invisible hand' that Adam Smith wrote about. Whereas Smith's *The Wealth of Nations* has been the dominant guide to his thinking, there is much merit in giving another of his books, *The Theory of Moral Sentiments,* greater prominence. This book is unequivocal that ethics and fairness are vital ingredients for maintaining a successful economy. Yet there are many who believe to even talk about morality and business in the same sentence is incompatible. I do not believe this canard. But I do believe the social economy and the market economy are different in their motivational driving force and while compatible with each other have to be managed and controlled in different ways.

In a foreword to a University of Manchester report published in April 2014, calling for the foundations of how economics is taught to be changed, the newly appointed Bank of England economist Andy Haldane still in post in 2020, wrote:

In the light of the financial crisis, those foundations no longer look so secure. Unbridled competition, in the financial sector and elsewhere, was shown not to have served wider society well. Greed, taken to excess, was found to have been bad. The Invisible Hand could, if pushed too far, prove malign and malevolent, contributing to the biggest loss of global incomes and output since the 1930s. The pursuit of self-interest, by individual firms and by individuals within these firms, has left society poorer.

The crisis has also laid bare the latent inadequacies of economic models with unique stationary equilibria and rational expectations. These models have failed to make sense of the sorts of extreme macro-economic events, such as crises, recessions and depressions, which matter most to society. The expectations of agents, when push came to shove, proved to be anything but rational, instead driven by the fear of the herd or the unknown. The economy in crisis behaved more like slime descending a warehouse wall than Newton's pendulum, its motion more organic than harmonic.[346]

Haldane's reference to the 'fear of the herd' is dealt with later in this chapter, but he went on to assert: 'We are a co-operative species every bit as much as a competitive one. This is hardly a surprising conclusion for sociologists and anthropologists. But for economists it turns the world on its head.'[347] Until the financial sector as well as the political one takes seriously the need to consider the research and knowledge gained from a multidisciplinary behavioural approach it will have difficulty in learning how to cope with the twenty-first century explosion of knowledge. To spend billions of US dollars on risk analysis and ignore the concepts – social, biological, philosophical, psychological and even anthropological – underpinning hubris and its stable mate hubris syndrome is little short of folly. The social market was designed to make us as individuals pay more attention to the extreme manifestations of overpowering greed, selfishness and high degrees of self-regard.

346 Andrew Haldane, 'Foreword', in *Economics, Education and Unlearning: Economics Education at the University of Manchester* (Manchester: Post-Crash Economics Society at the University of Manchester, 2014), pp. 3–4.
347 Ibid., p. 5.

In contrast, there has been more progress over introducing equal pay for equal work. Sexual equality has more support than social equality. These may have an effect medium to long term particularly because female decision makers often come to different conclusions on behaviour than males. There is almost certainly less greed amongst women. There are other differences. Ian Robertson, Professor of Psychology at Trinity College, Dublin has claimed that women have approximately half the risk of becoming addicted to drugs as men. He expresses this as a hunch – until it can be verified by much more research. There are differences too that need more study about women's behaviour in relation to sex, drugs and money.

Despite the hubristic claim by Gordon Brown to have abolished boom and bust, unlike Tony Blair, he never acquired hubris syndrome when he was Prime Minister, nor did he ever become blind to social needs and social priorities. The biggest problem he faced as Prime Minister was too much inner tension brought out from self-doubt. He found it difficult to admit mistakes, not because he was super-confident but because there was an underlying depression emerging mainly as anxiety and lack of confidence. One sensed he knew when he had made mistakes and regretted them. But as a tribal politician and a frequent practitioner of the black arts of politics, he believed, mistakenly, that the admission of error was a demonstration of weakness, so any apology had to be dragged out of him. His bitten-down finger nails reflected an inner anxiety, part of a depressive illness which anyhow excludes him from even being considered for hubris syndrome. Depression dictated his mood changes and made him at times very difficult to work with. Yet this was compensated for by real knowledge and a dedicated work ethic which he displayed as the chairman of G8, pulling together the G20 in 2008 in an attempt to formulate a coordinated response to the banking crisis.

Brown's Chancellor, Alistair Darling, who has no hubris in his make-up, had the courage to warn in a deliberately frank interview early on in the crisis that Britain was facing, arguably, the worst crisis in 60 years and then, when criticised by briefings from No. 10, compounded his offence by saying the worst in 100 years. He showed himself to be cool under fire and Brown's mistake was to veto his proposed cuts in expenditure before the election, which would have signalled the government's readiness to take carefully calculated steps for tackling the deficit. The new Conservative/Liberal Democrat coalition government, under Prime Minister David Cameron, then made far greater cuts, in part because international confidence in the UK's coalition government initially was weaker than before the election. When the banks ran out of money for the second time Brown and Darling took on, of necessity, vast liabilities through the so-called Asset Protection Scheme. Somewhat similar action had taken place under Bush and Poulson in the US. They were right to do so, but wrong to do so largely within Greenspan's financial services framework – the very framework which had brought about this disaster. Nothing has been more disillusioning to the bulk of the population than to watch heads of government and treasury ministers on both sides of the Atlantic combine to ensure that basic Greenspan attitudes continue on through the twenty-first century subject only to relatively minor adjustments. In fairness, that was not the response of the Bank of England under Mervyn King at the time of the crisis. He was far more conscious of the need to change fundamental attitudes and his book *The End of Alchemy* on what to do now to avoid another crisis is one of the very best.[348]

The inherent instability within investment banks and private equity is a relatively modern consequence of their links to retail banking. The two forms of banking, as long as that word has meaning, need separating out. There is a social necessity for government to underwrite retail banking in a crisis but there is no such necessity to underwrite investment banking and private equity

---

348 Mervyn King, *The End of Alchemy. Money, Banking and the Future of the Global Economy* (Abacus, 2017).

risk taking. By their nature these massive linked all-purpose so-called banks are 'too big to fail' and their senior executives know this. That is why they wish to restore the situation before the Dodd-Frank legislation. These banks make great sums of money for some and lose great sums of money for others. What most people think of as banking is retail, low risk banking. Combining the two under the name 'bank' is not an economic or technical question, alone it comprises a fundamental value judgement about how society sees itself and who needs protecting and from whom. As lobbyists these big bankers are very powerful. Their vested interests are so obvious that scepticism should meet their protestations.

In the UK, in a very troubling way, the 2014 revelations about Paul Flowers, the chairman of the Co-operative Bank in the UK, greatly damaged the ethical image of co-operative banking and shook the confidence of many of the Co-op's natural customers, of which I had been one for many decades. Yet people's confidence was being eroded well before that. The Financial Services Authority (FSA) in 2011 wrote an assessment of NatWest Bank saying it found no regulatory fault and its collapse in 2008 was the result of bad decisions. Initially the report was not designed to be made public. When under great pressure it had to be made public the FSA Chairman admitted there was no actual report despite 19 months work at a cost of £7.7 million. The problem in RBS was highlighted in the criticism by James Eden, an analyst with Dresdner Kleinwort who years before at a public analysts meeting had said directly to the RBS Chairman, 'Some of our investors think Sir Fred is a megalomaniac who cares more about size than shareholder value.' Sir Fred Goodwin was forced at this time to confront his own shortcomings and he considered resigning according to a report in the *Sunday Times* on 6 March, 2011. It is probable that had he done so then there would have been no acquisition of ABN AMRO which, in effect, precipitated NatWest's collapse. To this day the bank, despite some sales of government-owned RBS shares at a loss, is still substantially owned by the UK government.

Businessmen and politicians remain susceptible collectively to what Keynes called 'animal spirits'. Alan Greenspan after the crisis spoke of 'irrational exuberance' – note the word 'irrational'. He has had the grace to apologise for his own part in that irrationality, not something we have yet heard from many politicians. But his writings suggest a failure to understand that the irrationality is also inherent in his own thinking and actions during his long tenure as head of the Federal Reserve.

Risk taking goes with capitalism: yet sweep it all aside and you are left merely with a bureaucracy. What is needed, therefore, are specific solutions and tough sanctions against aberrant behaviour, amongst which the most important deterrent is the threat of imprisonment and the humiliation that for most people accompanies imprisonment. In 2020 we can be certain that the 'animal spirits' have returned.

Hubris and exuberance have not been kept in check. Greed is stronger than the slight fear of disgrace, bankruptcy, prison and penury. The fact is that there have not been major prosecutions in the big banks in the US and UK since 2008, the fact that the 'light touch' regulation of the Anglo-Saxon financial services industry, which encouraged the global crisis, is in large part still in place, have all combined to demonstrate that the system, despite so-called reform, is still rotten: probably to its core. The combination of crooked politicians world wide, corrupt officials and offshore secrecy jurisdictions, shell companies, criminal networks, some with links to Russia, have carried into New York and London and while present for some time in Monaco and Geneva, are evident in Miami and Los Angeles.[349]

The 2008 crisis stimulated the creation of the Tea Party in the US two years later. The disillusionment reflected in the Brexit vote

---

349 Oliver Bullough, *Moneyland: Why Thieves & Crooks Now Rule the World and How to Take It Back* (London: Profile Books 2018).

in 2016 was signalled in the European Parliamentary election on 22 May 2014 with UKIP winning the largest number of seats in the UK. The revolt of voters in the US rust belt states had much of its drive from the Tea Party which Trump widened out with a sustained attack on the Wall Street support given to his opponent, Hillary Clinton, and the Democratic Party. He cleverly used his claimed wealth as a sign he could be critical of Wall Street. The wealth accumulated by Bill Clinton and Tony Blair is one of the most disillusioning by-products of their globe trotting.

Young people in 2020 look in hope that the US Democratic Presidential candidate will challenge Wall Street.

Professor Adam Tooze referred to earlier in the *Observer*, writes 'Donald Trump is the most spectacular manifestation of that disillusionment and the one that matters most. He is an outright nationalist, pushing against the trend of globalisation. He has little respect for markets unless they deliver outcomes he likes. He is not afraid to boss the bosses or moan about the Fed. And he proclaims that everything from imports of German cars to Chinese "borrowing" of US chip technology is a matter of national security.'

The Regulators of the financial services industry are widely thought of as weak and compromised. Ambitious regulators tend not to challenge the power brokers when they wish to come back into higher-paid and more responsible jobs in what had been their industry. A very clear lesson from experience with regulation over the last ten years from 2008 should be that it is better to assemble older, wiser and more independent regulators who will, as part of accepting the regulators' job, agree never to return to the financial services industry. Canada, unlike the US, still retained much of its old banking legislation and traditional banking attitudes, so during the 2008 crisis they came out better demonstrating that not everything or everyone in the Anglo-Saxon world went along with the global model and Wall Street standards. That the Bank of England's new Governor, Andrew

Bailey, from March 2020 was the head of the Financial Conduct Authority makes the point.

As we look back on the global crisis of 2008 the uncomfortable views of Timothy Geithner, President Obama's first-term Secretary of the Treasury, will continue to have considerable influence, as it comes from the man who was before the crisis the chief executive of the Federal Reserve Bank of New York. That view is:

> The goal is to let the system start to adjust and deleverage without tipping into panic and collapse, which sounds a lot easier in theory than it is in practice. In any case, once the fire burns too hot, once the mania turns to panic, once the diagnosis is complete and dire, the time for tentative is over ...
>
> The financial crisis was a true stress test for the United States, a full-blown financial panic that obliterated $15 trillion in household wealth and triggered the worst recession in generations.

Throughout the crisis Geithner had no illusions about Europe, which had enjoyed a 'wild credit boom of its own, with much of the risky borrowing in the periphery funded by risky lending by banks in the German and French "core" ... The Eurozone was sixteen nations with sixteen fiscal policies and sixteen banking systems, all joined together under a common monetary policy.'[350] The Eurozone situation in 2018 in relation to Italy raises its vulnerability once again.

Geithner's perspective was that of a man who had wanted to bail out Lehman Brothers but when it was not saved, claims he lost whatever 'minimal tolerance' he might have had for letting moral hazard or political considerations impact on his decision-making. Understandable but brutal realism. Yet throughout it was a clever

---

350 Timothy F Geithner, *Stress Test: Reflections on Financial Crises* (New York: Crown, 2014), pp. 517, 525, 443.

technocrat's response following the lead set by President Obama, who was very cautious in this inherited crisis, the dimensions of which were large enough to bury his presidency. Unlike Franklin Roosevelt who had greater Congressional support for a public spending stimulus and was in his second term, Obama was inexperienced and determined his presidency would not be dismissed as a one off. Obama's caution did work in the sense that by 2020 the US economy appeared to be doing well, but it did not work in restoring the concept of moral hazard and changing the cultural climate of Wall Street. It is to that necessary concept of moral hazard that studies of hubris can contribute.

By contrast the issues for the aftermath of the crisis are still seen as mainly political. Are politicians willing in 2020 to challenge the broad global economic trend whereby the rich, fed by the financial services industry, are getting ever richer and cities like London and New York superficially prosperous? After his electoral success in the rust belt states it is damaging for Trump's re-election prospects that he has not delivered promised investment in infrastructure. Something which Johnson must deliver on. Trump's tax reforms have benefitted prosperous taxpayers, brought a greater deficit and reduced Republican support in Congress for infrastructure investment.

Hubris is an urgent problem for all business leaders, not just bankers and financial service specialists, which they still show few signs of recognising. The 1991 study on General Motors demonstrates that these issues are not new. It said: 'The Greeks called this hubris and they knew that the gods, whom we might refer to as reality, do not stand for it. They demand humility.'[351] It is a condition that does not pick its professions. Hubris among the top business executives was the central cause of the Enron scandal. In its aftermath, the US introduced a mass of new regulatory

---

351 Schwartz, 'Narcissism Project and Corporate Decay'.

procedures for audit committees and main company boards with the Sarbanes–Oxley legislation, billions of US dollars were spent, but as yet this has not resulted, even marginally, in higher research budgets about attitudes and behaviour patterns among business leaders which is still deliberately underplayed and even ignored.

For all the money and time business spends on risk management, building complex models and using quantitative statistical methods, it needs to devote at least as much money and effort to human resources research on personality and behavioural assessment. In March 2009 Stefan Stern in the *Financial Times* reviewed a lucid and technical analysis of risk management in the *Harvard Business Review* by Professor Rene Stulz. He added his own comment: 'True understanding of risk also requires a maturity of outlook, an ability to see the big picture, and deep experience. This last is a rare commodity; impossible to fake and acquired only over time.'[352] Still in 2020 we need to use all the necessary multidisciplinary skills to learn from the 2008 financial crisis.

The issue for those who are interested in human risk management is: how can you identify the exuberance which cannot be contained, the exuberance that is not a 'celebration' but a diminution, indeed a corruption, of life? Exuberance that is beyond the control of the individual or sometimes of the corporation is very dangerous. It is very difficult to mentor these individuals. Whereas it is possible to constrain a propensity to hubris. An article in the *New York Times* in May 2009 by David Brooks claimed that wise non-executives are well aware of research showing that the 'CEOs that are most likely to succeed are humble, diffident, relentless and a bit unidimensional. They are often not the most exciting people to be around.'[353] Yet Boards, often under assumed market pressure seem to want a CEO 'to be resolute, even at the cost of some flexibility' with a relentless

---

352 Stefan Stern, 'Six lessons to help negotiate risk: just add wisdom', *Financial Times*, 10 March 2009.
353 David Brooks, 'In praise of dullness', *New York Times*, 19 May 2009.

commitment to incremental efficiency gains. Quoting a study by Steven Kaplan and others, 'Which CEO Characteristics and Abilities Matter?',[354] Brooks identified the traits that correlated most powerfully with success as being attention to detail, persistence, efficiency, analytic thoroughness and the ability to work long hours. In his article, Brooks warns against fame, recognition and awards.

Tim Wray, as part of a study at the University of Surrey Business School, looked at the style of leadership of Richard Fuld, CEO and chairman of Lehman Brothers. He was nicknamed the 'gorilla' because of 'his aggressive attitude and history of ousting those who disagreed with him'. Much of this was present as a trader long before he became CEO. A 2009 book titled *A Colossal Failure of Common Sense* describes a meeting in 2007 at which Fuld is informed by a colleague of the increasing risk regarding the holding of assets backed by sub-prime mortgage.[355] The recommendation for reducing exposure to such assets 'was not anything Richard Fuld wanted to hear. He wanted risk, more risk and if necessary bigger risks'.[356] Something similar had been evident before, when in 2006 a remark from the chief risk officer had irritated Fuld, who told him to 'shut up'.[357] These sorts of stories were commonplace after the events of 2008 but they contained too much retrospective wisdom and were heard uncritically in the guilt ridden atmosphere following collapse. But in the absence of court action and transcripts of cross-examinations we are left with few court indictments to quote from or transparent investigation. Too much has gone on in private, politicians too eager to protect

---

354 Steven N. Kaplan, Mark M. Klebanov and Morten Sorensen, 'Which CEO Characteristics and Abilities Matter?', Swedish Institute for Financial Research Conference on the Economics of the Private Equity Market, 1 July 2008, available at http://ssrn.com/abstract=972446 (accessed 4 June 2014).
355 Lawrence G. McDonald, *A Colossal Failure of Common Sense: The Incredible Inside Story of the Collapse of Lehman Brothers* (London: Ebury Press, 2009).
356 Ibid., p. 233
357 Ibid., p. 269.

the names and reputations of political leaders. Nothing replaces the open cross examination of the court room.

An interesting recent book is *Think Again: Why Good Leaders Make Bad Decisions and How to Keep It from Happening to You*, which identifies four common sources of error: misleading experiences, misleading pre-judgements, inappropriate self-interest and inappropriate attachments.[358] Applied to the case of Sir Fred Goodwin, chief executive of the Royal Bank of Scotland, we can see how past experiences might give misleading guidance in making decisions: Goodwin's success in the NatWest takeover appears to have encouraged him and the RBS chairman to make a reckless decision in the light of some of its poorly performing assets, particularly in America, on acquiring ABN AMRO.

Two fascinating tables below (Tables 12.1 and 12.2) compare the hubris of two CEOs, Fuld of Lehman Brothers and Goodwin of RBS against the criteria of hubris syndrome as outlined in the *Brain* article written by Jonathan Davidson and myself and a table relating to media praise for the CEOs. These are drawn from an essay on 'The Role of Leader Hubris in the Decline of RBS and Lehman Brothers' by Tim Wray.[359] A recent article for *Organisational Dynamics* on 'Hubristic Leadership: Understanding the hazard and mitigating the risks'[360] argues that 'it is a relational and situational phenomenon . . . more likely to be alleviated by a palette of solutions rather than a "silver bullet" . . . only by understanding the characteristics, causes and consequences of hubris that the hazards it poses can be combatted and contained'.

---

358 Sydney Finkelstein, Jo Whitehead and Andrew Campbell, *Think Again:Why Good Leaders Make Bad Decisions and How to Keep it from Happening to You* (Boston: Harvard Business Press, 2009).

359 Ed. Peter Garrard and Graham Robinson, *The Intoxication of Power. Interdisciplinary Insights* (Palgrave Macmillan, 2016), Chapter 12, pp. 240-1, 243.

360 Eugene Sadler-Smith, Graham Robinson, Vita Akstinaite, Timothy Wray, 'Hubristic Leadership: Understanding the hazard and mitigating the risks' *Organizational Dynamics (2018)* https://doi.org/10.1016/j.orgdyn.2018.05.007

Table 12.1 Evidence for symptoms of Hubris Syndrome

Disproportionate concern with image and presentation

FULD: '[I]f ever a story appeared that was remotely negative, Fuld would give the press officer responsible a grilling – or worse one by one the most senior Lehman PR executives were fired because of stories Fuld had not liked' (Ward. 2010; 150)

GOODWIN: 'Gogaburn [location of new HQ] was a cathedral to his folly. . . . more resort than office . . . complete with oyster bar and office for Sir Fred that stretched the entire length of one of the buildings wings' (Wilson et al., 2011a)

Identification with the nation or organisation to the extent that the individual regards their outlook and interests as identical

FULD: '[T]wo things consumed Dick Fuld and Lehman; Getting the stock price to 150 and beating Goldman Sachs' (Ward, 2010: 147)

GOODWIN: 'Sir Fred – a renowned petrol head bought Dixons Motors in a £110m deal . . . Fred thought he could reinvent the processing of cars because he was so clever and because he loved cars . . . it was nothing to do with RBS's business' (Wilson et al., 2011a)

Excessive confidence in own judgement and contempt for the advice or criticism of others

FULD; '[O]nce threatening to ram his fist down a critic's throat and rip out his heart' (McDonald & Robinson. 2009: 224)

GOODWIN: 'Cryan wrote to Sir Fred warning him about ABN's exposure to subprime: "There is stuff in here we can't even value" Sir Fred replied saying: "Stop being such a bean counter" (Wilson et al., 2011b)

Exaggerated self-belief, bordering on a sense of omnipotence, in what they personally can achieve

FULD: 'Even when the writing was on the wall, [Fuld] had refrained from calling in the bankruptcy lawyers' (McDonald & Robinson, 2009: 319)

GOODWIN: 'Goodwin knew about, and should have understood the implications of the collapse of the German bank IKB after some AAA-rated assets turned out to be worthless. Yet Goodwin actually invested RBS further into the bubble' (Hancock & Zahawi, 2011: 98)

A belief that rather than being accountable to the mundane court of colleagues or public opinion, the court to which they answer is history or God.

FULD: '[I]t was as if he [Fuld] knew something that others didn't, as if he believed that in the end, all would be well' (McDonald & Robinson. 2009: 305)

GOODWIN: 'Sir Fred Goodwin went so far as to refuse to allow his Chief Economist to attend a parliamentary Select Committee until the Chair of the Committee was forced to call and explain that if he chose not to attend he would be summoned' (Hancock & Zahawl, 2011: 75)

Restlessness, recklessness and impulsiveness

FULD: '[I]t usually takes weeks if not months of assessments before appointing a CFO . . . deep into the reign of King Richard the Not-so-Great, it took about 12 minutes.' (McDonald & Robinson. 2009: 269)

GOODWIN; 'Sir Fred quickly decided to move ... due diligence and transparency on the Charter One deal were poor . . . the detail provided was so scant the numbers could barely be tested properly by analysts' (Wilson et al., 2011a)

Hubristic incompetence, where things go wrong because too much self-confidence has led to the leader not to worry about the nuts and bolts of policy

FULD: 'Dick Fuld could not understand the technicalities of market finance at the highest level. And when Mike tried to explain the boss just glazed over and tuned out' (McDonald & Robinson, 2009: 234)

GOODWIN; '[H]e now gave his investment banking deputies carte blanche to deliver growth . . . it was a mistake because [Sir Fred] doesn't understand investment banking' (Wilson et al., 2011a)

Owen and Davidson (2009) 7 of the 14 symptoms of Hubris Syndrome highlighted in bold

Table 12.2 Media praise for the CEOs

Year	Comment in praise of the CEO
2002	FULD: Even with the recent troubles, it was a dazzling year for Fuld. Lehman gained market share in global debt and equity issuance, and its market cap held steady as rivals saw theirs sink' (BloombergBusinessWeek. 2002)
	GOODWIN: 'Fred Goodwin has been named businessman of the year by the global edition of leading US business magazine Forbes' (Thisismoney.co.uk, 2002)
2003	GOODWIN: 'One has to hand it to Fred Goodwin and Royal Bank of Scotland. Their timing is excellent' (Thisismoney.co.uk, 2003)
2004	GOODWIN: 'Fred Goodwin, chief executive of Royal Bank of Scotland, was named European banker of the year by a group of journalists in Frankfurt' (Thisismoney.co.uk, 2004)
2005	FULD: 'Since Fuld took over as CEO on the eve of the IPO, Lehman has overcome a series of crises: an inadequate capital base and a credit rating downgrade in 1994 . . . Each setback has seemingly made Lehman stronger, with Fuld and a cadre of battle-scarred veterans cultivating an intensely loyal, us against-the-world culture that has fuelled the reclamation of the firm's lost glory. Today, Lehman again stands as one of the most admired investment banks on Wall Street' (Institutional Investor. 2005)
	GOODWIN: 'Sir Fred Goodwin, chief executive of Royal Bank of Scotland, can't abide journalists. In that, of course he is not alone. But then other haters of the Fourth Estate don't run the world's sixth largest bank, don't oversee one of the country's largest employers and most widely held companies, haven't grown their business through a spectacular programme of acquisition (NatWest and Churchill Insurance in the UK. Mellon and Charter One In the US. to name just some of his 20-odd purchases) and aren't seen as pillars of the communities In which they operate – be they Scotland, the City the UK or overseas' (Thisismoney.co.uk, 2005)
2006	FULD: 'Lehman Brothers, a 156-year-old firm that has had numerous brushes with death is now enjoying its greatest run ever. Richard S. Fuld Jr., 59, took over the notoriously fractious Lehman Brothers 13 years ago, when it was a forgotten subsidiary within the rat's nest that was Shearson/American Express. Driven partly by those who dismissed him and his firm as second- or even third-rate, Fuld transformed Lehman from Wall Street weakling to global powerhouse.' (Serwer, 2006)

Libor (London Interbank Offered Rate) is the benchmark interest rate based on the rates at which banks lend unsecured funds to each other on the London Market.[361] An international investigation into Libor starting in 2012 began to reveal a widespread plot by banks such as Deutsche Bank, Barclays, UBS, Rabobank and RBS to manipulate these interest rates for profit starting in 2003. Libor underpins over $300 trillion loans worldwide. The Financial Conduct Authority shifted responsibility for the supervision of Libor to the ICE Benchmark Administration (IBA), the independent UK subsidiary of the private US-based exchange operator,

---

361 James McBridge, 'Understanding the Libor Scandal' Council of Foreign Relations, 12 October 2016.

Intercontinental Exchange or ICE. When Libor rises, rates and payments on loans often increase; they fall when Libor goes down. In all 15 global institutions have been investigated. Libor was manoeuvred both upwards and downwards based 'entirely on a traders position' according to Ronald Anderson of LSE. It has been estimated that this manipulation could lead to banks paying $35 billion in private legal settlements. Investigations have focused on traders and more than 100 traders or brokers are likely to have been fired or suspended. The SFO prosecutors were set back when in January 2016 six brokers were acquitted on all charges. Three Barclays traders have received prison sentences. In New York two former Rabobank employees were sent to prison and the Department of Justice has charged, as of 2016, a further 16 people. In 2018 the SFO opened a legal case against five ex-traders for alleged rigging of the Euribor rate which affects some €150 billion of Italian floating rate debt which is tied to Euribor. The nature and depth of this scandal is such that it is beyond belief that no senior figures in these banks knew or suspected that it was going on.

One reason these situations are accommodated by government is that governments were, and still are, frightened of an ongoing global financial crisis. They tolerate, particularly within the Eurozone, large cover-ups of state finances. Governments hoped that financial organisations and banks could restore their balances over time without full exposure. The Bank of England has fortunately been tougher on this area than most central banks. Corporations have acted in ways that show they fear total exposure and want governments to cover up and protect them. Organisations claim that public exposure inhibits their ability to rebuild their balances. All this is to some extent understandable but the cover-ups reveal a frightening vulnerability. All the trumpeting of the vital importance of the 'rule of law', such a feature of Greenspan's writing, came to nothing in the actual crisis. The rule of law was set aside and there was little, if any, individual accountability in terms of the laws of the land. Everything was dealt with at corporate level with heavy fines brought in after a period of years when they could be paid even though the return to solvency in a true sense was delayed. Individual culpability was virtually ignored. Yet the penalty that society as a whole will pay for this conspiracy of silence from 2008 is huge. Unlike in the 1930s there have been very few prominent politicians in a position to act who have been brave enough to insist on using the courts and accept the publicity of prominent bankers going to prison. There is an overall cravenness to deal with greed.

Few authors have been more persistent in exposing the venal nature of some parts of Wall Street and also the City of London than Michael Lewis, first in 1989 with *Liar's Poker*, then in 2010 with *The Big Short*. In *Boomerang* (2011) he wrote about how Goldman Sachs's behaviour in Greece triggered the euro crisis and now in 2014 with *Flash Boys* he has demonstrated how on the US stock market the high-frequency traders, who make two-thirds of the trades in the public US market, are using every technical device to capitalise on the speed at which information arrives with the decision maker. In effect they are fraudulently gaming the system and this is being both used and abetted by very large banks.[362] These technological advances could be the factor which precipitates another global economic crisis. There is little room for judgement, holding back, keeping one's nerve when buy and sell signs are fixed in computers and appear automatically. Similarly, cyber warfare could be financial not military and in that area far more damaging and disruptive.

The American psychologist Robert Hare has written that business is the most agreeable vocation for psychopaths though this word is much less used today. In their book *Snakes in Suits*, Hare and his co-author, Paul Babiak, point out how difficult it is to spot a

---

362 Michael Lewis, *Flash Boys: A Wall Street Revolt* (New York: W.W. Norton, 2014).

psychopath coming when some core psychopathic personality traits may seem initially attractive to recruiting business people and traders.[363] Charm is one. Another is that 'some hiring managers may mistakenly attribute "leadership" labels to what are, in actuality, psychopathic behaviours'. Furthermore, the tendency of many businesses to abandon the old, massive, bureaucratic organisational structures in which people got on by not rocking the boat, in favour of what has been called a 'transitional' organisational style – one that has fewer layers, simpler systems and controls and more freedom to make decisions – encourages the recruitment of people who can 'shake trees'. As Hare and Babiak put it, in this changed business climate 'egocentricity, callousness, and insensitivity suddenly became acceptable trade-offs in order to get the talents and skills needed to survive in an accelerated, dispassionate business world'.

Some beneficial traits in potential executives, such as levels of confidence and the propensity to take risk, are vital elements in any successful business leader. These qualities may be, in part, related to levels of testosterone. It is claimed that the levels of testosterone in any individual are determined by the degree of exposure to it in the womb. What is extraordinary is that testosterone is detectable in what is known as the 2D:4D ratio – the relative length of the index finger to the fourth finger. Research on this has been conducted by John Coates, a former Wall Street trader interested in the boundaries between economics and neurology, together with Mark Gurnell, an endocrinologist, and Aldo Rustichini, an economist. They claim in an article in *Proceedings of the National Academy of Sciences*[364] that the advantage gained by those with a low 2D:4D score (and so high testosterone) derives from two things.

363 Paul Babiak and Robert D. Hare, *Snakes in Suits: When Psychopaths Go to Work* (New York: Regan, 2006) p. xii.

364 John M. Coates, Mark Gurnell and Aldo Rustichini, 'Second-to-Fourth Digit Ratio Predicts Success among High-Frequency Financial Traders', *Proceedings of the National Academy of Sciences* (2009), vol. 106, pp. 623–8.

First, high pre-natal testosterone shapes brains with quicker reactions and a greater ability to concentrate; and it amplifies what they call 'rutting stag' behaviour.[365] It would be very convenient if personality disorders, let alone hubris syndrome, could be detected simply by measuring the relative length of fingers or some such unequivocal measure. But it is most unlikely such a simple test will ever be devised. Nonetheless, there are tests which can alert people to the possibility that young executives may be vulnerable to orthodox personality disorders that could later wreak havoc.

A recent article on how cortisol shifts financial risk preferences shows that 'the stress response calibrates risk taking to our circumstances, reducing it in times of prolonged uncertainty, such as a financial crisis'.[366] This notion was conceived by Coates and Gurnell with inputs from two business schools. The article suggests that 'physiologically driven shifts in risk preferences may thus be a source of financial market instability that has been overlooked by economists, risk managers and central bankers alike'. This was followed by an article in the *New York Times* in June 2014, in which Coates postulated that cortisol can scale back our risk taking in periods of uncertainty where we no longer understand what is happening; whereas a potent cocktail of dopamine and testosterone can in a mood of certainty encourage us to expand our risk taking.[367] Coates has also written a more general account of these areas of brain function in a book, *The Hour between Dog and Wolf: Risk-Taking, Gut Feelings and the Biology of Boom and Bust.*[368]

365 Tim Harford, 'Why high-frequency traders are like rutting stags', *Financial Times*, 17 January 2009.
366 Narayanan Kandasamy, Ben Hardy, Lionel Page, Markus Schaffner, Johann Graggaber, Andrew S. Powlson, Paul C. Fletcher, Mark Gurnell and John Coates, 'Cortisol Shifts Financial Risk Preferences', *Proceedings of the National Academy of Sciences* (2013), vol. 111, pp. 3608–13.
367 John Coates, 'The biology of risk', *New York Times*, 8 June 2014.
368 John Coates, *The Hour between Dog and Wolf: Risk-Taking, Gut Feelings and the Biology of Boom and Bust* (London: Fourth Estate, 2012).

There is another difficulty which business has in relation to hubris, and it is one that the political world to some extent escapes. Both attract people with a propensity to hubris and who may already exhibit hubristic traits. But the modern commercial world is *collectively* more susceptible to hubris, making it harder to single out *individuals* who are especially hubristic. The professor of economics at the University of Warwick, Andrew Jackson wrote a letter to the *Financial Times* in March 2009, about herd behaviour:

> Herding happens when *relative* position matters. Think of sheep in a field or fish in a pool. They cluster together because safety from outside predators comes from being on the inside of the group. Although most do not recognise it in themselves, human beings are like other animals . . . Homebuyers paid extraordinarily high prices for houses, even though not justified by fundamentals, because they felt they were trailing behind the Joneses. Brokers sold unsound mortgages not because they were convinced of the absolute merits of those products but because they had to keep up with rival brokers. Most economists kept quiet about the house price bubble; they were frightened of speaking up.

This collective susceptibility operates at two levels. It operates globally within economies as a whole, for what else is a bubble? Indeed one might say that the expression 'boom and bust', describing a phenomenon which Gordon Brown believed he had permanently overcome, embodies the ineradicable condition of capitalist economies. It is merely a modern way of talking about hubris and nemesis in business. But collective hubris can operate also at the company level. Collective hubris at both levels provides camouflage to individuals working within the business world who may, in addition, be susceptible to the syndrome themselves. The reason why the business world is vulnerable to collective hubris is clear enough. The goals of business, unlike the goals of politics, are defined almost exclusively in terms of shareholder or personal wealth.

An independent study in January 2018 recorded a typical UK FTSE 100 chief is paid £3.45 million a year, 120 times average earnings. That is less than similar figures for 2014 of £4.5 million and 170 times average earnings. We can only hope that trend of narrowing the gap continues and that shareholders exercise pressure for greater fairness as part of overall good governance. If economic growth and profit were reflected in higher rewards for all employees and in dividends to shareholders few would object. If an increased share price additionally brings a return in share options and is followed by consolidated salary increases for those who work in the enterprise and, beneficially for those connected to the business, increased investment in corporate social responsibility, again not many would object. But all too often that close correlation between profit and reward is being fudged, for example with bonuses or the offer of restricted shares replacing share options when performance of shares is poor. Bonuses and restricted shares can easily come to be viewed as automatic, justified for retention and recruitment or quite unrelated to the success of the business. There is a cycle of reinforcement here too. Consultants suggest remuneration levels for pay, bonuses and restricted shares; they choose comparisons and establish new norms, which are reinforced by recommendations to compensation committees on which sit non-executive directors who are themselves being compensated as part of that very cycle as executives in other companies. Bonuses given in advance have hitherto proved virtually impossible to pull back even if the business declines, or is heavily fined or becomes bankrupt. Interestingly, mechanisms for clawback to cover a period of six years are being designed by the European Parliament.

Expanding the business and taking risks to achieve higher profits motivates endeavour. But if financial results are the only yardstick of success then expansive goals will not be challenged.

The willingness to take risks to achieve such goals will have no constraint. A readiness for the short term to dominate will become indigenous in the business and an acceptance of the need to consolidate, rebuild and reinvest, putting aside salary goals for a time and eschewing risk-taking, will rarely surface. Doing little for a year or more waiting for past investments to be reflected in the order book and performance is at times the responsible course to adopt when argued through. On rare occasions also doing nothing new is sometimes a wise course in business and in politics. The mantra of 'action, never inaction', espoused by Alan Greenspan, is wrong in every sense but few questioned Greenspan's totally uncritical acceptance of it. Fortunately not all business people follow such a mantra and many are ready to take the longer view, to invest for the future, to build companies where salaries are fixed not only according to financial criteria, but reflecting attitudes worth fostering that may not endorse the existing fiscal culture. We see this in the fact that implementing action to respond to current world environmental concerns can also have an economic pay off.

A good example of collective hubris operating at company level is the case of BP, well described in the *New York Times* by Sarah Lyall in 2010[369] and then revealed in the subsequent legal cases over compensation. Lord Browne, the former chief executive of BP, also discovered the dangers of invoking the power of a court of law to cover up a relatively minor lie. In this case Mr Justice Eady referred to Browne's 'willingness to tell a deliberate lie to the court' and said of the lie that 'it may be that it should be addressed as contempt or as some other form of criminal offence'. Somewhat surprisingly, given that Browne's behaviour might have been considered contempt of court, he added that he had decided not to refer the

---

369 Sarah Lyall, 'In BP's record, a history of boldness and costly blunders', *New York Times*, 12 July 2010. David Owen, *Time To Declare: Second Innings* (London: Methuen, 2009), pp. 602–3.

case to the Attorney General for possible prosecution. He did say, however: 'I am not prepared to make allowances for a "white lie" told to the court in circumstances such as these – especially by a man who prays in aid his reputation and distinction, and refers to the various honours he has received under the present government, when asking the court to prefer his account of what took place.'[370] When Browne's attempts to overthrow this ruling were rejected by what was then the judicial part of the House of Lords, now the Supreme Court, the injunction was lifted and Browne resigned at once from BP on 2 May 2007.

The late Peter Sutherland, as BP's chairman, had argued against extending Browne's term of office. According to *The Guardian* of 9 March 2009, Sutherland cited the relative recovery in the fortunes and reputation of BP since Browne's departure as a reason for making performance-related share issues to his successor, Tony Hayward, who later left BP. Browne was excluded from the incentive payment for which he was eligible for 2006. Hayward had pledged to make safety BP's 'number one priority, but it was under his watch that the *Deepwater Horizon* accident took place, involving an exploration rig in the Gulf of Mexico and a massive oil spill. The court case transcripts, as well as the judgement, if carefully studied will give clues as to how long it takes to remove a culture of cost-saving that damages safety provision.

With regard to misleading pre-judgements – a failure in recognising patterns – at HBOS Peter Cummings, the head of corporate lending, was apparently unable to 'read' the deteriorating situation and went on lending even after the world collapse had started and Lord Stevenson, the chairman, and Andy Hornby, the chief executive, failed to rein him in but their failure was brushed aside only to be followed later by the mildest of sanctions, no longer

---

370 Mr Justice Eady's judgement of 9 February 2007 in *Lord Browne of Madingley v. Associated Newspapers* (2007) EWHC 202 (QB).

of any real relevance to either of them. The business establishment is not alone in self protection. The House of Commons is a past master in protecting its own too which makes it a little harder for them to legislate for effective action and they worry about being seen to interfere in the post-Margaret Thatcher era of endless criticism of virtually all regulations.

What needs focusing on is appropriate self-interest in business. For those with hubris syndrome the identification of themselves with the organisations they run, one of the fourteen identifiable symptoms of hubris syndrome detailed in the Introduction, means that they see no difference between their own self-interest and the interests of their own organisations, a truly frightening condition with obviously potentially ruinous consequences. Andrew Fastow, who became Enron's chief financial officer in 1998, developed an excessive attachment to the company, whereby he saw himself as a 'hero' to Enron, and this led him to take decisions which helped cause the downfall of his company and sent him to prison.

Contempt of court should always be treated very seriously because it undermines an essential safeguard in our democracy, namely that the truth and only the truth be told in court. The same should apply in Parliament but as yet it does not. To be held in contempt of Parliament should be considered a very serious affair. Even if it involves only a relatively small point, contempt of Parliament needs to be recognised and attention and thought given to a worthwhile deterrent. This is particularly important where it involves high-profile leaders in any walk of life. Contemptuous behaviour often goes with hubris and was something the Greeks focused attention on. The Greeks were not alone, however, in recognising the hazards of hubris. A road leading to a tower that was said to mask the frontier between heaven and earth was known to the local Babylonians as 'May-the-Arrogant-not-Flourish'.[371]

---

371 Holland T. *Persian Fire* (Great Britain: Abacus 1ˢᵗ edition, 2005)

Contempt is hubristic. Lying is often hubristic because the risks entailed suggest the recklessness of someone who has lost touch with reality and the dangers that lie ahead, such as being found out. Also loss of touch with reality is itself one of the symptoms of someone in thrall to hubris. The penalty for such loss of touch with reality can be nemesis. There have been few bigger falls from grace than that involving the arrogance of Dominique Strauss-Khan, managing director of the International Monetary Fund and at the time a strong favourite to run against and defeat Nicolas Sarkozy for the presidency of France. Instead that post fell to François Hollande.[372] In December 2016 Christine Lagarde, the head of the IMF, was accused in court of 'negligence by a person in position of public authority' over a €400m payment made to a French tycoon while she was the country's finance minister. She was found guilty but no penalty was imposed and she did not appeal. Reappointed to the IMF in 2018, she became head of the European Central Bank in 2019.

Are the boards of public companies capable of holding their executives to account? A survey of 375 company chairmen and non-executive directors in the UK, conducted by the remuneration consultants MM&K and the headhunters Hanson Green, revealed that a quarter of non-executives said they were unsure they could control chairmen and chief executives and a further 10 per cent said they knew they could not.[373] Shareholders and the wider public cannot therefore rely on non-executives unless there are significant changes in the balance of power within a company. In this respect we need greater clarity and openness about the ownership structure of modern companies. A hedge fund shareholder is bound to seek a quick capital return from a company, while a pension fund or tracker fund is more likely to take a longer-term view. Shareholder

372 Ian Robertson, *The Winner Effect. How Power Affects Your Brain* (London: Bloomsbury, 2012), pp. 130–1.
373 Anthony Hilton,'Time for the magic circle to vanish', *Evening Standard*, 4 February 2009.

engagement is a positive when it is aimed at unlocking cash that has been hoarded for long periods. But it is not always beneficial in terms of helping to generate long-term growth. However, it is both necessary for shareholders to be offered a detailed explanation of the huge pay differentials that exist in more and more companies between the top executives and the rank and file, and right that they should be able to vote against remuneration packages that reinforce such differentials.

In her book *Fool's Gold*, Gillian Tett writes about how the banking crisis of 2008 had deep roots:

> I am still trying to make sense of the last decade of grotesque financial mistakes. I have found myself drawing on my training as a social anthropologist before I became a journalist ...What social anthropology teaches is that nothing in society ever exists in a vacuum or in isolation ... In recent years regulators, bankers, politicians, investors and journalists have all failed to employ truly holistic thought – to our collective cost. Bankers have treated their mathematical models as if they were an infallible guide to the future, failing to see that those models were based on a ridiculously limited set of data. A 'silo' mentality has come to rule inside banks, leaving different departments competing for resources, with shockingly little wider vision or oversight. The regulators who were supposed to oversee the banks have mirrored that silo pattern too, in their own fragmented practices. Most pernicious of all, financiers have come to regard banking as a silo in its own right, detached from the rest of society.[374]

A fascinating book is that by Lord Desai, the Emeritus Professor of Economics at the London School of Economics. Entitled *Hubris*.

---

374 Gillian Tett, *Fool's Gold: How Unrestrained Greed Corrupted a Dream, Shattered Global Markets and Unleashed a Catastrophe* (London: Little, Brown, 2009), pp. 298–9.

Why Economists Failed to Predict the Crisis and How to Avoid the Next One.[375] Lord Desai has also written interestingly about Donald Trump reported in *The Week:*

> You quite rightly say that Donald Trump is being "demonized" by the Europeans. The old order of liberal trade in a globalized world collapsed in 2008. The US paid for that arrangement by providing a rule-bound trade regime that allowed the EU to run a protectionist customs union, and paid for Europe's security. For Trump, that world has ended. The US can no longer pay for the free-riding Europeans, particularly Germany, while being lectured by them as to how the President should behave. Trump views the world not as a concert of Western powers orchestrated by the US, but as a series of bilateral relationships. It might be an idea for the world to listen to him more carefully than it is doing.[376]

Another interesting aspect of hubris is the extent to which it presents as unbridled intuition. This is something which I studied with two colleagues. In an article published in the journal *Leadership*, we said: 'Intuition involves a mental leap. It is not part of a logical continuum or the steady application of reasoning ending with a commonsensical judgement. The leap is often ascribed to being one of experience, instinct or faith.'[377] We believed that 'unlike hubris which has clearly negative connotations, intuition has recently come to be viewed as a positive management and leadership attribute to the extent that "gut instinct" or "gut feel" is considered to be as important an asset as rational analysis.' Yet we

375 Meghnad Desai, *Why Economists Failed to Predict the Crisis and How to Avoid the Next One* (Yale University Press, 2015).

376 Lord Desai, 'Trump and new world order' Letters page, *The Week*, 16 June 2018.

377 Guy Claxton, David Owen and Eugene Sadler-Smith, 'Hubris in Leadership: A Peril of Unbridled Intuition?', *Leadership*, 12 December 2013.

concluded that 'a hubristic predisposition allied to ideological instinct or to unbridled intuition is a perilous mix to have at the top of any political institution or business organisation.' Shakespeare in King Lear has good advice, 'Have more than thou showest, speak less than thou knowest' and he puts those words in the mouth of the Fool. Trump boasts about his time at business school.

Who is going to take on the Business School culture? One person who has is Duff McDonald in his book *The Golden Passport.*[378] He concludes his largely historical analysis:

> What's crystal clear today is that society is sick, with the victory of Donald Trump simply the most visible symptom. If there is a silver lining to all the ugliness it's that it's now more obvious than ever that it's time to get back to the things that really matter, which is not money or metrics, but people. And yet the Harvard Business School remains in its inward-facing huddle repeating empty mantras of enlightenment that fly in the face of simple, undeniable fact.

If we are to see the development, and the provision, of mentoring services for those leaders in all walks of life prone to hubris, there are important lessons to be learned. A distillation of other's wisdoms could run something like this:-

Do not appoint men or women not ready to challenge conventional views; there are too many in any bureaucracy already without adding to their number. Insist on a better gender balance, for some women find it easier to criticise male bosses than fellow males do, and male leaders often prefer to take criticism from women. Seek out contrarian advice in any field of activity; contrary views can be a stimulus. Deliberately encourage people to listen to and read criticisms of likely policy decisions, and indeed

378 Duff McDonald, *The Golden Passport. Harvard Business School, The Limits of Capitalism and the Moral Failure of the MBA Elite* (Harper Collins, 2017), p. 578

be very suspicious of people, who say they never read newspapers or watch television, claiming they have 'no time'. Encourage critics to attend meetings and demand that associates study and bring to attention the views of critics. Indicate clearly that no one should be shielded from criticism. Read a wide range of articles and newspapers, in particular those known to be critical of existing policies. Make time to watch television, news and comment programmes. Try and watch documentaries if they are critical of relevant policy areas or your decisions. In these ways leaders can quickly see what is troubling the people who have to live with their decisions. Leaders should not be afraid to tease out any scepticism by seeming to adopt a position that is not necessarily theirs to provoke argument; thereby demonstrating that they are not fearful of dissent. Probe the certainties of advisers to the extent of being one's own devil's advocate. Above all, insist on option papers, and refuse to accept papers that only discuss one strategy. Beware of the doctrine 'there is no alternative'. Very rarely is there, to use an American expression, a 'slam dunk' situation. Most of the time there are genuine options which any wise leader will ensure are examined seriously and considered carefully. The message from the top down should be to think 'outside the box' and to mean it – not just to espouse it. A readiness to listen, to ensure a process of genuine consultation is crucial. Every written submission should have an 'Options' heading. Without it, papers should be automatically returned by the leader's office for further work before re-submission. If there truly are no options, insist on a clear declaration that issues have been examined but no options found.

The other great strength of a leader comes from a readiness to trust subordinates and for them to know that they cannot do everything themselves, that they need to enable others in their leadership team to fulfil their potential. That means accepting that there is for everyone a learning curve, but that people will not learn without taking responsibility. So at an early stage the inexperienced will have to be stretched and given more responsibility than they are used to. That means the leader must take a risk on subordinates' potential to grow in the job, deliver more than they have yet delivered – in effect to gain in stature. Also develop so that they may be in a position to replace them as leader. The other key role for those in any leadership team is to go and talk to other important decision makers in other fields of activity and to come back with information and new ideas.

An interesting essay on 'Preventing and Curing Hubris in Leaders' by Karen Otazo writes about graciousness, 'a demonstration of tact, kindness, warmth, elegance or courtesy to others'.[379] Is it too much to ask that we learn one lesson from the global economic crisis of 2008 and turn away twelve years later from the hubristic image of leadership in all walks of life but particularly in business?

---

379 Ed. Peter Garrard, *The Leadership Hubris Epidemic. Biological Roots and Strategies for Prevention* (Palgrave Macmillan, 2018), pp. 193-221.

Chapter 10

Hubris of Neville Chamberlain, Margaret Thatcher and Emmanuel Macron

Neville Chamberlain became Prime Minister on 28 May 1937 and the public responded initially with enthusiasm to a conviction politician and a vigorous and active Prime Minister, even though already sixty-eight years old. He had for a long time been doing some of the work of Prime Minister Stanley Baldwin who passed the load of his decisions down to Chamberlain as he contemplated retirement to the Worcestershire countryside. When it came the transition was smooth and was helped by Chamberlain's five and a half years' tenure as Chancellor of the Exchequer, which some believed was the most successful since William Gladstone held that office. He was competent and decisive, and at home with figures, as befitted his experience in manufacturing industry. Yet Herbert Samuel, the Liberal leader, had detected a ruthless streak in Chamberlain's character that was to become much more evident when he became Prime Minister: 'What he says goes. When he puts his foot down and says something must be done, that decision settles it.'[380]

---

380 William Percival Crozier, *Off the Record: Political Interviews 1933–1943*, ed. A. J. P. Taylor (London, Hutchinson, 1973), pp. 48, 50.

Chamberlain's hubris which developed in No. 10 was accompanied by stubbornness and I have written about this in *Cabinet's Finest Hour* from which I have drawn much for this account.[381] Chamberlain was not malleable, in the sense that he resisted all attempts to improve his public image. Suggestions that he should go to the Derby horse race at Epsom or attend cricket matches, or even to buttress his support amongst his own MPs by going to the Smoking Room in the House of Commons, were brushed aside. He did not wish to be seen to act 'out of character'. For all that, he was, and remained for far longer than most people recognise today, a surprisingly popular Prime Minister.

As Prime Minister, Chamberlain seized with relish the opportunity to play on the world stage. His personal diplomacy during two weeks in September 1938 was judged disastrous and Munich still reverberates in history as the first summit conference, and for many diplomats a warning to all future summiteers of the dangers of believing that personal relations can overcome all problems. Politicians can become gripped by summitry; Lloyd George did and Trump may become addicted to one on one diplomacy. David Reynolds writes of Chamberlain's summitry, 'More dangerous still was the idealism (and hubris) of a politician who believed he could bring peace to Europe.'[382] Yet there was huge public support for Chamberlain's search for peace. At one stage there was almost public adulation, although for many people that subsequently vanished with the widespread recognition that his policy of appeasement fed Hitler's ambition and made it more, not less, likely that we would be forced into the Second World War. The Mass-Observation organisation sampled

---

381 David Owen, *Cabinet's Finest Hour. The Hidden Agenda of May 1940* (Haus Publishing, 2016), Chapter 2.
382 David Reynolds, *Summits: Six Meetings That Shaped the Twentieth Century* (London: Allen Lane, 2007), p. 91.

opinion on 15 September 1938, the day Chamberlain flew to Germany for the first time, and reported a 'sensational swing' of opinion in the Prime Minister's favour. No British Prime Minister had been to Germany since Disraeli attended the Congress of Berlin in 1878. One observer sampling opinion in a working-class area got a spontaneous pro-Chamberlain response from every second person questioned.[383]

But appeasement was ferociously attacked by its opponents such as Winston Churchill whose advocacy of rearmament meant that for a period he was condemned to be a prophet in the wilderness. Before that he had been written off by many commentators, one of whom had described him as a 'beached whale'.

Opinion polls showed a major turn-around following Eden's resignation as Foreign Secretary. According to Gallup, only 26 per cent favoured Chamberlain's foreign policy and 71 per cent thought Eden had been right to resign. Yet by March Gallup showed only 33 per cent wanted to express support for Czechoslovakia in the event of German aggression and 43 per cent opposed support and went along with Chamberlain. So much so that in a conversation with the Government Whips, Churchill made sure they knew that Eden's resignation would never become the rallying point to remove Chamberlain. Churchill was not prepared to play second fiddle to Eden.

There was admiration by Cabinet colleagues for a man nearing seventy flying off to confront Hitler, but after his return it was very clear to some in the Cabinet that Chamberlain had lost any critical judgement over Hitler. Chamberlain had said of Hitler on 17 September that 'when he had included the Sudeten Germans in the Reich he would be satisfied'.[384] As Andrew Roberts described it, 'Here was the hubris required by all the best tragedies before any eventual nemesis.' A European democracy was 'about to be

---

383 Charles Madge and Tom Harrisson, *Britain by Mass-Observation* (Harmondsworth, Penguin, 1939) p. 64.
384 CAB 23/95 39 (38).

dismembered according to an Anglo-French plan subject to the approval of the German Chancellor'.[385]

The degree of Chamberlain's self-satisfaction is very apparent in a letter written on 19 September to his sisters saying that Hitler was impressed by him and continues that Hitler was a man 'with whom I can do business'. He also claimed: 'I am the most popular man in Germany!'[386] It is these letters, written once a week, alternately to each sister, and passed between themselves, which highlight the hubris of Chamberlain: always trying to put the best possible interpretation on the week's events and putting himself in the best light. The letters provide a fertile field of evidence for a gathering hubris.

Yet by 22 September, when Chamberlain flew to Bad Godesberg, opinion was hardening against further concessions and protesters booed as he flew off. On his return war seemed imminent. Caution returned as people felt fearful. Hubris had gripped Chamberlain in his conviction that he, and he alone, knew how to handle Hitler. Halifax, the Foreign Secretary, however, had second thoughts and told the Cabinet that 'so long as Nazism lasted, peace would be uncertain. For this reason he did not feel that it would be right to put pressure on Czechoslovakia to accept.' Chamberlain sent Halifax a pencilled note: 'Your complete change of view since I saw you last night is a horrible blow to me, but of course you must form your opinions for yourself.' Halifax replied: 'I feel a brute – but I lay awake most of the night, tormenting myself.' Chamberlain retorted tersely: 'Night conclusions are seldom taken in the right perspective.'[387] After ambushing Chamberlain in Cabinet on 25 September Halifax progressively hardened his position. Even though Hitler had softened the

---

385 Andrew Roberts, *The Holy Fox: A Biography of Lord Halifax* (London: Papermac, 1992), p. 111.

386 Robert Self (ed.), *The Neville Chamberlain Diary Letters, vol. 4: The Downing Street Years 1934–40* (Aldershot: Ashgate, 2002).

387 Ibid., Roberts, *the Holy Fox*, pp. 115, 117, 118.

arrangements at Munich which he had demanded at Bad Godesberg. The Kristallnacht pogrom on the night of 9-10 November, which saw Jewish shops smashed and much bloodshed, shocked the public and revolted Halifax. Although in a letter to a friend in 1952 he admitted he had 'always been rather anti-Semitic', the events of Kristallnacht completed his 'about face on appeasement'. Halifax continued for the rest of the year to identify Nazism as the problem and argue for a tougher stance. At this stage the Foreign Secretary was not the main appeaser.

Hitler responded positively on 28 September 1938 to holding a meeting in Munich next day and the staid House of Commons went wild when the Prime Minister confirmed he would go. Members stood, cheered and waved their order papers. In the public galleries, against the rules, people clapped. When he returned from Munich it took the Prime Minister's car an hour and a half to drive from the airport to Downing Street. During this time, according to Roberts, Halifax performed the function of the slave in ancient Rome who constantly whispered in the victorious general's ear reminders of his mortality in the hope of curbing his hubris. Chamberlain publicly waved the piece of paper carrying his and Hitler's signature and was ill-advisedly invited by George VI to appear with him on the balcony of Buckingham Palace where thousands of people cheered below. Most newspapers were overwhelmingly supportive.

Not surprisingly, Chamberlin, who was used to living and working in Birmingham had his head turned by all this international attention. He now became a man of destiny. His relations with Halifax deteriorated as his policies of appeasement were progressively discredited. In the House of Commons on 5 October 1938 Churchill unleashed his full invective, calling the Munich settlement 'a total and unmitigated defeat'.

Halifax accompanied Chamberlain to Paris in late November; Chamberlain saw it as giving 'the French people an opportunity of pouring out their pent up feelings of gratitude and affection towards him' in a letter to his sister dated 27 November.[388]

At the meeting of the Committee of Imperial Defence on 26 January 1939 Halifax advocated 'tripling the British Expeditionary Force, doubling the Territorials and instituting immediate wide-ranging Staff talks and full military conscription'.[389] Chamberlain and John Simon, the Chancellor of the Exchequer, opposed these measures. This calls in to question the argument that appeasement was undertaken by Chamberlain to buy time so that the UK could rearm. This rearmament emphasis came later in 1939 from Chamberlain well after Munich. Not only were they worried about the financial implications of such policies, but, as Roberts points out, 'they saw Staff talks as symptomatic of the pre-1914 mood that they were trying at all costs to avoid'. These were the Military Conversations between France and Britain begun in 1906.[390]

What was it that made Chamberlain susceptible to and quickly acquire hubris syndrome as Prime Minister? It is interesting to analyse his state of mind at Munich. He was self-satisfied and exhausted but not depressed the day after his heady return to Heston aerodrome. Yet he admitted to his sisters that he had come nearer to a nervous breakdown 'than I have ever been in my life'.[391] His mood was exultant and he appeared then to believe he had been successful in ending the prospect of war. He had acted throughout with a small inner Cabinet and had marginalised any opposing opinion in the full Cabinet. He deluded himself about Hitler's trustworthiness and underestimated his sinister ambitions.

---

388 Zara Steiner, *The Triumph of the Dark: European International History 1933-1939* (Oxford University Press, 2011), p. vii.
389 Roberts, *The Holy Fox*, p. 128.
390 David Owen, *The Hidden Perspective: The Military Conversations 1906-1914* (Haus Publishing, 2014).
391 Reynolds, *Summits*, p. 91.

On 18 March 1939, three days after the destruction of Czechoslovakia, the Soviet Commissar for Foreign Affairs, Maxim Litvinov, made an attempt at a new rapprochement and proposed a conference in Bucharest of Russia, Romania, Poland, Britain, France and Turkey to form a peace front against an expanding Germany. On 23 March Chamberlain said the Government took a dim view of establishing 'opposing blocs'. In Chamberlain's mind Bolsheviks, not Nazis, were still the greatest threat. On 13 April Churchill in the Commons said that the 'deep, natural, legitimate interest' that Russia has against further eastward expansion of Nazi power was something the UK should offer 'the closest cooperation'. But Stalin on 23 August signed a non-aggression pact with Hitler.

Exhaustion and stress were taking their toll on Chamberlain. By March 1939 R. A. Butler, usually known as 'Rab', then a minister in the Foreign Office, described how, on learning that the Italians had invaded Albania, he went over to No. 10 to tell the Prime Minister what had happened. Chamberlain was at the open window of his study feeding seed to the birds, and was rather annoyed at Butler's arrival. He expressed amazement at Butler's distress at the news, saying: 'I feel sure Mussolini has decided not to go against us.' When Butler talked about the threat to the Balkans, Chamberlain dismissed it, saying: 'Don't be silly. Go home and go to bed,' and continued to feed the birds.[392] The capacity for self-delusion is the most worrying aspect of this story, and the fact that it was recorded by Butler, a politician who supported Munich and appeasement, makes the testimony all the more convincing.

A defence of Chamberlain is that certainly by 1939 he had become more realistic about Hitler and was buying time as the rearmament programme built up, knowing that Britain had to fight.

---

392 William Manchester, *The Caged Lion: Winston Spencer Churchill 1932–1940* (London: Michael Joseph, 1988), p. 421.

Gallup started polling approval ratings for the government in October 1938 and by February 1939 they were showing over 50 per cent levels of support for Chamberlain. Diplomacy had little to offer. President Roosevelt sent Sumner Welles to Europe in February 1940 who reported back 'I do not believe there is the slightest chance of any successful negotiation at this time', namely March 1940. When Churchill became Prime Minister Lord Halifax, highly intelligent, nicknamed the 'Holy Fox', somewhat surprisingly, but quite legitimately did advocate negotiating with Mussolini in May 1940, a position wisely rejected by the War Cabinet in nine meetings over five days chaired by Churchill. Yet Chamberlain did not connive with Halifax as recently depicted in the film '*Darkest Hour*'. Instead Chamberlain started fairly neutral. Out of office his hubris had waned somewhat and he was very skilfully won round by Churchill's personal warmth to him and realistic arguments. Had Halifax become Prime Minister and begun negotiations with Mussolini it is impossible to avoid the conclusion that Hitler would have demanded a ceasefire and it would have been conceded making it virtually impossible to restart the war and a humiliating Vichy-like government would have been imposed on Britain.

Clement Attlee, Churchill's deputy in the War Cabinet achieved in the General Election of 1945 a result that shocked not just Churchill but the whole of the Conservative party. Voting took place on 5 July and the results were declared three weeks later. Attlee became Prime Minister as Labour won 393 seats against 192 for the Conservatives. Opinion polls had shown a Labour lead since 1942 so the result should have surprised nobody. Attlee, who at long last has been the subject of a biography[393] worthy of him, was totally devoid of hubris so does not feature in this book any more than President Truman. Both proved to be popular leaders in the sense that they identified with the people

---

393 John Bew, *Citizen Clem. A biography of Attlee* (Quercus Editions, 2016).

they led. The House of Commons in its own unique way recognised this by including Attlee among the four leaders placed on plinths in the Members' lobby – Churchill and Lloyd George, then Attlee and then Thatcher.

Margaret Thatcher's handling of the Falklands War is described in Chapter 8 'Hubris and the Military Mentality'. During that war as I closely witnessed, she was not hubristic. Nor was she during the year long miners' strike of 1984-5 when she was utterly determined, some would say ruthless, but also careful and cautious.

The UK's relative economic decline could only have been reversed by a conviction politician and Margaret Thatcher's pursuit of monetary discipline, trade union reforms and privatisation transformed the British economy, ensuring a considerable legacy but leaving in its wake considerable social division, deprivation and the hollowing out of the state and much of industrial Britain as it had developed under the Premiership of Clement Attlee from 1945-51.

In 1975 on the eve of the first ballot in the Conservative party leadership contest after Heath resigned, Thatcher said on television: 'All my ideas about (Britain) were formed before I was seventeen or eighteen.' There is a good deal of truth in this comment. It explains her black-and-white view of life, which was part of her appeal, as well as the source of an off-putting certainty. On the day of her election as leader, she told ITN: 'You don't exist as a party unless you have a clear philosophy and clear heritage.' The philosophy was kept in her handbag – Friedrich Hayek's *The Constitution of Liberty*, of which she is supposed to have said: 'This is what we believe.' Some of it was both populist and popular. She used the word, 'swamped' deliberately in relation to immigration on Granada's *World in Action* on 30 January 1978 and years before that had gone to a dinner of her own constituency party where Enoch Powell was the guest of honour when she could have dined with the rest of the shadow cabinet at Selsdon Park where there was a conference to hammer out the 1970 election campaign.[394] During that 1970 election Powell made a series of speeches about 'the hidden enemy within'. Without doubt Powell was both a populist and part of a political agenda that owed much to populism but sadly his language became racist.

Thatcher was more pragmatic as Prime Minister in 1979 than is sometimes recognised. Encouraged by her Foreign Secretary, Lord Carrington, she dumped some of her previous prejudices, such as her passionate support in opposition for Bishop Abel Muzorewa and the internal settlement in Rhodesia in 1978. In February 1981, when the moderate miners' leader Joe Gormley was close to calling a strike, without any Cabinet discussion she told her Energy Secretary, David Howell: 'Bring it to an end, David. Make the necessary concessions.' But she carefully prepared for the inevitable confrontation with Arthur Scargill, the Communist miners' leader, by stockpiling coal at power stations and elsewhere.

The economic gloom deepened throughout 1981 and the Cabinet grew increasingly divided. William Whitelaw, having put his defeat in the leadership election behind him, was now Home Secretary and Thatcher's confidant. He warned her: 'There comes a moment in politics when you have pushed the tolerance of society too far. We aren't there but we aren't far off.' Outside Parliament, John Hoskyns, the first head of Thatcher's policy unit and her leading non-career civil servant, sent her what he called a 'blockbuster' memo entitled 'Your Political Survival'. It recognised that 'your government has achieved the beginning of a near-revolution in the private sector and especially in industry'. It even ventured: 'Things in the economy are better than people realise.' But it went on: 'Your own credibility and prestige are draining away very fast... You lack management competence... Your own leadership style is wrong... You bully your weaker colleagues... You give little praise or credit, and you

---

394 Charles Moore, *Margaret Thatcher. The Authorised Biography. Volume One. Not For Turning* (Allan Lane, 2013), p 382 and 195.

are too ready to blame others when things go wrong.' A few weeks later, after no discussion, she hissed at him: 'I got your letter. No one has ever written like that to a Prime Minister before.' True but no one had ever been a Prime Minister like her before and not just because she was the first female Prime Minister.

Her victory over the miners, particularly in the shape of their leader, Arthur Scargill, defied the conventional wisdom of Conservative leaders, which would have had her compromise. Yet it meant that she began to be dangerously overconfident about her own judgement and contemptuous of other people's. Nemesis came over the European Monetary Union. Thatcher claims that right up to the beginning of the December 1985 Luxembourg Council she thought she could rely on Chancellor Helmut Kohl's recent conversation with her that the Germans were totally opposed to any wording to cover economic and monetary union in the revisions of the treaty. That was not to be the case. Her Chancellor of the Exchequer, Nigel Lawson, had warned her twice on accepting any wording on monetary union, EMU, in memos of perception and wisdom.[395]

Contrary to many people's view, Margaret Thatcher was not always hubristic. The roots of her hubris lie after her third election victory on 11 June 1987. William Whitelaw stepped down from the Cabinet at the end of that year following a minor stroke and collapse at a carol service in Westminster. Nigel Lawson, Chancellor of the Exchequer for much of Thatcher's time in office, wrote in his autobiography about Whitelaw's departure from government in very moving terms and with considerable insight:

> Only someone who served at the heart of the Thatcher Government can fully appreciate the key role Willie played. He was irreplaceable. It was not simply that he was a wise elder

---

395 Nigel Lawson, *The View from No 11. Memoirs of a Tory Radical* (Transworld Publishers, 1992), p. 893.

statesman of immense experience and acute political instinct, unfailingly loyal and devoid of personal ambition, to whom Margaret could always turn. He also resolved many of the tensions that arise between Cabinet colleagues in any government before they even reached Margaret. And when she was involved, it was he alone who could sometimes, although inevitably not always, prevail upon her to avoid needless confrontations or eschew follies ...When she needed him most she ignored him completely, and instead retreated even further into her Downing St bunker.[396]

Thatcher's insistence on introducing the poll tax perfectly illustrates how she was succumbing to hubris syndrome. The tax was almost universally regarded as unfair but she was convinced it was not and ploughed on with the policy. The proposal was dropped. But the weight of mere public opinion was not something that was going to stop Thatcher in her tracks. Even here, though, she did not manifest that cavalier inattention to detail that is often symptomatic of hubris syndrome. There were extensive studies conducted about the whys and wherefores of the tax before it was introduced. Colleagues were also very fully consulted. But the momentum behind it was undoubtedly Thatcher's unwavering conviction that it was 'right'. At a more comical level it started to become clear she was suffering the effects of hubris when she greeted the arrival of her first grandchild with the remark 'We have become a grandmother!'

Even a leader as self-confident as Winston Churchill recoiled from such hubris. In preparing the Conservative manifesto for the 1950 election he had cursorily dismissed the complaint of a young member of the party's Research Department, Reginald Maudling, that a particular proposal was unfair; but when Maudling had the temerity to come back with the observation that the 'British people' would regard it as unfair, Churchill paused and remarked: 'Ah!

---

396 Nigel Lawson, *The View from No 11*, p. 427.

That is a horse of a very different colour!' The man who could have provided the 'toe-holds' for Margaret Thatcher as Louis Howe did for Franklin Roosevelt, another hubristic leader, was Willie Whitelaw and he was ignored from 1988.

By 1989 Thatcher's grasp of the realities in which she was operating seemed to be deserting her. When the Berlin Wall came down in November, she refused to recognise that reunification of East and West Germany would come immediately onto the political agenda. An underlying fear of a larger Germany developed into her privately talking emotionally about a Fourth Reich. She had had an amazingly warm relationship with Ronald Reagan but she warned President George Bush Sr that 'if we are not careful, the Germans will get in peace what Hitler couldn't get in the war',[397] a quite extraordinary remark. The fact that she totally miscalculated the speed of the political imperative that was driving German reunification was one of the signs that her political judgement was being jeopardised by her political prejudices and that her self-confidence was overriding her caution. By then, her contempt for the Foreign Office was allowing her to disregard much diplomatic advice.

Sir Geoffrey Howe was reshuffled out of the Foreign Office to Leader of the House of Commons. As Lawson wrote, 'over the years she felt compelled, to the acute embarrassment of everyone else present, to treat him as something halfway between a punchbag and a doormat. She wanted to humiliate (Howe) at every turn, berating him in front of colleagues and conspicuously excluding him from ad hoc meetings of senior Ministers. It was extraordinary conduct . . .'[398] It was also a further manifestation of contempt, one of the key signs (No. 7) of hubris syndrome as enumerated in the Introduction to this book. Another is being reckless (No. 11) and Lawson records that this episode 'was yet another example of her

---

397 George Bush and Brent Scowcroft, *A World Transformed* (New York: Alfred A. Knopf, 1998), p. 249.
398 Lawson, *The View from No 11*, p. 653, 936, 592.

recklessness which one senior official, a particularly shrewd and close observer, described to me as the outstanding characteristic of her long-drawn-out final phase.'

She had begun to be reckless over the European Union. Very surprisingly she had brushed aside Lawson's warning over accepting wording on European Monetary Union as far back as 1986 over the Single Currency Act. She would be appalled in later life to see her successor, John Major, accept the euro, not for the UK, but for a Eurozone of EU countries in the Treaty of Maastricht. The Italian Prime Minister Giulio Andreotti, in 1990 at a summit in Rome, arranged for a political ambush to which Thatcher responded with her famous series of 'No! No! No!' statements. She appeared in the House of Commons on 30 October on an emotional high, full of adrenalin or serotonin, perhaps both, as I sensed from sitting across from her, on the front bench below the gangway, she figuratively hand-bagged every European federalist proposition.

Howe, now Leader of the House, sat watching as Thatcher opposed a single currency and even backtracked from the government's position over the hard ecu, his face a picture of misery. He looked like the 'dead sheep' of Denis Healey's famous jibe about being 'savaged by' but we were soon to discover fully his capacity to 'ravage' her in a way which neither Healey, nor any opposition parliamentarian, including myself, had ever been able to do.

The scene in the Commons was well imaged by the *Guardian*'s political commentator, Hugo Young, describing Margaret Thatcher: 'Returning home, she had not cooled off. True, as quite often happened in the Thatcher decade, the relevant Whitehall officials effected a certain hosing down' so that the text of what she read out was controlled. But in answer to questions,

it became in its monosyllabic brutality, the rubric of one of her most famous parliamentary moments, leaping with rage, ringing round the chamber, startling even those who in eleven years had much experience of the Thatcher vocabulary on Europe. 'No . . . no . . . no,' she bawled, her eye seemingly directed to the fields and seas, the hills and the landing grounds, where the island people would never surrender.[399]

At a Cabinet meeting shortly before Howe resigned Margaret Thatcher 'lost it' in the sense that there was no longer any reserve in her handling of him, sitting beside her on her left with the Cabinet Secretary on her right. The incident was well captured in the film about Margaret Thatcher, who was played by Meryl Streep. Had Willie Whitelaw been present, however, there is little doubt that she would never have embarked on what can only be called a rant and a humiliating evisceration of Howe in terms which made many members of the Cabinet ashamed and angry at her behaviour. Howe resigned as Lord President of the Council and Leader of the Commons on 1 November 1990.

The touch paper was now in place for a challenge to her leadership but it was not to be lit until the debate on the Queen's Speech on 13 November. Geoffrey Howe then used his right to make a resignation speech after becoming very annoyed by days of briefing from No. 10, which tried to portray his resignation as an argument about style rather than substance. Having thought long and hard on what to say and consulted close friends, he decided in a measured tone to deliberately focus on one central purpose: namely to encourage an election to choose a new party leader and Prime Minister. He made a full-frontal attack, the speech of an assassin, with every word crafted and sharpened to penetrate ever deeper. 'Cabinet government is all about trying to persuade one another from within.' He ended: 'The time has come for others to

---

399 Hugo Young, *This Blessed Plot: Britain and Europe from Churchill to Blair* (London: Macmillan, 1998), p. 368.

consider their response to the tragic conflict of loyalty with which I have perhaps wrestled for too long.'

Michael Heseltine, who had literally walked out of the Cabinet a few years earlier, protesting at the Thatcher style of government, announced he would challenge her for the leadership. On 19 November, Thatcher was in Paris attending an international conference when she would have been better advised to have remained in London gathering the support of a few more MPs in personal meetings. In the first ballot she came out fifty-two votes ahead of Heseltine: four short of the fifty-six majority she needed to avoid a second ballot.

A defence of Margaret Thatcher by a close adviser, Robin Harris, was included in his book published in 2013, long after her death. He claims she was insensitive but not hubristic and not a Greek tragedy.[400] But insensitivity is part of what the Greeks identified as a condition of growing contempt.

On Thursday 22 November at 10 a.m., after it had become clear to her from talks with every Cabinet minister that she had lost the confidence of her parliamentary colleagues, Margaret Thatcher resigned. She was succeeded as Prime Minister by John Major, a person as different from Margaret Thatcher as it is possible to conceive. He went on to win the General Election of 1992 serving a full term but losing to Tony Blair in 1997.

Thatcher's removal was the ultimate demonstration of how hubris is followed by nemesis and that in the UK based on the fusion of powers between the Executive and Parliament, a Prime Minister has to retain the support of colleagues. It is not enough to be a conviction politician.

President Macron's victory in France on the second ballot on 14 May 2017 was spectacular having only launched his new movement 'En Marche' on 6 April. I warmly welcomed his election victory

---

400 Robin Harris, *Not for Turning. The Life of Margaret Thatcher* (Bantam Press, 2013).

believing that anyone who had the full support of my lifelong friend, Michel Rocard, would make a good President.

Yet just over a year later an article in *The Times* of 7 September 2018 headed 'Macron is given a lesson in hubris' confirmed my growing concern. It followed a You Gov poll in France which showed only 23% of voters thought the President was doing a good job. Gérard Collomb, aged 71 and one of the few seasoned politicians in President Macron's Cabinet warned his colleagues on television, obviously including Macron himself, who was increasingly being depicted in the French press as a haughty leader, to 'listen to what people are saying because you can quickly lose your capacity for listening to the population in the palace of the republic.' Adding 'There is a saying that the gods make blind those they want to lose. We must not therefore fall into blindness.' He said that he used to be a teacher of Greek, 'there is a word called hubris, which is the curse of the gods when you become too sure of yourself, you think you are going to carry everything before you.' Later Collomb resigned from Macron's government.

President Macron's book *Revolution* translated into English and published by Scribe not only reveals the ambition of his project for France but there is a single-minded revolutionary ethos running through it. He knows the answers to France's problems; he has the solution. In that sense, he has the hubris already that both Neville Chamberlain and Margaret Thatcher developed in office and like them he is ready to be unpopular in pursuit of his policies. All three can be described as conviction politicians.

It was President Macron's carbon charge that triggered the French phenomenon, the 'gilet jaunes', still active at the start of 2020. It is very different from the Brexit phenomenon or the rust belt states' revolt in America. The yellow vests they wear have been described by James McCauley, the Washington correspondent in France, as a symbol of car ownership. Outside Paris where there are no other transport options open to them with abandoned train stations, new carbon taxes can seem like sneers from the Paris elite'. In Macron's language 'Ceux qui ne sont rien' the precarious ranks of the lower middle class, feel they are – nothing. They return the perceived insult with 'an intense and deeply personal hatred of Macron'.[401]

France, like Italy, does not easily conform to EU budget deficit limits. The German stance towards the Eurozone is agreed to by the other seven northern EU countries, called the 'New Hanseatic League' including the Netherlands, Denmark, Sweden and Finland.

On the urgent issues relating to the Eurozone the German-French relationship is crucial. The Merkel coalition Christian Democrats and Social Democrats was threatened in December 2019 by her partners electing two new left wing leaders demanding extra spending and new social justice policies.

The new player is Annegret Kramp-Karenbauer, AKK, as she is often referred to, and German Chancellor designate. She has made it clear that she rejects the three key economic shifts in policy advocated by President Macron. Firstly, a European minimum wage. Secondly, making social security systems pan European and thirdly, and most importantly for the future of the Eurozone, French proposals for "communitising" debt. There may be some room for a compromise over Macron's wish for a Eurozone Treasury headed by a Eurozone Finance Minister with a Eurozone budget. But behind Macron's reforms for the euro is the conviction that a Federal Europe is the true destiny and a readiness, unlike any other French President when in office, to champion such a Europe, strong in the certainty that logically it is the true path.

President Macron, undoubtedly, shows many signs of developing hubris. His interview 'Emmanuel Macron in his own words' in the *Economist* of 7 November 2019 is well worth reading and analysing. I first recognised his importance in Paris early in 2013 where I had gone to talk to Michel Rocard about my new book *Europe Restructured*. He said 'David you have come on the wrong day.

---

401 *The New York Review of Books*, 2 March – 3 April 2019, p. 58-62.

Tomorrow *Le Monde* has an article by me saying the UK should leave the EU with friendship. Your UK presence will be a persistent refusal to build Europe.' I replied there were ways of keeping the UK in a wider European circle like the EEA but without some of the EU founding principles like freedom of movement of labour and commitment to binding European defence and foreign policies. 'Who should I talk to in the Elysée', I asked. Without hesitation, Michel said 'Macron, he is your man.' Macron was at that time an adviser to President Hollande. After an exchange of emails we had a good conversation on the telephone but it did not take long to recognise Macron's deep-seated commitment to a federal Europe, very similar to Michel Rocard's. On the propositions within my book there was interest, but he was on a mission and it did not involve compromising on his core vision − a fully integrated Europe. Everything I have read or heard of him since convinces me he will either build that Europe or he will fail openly and even ignominiously.

According to Macron, with reference to Syria, NATO is 'brain dead', a description repeated in front of all NATO leaders at the NATO summit in the UK in December 2019 to the dismay even of Trump who called it 'insulting'. Early on taking office President Macron made 101 trips to over 50 different countries, including twice to China. A cynic might say all this travel is to deflect from the continuing crisis at home with the 'gilets jaunes' protestors. In December 2019 he faced mass public service strikes all over France. French Presidents have had to deal with this before as have British Prime Ministers but he will not convince his fellow EU partners about his ideas for the future direction of Europe until he can demonstrate that France is at ease with itself and set on a course of economic strength. Macron wants a Europe that can project power but he lives in a Europe that is reluctant to build, let alone project, power. He can and does hold many meetings to broker a power that at present does not exist. His advisers claim he is a realist and a pragmatist. But from across the Channel in the UK he appears to be neither. One of the many challenges for Boris Johnson will be to engage with him and assess his true metal and, if possible, to weld together another *entente cordiale*, based not only on a bilateral foreign and defence policy but on building mutual prosperity in our two countries.

Macron talks of the 'grammar of power'. He is stopping, for a time, further EU enlargement. He is ready, it appears, to appease Russia raising concerns in the third largest military power in the EU, Poland. We have yet to see whether he is a sufficient realist to know that it would be wise to allow for continued economic engagement with a UK outside the EU. That is an *entente* the French people, particularly those in the socialist Calais region might find very attractive and as being in their self-interest, rather more easily than their President. Our more populist UK Prime Minister might well champion this to great effect in his fluent French. In combination they might be able to include President Trump and his successor whoever that might be. In 2019 France saw US tariffs biting hard on their wine industry in retaliation for subsidies to Airbus which were judged to be illegal by the World Trade Organisation and lurking in the background is a fiscal ruling from WTO on US subsidies to Boeing which could well lead to EU tariffs on American goods in 2020, a presidential election year.

President Macron's handling of President Trump has been both distinctive and interesting. He very quickly hosted him, with wives, for a meal on the top of the Eiffel Tower. This was followed the next day by Trump marching down the Champs Elysée during the Bastille Day celebrations. As their oldest ally the full honours were returned during Macron's visit to the US by Trump hosting a dinner at the White House. President Macron tried to have it both ways with Trump and was initially successful but the mood music shifted. A Berlin official is reported in the *FT* in November 2019 as musing that Macron is indulging in 'intellectualised Trumpism'.[402] At the first G7 meeting in Canada, Macron and Trump clashed on climate change and then over NATO at the Summit in the UK.

TV cameras in Buckingham Palace caught Macron laughing while Trudeau, the Canadian Prime Minister, joked about Trump. Johnson was with them in the group, but not so obviously laughing. To some extent, Trump is like Macron in putting 'America first' but Macron follows a familiar French presidential pattern putting France first but wrapped up in the EU flag. The unanswered question is will Macron stay true to his federalist beliefs? I believe he will because like Chamberlain and Thatcher he is a conviction politician but first he has to win a second term.

402 Gideon Rachman, 'Brexit has destabilised the Franco-German couple', *Financial Times*, 25 November 2019. https://www.ft.com/content/000e9634-0f63-llea-a7e6-62bf4f9e548a

Chapter 11

Donald Trump's Populism

President Donald Trump presents a completely new challenge to handling US-UK relations. As a businessman Trump approaches negotiations as transactional, highly personal and held at the highest level. Usually about money and based on numbers. The starting points tend to be very different between high and low and game playing is normal. Self-interest and short termism are commonplace, boasting about the outcome and claiming victory frequent. Whereas government negotiations are usually more relational than transactional, start at a lower level, involve leaders at a later stage, and cover a wider field than money and numbers. The national interest is also more complex and harder to define than a financial business interest. Flamboyance is prevalent and acceptable in business, not so for intergovernmental negotiations.

President Trump shows no sign of changing his style but it is not necessary to ape his style to continue to work with him. He may be in power for a total of eight years since impeachment failed. Every UK-US negotiation should be examined critically for the best style to achieve lasting results. Making adjustments even on a short term basis with Trump has its own problems.

It is a UK interest to negotiate a Free Trade Agreement with a US President who makes no secret of his wish to achieve this well before the summer of 2020 and a good deal of preparatory work has already been done.

Mark Leonard an interesting writer on international affairs, on 24 July 2018 in the *Financial Times* wrote after having spent time in Beijing talking to officials and intellectuals. 'Donald Trump is leading a double life. In the west, most foreign policy experts see him as reckless, unpredictable and self-defeating. But though many in Asia dislike him as much as the Europeans do, they see him as a more substantial figure and 'are awed by his skill as a strategist and tactician.'

Adjusting to Trump's style is therefore not the same as accepting his agenda. His methods do require adjusting to, for there is good sense behind some of them and a few have a welcome radicalism in challenging status quo attitudes. For the most part, Trump has yet to demonstrate he sees merit in the concept of international agreements, coordinated actions and striving for coherence. The President of the EU Commission, Jean-Claude Juncker announced in his 25 July 2018 meeting in Washington with President Trump 'both sides would work together towards zero tariffs, non-tariff barriers and zero subsidies on industrial goods. Trump called it 'a very big day for free and fair trade' and claimed that 'we will also work to reduce barriers and increase trade in services, chemicals, pharmaceuticals as well as soya beans.' If real progress is made, Trump will explain it as the EU responding to threatened actions. Yet Trump's impact on the world is one that could easily slide back into 'beggar my neighbour' policies under a misplaced assertion internationally of 'my nation first'. So a combination of firmness and flexibility has to be upheld, meaning most countries linked to the US are in for an uncomfortable ride. Unlike some, I believe there has been real progress on important issues under President Trump, but international cohesion has suffered overall.

In that Trump's methods are different it is prudent to analyse why they are different and what are the potential benefits as well as disadvantages of them. That there is some method I have few doubts; but some of these have not stood the test of time. His is a largely unproven methodology in government to government negotiations. But he is seemingly not rigid. He does understand it is best if both sides have something they can claim as their victory at the end.

Trade disruption on a unilateral basis has been the initial policy of the Trump Administration. If Trump wants to develop a more coherent strategy, which is open to doubt, there is one detailed scheme available to him named by its author 'Masch 403' as Compensated Free Trade, CFT. It is rooted in Article 7 of the Breton Woods Agreement on the creation of the International Monetary Fund sometimes referred to as the 'scarce currency' clause which Robert Skidelsky describes in his major latest book, *Money and Government. A Challenge to Mainstream Economics.* (Allen Lane, p. 380-1). It could be a mechanism whereby members of the IMF could 'restrict their purchases of goods from countries whose currency was declared "scarce", ie which ran persistent current account surpluses.' Under this suggested CFT the US would decide on the maximum amount an overall trade deficit would be acceptable. In order to keep within range of that figure it would fix limits on the surpluses of key trading partners. The more transparent the fixing of these limits were to be the more tolerable the unilateral measures might become.Skidelsky notes that of the $677 billion trade deficit that the US had in 2016 China contributed $319 billion, Japan $62billion, Germany $60 billion and Mexico $59 billion. The surplus country could exceed their allocation subject to paying a specific charge on the difference between their allocation and their allowed exports. Without such payments the country's exports would be blocked. To many countries such a scheme would be totally unacceptable until perhaps it was introduced as a *fait accompli*, at which time realism and some modifications might lead to reluctant acceptance. The question for

---

403 Ref Masch,V.A.(2017) Balancing global trade:'compensated free trade'.World Journal of Social Sciences, 7(1), March, pp. 49-63.

the UK is whether to advocate it as the logical extension of Keynesian thought and with modifications and transparent mechanisms. Arguably it would be the sort of intellectual internationalism that the UK should undertake outside the EU and trying to make WTO more effective.

Trump definitely exhibits many signs of hubris. The question is has that hubris been present for a very long time? It would help to know more about why at the age of thirteen, his parents decided to send him to the New York Military Academy. More uniform than soldiering. But a more disciplined school and environment. I have talked to a number of people who have known him at school, university and in his business life. It is very common to learn there has been little change over these years.

A journalist, Leslie Marshall, sent me an article she wrote two decades ago in a magazine called *Style*. Set in Trump Tower with lavish interior photographs there is a revealing one of Trump on a large bed with young teenage daughter Ivanka, telephone in hand, conducting business. And another with his second wife and young two year old daughter Tiffany. Comparing that interview with the many, many interviews he has given since, I am convinced Leslie Marshall's words to me that he is 'irretrievably Trump' sum him up. Most presidential lifestyles would be different; his seems even as President surprisingly unchanged. Trump Tower has come to the White House. The interweaving of business and family life is not much changed. As to his business life, we know enough about it to be sure he has lived at times under considerable stress associated with bankruptcies. He has also managed to develop not just business skills but the skills one needs to handle TV programmes such as 'The Apprentice' which he had made his own, changing his language to be simpler, direct and effective.

The American psychiatrist, Dr Bandy X. Lee from Yale University when briefing a dozen lawmakers from the US Senate and House of Representatives on 5/6 December 2017 said about

President Trump that there were 'signs that he is going into attack mode when he is under stress. That means he has the potential to become impulsive and very volatile.' She also noted, 'as he is unravelling he seems to be losing his grip on reality and reverting to conspiracy theories'.

We all need to be careful about using words like 'unravelling'. It implies someone is veering out of control, quite unable to handle the strains and stresses of normal life. President Trump has been under huge personal and political pressures and much stress since taking office. Therefore the unravelling charge is something that needs to be monitored carefully. Dr Lee got around Section 7.3 of the American Psychiatric Association's guidelines against using such a term, sometimes referred to as the Goldwater Rule, that 'member psychiatrists should not give professional opinions about the mental state of someone they have not personally evaluated' by invoking the other part of APA guidance that it is 'fine for a psychiatrist to share their expertise'. (See President Johnson's mental health, Chapter 6, pages 158–162.)

As well as 'unravelling' we also recently have the word 'unhinged' being used as in Omarosa Manigault Newman's book *Unhinged. An Insider's Account of the Trump White House.* Best known as a reality television show participant, she was assistant to the President and Director of Communications for the Office of Public Liaison in the Trump White House, having known Trump for a span of 15 years, from the time she was the only African American woman on the first season of 'The Apprentice' in September 2003. She has been described as a divisive character and a self-publicist and worked on the *National Enquirer* for two years in a job brokered by Donald Trump with his friend, the proprietor, David Pecker. She also worked in the office of Vice President Al Gore during the Clinton Administration. She was ordained a Baptist minister in February 2012 and became a chaplain in the California State Military Reserve. She signed on for Trump's campaign team in

September 2015, yet within a year in the White House left, having as her book reveals undertaken over 200 secret recordings, including one in the Situation Room. She writes 'The Donald Trump of 2018 is not the same man as he was in 2003.' . . . 'The change in him since his prime was dramatic. Back on season one of The Apprentice . . . Donald Trump repeated a lengthy numbers sequence with no notes in front of him, calculated them in his head in moments, and came to his conclusion that the math-addled contestant should be fired. That was how sharp he used to be. Now? The blade had been dulled.' . . . 'Donald is very street-smart and is talented at making quick adjustments. His adaptability has been a skill that benefited him as a businessman. But for the job he had now, he needed to be able to read, and he struggled . . . he has only a surface-level understanding of the content he's signing into law.' She goes on to describe 'I'd been watching Donald for two months day to day in the White House with growing concern about his mental state. He seemed to be showing signs of deterioration . . . His forgetfulness and frustration were getting worse.' That could well be a description of aging. As one gets older the processes of the brain change and one is more easily stressed.

I am not convinced anything warrants the description of 'unhinged' but the fact that his personality and abilities have changed does give cause for concern.

A 'nervous breakdown' in Trump's presidency is part of the title of an article in the 4 September 2018 issue of the *Washington Post* by Philip Rucker and Robert Costa commenting on *Fear: Trump in the White House* by Bob Woodward. The book 'depicts Trump's anger and paranoia'. The title of the book is taken from what Trump actually said, 'Real power is, I don't even want to use the word, "Fear."' Woodward describes a staffer called Porter who left the presidency in February, 'It felt like we were walking along the edge of a cliff perpetually.' And also saying 'This was no longer a presidency. This is no longer a White House. This is a man being who he is.' We know Trump's former doctor, Bornstein, told CNN in an interview on 2 May 2018 that Trump had dictated the whole letter which he, as a candidate for President, published in 2015 which declared that Trump's health was 'astonishingly excellent'. Also Bornstein said to CNN that Mr Trump's bodyguard had carried out a raid on his offices in February 2017 removing all of Mr Trump's medical reports. Bornstein further said that the letter which used the following words that Mr Trump would be the 'healthiest individual ever elected to the presidency' was not his professional assessment. Since then the White House doctor Ronny Jackson, a Rear Admiral in the US Navy who has cared for three Presidents over 12 years, said on 17 January 2018 'I have no concern about his cognitive ability or neurological function.' The White House issued a statement also which said it had not been a raid on Bornstein's offices but 'standard procedures for the White House medical unit to take possession of the President's medical records'.

In some ways it is essential in examining Trump's personality to consider it in the round for the man is more than unusual. He is capable of making statements that are completely at odds with each other within a matter of hours. It is as if he compartmentalises different issues in his mind and different solutions. He also deliberately talks differently to different audiences at the same time. In that sense he demonstrates that the truth does not matter to him and he is ready to flaunt that disregard.

Trump as President displays the uncharacteristic feature of almost all other Presidents in history in that he does not make a distinction between how he behaved as a candidate and how he behaves in office. He claims to have systematically set out to follow through on all his policy commitments that he espoused as a candidate and continues to use much the same language. Trump's inaugural address which shocked some and delighted others was not markedly different from his speeches on the campaign trail.

For too long, a small group in our nation's capital has reaped the rewards of government while the people have borne the cost. Washington flourishes, but the people did not share in its wealth. Politicians prospered, but the jobs left and the factories closed. The establishment protected itself, but not the citizens of our country. Their victories have not been your victories.

He has been on the campaign trail since being elected and continues to hold campaign meetings in a style similar to that in 2016 as a candidate and with a frequency that appears to surpass those of most of his predecessors. Perhaps because of the need for security they are announced without much prior warning and they give the appearance thereby of being more spontaneous. Yet their locations are carefully chosen to rally his support base.

The most interesting example of a readiness to continue with his past practice is his determination to go on using his Twitter account. His tweets are starting to be subjected to the new science of linguistic analysis, referred to in Chapter 7 in relation to Blair. This technique is described fully by an international expert, Professor Peter Garrard, in an essay in a book he helped edit, *The Intoxication of Power: Interdisciplinary Insights*.[404] In it he reports on his analysis of words spoken in transcripts from the Official Report of proceedings in the House of Commons during Question and Answer sessions of three Prime Ministers: Margaret Thatcher, John Major and Tony Blair. To no one's surprise Major showed no hubristic features, Thatcher was hubristic and Blair manifestly hubristic. That technique Garrard is now using to understand hubristic and non-hubristic leadership in terms of multiple influences and indicators and Trump will be part of that study. This may give some guide as to whether Trump is becoming intoxicated

---

404 Ed. Peter Garrard and Graham Robinson, *The Intoxication of Power: Interdisciplinary Insights* (Palgrave Macmillan, 2016).

with power acquired as President, a key feature of hubris syndrome.

A fascinating account is already available covering Trump tweets from 4 May 2009, when he started, to 4 March 2017 written by Peter Oborne, the British political journalist in *How Trump Thinks*.[405] The early years are ones where Trump is developing his style, he is building up followers and not very partisan politically. He is pleasant about Bill and Hillary Clinton and even Barack Obama. Gradually this changes; he ceases to be a Democrat voter and changes his registration to independent on 27 December 2011. Then on 16 June 2015 he declares as a Republican candidate after supporting Romney as the Republican candidate in 2012. There is after 2012 a very definite, no doubt calculated, progressive change in using a far tougher and emotional language about Hillary Clinton. Again one might expect on past precedent that personal aggressive language would ease down when someone becomes President but with Trump it appears to be increasing. This may be a reflection of the strained circumstances arising from the appointment by the Deputy Attorney General Rod Rosenstein, not Trump's own appointed Attorney General, of Robert Mueller as Special Counsel to 'ensure a full and thorough investigation of the Russian government's efforts to interfere in the 2016 presidential election.' Trump never ceases to reiterate there was no collusion. The legitimacy and authority of Mueller's appointment was challenged but his report eventually was a disappointment to those who wanted to use it for impeachment.

On 13 April 2018 Trump issued two tweets, not unreasonably called 'tirades' about the former FBI Director, James Comey calling him a 'slime ball'.

---

405 Peter Oborne & Tom Roberts, *How Trump Thinks. His Tweets and the birth of a new political language* (Head of Zeus, UK 2017).

Donald J. Trump @realDonaldTrump Apr 13
James Comey is a proven LEAKER & LIAR. Virtually everyone
in Washington thought he should be fired for the terrible job he
did until he was, in fact, fired. He leaked CLASSIFIED
information, for which he should be prosecuted. He lied to
Congress under OATH. He is a weak and

Donald J. Trump @realDonaldTrump Apr 13
. . . untruthful slime ball who was, as time has proven, a terrible
Director of the FBI. His handling of the Crooked Hillary
Clinton case, and the events surrounding it, will go down as one
of the worst 'botch jobs' of history.
It was my great honor to fire James Comey!

This could be seen as an anomalous reaction to stress and a
growing intoxication from his position of power and of a gathering
hubris. Yet he made similar tweets before becoming President,
however the strain and stress to which he has been subjected
throughout his early period as President, have been of a very high
order right up to impeachment.

The conduct of Trump on Twitter in the campaign about which
I suspect many of his supporters would agree was indefensible when
he deliberately used vilification extending to a wife, not a cam-
paigner. Long before Senator Ted Cruz endorsed Donald Trump,
they spent months slinging insults with one of the worst from Trump
being: 'Be careful, Lyin' Ted, or I will spill the beans on your wife!'

Using as President language like 'slime ball' about any other
person is another form of vilification. He sees no incompatibility in
using such tweets and such words as President while upholding in
public ceremonies the dignity of the office of the presidency. His
words jar with many but they also chime with others. He wants his
presidency to mark this apparent contradiction; he has no intention
of losing touch with the frustrations, anger and feelings of those
people in the rust belt states who voted him into office against the

odds. Just as he developed his skills of communication in his long running TV appearances, so he has developed a new political language simpler and more direct for political rallies. Some claim this poverty of language is a sign of mental deterioration not deliberate wording. It could of course be both. The result is few in America can claim not to know where Trump stands on many issues.

Trump has also been prolific in writing between 1987 and 2012 nineteen books, mostly co-written, one of which is acknowledged as fiction called *Trump Tower* and claimed as the sexiest novel of the decade. He has as President now credited the book as having a sole author, Jeffrey Robinson.

Trump is an unashamed populist President, intent on bypassing the conventional media. What is of considerable concern is that part of his strategy which is to challenge what he calls 'fake news'. To some extent there is an intention that facts no longer matter. Trump himself is casual with the truth. His facts are often plain wrong on his tweets and in his spoken and written words. A danger of a second term is that it could create a lying culture across the US which would be devastating. This is what happened in the old Soviet Union and it is still present in the Russian Federation and in many of the new nations that emerged after the break up of the Soviet Union. A culture where many are 'strangers to the truth', where people lie without remorse or sanction is both damaging and destructive.

Other Presidents have used the 'bully pulpit' but Trump uses it not only in a different way but in a way that does not respect facts. Disobliging facts are rubbished or ignored. 'Trump news' is often a stream of consciousness, involving the misquoting of facts, the manipulating of evidence and playing on emotions. Yet it is foolish to ignore that behind this Trump technique is research, intelligence, marketing skills and expert use of all forms of social media.

To carry this complexity he needed and developed a team. It is not possible to read *Let Trump be Trump. The Inside Story to the Rise to the Presidency* [406]without realising what an effective campaign team he put in place and is assembling now amidst what to some appears as chaos to fight a second term he is sure he will win. His White House team as distinct from his election campaign team has had its ups and downs to put it mildly but there is a sense that that is in part deliberate. Trump wants controversy, thrives on it and is not himself a team player. He watches television news in the early evening as a boxer will watch videos of his fights in order to improve his performance. TV is 'meat and drink' to him. He does not touch alcohol because he wants to be in control of himself and events at all times.

The White House is also developing new ways of using TV. Destiny Pictures produced a short propaganda video with the White House logo in the right hand corner. It is described in some detail by Tony Patterson of the *New Yorker* to coincide with Trump flying to Singapore to meet the North Korean leader Kim Jong-un. Some will feel that nothing of substance emerges from watching the video, others will absorb from this four minutes an image of a President of the US grappling as no other President has done with formidable problems.

President Obama wisely warned Trump immediately after his election that North Korea was the coming issue. Trump took the advice and chose to lead on Korea. But from the start he has dealt with it in his own way. As Patterson describes it and I have seen it, 'stock footage finds the sun shining like a dime beyond the curve of a turning world. Is Trump inviting Kim to take command of Universal Pictures? Or join him as playing God? Does either of them know the difference?' He explains the midpoint in the fulcrum of the film 'the prospect of Kim failing to show leadership is symbolised by the use of a burning – celluloid effect as in Bergman's

---

406 Corey R. Lewandowski and David N. Bossie, *Let Trump be Trump. The Inside Story to the Rise to the Presidency* (Center Street, 2017).

"Persona" or "The Muppet Movie." The image disintegrates implying the destruction of North Korea.' The video ends with TV control rooms and a woman alone on a sofa watching TV.

When Trump began his approach to North Korea with flamboyant language it was met with very close to derision from the conventional news media and Korean experts, then when it seemed to make a little progress that started to be toned down and in the run up to the Singapore meeting pundit after pundit began to hedge their bets. The Korean problem appears defused but no concrete nuclear disarmament has taken place.

Trump has never liked the Washington diplomatic machine and was content to have the smaller State Department delivered by Rex Tillerson, the former head of Exxon and his first Secretary of State. Trump was in no hurry to appoint career ambassadors. He now appears happier with Mike Pompeo, initially his head of the CIA. Trump's choice of General Mattis as Defense Secretary was initially a success and Mattis appeared to be given considerable freedom to choose on what to spend extra defence money but he resigned. A big Trump success was his choice of representative at the UN, Nikki Haley who stepped down while still supporting Trump and is tipped as a future president. But in other parts of his Administration there have been serious failures and the appointment of John Bolton as National Security Adviser, ended in acrimony.

Trump is both creative and destructive; efficient and inefficient; thoughtful and unthinking; intemperate and cool headed. He intends to be a deal maker and a deal breaker. As with all such people, there will be many predictions about him that will turn out to be wrong, but some will be right. He relishes the 'one off' initiative as well as the 'off the wall' initiative. Trump makes frequent mention on Twitter of his book *The Art of the Deal*. The book itself sold over one million copies. On 7 July 2011 he quoted himself from the book, 'The best thing you can do is deal from strength, and leverage is the biggest strength you have.'

Much international diplomacy of the Trump Presidency involves leverage and is at different stages in development. NATO which, within days of his inauguration in January 2017, started as the most acute issue in Trump's relations with Europe was to many people's surprise and delight addressed convincingly by Mattis. Trump was put under immediate pressure from Europe, to fully sign up to the automatic commitment in Article 5 of the NATO Charter to come to defend another member state if attacked. His early Washington meeting with the UK Prime Minister Theresa May was when this troubling question was meant to have been answered: Trump would honour the wording of Article 5 in full. Yet in preparing for the July 2018 NATO annual summit, the question returned with Trump saying 'NATO is as bad as NAFTA. It's much too costly for the US.' Trump has since renegotiated NAFTA and is expected to be approved by Congress in 2020.

Why did the outgoing President of Mexico and Trudeau the Prime Minister of Canada reach an agreement in a short time? This is important for the UK who might like to link to NAFTA at some stage.

Trump cleverly started to negotiate first with Mexico and made unexpected progress and then used the time pressure of when its President would lose his authority to bind his successor to tell Canada 'sign up or I do a bilateral deal with Mexico'. In using this tactic he was belittling Canada. But he was not the first President to do this.

President Johnson's famed angry outbursts reached a high point over the Prime Minister of Canada Lester B. Pearson, a winner of the Nobel Peace Prize. Pearson while visiting Philadelphia called for a suspension of the bombing in Vietnam. Next day he was unwise enough to visit Johnson at Camp David where, according to Professor Robert Bothwell of the University of Toronto, the President was so enraged that he lifted Pearson up by the lapels of his coat and bellowed into his face 'You pissed on my rug.' That was in the days when this sort of behaviour did not instantly become public. President Trump's relations with Prime Minister Justin Trudeau have been somewhat abrasive. Trump preferred open abuse while invoking steel and aluminium sanctions against Canada and claiming as his justification of all things national security. After what Trump called in public 'testy' relations over the NAFTA renegotiation Trudeau's low key reply contained a warning that Canada would use the 16 years in the new agreement 'to adjust, to diversify our trade beyond the United States'.

A perceptive article in the *Financial Times* on 1 October 2018, 'Time to grapple with global trade' holds many truths. Rana Foroohar writes 'Donald Trump can embed a single, visceral truth in a welter of falsehoods. So it is with the US President's anti free trade stance.' Many of us know that like other aspects of the market economy the global free trade system needs reform. The large exporting companies dominate and make record profits while wages mark time. Cheating abounds. Intellectual property is stolen. Corporate concentration increases. Trump says and acts on trade where the world anguishes. At least he is stirring the pot and forcing a response.

Whatever Trump's real attitude to Russia he never stopped Mattis completing NATO's agreed response. That is the claim of a previously ardent and persistent critic of NATO's response, Edward Lucas, writing in *The Times* on 18 May 2018.[407] On the Russian Federation's annexation of Crimea, military re-equipment programme and provocative deployments Lucas clearly wrote, 'we can rest assured' and asserted that America has boosted with strong Congressional support its contribution to Europe's security. They had been 'splurging money in Eastern Europe and sending

---

407 Edward Lucas, 'Trump makes western alliance great again', *The Times*, 18 May 2018.

back the heavy armour that the Obama Administration withdrew'. In April the 'Pentagon announced the restoration of the Second Fleet, the US navy's North Atlantic command.' Lucas further claimed that NATO was now well positioned to focus on its core mission: territorial defence. 'The multinational tripwire forces recently deployed in the Baltic Republics and Poland have transformed the security of these frontline states, while the danger of a Russian sneak attack has receded. We are all safer as a result . . . The US have also beefed up its military ties with non-NATO Sweden and Finland.'

Trump's problem – and it is not just his, but should be ours as well – is that to achieve this welcome NATO response the US paid for most of it. Trump was vocal in his condemnation of the inadequacy of the EU nations' defence contribution. Yet Trump left the 2017 NATO summit typically claiming victory with promises of extra money from Europe for NATO's budget over the next few years. But those promises are not being fulfilled. Thereby lies danger.

Trump will continue to rough up recalcitrant European nations on defence and many Americans think he should. The UK does not have to add much in public to Trump's demands for more European countries to spend more. Boris Johnson's government crucially has been ready to lead by example and said it will be increasing defence spending from just over 2% of GDP to 2.5% immediately and 3% may be necessary. To do this is the only way of showing American voters that some Europeans in NATO are more than paying their way. There has been no formal commitment announced in Parliament and Secretary of State Ben Wallace has only talked about reviewing procurement and "cutting their cloth to fit ambition." The UK's National Security Council mechanism which started in 2010 is looking anew at how Defence and Overseas Development Budgets can be linked and it means changing the OECD wording on allocation of resources criteria. The need is to link the eradication of poverty with the maintenance of security and stability in the poorest countries. If this is done the UK will legitimately increase its level of defence spending. Germany can also divert non-defence budget resources to building up the new NATO Joint Support and Enabling Command in Germany at Ulm. At the same time the US and UK must not abandon its longstanding criticisms of a separate EU defence command and control.

In giving a far greater priority to China's trade abuses than any of his predecessors, President Trump made a good early decision. He invited President Xi to Florida after his inauguration and his daughter Ivanka's small children singing a welcoming song in Chinese went around the world on social media. The meeting involving Trump and Kim Jong-un in Singapore wisely has Secretary of State Pompeo doing the follow up diplomacy. A decision prompted, in part, by the earlier off-message comparison of North Korea with Libya by John Bolton.

As yet President Trump has held back from a joint initiative with President Putin on the Middle East. It should become the region Trump and Putin focus on. Trump can help peace in Eastern Europe over Ukraine but this should be done in close association with Germany, France, Poland and the UK. Putin can help in the Middle East, for Putin personally is in constant touch with all the parties including Iran and Israel. The American groundwork for a Middle East settlement, in particular over Gaza and the West Bank, started by Trump's son-in-law, was published in January 2020.

Trump chose deliberately to give it a high profile at the White House with Netanyahu standing beside him. At this stage the world will see this as predominantly a further step to bind the evangelical vote for Trump into continued support through to the Presidential election in November. The main value of the report, however, is that it is the first time that any US initiative can claim to have the understanding of Arab opinion in the Middle East. It was noteworthy that Ambassadors from Oman, Bahrain and the UAE were present when Trump spoke of "his vision". In Jordan, Egypt and Saudi Arabia there is a sense of involvement in finding a solution which has not been present hitherto.

Of course, much will be made of the hostility of the Palestinians. Previously Hamas anger and the Palestinian frustration over Trump's decision to move the US Embassy to Jerusalem was contained. Trump's critics inside the US are tending to fall along Republican/ Democrat lines but it is an inescapable fact that the three previous US Presidents had all claimed during their election campaigns they would move the embassy to Jerusalem; then having been elected they conveniently forgot their promise. It was typical and tactical that Trump undertook the move of the embassy early. He was never going to accept that a US Embassy in Jerusalem should be used as a negotiating lever but it is an open question what sort of Palestinian presence should be in old Jerusalem.

It has surprised some that Trump has not chosen to encourage a one state solution. This is a different and new Middle East diplomatic approach and much of it is supported by the Saudis and there is an ongoing dialogue about Israel with Egypt. Nevertheless there will be defiant voices amongst the Palestinians who will not read carefully page after page of detailed wise economic planning for where they live backed as never before by billions of dollars. What is necessary now is for this document to become part of a wider Middle East negotiation. At that stage Russia and Syria will be wanting recognition from the international community for President Assad. That will not be conceivable unless Syria accepts that the Golan Heights will continue part of Israel. The Lebanon too will be wanting out of a Middle East settlement money and stability, neither of which will be remotely possible if Iran continues, through missiles and military personnel, to force, confrontation with Israel.

One of the most important aspects of the Trump plan and a surprise is that Israel should freeze settlement construction for four years during which they will be expected to increase the amount of territory under direct Palestinian control. The US proposed map will not survive an overall Middle East settlement in every respect. But it is very likely to focus minds and provide an essential framework for discussion, debate and perhaps even an agreement. An aspect that might emerge from a Middle East Conference would be to give the people of Gaza the opportunity to expand into leased territories by Egypt. The tunnel proposed for Gaza to the West bank will not, of itself, solve its present tight boundaries.

The Camp David Agreement made in 1978 ensured Egypt had every hectare of Sinai returned by Begin. It was hoped before Sadat was assassinated that there might be some Egyptian flexibility to help ease the overcrowding in Gaza, but this might now come with Saudi economic development with Jordan, Egypt and Israel helping to beat ISIS in Sinai.

How to bring all this together is difficult and Trump must involve himself in it with Putin. Establishing diplomatic linkage between Ukraine and Crimean discussions and those in the Middle East makes sense, if for no other reason than it widens the canvas of giving ground and taking ground figuratively and practically. It is not enough to say Putin can help Trump in the Middle East and Trump can help Putin over Crimea and Ukraine. The problems are too complex for that but linkage has a place in many negotiations.

In both the UK referendum and the US presidential election in 2016 – the word 'populism' emerged as the elite's explanation for their defeat. This was despite, or perhaps because of, there being no widespread agreement as to what the actual word populism meant.[408] A cynic might well define populism as that which the elite deplores.

An interesting article in the international edition of *The New York Times* on 16 July 2018 by Roger Cohen describes the word

408 Richard Hofstadter, 'Everyone is Talking About Populism But No One Can Define It.' In Isaiah Berlin et al ., 'To define Populism' *Government and Opposition*, 3,2, April 1968 pp 137-180.

populism as 'freighted with contempt. . . . a term for everything urban elites won't make the effort to understand.'[409] He acknowledges as touched on in Chapter 1 of this book the history of populism going back into the late nineteenth century in the US when it signified 'a belief in the wisdom of the common people'. Cohen argues, rightly I believe, that Trump supporters have 'not been seduced by populism'. They are not 'populists'. They have few illusions about the President. They think he is a loose cannon, needy, narcissistic, erratic. They like the way he is an outsider and 'tells it like it is'.

In the US presidential election in November 2016, Donald Trump, to the surprise of almost all commentators and opinion pollsters, beat Hillary Clinton in the electoral college vote by 304 to 227 with Trump's success stemming from winning the so-called rust belt states. Yet Clinton won the popular vote by nearly 2.9 million, and questions about the electoral college began to be asked. Trump had tweeted his dislike of the electoral college voting system when Romney was beaten by Obama perhaps mistakenly because he thought Romney had won the popular vote. Unsurprisingly, as the victor, he now supports the electoral college unlike his role model President Jackson.

Another perhaps too cynical an explanation for why the word populism began to be used extensively as a pejorative term by the press and TV commentators after Trump's victory was those same commentators were part of the defeated elite on both sides of the Atlantic. Thinking that to leave the EU was inconceivable or totally convinced that Hillary Clinton would win the election these commentators missed or excluded a large body of evidence, more sociological rather than psephological, which was there in the small print, indicating that a Trump win and Brexit victory were possible or even likely.

---

409 Roger Cohen, 'Think twice before you cry 'populist'', *The New York Times*, 16 July 2018.

In the UK, David Goodhart in *The Road To Somewhere. The Populist Revolt And The Future Of Politics*, provides much useful political and social background information about the voters' reasons for choosing Brexit.[410] In the US, an eminent sociologist, Arlie Russell Hochschild in her book *Strangers In Their Own Land. Anger And Mourning On The American Right* moved out of her liberal academic enclave at Berkeley and travelled widely to explore person by person the emotional draw of the Tea Party. That organisation for many on the right wing of politics had indirectly prepared the way for Donald Trump's electoral appeal.[411] Another preparatory move was when Senator McCain chose Sarah Palin from Alaska as his running mate in his presidential campaign against Barack Obama. A decision he later regretted.

It has been a travesty of journalism on both sides of the Atlantic that so little of this in-depth explanation of voting patterns and intentions emerged at the time in papers like the *Financial Times*, *Guardian* and *New York Times*. There was an almost wilful neglect by serious analysts to try to explain why Senator Bernie Sanders had started to poll so well amongst voters in the Democratic primaries. They also failed to examine with objective reporting grassroot opinion of Trump's appeal. I was reminded how my old journalist friends, David Watt of the *Financial Times,* Johnny Apple of the *New York Times* and Peter Jenkins of the *Guardian,* all of whom have sadly died, used their long contact lists of people and personal visits away from London and Washington to detect shifts in opinion. Polling reigned supreme but like Humpty Dumpty it has had a great fall. The sophisticated attitude and awareness surveys with opinions recorded on a scale of +5 to -5 were abandoned in the 1970s because they were too expensive. It will be a long time before

---

410 David Goodhart, *The Road To Somewhere. The Populist Revolt And The Future Of Politics* (C. Hurst & Co Publishers, paperback Penguin, 2017).

411 Russell Hochschild, *Strangers In Their Own Land. Anger And Mourning On The American Right* (The New Press, 2016).

opinion polls on voting intentions become as respected again. Perhaps they never will.

In America the rust belt revolt is underpinned by many fascinating statistics. Whereas 33% of Americans described themselves as 'working class' in 2000, by 2015 that had risen to 48%. So the pool of voters to which both Trump and Senator Bernie Sanders, the Democrat challenger to Hillary Clinton for the presidential nomination, were paying special attention was an expanding one.[412] While those earning less than $50,000 split 52% to 42% towards the Democrats, those who switched from Democrats to Republicans were by a large majority from the middle and lower income groups. The Resolution Foundation reported that 16% of voters earning less than $30,000 switched to Trump. So it was not so surprising that mid-western states like Michigan and Wisconsin went for Trump rather than Hillary Clinton. There may have been an anti-incumbent, President Obama, factor as well as an anti-Hillary Clinton factor and this may be why Trump frequently attacked Obama in his tweets right up to election night. Trump drew attention in both speeches and tweets to Obama's Wall Street personal links as well as money links. He persisted outrageously in his charge, against all the evidence, that Obama was disqualified from being President because he had been born outside the US. This was a racist 'dog whistle' issue well established before Trump took it up. Presumably Trump had some polling evidence that this issue was a factor in determining voting intentions. In 2012 Obama took 39% of the white vote. Hillary Clinton in 2016 only took 37%. Trump polled 8% of blacks, 29% of Hispanics and 29% of Asians.

Immigration in the US hitherto had not appeared to be as big an issue as some might expect given American history. One reason is because high immigration levels from Europe and elsewhere to

412 Frank Newport, 'Fewer Americans Identify as Middle Class in Recent Years', *Gallup*, 28 April 2015.

the US fell away for nearly 50 years from around 1922-1968 and in 1970, 84% of Americans were white and only 4% were foreign born. The present surge of immigration has meant, however, that the non-Hispanic white population has fallen to 62%.

When all these statistics are absorbed, Trump's vote is easier to understand. Behind them was the projection of Trump as an unashamedly rich leader, who with no embarrassment made it clear at every stage of the campaign that he paid his way, in marked contrast to others; travelled in his own plane, played golf on his own courses. This was all deliberate to reinforce the message that Trump was a 'one off' man who could not be bought. What was conveniently ignored was his past financial dependence on others and the size of his debts. He made four trips to the bankruptcy courts. Bondholders had to accept more than $1.5 billion losses. One of the features of the special prosecutor is that he is opening up this whole area. (Ref. Craig Unger, *House of Trump, House of Putin: The Untold Story of Donald Trump and the Russian Mafia* London: Random House, 2018, pp 91-2.)

Trump also played to journalists' and TV broadcasters' fascination with any powerful hubristic, sometimes contemptuous, and often impetuous, narcissistic leadership style, which he contrasted with Hillary Clinton's weakness and unspecified health issue. This image of the great charismatic leader is not new and other US Presidents have portrayed it. Also other Presidents have gained from having greater access to money than their opponents. But this was not true for Trump. Hillary Clinton raised substantially more campaign funds. Hence Trump's focus on personal shocking TV news headlines to counter her spending on advertising.

It is a depressing fact that a consistent, evidence-based, thoughtful, concerned leadership style may not be appreciated today by as many voters or shareholders as hitherto. The media sense this and push the charismatic model for all its flaws. Democratic politics worldwide cannot afford to let this manipulation of good leadership qualities go unchallenged. In the 2017 presidential election campaign it was true, but not widely known or acknowledged by the electorate, that Trump had spent time on the edges of bankruptcy. Even among those who knew, some saw his turnaround in fortunes as a positive. His reputation as a businessman had been artificially boosted by his long TV exposure on the successful 'Apprentice' programme. By contrast, his less successful business record had either been dismissed or not fully focussed on. Why did Trump escape much of this personal criticism? The answers are complex but they reflect a troubling neglect of temperament, character and trustworthiness by voters' and shareholders' greater regard for business leaders than political leaders.

Dollars, euros, yuan and pounds are spent in very large quantities on financial risk assessment, on building financial models, employing management consultants and attending business schools; but research on human risk and behaviour which contributed so much to the global financial crisis of 2008 is an orphan by comparison. The reason, in part is that our leaders in many walks of life are afraid of their character or behaviour in their business life being examined and so they unconsciously or consciously starve the behavioural sciences of sufficient financial resources. Without many of these wider issues being addressed, researched and lessons learned from the Trump presidency, particularly the growth of at least two truths living alongside each other, that culture will become a way of life challenging objective truth. There will be a greater acceptance even than at present, of public figures presenting known lies or covering up acknowledged facts and that is a very serious development not just for the US but for the world.

The US hitherto has appeared to have a strong constitution. But many question whether its legal checks and balances are operating effectively when bipartisan politics break down. Trump had in the Kavanaugh hearings real opposition yet his nominee was approved by the Senate regardless of merit. Added to his earlier appointment there is now a shift in the balance of opinion in the Supreme Court. Elsewhere too, on controversial issues like abortion and the environment, and what are federal or state matters. Supreme Court Justices are elected for life and approximately one third of members of the Senate are elected every two years so it's not possible to predict when the balance will shift back.

The implications for the Supreme Court will last longer than mid-term election results and it has the potential to bind the Republican Party closer to Trump and to some extent he to them. This might be a stabilising factor for the Republican Party. A contrary view came from a *Financial Times* editorial on 28 July 2018. 'The steady debasement of a grand old party makes the point' adding 'Trump's capture of the Republicans is a problem for the world.'

Internationally there has been some agreement between the US, UK, France, Russia and China on many of the big issues. The UN Security Council found real common ground in the 1980s and 1990s. More recently this has eroded. The consensus those countries forged on how to deal with the Iranian's nuclear programme Trump has challenged in a fundamental way using the US practice of extraterritorial legislation to enforce sanctions. The best way on Iran is for Trump and Putin to work together on a plan for the Middle East, and for Putin to insist with China on keeping the Iran nuclear issues as a legitimate factor to be discussed in any wider Middle East settlement. Trump and Israel can oppose Iran, but Russia, China, France, Germany and the UK should hold firm against allowing any Sunni-Shia war to unfold. Yet they must also insist that the undoubted serious problems that Iran's military are creating in the Middle East are addressed in the round. Not just Iran's military presence in Syria and Lebanon but their importance in exacerbating the Shia-Sunni divide which Iran is doing in Iraq and in Yemen and elsewhere.

President Trump hopes to readmit President Putin and the Russian Federation before the G7 meeting in America in 2020. Building on any common ground while not hiding differences and learning from the past is possible despite deep differences on domestic political matters in Russia. The UK has not followed Trump in opting out of the UN Commission for Human Rights despite the problems that still persist with this organisation. There has been a tendency to mix everything up – domestic and international human rights differences and this is a highly questionable route to travel. Sometimes human rights abuses have to be challenged and there is no escape from international and domestic confrontation.

Myanmar, a predominantly Buddhist country supported by China is facing the charge of genocide by the military of the Rohingya Muslims. China too is repressing Muslim Uighurs in Xinjiang Province.

Human rights are of universal concern. But human behaviour will always have limits, set by different cultures and religions, to what can be ruled by international standards. We have erred in this regard in the US and EU in relation to Russia and China. Our western democracies will not be replicated in those two countries any time soon. To keep up the pretence that they will is unwise.

The discipline of not getting involved in other countries' elections, whether they be friends or foes, has served the western democracies well. But there have been two fairly recent examples where this discipline has not been adhered to. In 1996 Clinton, Major, Chirac and Schroder overtly supported the incumbent President Yeltsin against the Communist challenger, Gennady Zyuganov. We never criticised 'Loans for Votes' and the buying of that election. That was a mistake and has served retrospectively in Russian minds, particularly Putin's, to legitimise interference with other countries elections. He claims some evidence of US interference in his election in 2012 and the role of Hillary Clinton as Secretary of State. What the western democracies can do is to influence inward investment so that it helps build up the rule of law in the Russian economy. The Western democracies did nowhere near enough to support and sustain the rule of law during Gorbachev's and Yeltsin's time.

What did happen in the US presidential election between Donald Trump and Hillary Clinton as far as Russian interference goes is very important to nail down, expose and prevent any reoccurrence in the UK. Ben Rhodes, who from 2009 to 2017 was Obama's deputy National Security Adviser and saw many aspects of US-Russian relations, as well as bearing overall responsibility for input into Obama's speeches writes perceptively:

> To understand what ended up happening in the 2016 presidential election, you have to understand this: When protests toppled the Ukrainian government, Putin interpreted that as the United States coming into Russia, akin to an act of war; when he launched his counterattack – annexing Crimea, creeping into eastern Ukraine – he weaponised information and showed a willingness to lie, using traditional media like television, and new media platforms like Twitter, Facebook, and YouTube, to spread disinformation into open, Western societies like a virus. Eventually, the Russians would come into America, as they believed we'd gone into Ukraine. They took advantage of the fact that we were worn down by decades of political polarization and the balkanization of our media. America's antibodies to the sickness of Russian disinformation were weak, if they were there at all.[413]

On NATO, both President Obama and President Trump are totally right to express publicly their concern that many European

---

413 Ben Rhodes, *The World As It Is. Inside the Obama White House* (Bodley Head, 2018) pp. 383-386.

countries are not contributing enough money into the funding of NATO. Trump is not out on a limb on this issue. It was President Obama who first used the term 'free riders' when in an interview for the *Atlantic* magazine, he criticised us in Europe for 'freeloading' on the NATO defence budget. It is clearly not tolerable for the US voters that they should pay 73% or 75% of the NATO budget. That position must be corrected and soon. In the short term the UK is correct to move to 2.5% of GDP but it may need 3% to avoid announcements of defence cutbacks because current commitments are not being properly funded. It was President Obama who told Prime Minister Cameron straight that if you want the 'special relationship' to remain intact 'you have to pay your fair share.'

The U.S. Defense Department has for decades rightly been hostile to EU 'common defence' and to 'autonomous defence' in the EU because of its duplication and its pretension but also the danger of having two planning centres for defence in Europe, one in the EU and one in NATO.

NATO is not dysfunctional but it is underfunded. It will benefit from a committed British voice no longer in the EU but it must not be one hovering between NATO and EU defence after we leave the EU. NATO must become the core UK international organisation and the UK must be seen to strengthen NATO and to help improve the Alliance's capability to act cooperatively to preserve peace and security worldwide. That means increasing the UK's defence budget some claim at present 2.2% of GDP immediately to 2.5% and as soon as possible to 3% over the next few years.

The former Secretary of Defense, Robert Gates, who served George Bush and Barack Obama records in his book *Duty* that the then Secretary General of NATO, Anders Rasmussen 'had shared with him his concern that Germany would not agree to any NATO action on Libya, mainly because it wanted the European Union to be in the lead.' We should note General David Richards, the then UK Chief of Defence Staff, in his autobiography has claimed that he 'insisted in the National Security Council that any military operation in Libya had to be a NATO operation' and that President Sarkozy was advocating an essentially Anglo-French operation. Richards writes, 'we could not have done it with the French alone'. As it turned out the handling of the aftermath in Libya was a failure which President Obama admits more openly than David Cameron has done. Robert Gates publicly said, 'while every alliance member voted for the Libya mission, less than half have participated at all and fewer than a third have been willing to participate in the strike mission . . . The military capabilities simply aren't there . . . I've worried openly about NATO turning into a two-tiered alliance: between members who specialise in 'soft' humanitarian development, peacekeeping and talking tasks, and those conducting the 'hard' combat missions . . . This is no longer a hypothetical worry. We are there today.' That was said in 2011. The situation nine years later over EU countries' attitudes to fighting capabilities is far worse in 2020 and President Trump is right to say so.

Chapter 12

Boris Johnson's Populism

So far the policy elite in Washington, London, Paris and Berlin are having great difficulty in embracing any new Trump approaches on trade, defence spending and foreign policy, particularly on China.

In 2018 Aeron Davis wrote *Reckless Opportunists. Elites at the end of the Establishment.*[414] In the Introduction he writes,

> 'The great transformations of the 1980s onwards have not only upended societies, they have reshaped leadership itself. Globalisation, turbo capitalism, financial engineering and new communication technologies have destabilised and disorientated elites as much as anyone else. This has produced a new generation of leaders who are struggling to maintain some form of command. Regardless of intent, they lack expertise and vision. They are precarious, rootless and increasingly self-serving. Although many have done exceptionally well in material terms, their ability to shape events and influence perceptions is in steep decline. And they have yet to come to terms with the economic and political gulf between themselves and the rest of the population.'

Aeron Davis is unashamedly writing about an alternative view when he states, 'the modern generation of leaders are neither expert

---

414 Aeron Davis, *Reckless Opportunists. Elites at the end of the Establishment* (Manchester University Press, 2018)

nor visionary; nor are they socially conservative or in control. Too many are just reckless opportunists making the best of what they have amid the chaos they have helped to create.'[415]

The author claims 'The ways elites are selected, constrained and incentivised everywhere has meant we are producing a generation of self-serving, insecure and less competent leaders. They have the abilities and skills sets needed (*to become*) good leaders but not those required (*to be*) good leaders. They are always on the move and can't afford to invest meaningfully in personal relations or in gaining expert knowledge.'[416] This impoverishment of political leadership must change. To have lasting appeal it needs to be built on strong foundations, where people acquire political skills based on prior time serving as junior government under secretaries of state and learning government skills. This problem is seen on both sides of the Atlantic. George W. Bush and Tony Blair recorded both the highest and lowest post-war approval ratings for leaders in the US and UK respectively. President Macron after nearly a year and a half in office, suffered a massive fall in public opinion. In part because like Napoleon Bonaparte he has acquired hubris syndrome.

In 2013 Prime Minister Cameron called for a referendum after the next election while in coalition with the Liberal Democrats from 2010–2015, who were totally opposed. Cameron acted to spike the guns of the UK Independence Party. He was right about the threat; UKIP won the 2014 European elections under proportional voting. Yet Cameron's referendum commitment delivered him a working majority in the 2015 General Election, under 'first past the post' voting. But by the time of the referendum in 2016 there had been no official consideration on ways of handling a result which would involve leaving the EU. Just before the referendum Cameron in an offhand comment in the House of Commons

415 Ibid, Aeron Davis, p. 3.
416 Ibid, Aeron Davis, p. 4.

advocated Article 50 of the EU Treaty as the mechanism for leaving without any study of the alternative option of using the procedures of the Vienna Convention. The fact that the then Cabinet Secretary tried to abandon the normal 'purdah' period for civil servants for the period of the referendum with no apparent Cabinet sanction was a serious erosion of Cabinet responsibility. Fortunately it was rejected by Parliament. There are signs that Cameron's concept of Cabinet government, fragile at the best of times, had ceased to exist by 2016. Having promised to continue as Prime Minister, regardless of the result, Cameron resigned immediately on losing the referendum when 16,141,241 voted to remain and 17,410,742 voted to leave. A new Conservative leader Theresa May had to try to implement the will of the people. She failed and a three year deadlock in the House of Commons fed public cynicism for so-called democratic politics. The last straw was parliament rejecting its own referendum.

In July 2018 Larry Elliott of the *Guardian* pointed out another interesting grassroots change. In 1966 when England won the World Cup football championship fans were waving the Union Jack flag. Gradually this changed to fans waving the flag of St George but in the case of those English fans who travelled to Russia in 2018 some waved the flag of St George with the names of towns and cities of northern England on them. It was a grassroots expression and a post-referendum assertion that their voice from now on was going to be heard in London and in other countries.

What follows are some of the uncomfortable facts around, first, Brexit and then the election of Trump which may give some leads to a better reporting and general voter understanding of attitudes, particularly outside London and Washington. Also why Trump's criticism of 'fake news' landed on fertile ground. This was not a sudden change, the deep suspicion of politicians, and of the 'blob' as some people call the governance of a self-regarding elite, as distinct from genuine experts, has been coming for some time.

On Brexit there was a fundamental divide in the UK in that support for Remain was highest at 57% in the top social classes (ABs) dropping to 36% in the lowest (C2, D, Es) with 49% in the middle C1s).[417]

It was estimated that 3 million people who did not vote in the 2015 General Election voted in the EU referendum. This much higher turnout of 72% contained a clear majority of Leave voters.[418]

The UK was geographically divided. London, Scotland and Northern Ireland voted Remain; the North East, West Midlands, Wales and the West Country voted Leave.

I was born in Plymouth and represented the city for longer than any other MP in its history. In the referendum Plymouth voted 60:40 for Leave. It baffles many people who live in London still why there were so many Leave voters. Provincial England is not opposed to a more global economy but they want a fair share of that economy. They felt the austerity-driven policies were not being fairly applied. That outside the EU protected economy the wider global economy offered opportunities. Leave voters were and still are influenced by many factors that were not strictly related to their own standard of living. The potency of the Leave campaign theme of 'take back control' of their own country affected many issues.

On the sensitive issue of immigration, it was the fact that the EU refused David Cameron's negotiating request to change the so-called founding principle of the EU about the right to free movement of labour that was a significant vote changer in early 2016. Free movement is a federalist project as is the single currency. Wiser EU leaders might have listened to the argument that it would make more sense to restrict freedom of movement to those countries that were or wanted to be in the Eurozone. People had and still have very different

---

417 Source: You Gov 2016/06/27.
418 Matt Singh, 'The 2.8 Million Non-Voters Who Delivered Brexit', *Bloomberg*, 4 July 2016.

views on what levels of immigration are acceptable and to whom immigration controls should apply for those wanting to come to the UK. It was the automatic right of people from the other 27 EU countries to enter and stay in the UK which to many defied all logic, particularly since the UK was not part of the Eurozone.

The ability to take more control of the UK once outside the EU had an appeal to people who were liberal in their attitude as well as those who were restrictive in their attitude to immigration. There was a difference in relation to age and a difference on where people lived on both this and on some other issues, but the overriding wish to have more of a say and influence was strong.

After Brexit wise politicians will channel these feelings into refining the UK's devolutionary settlement. I have written in some detail on how we could develop a Federal UK Council similar to that which was designed for the German constitution around their Lander system.[419] This should happen whatever we might do to replace our outmoded, undemocratic House of Lords. There is also a strong case for a UK Bill of Rights to justify the wise decision of the UK Parliament not to continue with the EU's own human rights legislation. However the UK should remain under the jurisdiction of the Human Rights Court in Strasbourg which the UK helped found in 1947 after the Second World War, at least until we have our own Human Rights Act.

The other determining factor in the referendum was social attitudes. The British Social Attitudes Surveys have charted since 1983, when they began, a definite decline in homophobic, male chauvinistic and racist attitudes in the UK and far more concern on environmental issues. Much of this began in the UK Parliament when I became an MP in 1966. It has been a fundamental mistake however to assume that these attitudinal shifts mean automatic

---

419 'Lord Owen sets out the case for Federal UK Council' http://www.lorddavidowen.co.uk/category/domestic/other-domestic/

endorsement of post-modernist views that the nation state has had its day. Post-modernism is a very slippery, somewhat trendy, concept and in the UK it is still clearly a minority view and that should be one of the abiding lessons of the Brexit referendum. The British people believe they are part of a nation and wish to remain a nation.

On entering No 10 as Prime Minister, without a contested election, Theresa May continued with Cameron's lofty approach to the Cabinet but without a close relationship with the Chancellor of the Exchequer. She promised simply and with constant repetition that 'Brexit means Brexit' and ruled out an early election. Yet only a year later on seeing a poll lead of 20% and more opening up, opportunism reared its head and she called an election and the five year fixed term Parliament threshold meant Jeremy Corbyn had to agree, which he did relishing the chance to prove the opinion polls wrong. The electorate, sensing they had been grossly misled, not unreasonably deprived May of a workable majority and the Conservatives had no option but to form an alliance with the Northern Ireland Democratic Unionist Party, DUP. The Labour Party's manifesto was a coherent document and surprisingly strong on defence. The huge volatility in public regard for politicians was apparent during the six weeks' election period and Theresa May dropped 44% in her approval ratings.[420]

The way of leaving the EU was disputed in Parliament for three years and MPs went back on their word to honour the referendum result. I argued that the UK, instead of exiting under Article 50 without an agreement should exit the EU by simply asserting our right to become a non-EU contracting party to the European Economic Area Agreement (EEAA) for a transition period, and then when a Free Trade Agreement had been reached leave the EEAA by giving 12 months' notice.

What is popular is not the same as what is populist, but the

---

420 Ibid, Aeron Davis, p. 53

difference can be a fine one. No democrat should sneer at what is popular. A particular policy may be wrong, it may need to be revised or rejected but if it is popular it cannot be ignored in a thriving democracy. When it is ignored or even not subject to discussion or debate, then comes disillusionment. Populism can be a movement of opinion before its time that sometimes breaks through from a minority to a majority opinion. There are very few well-regarded democratic political leaders who have not at some stage in their careers supported populist causes, sometimes to their advantage, but also at times to their disadvantage. Theodore and Franklin Roosevelt and Bill Clinton as US Presidents were populists in many of their policies. In the UK, Lloyd George was a populist and in some ways so was Churchill. Margaret Thatcher was a populist in many of her stances and was rewarded by the electorate. Tony Blair had many characteristics of a populist. Boris Johnson is a populist to his core. This was apparent well before he became an elected politician. He was a populist as a journalist despite, or perhaps because of, writing predominantly for the *Daily Telegraph* and the *Spectator*. He chose to use wit and words which made his book on Churchill easy to read.

The current mood in Europe amongst intellectuals is to be dismissive of all forms of populism (see p. 41) but that is absurd. Populism can be reasonable, it is not always damaging. It can be racist or fascist in government and then there must be zero tolerance. Populism can also be mendacious in that its justification and implementation are based on a lie or lies. When it is, it is imperative that the lies are challenged and its proponents held to account. Yet not all populism demands brazen lies as Catherine Fieschi, Director of the new Global Policy Institute at Queen Mary University of London, argues in an article, 'Art of telling whoppers'.[421] She

---

421 Catherine Fieschi, 'Art of telling whoppers', *The World Today*, October & November 2019.

compares Matteo Salvini, the Italian populist, with Boris Johnson and reminds us that "one of the lessons that Machiavelli enjoins on the Prince is that he might lie occasionally, but he should not lie routinely." She claims, "Johnson's trademark is what one might call the lie of assertive approximation." Also, in relation to Salvini "telling blatant lies is the currency of Italian politics." Berlusconi, as Prime Minister, was in many ways a prelude to Trump as President.

In his important book *The Myth of the Strong Leader*, Archie Brown writes of a much-needed check on the merits of charismatic leadership.[422] It ends: 'Leaders who believe they have a personal right to dominate decision-making in many different areas of policy, and who attempt to exercise such a prerogative, do a disservice both to good governance and to democracy. They deserve not followers, but critics.'[423]

The opportunity to exercise decisive and sometimes controversial leadership is one of the strengths of representative democracy and there is undoubtedly a need from time to time for boldness and even instinctive leadership but these should be the exception not the rule. Under the UK parliamentary system representative democracy demands that leaders' decision-making be open to democratic scrutiny in full Cabinet in times of peace and in times of war in a smaller War Cabinet. The most alarming circumstance of the first part of the 21st Century is the way British Prime Ministers, starting with Tony Blair in 2001, have begun to assume some of the powers of a President, particularly those of a US President. There is now a political imperative to challenge and curtail the imperial presidency that has arrived in British politics from the US.[424]

---

422 Archie Brown, *The Myth of the Strong Leader: Political Leadership in the Modern Age* (London: Bodley Head, 2014).
423 Ibid, p. 362.
424 SA Goodman, *The Imperial Premiership: The role of the modern Prime Minister in foreign policy making 1964-2015* (Manchester University Press, 2016).

The Iraq Inquiry established by Gordon Brown and chaired by Sir John Chilcot was published on 6 July 2016, thirteen years after the war started. Commonly referred to as the Chilcot Report, its publication was delayed by successive Cabinet Secretaries for a combination of good and bad reasons. The good reason was to take account of the International Criminal Court; the bad reason was to use delay as a protective device for Tony Blair. The report provides both a history and a forensic analysis of the Iraq War. It considers there should have been collective decisions made on eleven specific occasions before the invasion.[425] That is of itself a damning verdict.

Tony Blair's written statement issued on the same day as the Chilcot Report was published has correctly been challenged. Defiance is the only way to describe his words: "If I was back in the same place with the same information, I would take the same decision." A leading article in *The Times* rebutted Blair's statement the following day declaring we went to war

> on the basis of intelligence on weapons of mass destruction that remained privy to the Prime Minister and his closest aides but which he insisted, in private as well as public, was incontrovertible. It was anything but. Still defiant 13 years on, Mr Blair insisted in a written statement that the Chilcot report alleged "no falsification or improper use of intelligence". In fact, the report states that the intelligence "was not challenged and should have been". Many will conclude that amounts to improper use.[426]

Parliament disgracefully never properly considered whether Blair's conduct had or had not brought Parliament into disrepute. In my view it had. The use Blair made of the available intelligence,

---

425 The Report of the Iraq Inquiry, Executive Summary, 2016, pp. 58-59.
426 'Catalogue of Failure', *The Times*, 7 July 2016.

quoting it inaccurately and ignoring caveats and concerns, was 'disingenuous', the word used in the House of Lords by Lord Butler, a contribution bizarrely ignored in the Chilcot Report. (See p. 200.)

On the face it, Tony Blair committed an impeachable offence as defined by Lord Sanderson in 1906 (see pp. 216-7) when on 28 July 2002 he wrote to President Bush, "I will be with you, whatever." That both a senior diplomat, David Manning. and his political chief of staff, Jonathan Powell, advised him not to use those words showed they shared some of Sanderson's caution. It was only eight days after this expression of support from Blair to President Bush that the path to invasion had been set, if not in concrete terms at least in the minds of the key decision makers in Washington and London.

In November 2004 a motion was tabled in the House of Commons by Plaid Cymru calling for the Prime Minister Tony Blair to be impeached for 'high crimes and misdemeanours' but a vote could not take place since it was not supported by the three main parties. It would importantly have allowed MPs to debate whether they thought Blair had lied to the House, a word which is normally not allowed during Commons debates due to restrictions on Parliamentary language.

The war was deeply unpopular by then and Boris Johnson, when he was MP for Henley, was interestingly a supporter of the motion and wrote a comment for The Daily Telegraph in which he accused Blair of deliberately misleading Parliament:

> It is not so much that he lied (though many of his statements were at odds with reality): it is rather that he used all his lawyerly arts, and all the trust that is naturally reposed in his office, to communicate to the public a vast untruth.

November 2004 was the month that Boris Johnson's public and private life intertwined leading to him being sacked as shadow arts minister and vice chairman of the Conservative Party by Michael Howard, the Conservative Party leader later defeated in the 2005 General Election by Tony Blair. Howard stepped down from the leadership and was succeeded by David Cameron elected by the whole party membership. In normal circumstances Boris Johnson might have hoped to be a candidate for the leadership but there was practically no support for him amongst his parliamentary colleagues and Cameron did not feel the need to even appoint him to the shadow cabinet in December 2005. This exclusion was followed by a story that Johnson might run for Mayor of London and the Conservative HQ denied the story only to be embarrassed when Johnson issued a statement

> Being Mayor of London would be a fantastic job and anyone who loves London would want to consider the possibility very carefully.

Johnson delayed until the last possible day before declaring his candidacy on 16 July 2007 and in September he easily beat three other potential Conservative candidates in an open primary. His opponent in May 2008 was by then the independent incumbent Mayor of London Ken Livingstone, another populist who had left the Labour Party. To many people's surprise in the first round Johnson led Livingstone and in the second preference votes he won by 1,168,738 votes to 1,028,966 votes; 53% to 47%. By any standard this was a formidable triumph and from that moment on it was not possible for serious political analysts to join in the widespread laughing off of 'Boris'. He had become by dint of his electoral success a politician who had to be taken seriously. Particularly so when Johnson won a second term against a strong Labour candidate, the former Cabinet Minister, Frank Dobson. During those eight years he oversaw the Olympics with skill and attention to detail and succeeded in putting London on the international map as one of the most attractive cities to visit. But it was not long before he began to contemplate returning to the House of Commons and in 2015 while still Mayor won the constituency of Uxbridge and South Ruislip for the Conservatives with a majority of 10,695.

As Mayor, Johnson collected enemies as well as friends. But most fair-minded people considered his two terms of office were a success. In large part this was because he assembled a team of serious and accomplished people around him. Kit Malthouse, now an MP and in his government, became Deputy Mayor and Johnson was helped greatly by Simon Milton becoming Deputy Mayor for Policy and Planning, a very experienced Leader of Westminster City Council. When Milton tragically died young a service was held at Westminster Abbey in October 2011 and Johnson gave one of the addresses. He talked of Milton's ability 'to sum up in about 50 words, what I had been trying to say all morning.'[427] According to Johnson's biographer, Milton was 'the man who did more than anyone else to bring order out of chaos at City Hall.'[428] I stress Johnson's capacity to attract people of talent and work well with them as Mayor because if repeated his capacity to grow in office as Prime Minister will be considerably enhanced. Time alone will tell.

Johnson, while still Mayor, wrote again in *The Daily Telegraph* about Blair and Iraq on 15 June, 2014

When we voted for that war -and I did, too – we did so with what now looks like the hopelessly naïve assumption that the British and American governments had a plan for the aftermath; that there was a government waiting in the wings; that civic institutions would be preserved and carried on in the post-Saddam era.

In other words, I wanted to get rid of Saddam, and I fondly imagined that there would be a plan for the transition – as there

427 Andrew Gimson, *Boris. The Adventures of Boris Johnson* (Simon & Schuster, paperback 2016), p.303.
428 Ibid, p. 299.

was, say, with Germany in 1945, where the basic and essential machinery of government was continued, despite the programme of de-Nazification. I felt so nervous (and so guilty) about this assumption, that I went to Baghdad in the week after the fall of Saddam, to see if I was right. I was not.

Somebody needs to get on to Tony Blair and tell him to put a sock in it – or at least to accept the reality of the disaster he helped to engender. Then he might be worth hearing. The truth shall set you free, Tony.

The populist instinct in Johnson meant he went much further in criticising Blair on Iraq than many dared. When eventually, after the Chilcot Report, an attempt was made to call Blair to account on 30 November 2016, the House of Commons rejected the motion moved by Alex Salmond by a large cross-party majority of 439:70. Johnson did not vote. John Prescott, by then a Peer, but in 2003 Blair's deputy, wrote his own verdict in the *Sunday Mirror* that following Chilcot he had come to the conclusion that the war was illegal. 'I will live with the decision of going to war and its catastrophic consequences for the rest of my life.'

A very big milestone in Johnson's life was his tortured decision to be one of the leaders in the Vote Leave campaign in the 2016 EU referendum called by David Cameron. Much has been written about this decision. How could a convinced European, some asked, reach such a decision? Most commentators gave the answer ambition, naked ambition to displace Cameron as leader of the Conservatives. But Johnson knew Cameron had already indicated he would step down in a year or so and that he would time this to help his Chancellor of the Exchequer and close friend, George Osborne, become Prime Minister.

Johnson himself admitted he had been 'veering all over the place, like a supermarket trolley' before his decision to join Vote Leave. He was much criticised because he wrote for himself two articles for his main statement in the *Daily Telegraph* arguing the case for Remain and Leave, I believe he was doing no more than many people do finding comfort from the patience of paper and listing the pros and cons and weighing up a decision on which there were bound to be conflicting views amongst his friends.

Thereafter at the weekly meetings of the Vote Leave campaign I watched as Johnson and Michael Gove who came, unlike Boris, from Cameron's Cabinet, combine with Gisela Stuart, a Labour MP, to lead the campaign. First, Vote Leave had to convince the Electoral Commission they should be the official body to represent Leavers as against the official Remainers lead by Cameron and many other leading politicians from the Labour and Liberal Democrat parties. It was not inevitable that Vote Leave would be chosen in preference to Nigel Farage and UKIP. I was asked to write to the Commission and in a long letter explained the tortured history of Labour's relationship with the Common Market under Gaikskell, Wilson, Callaghan and Blair.

All along Johnson saw that Vote Leave needed support across the parties, but more than anyone else he identified with the appeal to those who had no party political allegiance. I am sure that the combination of Boris Johnson, as a Conservative MP, and Gisela Stuart, a Labour MP, together on the bus and putting the Leave case at the Wembley stadium ensured that Vote Leave was never seen as a purely Conservative campaign. If conventional ambition to be the next leader of the Conservative Party was Johnson's only motive, I do not believe he could have been so successful in Vote Leave.

As Prime Minister, Cameron's decision to walk away from office in the early morning after the referendum, after telling everyone throughout the campaign he would stay, was the most important untruth of a referendum campaign full of them – for it doomed the British negotiating strategy with the EU. Cameron's autobiography gives his own justification for the untruth.

"So why had I promised that I would stay on if we lost? Initially I hadn't believed that losing would mean an immediate announcement of my departure. But more importantly, I knew that I must do all I could to keep my future separate from the issue of the EU in the public debate. If I had admitted that there was *any* chance of my stepping down if Remain lost, [Cameron writes grandiosely or modestly the reader is left to judge!] I would have jeopardised the referendum entirely."[429]

Few in the Conservative Party or in the country wanted Cameron to complete the negotiation but his duty was to start a credible and open discussion about the best options on how to leave. It was Cameron that had prevented the civil service from preparing for a leave scenario. In fairness, he writes in his book that leaving the EU is "legitimate'. Furthermore, he quotes John Major writing to him soon after he left office. "History will acknowledge that a referendum was becoming inevitable – if not now, later – and delay would have made Brexit more likely." The inclusion of that confidence in his book cannot be read other than as a justification for his referendum stance and implied criticism of Major's own subsequent rejection of the referendum result along with that of Tony Blair's. It was also an important fact that Cameron declared his intention to have a referendum on our EU membership in 2013 before the Scottish referendum in 2014. The result is deeply unpopular in Scotland but they were aware it was coming.

What about Cameron's personality? I judge on no direct knowledge, just watching, that he is far more 'cocky' than hubristic; self-confident to the point of 'not giving a damn'. In walking out in the very early morning after the referendum, he was acting in character. Any Prime Minister in that situation had one responsibility. It is a simple word – duty. It was Cameron's duty,

---

429 David Cameron, *For The Record* (William Collins 2019), pp. 681, 701-702.

having given his word, to all those who voted in the referendum, to stay and use his experience and authority having been Prime Minister for six years to get his country out of the mess he had created. There was no need to stay any longer than to set a course. All he had to say was 'I promised to stay and I will keep my promise and ensure an informed debate in government and in Parliament to find the best way or ways to leave the EU but I will leave before the final decision on the way ahead to implement the people's decision to leave.' His duty was to ensure options would be on the table for his successor to assess, for Cabinet to reflect on and for Parliament to debate and then enact. An uncomfortable few months for Cameron, undoubtedly, would have followed but the path of duty is often uncomfortable. Final decisions would only have been made, following an election in the Conservative Party for a new leader, by Cabinet Ministers, by then much better informed and more aware of the complexities as well as the challenges of leaving the EU.

Another attitude taken on the referendum result was that of Paddy Ashdown, the former leader of the Liberal Democratic Party

> Those who asked for this, and I was the first leader ever to ask for a referendum in 1989-90, have said so because they believe in the act of democracy. I will forgive no one who does not accept the sovereign voice of the British people once it has spoken, whether it's by one per cent or 20 per cent. It's our duty to serve the public and make sure our country does the best it can with the decision people have given us...When democracy speaks, we obey.

That was in stark contrast to the policy of outright rejection, even to revoking Article 50, adopted by his party in the 2019 General Election after he had died.

The sentiments expressed by Paddy Ashdown are why so many people, like myself, never accepted the legitimacy of the referendum decision being challenged by Parliament for three and a half years and why many people took the opportunity to 'tell them again' of that truth in the General Election. Having no vote in that election I made my view clear in an article in October 2019 in the *Mail on Sunday* that the referendum result should not be reversed and must be honoured.

It appears now Cameron would have left office if he had lost the Scottish referendum so for him the decision was in part at least settled in his mind. Yet to stay after the UK referendum was far more important. Harold Wilson well understood this and is why he pledged to stay in office in 1975 if despite his recommendation the country voted 'no' to the EU. A view that was upheld during the campaign by the then Foreign Secretary, Jim Callaghan, when correcting a senior civil servant and insisting that the government would be bound to 'act immediately' to legislate to leave if 'no' was the voters' decision.[430] By contrast, during the December 2019 General Election, Jeremy Corbyn likened, wrongly, his decision to remain 'neutral' in any second referendum to that of Wilson's. It was Fiona Bruce, chairing a *Question Time* event, with Johnson present, who reminded Corbyn and the audience that Harold Wilson had stated his recommendation to stay in the EU as well as that of his government and he had not therefore been neutral but was still ready to carry out the wishes of the people. I suspect this neutral stance which was forced on Corbyn by his friend and hitheto close ally, John McDonnell, did much to help Labour lose the General Election so badly. In the 2017 General Election in which Corbyn did well he was still seen by Labour voters to be open to leaving the EU as he had always been in the past. He was progressively driven off his position through 2019 by the vast majority of London Labour MPs who were remainers. Being neutral on the dominating issue of the election was not seen as

---

430 *The Official History of Britain and the European Community Vol II: From Rejection to Referendum, 1963-1975* (Routledge, 2012), p. 588.

credible by voters in the UK for a potential Prime Minister committed to renegotiating a new Agreement with the EU. When Corbyn compounded his position by refusing to recommend his own agreement on the ballot paper in a second referendum, some voters realised it was a crafted 'gimmick', not a serious policy.

Boris Johnson, at the time of the 2016 referendum, had not even served in Cameron's government, let alone as a Cabinet Minister. I have little doubt Johnson becoming Prime Minister in the wake of the referendum, despite Gove's challenge, would not have been the optimum solution – whereas five months after being Foreign Secretary or another Cabinet post under Cameron during such an interregnum period he would have been a far better prospect. Cameron's failure to act in this way ensured his successor, Theresa May, had a very difficult challenge and it was sadly one she could not handle. But it was her failure that paved the way for a populist Johnson to become Prime Minister on 24 July 2019.

It was one of Theresa May's great mistakes to pitch her Brexit appeal for at least the first two years solely to Conservatives. Belatedly, she recognised this mistake only to be spurned in formal talks by Corbyn and McDonnell's Labour Party.

In essence, I believe joining Vote Leave was to be the moment when Johnson decided, for better or for worse – and perhaps unconsciously – to eschew the conventional route to becoming Prime Minister which he recognised was closed to him. The populist streak, on which he had built his appeal as Mayor of London, gave him, unlike any other candidate for the Conservative leadership, a choice – to identify with the established view of Britain's role in Europe and with Cameron and Osborne or to side with the views of, by then, a very obviously large body of opinion going far wider than the Conservative Party, who wanted to leave the EU. Johnson, I think, began to sense this feeling represented in the country as a whole particularly in the Labour Party outside London had the potential to help him force his way to becoming

Prime Minister as a Conservative but on his own terms. He felt the anti-EU feeling had, with luck, the popular appeal to take him to No 10 even if the referendum was to be lost. When it was won for a moment it looked as if Boris would be elected the Conservative leader to succeed Cameron.

But, at the last possible moment, Gove decided to run as well declaring Johnson was 'not capable' of uniting the Conservatives and leading the country. Johnson, just minutes before he was due to launch his campaign, to the surprise of many of his supporters in the room, promptly withdrew his candidacy. Why? At the time Johnson's decision dumbfounded many of his close friends and delighted his enemies, with both thinking his political career in the Conservative Party was over. The fact that three years later he became the leader of the Conservative Party and Prime Minister might indicate that his judgement then was again a very shrewd one. He assessed, I believe, with clarity that the clash between the two leading Conservative Brexiteers would be very damaging to his personal credibility and could well lead to Theresa May coming up through the middle. He feared that the personal price he would pay for this was that he would be seen to have lost his unique appeal as a Conservative vote winner, first in London, now in the country at large because of the referendum victory. He realised he would be blamed – not Gove – by the many Conservative MPs who had voted to remain in the EU and his popularity in the country dented. Better to sit this election out, he concluded.

Johnson used the word, 'Brutus' – who killed Julius Caesar – for Gove's decision to challenge him but after bowing out he wasted little time in indicating to Theresa May his support, though nominally supporting Andrea Leadsom, thus helping to secure the position of Foreign Secretary in May's Cabinet. In the aftermath of the referendum Johnson did become a hate figure amongst Remainers. What eventually the referendum revealed, however, was that there was a deep split amongst both Labour and Conservative voters and that Boris, with his populist instinct, was judged by his fellow MPs as the Conservative MP alone able to bridge that divide. From then on, as Foreign Secretary it was only a matter of time before he resigned. Then by rather surprisingly voting for May's last attempt for an 'ambitious, bespoke' Agreement, Boris was astute enough to realise this would win the support of some more Conservative MPs in the House of Commons while not damaging his popular appeal. This populist appeal became his unique selling point in getting the votes of many Conservative MPs in the leadership election in the summer of 2019 and it was also the reason a number of hitherto Labour supporters voted for him in the General Election of December 2019.

I first noticed Boris with some amusement at the time I was Leader of the SDP from 1983. Johnson had started at Oxford that year and then proceeded to pass himself off as a Social Democrat and even telling people when standing for President of the Union he was an environmentalist. He became President at the second attempt. So effective was his deception that the Master of Balliol, Sir Anthony Kenny, was approached by an SDP MP to recommend a young man to work for him and when Kenny asked Boris if he was interested, Boris laughed and said, 'No, I'm a true blue Tory.' Anyone watching his career with any degree of objectivity knows he has always been far from a true blue Tory. He is liberal on many issues and has eclectic views. Labour and even the *Guardian* in the 2019 General Election spent time foolishly trying to pretend that he was on the right of the Conservative Party. This was palpable nonsense which backfired as not being credible. As to his private life, which was fully exposed but on which he personally refuses to comment, it appeared to have only a limited 'turn off' effect. A defence of the right of politicians to lie about their private lives was written years before by Boris Johnson in January 1998 in *The Daily Telegraph* in the form of a defence of Bill Clinton. He wrote, 'Is Gladstone to be condemned, because of what we know about his weird work with prostitutes? Was Thomas Jefferson a failure as a President because he had an affair with a slave girl? Does it really *matter* what Palmerston got up to with women in Hyde Park?'[431]

As Mayor of London and day by day at City Hall Johnson showed he was a 'people person', riding around on a bicycle, championing a particular new design for buses, or wanting to build a new airport to the east of London and not at Heathrow. Very little was done by accident. All the time, he was building an image. He was intent on putting down a marker that was potentially powerful for the future. Johnson has also chosen as his role model Churchill and he admired his ruthlessness. He does not mention it but I suspect Johnson was familiar with Churchill's attitude to Anthony Eden in 1938. At the time of Eden's resignation as Foreign Secretary, Gallup polling reported 26% support for Chamberlain's foreign policy of appeasement and 71% against. Eden had widened his protest at Chamberlain's interference in his role as Foreign Secretary to also include appeasement. Handsome, young Eden was a potential threat to Churchill but Churchill was not about to vacate the position of leader of the anti-appeasement group of MPs. So Churchill told the Chief Whip, Margesson, on 17 March 1938 that the Prime Minister's views and his were not divergent and they need not, therefore, group him and his supporters with Eden. Churchill ruthlessly knew he had to remain the key anti-appeaser and populist and Eden was never able to mount a challenge.[432]

What Johnson brought to the Vote Leave campaign was zest, humour and an unerring capacity to go for the 'jugular'. Populists do not like being unpopular. In Boris's case he also needs to be loved: and that vulnerability is attractive to many older women. Arriving on the bus in Newcastle during the referendum women

---

431 Ibid, Andrew Gimson, p. 212
432 David Dutton, *Neville Chamberlain* (Arnold, 2001), p. 112.

could be seen shouting "Boris, Boris" who were identifiable Labour members.

The UK experienced two US Presidents visiting the UK and expressing views on Brexit. First, Obama actually during the referendum in 2016, and Trump's visit in 2018 while the withdrawal legislation was still being discussed in Parliament. I wrote to the US Ambassador when there was first speculation about a visit by Obama and opposed it strongly and reminded the Ambassador that there had been no visit by President Ford surrounding the 1975 EU referendum on coming out of the Common Market. Quite correctly, Obama was initially advised by the US Embassy in London against intervening in the UK referendum on whether to remain or leave the EU. The effect of Obama's visit was totally counterproductive to his personal preference of the UK remaining in the EU. During Obama's stay the official Leave campaign recorded in opinion polls the only large spike in voting intentions throughout the campaign of a 3-5% shift in favour of leaving the EU. The British people did not like a US President, even one as popular as Obama, coming into their domestic campaign and telling them how to vote.

It was a very bad mistake for Prime Minister Cameron to persuade President Obama to make 'a hastily arranged trip to help' and campaign in the UK's 2016 referendum on the EU. We know from Ben Rhodes's book what happened.[433] Ed Llewellyn, Cameron's chief of staff in No. 10 had emailed Rhodes a couple of months earlier urging Obama to visit; saying they were barely ahead in the polls and fearful, and keen for Obama, whose opinion poll ratings were more than 70 per cent in the UK, to make a strong expression of support. On the flight over, Rhodes admits to having emailed back and forth with Cameron's staff about an op-ed that Obama was publishing in the *Daily Telegraph* making the case

---

433 Ibid Ben Rhodes, *The World As It Is Inside The Obama White House*

for Britain to stay in the European Union. Rhodes admits, 'It was unusual to coordinate so closely with a foreign government, but the Brits were different, and Brexit would be calamitous, a crucial piece of the post-World War II order drifting off into the sea.'[434] This view of Brexit from President Obama contrasted with my meeting on 3 May 2016 with Henry Kissinger in New York, during the referendum campaign. He was facing a deadline to decide before the end of the day whether to sign a letter with other prominent members of the American foreign policy establishment arguing that Britain should not leave the EU. It soon became clear that he had no intention of signing and his reasoning was clear and simple. 'I do not want a world in which there is no independent British voice', a view which I published later with his consent but only after the referendum result was known. It was to help establish that independent British voice that in 2017 I wrote with David Ludlow, a former diplomat 25 years younger than me and a Remain voter, *British Foreign Policy After Brexit*.[435]

Rhodes goes on to record how he showed Obama an op-ed that had been written by Boris Johnson in which he said the removal of a bust of Winston Churchill from the Oval Office, as Obama had done, 'was a symbol of the part-Kenyan President's ancestral dislike of the British Empire – of which Churchill had been such a fervent defender.'[436] We could have done without Boris's implicit reference to Kenya, for which there was no justification whatever. Obama gave a memorable speech in Westminster Hall six years previously on 25 May 2011 which included these words, 'the example of our two nations says it is possible for people to be united by their ideals instead of divided by their differences; that it's possible for hearts to change and old hatred to pass; that it's possible for the sons and

---

434 Ibid, p. 384.
435 David Owen and David Ludlow, *British Foreign Policy After Brexit* (Biteback Publishing, 2017).
436 Ben Rhodes, p. 384.

daughters of former colonies to sit here as members of this great Parliament, and for the grandson of a Kenyan who served as a cook in the British Army to stand before you as President of the United States.'

Rhodes writes about Obama's reaction to Boris Johnson:

'Really?' Obama said. 'The black guy doesn't like the British?'

'They're more subtle back home' Rhodes said.

'Not really' Obama said, 'Boris is their Trump.'

'With better hair.' added Rhodes.

Obama chuckled. 'Talk to Cameron's folks,' he said. 'Get me the best arguments for and against Brexit.'

Obama apparently had a long, friendly meeting with Cameron at 10 Downing Street and Cameron explained that Brexit campaigners were claiming that the UK could quickly negotiate a trade deal with the United States if they left the EU, and Obama said, 'What? There's no way that could happen . . . .'

The Brits laughed. 'We'd be at the back of the queue', one of them said.

'It'd be great', Cameron said, 'if you could make that point publicly.' And so Obama did, revealing in his use of the word 'queue' rather than the American 'line' that his comments were drafted in Downing Street.

When President Trump visited the UK in July 2018 he inadvisably went out of his way in an interview in *The Sun* newspaper to praise Boris Johnson and criticise the Government's EU Chequers Statement, named after the British Prime Minister's country residence. As Prime Minister, Boris Johnson should resist any temptation to act in a similar way before the Presidential election in November 2020. All politicians should learn the lesson of these interventions in another country's domestic politics.

It was Johnson who took on President Obama in the four days of Obama's visit. He ignored the arguments about whether Obama should or should not have intervened in our campaign and instead he scoffed at a US President coming over to tell us not to regain control of our foreign policy when that was the very issue on which America had broken away from us. But it was the moment when a 3-5% rise in the opinion polls made it possible for Vote Leave to win the referendum and Johnson was the main reason for that rise.

When May entered No 10 as Prime Minister on 13 July 2016 after the referendum vote there were no papers on her desk spelling out the many different options for handling Brexit. Instead, she developed her vacuous mantra, "Brexit means Brexit". On May's second day in office two new departments were officially created without any Cabinet discussion. The Department for Exiting the EU and, of greater relevance, the Department for International Trade which for some in the civil service "signalled a full-blooded Brexit was coming." Other civil servants felt that with Brexit international trade "needed to be part of the Foreign Office as in other countries."[437] On trade, there is no question, however, that for Conservatives in the Cabinet and most backbenchers the option for leaving the EU contained within it the opportunity to break away from a gathering protectionism in the EU, for negotiating Free Trade Agreements, FTAs, as the Norway option allowed for and as the WTO option involved. This was the moment in the early months after the referendum to explore transitioning out of the EU through the European Economic Area Agreement, EEAA, though not staying in it permanently.

The French President of the European Commission, Jacques Delors, a dedicated federalist yet in office a servant of the EU, always understood and ensured that there was an option for a close association for non-EU countries who wanted to make their own trade agreements and not follow the pattern of full integration into the EU. He saw merit in helping to design the EEA after Norway

---

437 Anthony Seldon, *May at 10* (Biteback Publishing, 2019), p.103-104. On Boris Johnson, p. 74, 322-324.

380

chose through a referendum not to join the EU. The Norwegian government recommended full membership but this was rejected by the public. I went to a meeting in Norway in 1972 to speak in favour of joining the EU at the request of the then Labour Prime Minister who wanted a young Labour MP to put the case for joining. Willy Brandt, the German Chancellor, was the lead speaker before I spoke and he was popular in Norway, having gone into exile there from Germany in 1933. But even he was barracked and catcalled. When my turn came I was very low key and sensitive to the hostility in the room but I vowed then and there never again to intervene in another country's election.

The EEAA was signed in 1992 and brought into operation in 1994. The 31 contracting parties comprise the 28 EU member states and Norway, Iceland and Liechtenstein who are EFTA members with their own governance. The EEAA allowed for EFTA countries to join the EU and it was the vehicle which was used by Austria, Sweden and Finland to make the step to leave EFTA for the EU in 1995 while remaining in the EEAA. After Delors stepped down the Commission became evermore defensive, too rigid and began to worship the four founding principles including freedom of movement of labour. It should have been no surprise that the Juncker-led Commission would use Article 50 in the way for which it was designed – as an instrument to make leaving the EU as difficult as possible. Was Cameron ever briefed in detail and warned about Article 50 before he spoke in the House of Commons about it being used if the referendum result was to leave? I very much doubt he was.

During the 'purdah' referendum period in 2016 when the civil service had to be impartial the then Cabinet Secretary, Jeremy Heywood, should have ignored Cameron's wish for no civil service studies to be undertaken and instead should have asserted his constitutional right to undertake detailed work during the referendum period, when the civil service has to be neutral, on all possible options if the vote was for leaving. A civil service study on an

EEAA transition should have been ready for Theresa May as Prime Minister on day one, along with the option of using the Vienna Convention, not Article 50. That this was not done was a fatal mistake leading inexorably to delay, division and discord under the disastrous three and a half years of parliamentary indecision up until the decisive General Election of 2019.

At all stages it was open to the UK to change our UK membership of the EEAA from being an EU member to being a non-EU member without using Article 50 and to proceed to negotiate our own fishing and agricultural policies and come under EFTA governance. If that had ever been challenged by the EU the UK could have gone to the International Court in Vienna and used its arbitration procedures and not gone near Article 50 which was specially designed by two distinguished European federalists, the former Italian Prime Minister, D'Amato and the Scotsman and former head of the Foreign Office, Lord Kerr. Our eventual withdrawal from the EEA would have taken place after giving the one-year statutory notice.

There is still a major possibility by the end of 2020, if the EU continues to insist on a common rule book and that UK fishing rights cannot be fully restored, that there will be no EU-UK FTA. Michael Gove is seemingly ready for this, warning that border formalities are inevitable and free trade will not be frictionless. It is an open question too whether a major US-UK trade deal will be possible because of the current disagreement on the UK's decision to continue using Huawei for its 5G development, previously agreed by Mrs May with the Cabinet Secretary and the head of MI6. The belief then and now was that US security professionals were relaxed on this issue so it was decided that the UK would only curb and cap exposure to Huawei technology, not abandon it. This, it is now clear, is a serious misjudgement. Our Five Eyes partners are very far from relaxed and it is time our security advisers woke up. It is not just President Trump's view but the all-party view of Congress confirmed by Democratic Senator Nancy Pelosi at the Munich Security Conference in February 2020. This is a very serious geopolitical development. We need to look again at an alternative industrial approach to 5G development. France is using Nokia and Ericsson, Germany sticking with Huawei. For the UK to fail to reconsider would not just risk our partnership in the Five Eyes, but undermine our increased commitment to NATO outside the EU. Relatively recently in relation to their national security these four countries now regard China as a hostile power and are refusing to continue to gloss over the size and sophistication of the Chinese rearmament programmes and the penetration of their intelligence activities. This shift in policy has also been flagged up by the FBI's broad-ranging effort to root out scientists in US universities working on behalf of China. This is another warning because the fields of nanoscale electronics and biomedicine have very important security dimensions in relation to China and tightening up on these is another portend for the future.

International politics is about partnerships. When the US changes its view on a cross party basis and their judgement is shared by three other Commonwealth countries any UK government would reconsider. On this issue Boris Johnson can no longer have his cake and eat it. When he was appointed Foreign Secretary Nick Timothy, Theresa May's Chief of Staff, recalls her saying to Johnson, "You and I have a patchy history, but I know there are two Borises. A deadly serious, intellectual, capable and very effective person: and a playing-around Boris. I want this to be your opportunity to show you can be the former." Timothy commented to Seldon, the author of *May at 10* about the meeting and Boris's reaction. "I remember thinking at the time if that was a bit supercilious and wondered if she had been wise to say it. But any way he took it on the chin."[438]

---

438 Anthony Seldon, *May at 10* (Biteback Publishing, 2019), pp. 109-110.

A view expressed by a Foreign Office official of May's decision to appoint Johnson is recorded by Seldon as saying it "was a mistake to appoint a known enemy as Foreign Secretary. She never trusted him and he knew she never trusted him." There was much "hostility. It was awful" said one civil servant on relations between May and Johnson. It is my strong view that for the relationship between Prime Minister and Foreign Secretary to work, there has to be trust. Tensions involving other Cabinet posts and the Prime Minister are easier to handle. Although relations between Theresa May and Philip Hammond, her Chancellor of the Exchequer, were also very bad and she had plans to sack him after the 2017 General Election but was then too weakened to do so.

Seldon reveals starkly and savagely the lack of any real Cabinet input to Brexit. "May had absolutely no intention of letting her Cabinet Ministers loose on subjects she herself was finding it hard to grasp. Instead, she wanted the key discussions and decisions on Brexit to be taken in No 10 – specifically in her own room. No politicians welcome." Cabinet Ministers say that before her first agenda-changing Party Conference speech in October 2016 they had little chance to read what she intended saying on Brexit, much less to change it. Her line to the conference "There is no such thing as a choice between 'soft Brexit' and 'hard Brexit'" was nonsense. A soft three-year transition to a hard Brexit through the EEA was not only always available to the UK but was the best route to follow. Officials only saw her first Conservative Party conference speech 36 hours before she made it. Not all the blame should fall on May as one fellow official put it. 'Heywood had very many qualities. But a weakness – or was it for a civil servant? – was an over-eagerness to please his political masters.'

In a lengthy courteous correspondence with Theresa May, which she was under no obligation to either start or to continue with me, it became clear to me that the civil servants and/or special advisers who drafted her replies were themselves unaware of some of the detailed facts.[439] I have never actually talked to her. She came into the House of Commons when I left it, but I admire hugely, however, the way she handled her diagnosis of diabetes. She had to have chocolate passed up to her while at the Despatch Box when being questioned by MPs for three hours. She was particularly good in talking to children about her condition to encourage them to aim high in life and not be discouraged by such a diagnosis. May has been subject to much criticism by officials. 'She was the least collegiate Prime Minister I ever worked with, worse even than Gordon Brown because she was not as bright and lacked his intelligence and vision. She was very insular and couldn't communicate. She shared one trait with Brown, though; neither trusted people, and both were very tribal.'

There is also another interpretation of her character to the selective quotations of mainly civil servants in Seldon's book. In an article 'A flawed first draft of history' by Lord Stephen Parkinson, who worked for May in the Home Office, he writes of Seldon's many criticisms that they 'do not fit the down to earth, well read and cultured woman I got to know over seven years working with her.'[440]

It was emblematic of May's whole approach to Brexit that she stuck to her position on immigration as Prime Minister which she championed for six years as Home Secretary but had never delivered trying to fulfil Cameron's insistence in the 2010 and 2015 manifesto of cutting immigration to the 'tens of thousands'. It was not a remotely feasible target economically for immediate effect under Brexit from 2016-2020. Given that fact, it was amazing that the EEA option was never presented to Cabinet to show how out of the EU but within the EEAA for a transition period we could have used the Liechtenstein wording on immigration legitimately to

439 See Letter of 17 September 2018 between Lord Owen and the Prime Minister and other correspondence between 2016-2018 published on Lord Owen's website: www.lorddavidowen.co.uk.
440 *The Critic*, Issue 2, December 2019, pp. 52-55.

open up the small flexibility implicit in the wording covering Liechtenstein. The EU works on precedent. They are not geared up for ambitious, new schemes or bespoke solutions – May's two much trumpeted negotiating aims. The EU prefers modest, evolutionary changes. Diplomats know this and it has been the particular skill of the Foreign Office to guide that process to the UK's advantage in Brussels over four decades. Again that option, if only for the transition, was ignored.

After the disappointing 2017 General Election, everything changed for May. The DUP in Northern Ireland was now a big factor in the negotiating process. In the run up to the away day Cabinet meeting on 2 July 2018, May met with David Davis to discuss her "common rule book". He, as her appointed head of the Department for Exiting the EU, had been humiliated having to swallow only four weeks earlier her 'Irish backstop'. Davis said of her common rule book, "What you have here, Prime Minister, is incompatible with your conference speech and your 2017 manifesto".[441] And he was correct. On 6 July at Chequers, the Prime Minister's official house in the country, the Cabinet met and the press were briefed the ultimate humiliation that if anyone wanted to resign they would no longer be able to use their official car to go home and taxi numbers would be supplied. Davis correctly fumed, "The children have taken control of the kindergarten." Davis was only allowed to speak in Cabinet when his turn came up, a sign in front of his colleagues that he had been totally sidelined. "If we go ahead with your proposal, we'll be agreeing to a European rule book not a common rule book."[442] Johnson spoke next – some claim not very well – in favour of a rethink of her strategy. Then Gove spoke for accepting the deal, as the only alternative was rejection. It was a speech which was later

441 Ibid, *May at 10*, p.428.
442 Ibid, *May at 10*, p. 436.

categorised to the press by a colleague, as having "pulled the rug from under Boris Johnson and David Davis's feet." May's common rule book was then endorsed for industrial and agricultural products in the hope of frictionless trade. Davis resigned and went on BBC *Today* to explain. Johnson talked to his parliamentary private secretary, Connor Burns, from the car coming back from Chequers saying it was a "terrible proposal" and left him with the impression he would resign by Monday. But Johnson was meant to be hosting a meeting with other Foreign Ministers on a Balkans Summit that day. May tried to ring him and eventually found he was resigning and promptly appointed Jeremy Hunt in his place as Foreign Secretary. It was from then on obvious to all that power was daily moving away from Prime Minister May and it was only a matter of time before she was forced out by her own MPs.

Chequers was the point, according to Seldon, when the rebels in the European Research Group turned on May. What they were demonstrating was why properly run Cabinet government is an essential in the UK model of the fusion between the executive of government ministers and Parliament, meaning in most cases backbench MPs all of the same party. Different opinions in one political party can be contained by Cabinet where a Prime Minister is seen by backbenchers to ensuring Cabinet consider carefully opposing views. Cabinet government, as we have experienced over the Iraq War, and now over Brexit, only works where there is Cabinet debate and discussion where all sides of the argument are recognised by their own party's MPs to have had a fair opportunity to express their views within Cabinet. In this way it is possible to manage policy differences. It is only when that debate in Cabinet ceases to be meaningful, when a Prime Minister does not listen, closes down debate and acts autocratically as May did, that the fractures become apparent, the Cabinet ceases to function and Parliament loses its way.

It is absolutely vital if this new Parliament is to function properly from 2020 onwards under Speaker Hoyle and Prime Minister Boris

Johnson that Johnson restores Cabinet government. He has written in detail about how Churchill ran his Cabinet and War Cabinet. Churchill's conduct was about as far removed as it could be from that of May. It is now essential, if Johnson is to be successful, that he follows Churchill's example of discussion. It will be good for that process if he reduces the size of the Cabinet which has become ever larger, ever more prone to leaks and in part, for those reasons, is frequently sidelined. Johnson should also return full Ministerial responsibility for MI6, the international security services, to his Foreign Secretary while retaining the Prime Minister's overall responsibility. No Prime Minister can devote the time and attention to give the democratic political control to this delicate area of responsibility that it requires and it should not be delegated to junior ministers. It is not possible for the National Security Council to oversee MI6 any more than to oversee MI5. It would be a demonstrative sign of Boris Johnson's readiness to return to proper Cabinet government, and not government by diplomats and civil servants in cahoots with the Cabinet Secretary in and around No 10, if he gave back powers to a small number of Cabinet Ministers. Cabinet has not functioned as it should under Blair, Brown, Cameron or May.

In many ways the best hope for the UK post-Brexit in 2020 is that Johnson can learn from his hero Churchill. He is not of Churchill's stature and I think he knows it, but with Churchill as his model and his historical mentor, there is a chance he will become more disciplined as well as more truthful. Both changes are essential.

On another area of key importance for any Prime Minister: how to handle people. Johnson writes with great admiration of a virtue not many associate with Churchill – charm.

> "Never mind the speeches, sublime though they were. Set to one side the strategic decisions, not all of which now look flawless. If you want to understand how he won the war, look at the way he

wangled and wheedled his way to Washington and his subtle but unmistakable manipulation of the priorities.

He used a tool of diplomacy that was as old-fashioned and erratic as the man himself. It was called charm. That was the secret of Churchill's success. It wasn't easy, and there were times when it didn't look as though it would work at all."[443]

Johnson undoubtedly has bumbling charm. He does not mind looking foolish and cultivates this as an endearing quality in some people's eyes. Yet he has a very serious side to him too. He is, for example, very knowledgeable on the detailed environmental case against a third runway at Heathrow. I believe he fully expects the proven environmental figures about particles in the air of London will ensure in the courts of law that it is never built.

As to Cabinet, Johnson movingly describes Churchill's War Cabinet and his handling of it in the first pages of his book on Churchill. Initially consisting of five fellow ministers expanded to six and the Cabinet Secretary taking notes, "It is a measure of the depth of their crisis that they had been meeting almost solidly for three days. This was their ninth meeting since 26 May [1940] and they had yet to come up with an answer to the existential question that freed them and the world . . . The question before the meeting was very simple, and one that they had been chewing over for the last few days as the news got blacker. No one exactly spelt it out, but everyone could see what it was. Should Britain fight? Was it reasonable for young British troops to die in a war that showed every sign of being lost? Or should the British do some kind of deal that might well save hundreds of thousands of lives."[444]

No one who has written these words and then gone through the experience of the absence of Cabinet government under

---

443 Johnson, *The Churchill Factor.* (Hodder paperbacks, 2015), p. 241-242.
444 Ibid, p.8.

Theresa May, and who felt obliged to resign, should now as Prime Minister be anything other than committed to restoring Cabinet government. But will he be so committed? Only time will tell.

Will he stop telling untruths and lying? Will he, in short, live up to the adage, 'Office maketh the man'? It is in all our interests that as Prime Minister he does. Traditionally, new governments have a honeymoon period. After all that has happened, particularly over Brexit, it will take time for the passions to die down, for the anger to abate. Bagehot in the *Economist* on 7 December in a piece headlined, 'Liar, liar' wrote that the 2019 General Election had been 'marinated in mendacity'. Mendacity is another word for untruths, whereas to lie has to have the intention to mislead or deceive and disingenuous is a lack of candour or sincerity. All of these terms merge around each other.

Yet for all the proven lies, the distorted facts and misrepresentation on all sides, the people from different parts of the spectrum decided on 12 December 2019 that Boris Johnson, 'warts and all', should continue to be our 77th Prime Minister. Potentially he could be there for the next five years, maybe even ten years, having only been in office prior to the election for a mere 141 days. His first words towards Remainers about 'healing' and to those who had for decades past voted Labour about 'repaying the trust' were very encouraging.

As a Parliamentarian, I have lived through 21 elections and looking back over all these, with the benefit of hindsight, the electorate I think made the right choice in all of them. To admit this means admitting that in 1970 and 1979 the electors were right to kick me out of government, firstly when I was a junior Minister for the Royal Navy in 1970 and secondly as Foreign Secretary in 1979. The best definition of a democracy is where its people can vote out of office their political governors. I hope history will show that the decision to let Boris – as many still call hm even if they disapprove of him – continue as Prime Minister was correct. It was for many a Hobson's choice – Johnson or Corbyn.

There is much dispute as to how the General Election was agreed in October. The SNP knowing the full court trial of their former leader Alex Salmond was due early in 2020 had been pushing hard for an election before this. Labour MPs, who wanted a second referendum in the early summer of 2020, were in favour of postponing the election and Emily Thornberry wrote to her leader's office to warn that supporting an early election would be 'an act of catastrophic political folly'. Jeremy Corbyn told the *Guardian* at the outset of the campaign that he made the decision to support an election at a shadow cabinet meeting. 'I put it to them quite clearly', he said. 'Our objections are now gone. We are now supporting a general election... And everybody gulped. I didn't alert anyone in advance – it was my decision.' Corbyn, a lifelong supporter of leaving the EU, had had enough of dancing to the tune of remaining in the EU being pushed on him by his supposed close friend, John McDonnell, his shadow Chancellor of the Exchequer.

It is a vindication of the referendum that after three and a half dreadful years in which Parliament itself totally failed to make up its mind as to whether to honour the referendum result, the voters took the decision to honour it with a decisive result in the General Election. The Conservatives now have an 80-seat majority in the House of Commons and by taking 24 Labour heartland seats that have historically been Labour for decades, Boris Johnson has a unique opportunity to reposition the Conservative Party in British politics. It will now no longer just be a question of opinion polls but instead of having to listen to these voices from the north of England on the Conservative benches in the House of Commons, many with their regional accents.

The underlying statistics behind the Election results are even more revealing. The Brexit Party by not standing candidates in Conservative-held seats undoubtedly helped at the start of the campaign to establish that the Conservatives already ahead in the polls remained in that position throughout. In those seats the Liberal Democrats assess having no split in the Leave vote damaged their chances.

On previously held Labour seats, any post-election analyses must always be subjective as one cannot be absolutely certain where Brexit Party votes might have gone, but there is no doubt that many of the Conservative gains from Labour were helped by the Brexit Party vote. For example, seats like Blyth Valley and Heywood and Middleton, Labour might have held on if the Brexit Party had not taken away votes from Labour.

Conversely, an optimistic internal Conservative Party post-election assessment, was that Nigel Farage's decision to put up Brexit candidates in some other seats, and where the Brexit vote was quite sizeable, prevented them from potentially winning 20 more seats. In Wales they name 3 seats: somewhat surprisingly listing Blaenau Gwent (the old seat of Michael Foot, the former leader of the Labour Party), but also Rhondda and Cynon Valley. In Labour's so-called Red Wall there were 12 seats that they claim could have been won, from Wigan across to Hull West & Hessle and Doncaster North, the former Labour Leader, Ed Miliband's seat where a previous massive majority was cut down to 2,370 votes. In the North East they claim five Labour seats were vulnerable and surprisingly list Jarrow from where the famous march of the unemployed headed for London in October 1936. Even in London in Dagenham where the Ford car factory is situated and a rare Vote Leave constituency, the Labour candidate Jon Cruddas, well known for seeing off the National Front in earlier elections, had his majority cut to 293 but might well have lost if the Brexit Party had not polled 2,887 votes.

So, the Conservative Party now have a large vote amongst the working class, hitherto the preserve of Labour. Further evidence from YouGov polling after the election on how people had actually voted found that among the unskilled workers and those not working who are classed DE the Conservatives had a 13-point lead whereas in the 2017 General Election Labour had had a 3-point lead. This points to a Boris Johnson factor not dissimilar from Donald Trump and his victories in the 'rust belt States'. Amongst voters in households with an annual income of less than £20,000 45% voted Conservative and 34% Labour. No wonder Boris after the result rechristened his Conservative Party as the 'People's Party'. Time will tell whether this name change lasts.

One thing is certain: Boris Johnson now sees himself as the 'People's Prime Minister' and he would be wise to keep remembering this over the next five years as his new MPs from the North and the Midlands hold the key to him winning the next election.

As these voices are heard in the House of Commons, it could become daily ever clearer that the Conservative Party is different and is now rooted in parts of the country where they have never before made inroads. Boris Johnson knows that he will need to retain their support. These MPs will be demanding that their constituency problems must be taken into account immediately in spending priorities. New creative policies must be addressed to their voters. Boris Johnson showed he understands this in his acceptance speech

I have a message to all those who voted for us yesterday, especially those who voted for us Conservatives, one-nation Conservatives for the first time.

You may only have lent us your vote and you may not think of yourself as a natural Tory.

And as I think I said 11 years ago to the people of London when I was elected in what was thought of as a Labour city, your hand may have quivered over the ballot paper before you put your cross in the Conservative box and you may intend to return to Labour next time round.

And if that is the case, I am humbled that you have put your trust in me, and that you have put your trust in us. And I, and we, will never take your support for granted.

This will be the test of Johnson the Prime Minister. Can he, as Prime Minister, become a better person or will he, as President Obama jibed when in the UK in 2016, prove to be our Trump but with, as Ben Rhodes, his speechwriter, added 'better hair'.

There is precious little generosity in politics. Good ideas are pinched from other parties without acknowledgement. Distortion of other parties' policies are the name of the game. Yet it is a fact that without Nigel Farage, Boris Johnson would not be Prime Minister. Nigel Farage, first with UKIP and now with the Brexit Party, has slowly, and helped by proportional voting for European MEPs, had a transformative effect on British politics. He is a clever populist and plays with immigration fears but generally stops short of racist language, judging it wise not to alienate his wider voter base which would desert him if his appeal was based only on race. In Vote Leave during the 2016 referendum, it was determined the campaign should keep its distance from Farage and win by itself the Electoral Commission's choice as the designated official group campaigning to leave the EU. It was feared that Vote Leave would be damaged by Farage at some stage without any consultation going off on some venture which would be perceived as racist. This he did in fact do, appearing with a poster which caused great offence and when later that same day Jo Cox the Labour MP was killed by a right-wing extremist, the poster was withdrawn.

In Plymouth, however, I invited Lord Dartmouth then the South West UKIP MEP to share my public meeting platform. He had a good reputation and was very knowledgeable on trade negotiations.

Farage now in 2020 aims to form yet another vehicle for his populism and he has already said he will call it the Reform Party based on reform of the Lords and electoral reform. Farage is a populist leader who goes his own way without any party discipline but if anyone can force changes in these two areas it could well be Farage. The hereditary principle and first past the post voting system are historical legacies for Conservatives. They are not sustainable over the next decade. The House of Commons has never truly accepted an elected Second Chamber and on this issue even with a large majority Johnson could come unstuck.

The idea of reconstituting the Council of the North established in 1472 by Edward IV in York is an interesting concept. Any siting would need to be subject to full consultation. But why not constitute it with elected members from Edinburgh, Cardiff and Belfast and with English representation from the big cities and local government bodies, along the lines of the German Bundesrat with attendance based on expertise. It would be a very worthwhile federal innovation reflecting the federal nature of the UK but retaining the Commons as the only elected place where all of the UK is represented by direct elections and the only body covering defence and foreign policy.

The fact that Farage's Brexit Party stepped down in all Conservative-held seats before the 2019 General Election is to his credit. Not to have done so would have jeopardised Brexit. He has been a thorn in the flesh of the Conservative Party and has developed taking votes off other parties into an art form. Restless now that the Conservatives have won the election so handsomely, and no doubt feeling unloved and resentful that he has not received the credit he believes he deserves, he is a loose cannon. There is clearly an open welcome for Farage in Trump's Presidential campaign and perhaps for a while that will be sufficient at least until November 2020.

I doubt that Boris Johnson will go out of his way to help or contain Farage at present. He may be more tempted to wait and see if Farage's Reform Party is launched and if it appears to be in danger of taking off and damaging the Conservatives seek some accommodation while making Farage's reforms his own.

Personally, I do not believe Boris is narcissistic, at least no more than many past Prime Ministers, including Churchill with whom Johnson admits to being 'obsessed'. He is not therefore like Trump, on his key characteristic of being a world class narcissist. Johnson is hubristic as are most 'actor' politicians. His gusto, his energy is an important part of his attraction. I do not believe he is contemptuous of others, a characteristic of some Prime Ministers who acquired hubris syndrome when in office and other related features described in Chapter 1 which Lloyd George, Chamberlain, Thatcher and Blair all acquired in office. But if he attempts to sideline Cabinet and take all power into No 10 that will be his downfall.

If there is a single word to describe Johnson it is that he is 'promiscuous' in everything; promiscuous in the sense of the Oxford Dictionary definition:

1. Consisting of members or elements of different kinds massed together without order; of mixed and disorderly composition or character . . .
2. That is without discrimination or method: confusedly mingled, indiscriminate.

Martin Hammond, Master in College at Eton, to which Johnson won a scholarship after being at a state primary school and an international school in Brussels, wrote to his father on 10 April 1982. It is a letter which showed great perception on Johnson's unfurling character which stands the test of time and is highly relevant today. 'I think he honestly believes that it is churlish of us not to regard him as an exception, one who should be free of the network of obligation which binds everyone else.'[445] Hitherto,

---

445 Andrew Gimson, *Boris. The Adventures of Boris Johnson* (Simon & Schuster, 2016) p.43

Johnson has shown at times total contempt for those obligations, particularly in his private life.

What significance should we attach to Boris's hair? All the time on TV we see him deliberately ruffling it up before facing any camera. The explanation probably lies in how Johnson in an interview in 2014 well before the 2016 referendum himself describes Churchill: "he had a naturally eccentric, orotund character, and he became aware of how he was seen. I think that he then realised there were certain gimmicks and characteristics that he would play up" . . . "there was the cigar: never be without your trademark, he [Churchill] said.

For Boris, his hair – for the present at least – is his trademark like Churchill's cigar. He will develop others. He has written,

'I think he [Churchill] was also quite shrewd in knowing that the English as an electorate don't really mind that a great man should occasionally touch a spot of drink. So that you can see that, to some extent unconsciously – but also, to some extent, consciously – he began to morph into the incarnation of the country, of John Bull-type character that he slightly played to. It was a Falstaffian, John Bull-type character that he slightly played to, I think. In reality he was also a highly poetic soul, and a deeply literary guy: he was fascinated by poetry... He was a kind of bouncy-castle personality: he filled the room and, of course, was a tremendous bully in some ways, but we needed a bully! We needed someone who was going to drive the whole flywheel of the war effort to get stuff done. And thank God he was as he was.'

Johnson knows John Bull died with the British Empire but the British affection for a 'character' continues. Writing before he was a Brexiteer, nevertheless he again rationalises how he sees himself with an accurate description of Churchill's view of Europe. "He wanted a united Europe with France and Germany at its core, but I don't think he would have wanted the UK to have been solely committed to that. I think he would have seen us as assisting and participating, but also having an eye to our primary relationships with America and former imperial countries. He would have wanted to have his cake and eat it.'[446]

When the UK leaves the EU, we must be prepared to deploy militarily worldwide and return to blue water diplomacy. We must be selective, already a base for our two aircraft carriers is being prepared in Oman and that will be an excellent geographical position for a multinational maritime Rapid Reaction Force to be used either by the UN or NATO. Operating aircraft carriers from Oman, with Australia, New Zealand and hopefully India supplying escort vessels would be both feasible and globally strategically enhancing. The UK no longer in the EU should not contribute to EU 'common defence'. We must also focus the UK's defence effort on 'hard' defence within the NATO European area. On 11 July 2018, the day of the NATO Summit, an advertisement appeared in *The Times*, which bore my name as a contributor to the cost. It was signed by prominent former UK fighting commanders and the contents reflected their views with which I agree. The figure 8 was a play on the popular demand from the British public to build more Dreadnought battleships before the First World War, 'we want eight and we won't wait.'

1   Spending precisely targeted to **rebuild our hollowed-out key front line capabilities – capability means systems *and* people – to provide decisive assets *across the whole spectrum of modern conflict*.** Special funding should be directed into complementary technical investment in Artificial Intelligence

446 Johnson talking to Matt Elton of the BBC History Magazine, December 2014 (www.historyextra.com) attached to his biography, *The Churchill Factor. How One Man Made History* (Hodder paperbacks, 2015)

and autonomous systems, active and passive cyber and secret Intelligence *but without reduction in other areas.* A further eternal truth of war is that the enemy does not attack in the area of latest vogue, *but in whichever area has been allowed to decay.* All must be strong across the full spectrum of modern and future warfare.

2 A **Royal Navy** restored as a truly world-wide power and a Brigade level amphibious capability for the Royal Marines reinstated.

3 A **Field Army** based on a Corps of 3 Divisions.

4 An **Air Force** capable, sufficient and resourced both to secure our airspace and to conduct successful full-spectrum joint operations.

5 A **multi-service capability** to secure all our borders, waters and territorial assets.

6 Withdrawal from the EU Galileo satellite programme and the building of a **national 4i GPS satellite system** to enhance Five Eyes secure capabilities.

7 A **Defence Budget** sufficient for all these needs, just like in the later 1930s, *we can't afford not to;* and for as long as it takes, with a cast iron commitment to our NATO and Five Eyes allies.

8 **Arbitrary manpower caps lifted,** the Forces re-recruited as restored capabilities demand, and the return of recruiting from out-sourced companies to the Services including MI6.

President Trump saw the advertisement while flying in to the NATO Summit and apparently liked it. The US people need to understand that the British value NATO far more than EU defence. Of course the UK must always be ready to go on working with European allies, particularly France, on difficult UN and NATO missions and contribute troops to the Rapid Reaction Force, outside of EU defence structures, already agreed with President Macron.

The UK does not leave Europe when leaving the EU. We do not become a satellite of the US either. We become an independent nation again as we were before 1973. The EU has not worked for us as judged by the clear majority of voters in the 2016 referendum and reinforced by the 2019 General Election. That referendum only took place after a long and painful party political debate which has split all major parties for 47 years. In 2016 MPs voted for the referendum legislation by 544 to 53. Yet many of those same MPs shamefully failed to honour their promise to implement the result. This was one reason why another General Election was held in December 2019. Another reason was Jeremy Corbyn was coming under pressure to step down as party leader. Boris Johnson was well aware that any election would be far harder to win if Corbyn was replaced as leader. I have no doubt that that consideration weighed extremely heavily, despite the risks, in holding an election in December. Nevertheless, it was a brave decision. Other Prime Ministers have been known to hesitate and pull back from calling an election. It was definitely true of Gordon Brown and arguably so of Jim Callaghan. 'Fortune favours the brave' is an old saying and so it has proved once again. Johnson's was a very personal victory. He had personally become a symbol of Brexit and it carried him to victory in his own party as Prime Minister and Brexit carried him to victory in the country ensuring he continued as Prime Minister.

Whether a supporter or a critic it is not hard to see in Johnson's choice of words in 1994 the same Johnson that is with us still as Prime Minister. 'stuff done'; 'cake and eat it'. These are not ad men slogans he spouts, they are how he has always expressed himself and probably will continue to do so.

So we can conclude that Boris's ruffled hair will stay together with many of his mannerisms. But does he realise that he himself must change as Prime Minister? Some reading this will say he cannot change. I profoundly hope that they are wrong and as Prime

Minister Johnson will change. Let us hope fewer facile statements like when being asked on the campaign trail about politicians who lie. 'Well they should be made to go on their knees through the chamber of the House of Commons scourging themselves with copies of their offending documents which claim to prove one thing and actually prove something quite different.'

Judged by his first short period as Prime Minister in 2019 he did achieve far more in negotiations with, and in the handling of, the EU than all his many critics believed possible. But while Boris would like to be like Churchill, it is hard to find examples where Churchill in his long life – and certainly as Prime Minister, except as part of wartime propaganda – deliberately lied. Sadly, it is not hard to find many examples of Johnson lying.

Most Prime Ministers in my lifetime during periods in No 10 became a bigger and better person than the one who first entered, even Chamberlain. Some steadily improved in statesmanship, some deteriorated with illness, some began better than they finished, others finished better than they started. The electorate has chosen to continue with Johnson as Prime Minister. Whether people voted for him or not, he won with a substantial majority and most people will give him a measure of the respect we try to give to all newly elected Prime Ministers. We know the good parts of his character, his ability to make us laugh, to not take himself too seriously. To be intelligent and thoughtful and move with the times. To have no side. He is not a racist. He wants to be 'a one nation Conservative', although I have been trying to discover what that term really means in over 50 years in Parliament! He has the potential, against predictions, to enable Scotland and Ireland to become the focus of re-establishing a different and better United Kingdom. It is not inconceivable the piecemeal changes so far could yet gel together into something stable and yet dynamic.

After this General Election Johnson must be forced to recognise what is well understood by the public that mendacity has entered the practice and the soul of British politics. I say forced because he will only stop lying if he knows humiliation awaits him if he continues to lie. Mendaciousness started in 2003 over the invasion of Iraq under Prime Minister Blair and it has grown massively since then. It must be eradicated.

One mechanism which should be introduced urgently was presaged by the new House of Commons Speaker Hoyle in his speeches before and after his election by his fellow Parliamentarians. He sensed that the world no longer sees the House of Commons as the respected mother of parliaments and that the 'tarnish left needed polishing away'. The House of Commons can remove that tarnish. As a minimum over lying and misrepresentation it must create a Code of Practice. The Code must then be overseen by the Speaker as his high priority and around the Code real powers of enforcement must be established assisted by the Parliamentary Ombudsman with extra resources to investigate proven misinformation and lies by members of Parliament whether spoken or written and not just in the House of Commons but outside as well. I cannot see a role for making lying illegal and involving the courts of law more than they are already involved. Contempt of Court is a serious offence. Contempt of Parliament must become a serious offence too. The ultimate penalty for MPs is not a new one; but has fallen into disuse, namely being forced to resign. Serious breaches should not just involve an oral statement, but involve being called to make an apology at the bar of the House of Commons and reading out a statement of apology, the content of which has been previously agreed by the Speaker. This change in behaviour must start from the top with the Prime Minister Boris Johnson. If he does not mend his ways and discover the value of truth, then he will not only be compared with Trump, but he will be perceived to be a populist modelled on Trump's populism. That is not the present situation. The populism of Boris Johnson could well be seen, in retrospect, as the British way of adjusting through a referendum to much needed changes in our parliamentary democracy. Changes demanded by the people and thoughtfully introduced over a decade by a renewed smaller House of Commons and the abolition of the present House of Lords, are essential.

In January 2020 Prime Minister Johnson was faced with an important decision in addition to positioning the country outside the EU after the transition period at the end of the year. The high speed railway HS2 project was vastly over budget, controversial but could have been politically axed and the public expenditure saved invested in the North of England. Johnson nevertheless guided the Cabinet to continuing it, with important changes to its Northern linkages.

Following these decisions Boris Johnson moved to a Cabinet reshuffle which will be remembered most for the resignation of his Chancellor of the Exchequer, Sajid Javid, and replacing him with the Chief Secretary of the Treasury, Rishi Sunak. Nominally the aim was to have a joint unit of special advisers between No 10 and No 11. Boris must have expected that this would likely be refused. He now has in place, perhaps a year or so earlier than anticipated, the man he had wanted to be his next Chancellor. That is no bad thing provided it is not accompanied by the emasculation of Cabinet Government. Prime Minister Callaghan, who believed in Cabinet Government, also believed that the Chancellor, Foreign Secretary and Home Secretary should only disagree openly in Cabinet with the Prime Minister if they had first failed to agree privately. From time to time even amongst friends, but particularly amongst rivals, that will happen and Cabinet is where the matter should be resolved, not in the newspapers by briefings all of which erode confidence. This friction was a feature of the Blair/Brown rivalry for ten years and a sign that even with a large majority friction between the Treasury and No 10 is deeply destructive.

Chapter 13

Conclusion

George Washington was America's first and arguably best ever President. He is known for telling his father when a young boy when challenged over whether he had cut down his father's favourite cherry tree, admitting doing so saying 'I can't tell a lie, Pa. You know I can't tell a lie.' But this story written after Washington's death in 1799 comes from a book *The Life of George Washington* by Parson Mason Weems. On his way to his inauguration in 1861 Abraham Lincoln cited Weems's book as his greatest inspiration. Yet almost certainly the cherry tree story, which was only added in the fifth edition, is a fable. And the reason it has resonated down through history was that 'truth was one of the biggest casualties in the political battle that raged in the early years of the United States. As the protagonists argued they traded lies about each other, their loyalties and their love lives, often secretly financing newspapers to spread libels. Weems sought to raise Washington above such unseemliness.'[447]

The US has had different Presidents, Republicans and Democrats. Many of them at some stages in their presidency were populists. President Franklin Roosevelt was no more ready to declare war against Germany than President Woodrow Wilson had

---

447 Daniel Finkelstein, 'Truth will overcome peddlers of fake news', *The Times*, 31 December 2019.

been before him. Both waited until after they had secured their next presidential term of office. Wilson won his second term in 1916 and Roosevelt his third in 1940. Only then was either ready to declare war. Both Presidents waited in the event to be attacked first sensing the populist isolationist mood. Wilson waited until a number of ships had been sunk by German submarines. Roosevelt waited until the attack on Pearl Harbor by Japanese planes in December 1941. Was that the response of a populist President or was it responding to populism? Perhaps pragmatism best straddles the meaning of the two words populism and populist when applied to most elected politicians. Popular does not mean loved by all. In the latter stages of his 1936 campaign for a second term, Franklin Roosevelt made a highly partisan speech.

> For twelve years this Nation was afflicted with hear-nothing, see-nothing, do-nothing government . . . .They are unanimous in their hate for me – and I welcome their hatred . . . . I should like to have it said of my first administration that in it the forces of selfishness and lust for power met their match. I should like to have it said of my second administration that in it these forces met their master.[448]

Nor are democratic politics a polite exchange of views. Politics is a blood sport. Presidents Theodore Roosevelt, Franklin Roosevelt, Harry Truman, Ronald Reagan and now Donald Trump have all identified in various ways with President Jackson. It may or may not be significant that while holding a rally of his supporters, President Trump chose to visit Andrew Jackson's tomb at The Hermitage in Nashville, Tennessee on 15 March 2017, the 250th anniversary of Jackson's birth. Trump was the first sitting President to do this since Ronald Reagan. He laid a wreath on the tomb and gave a short speech to invited guests. He has also put up a portrait of Jackson in

---

448 Ibid, David Owen, *In Sickness and In Power*, p. 52

the Oval Office. In doing this Trump can be seen as identifying with a populist President who, like Truman, often spoke about 'the common man'. Some Jackson critics will always choose to highlight his Indian Removal Act, a law that enforced the moving of the Cherokee nation in what became known as the 'Trail of Tears'. Others will highlight his military battles, others his legislative record. It may be that his campaign to make the popular vote the ultimate decider of who becomes President may yet return to be fully debated again by Congress. Each year during his presidency Jackson proposed that the constitution should be changed and the electoral college vote should be abolished. Each year Congress rejected his proposal.

This book does not judge the morality of US Presidents or UK Prime Ministers, their sexual conduct, their underlying moral attitudes or the way they use religion. That is for voters.

A puzzling aspect of Donald Trump's electoral appeal, as viewed from outside the US, is how many evangelical Christians vote for him despite his own behaviour, to put it mildly, not fitting into a normal Christian lifestyle. It is commonly known that his Vice-President Mike Pence is a born again evangelical and on formal occasions is frequently pictured with the President. What is less well known is how the Republican Party in the 1940s and early 1950s linked up with Billy Graham and other well-known preachers and their religious teaching became linked with anti-communism. Graham was visibly seen to support President Eisenhower. Religious affiliation weakened over the years in both main parties but the evangelical right became evermore identified with the Bible lands and in particular Israel and Jerusalem.

For his eight years in office President Obama identified with Rick Warren, author of *The Purpose Driven Life* the best-selling, non-fiction hardback after the Bible in American history.

Not surprisingly, Donald Trump has his own distinctive approach to evangelicals and moving the American Embassy from Tel Aviv to Jerusalem was one important manifestation. He has now chosen Paula White as his new link to the evangelicals. She is an attractive evangelist, married three times, who is identified with the 'prosperity gospel' wanting their followers to achieve good health and increased wealth. She has known him since 2002 and has been appointed formally to his administration to boost his Faith and Opportunity Initiative.

The Reverend William J. Barber II who addressed the Democratic National Convention in 2016 was reported in the *New York Times* on 6 November 2019 as describing her appointment as "a very ominous sign" a sign that "Christian narcissism" has come into the White House. Yet what is important for Trump is that some other evangelicals appear to think she may be able to bring together people from parts of Christianity that would ordinarily never intersect. If true, that could provide crucial new votes in 2020 and may counter the upset that Trump's decision over breaking the US Army's link with the Kurds fighting together in Eastern Syria created amongst his evangelical supporters.

All these issues have to be resolved at the ballot box in their own countries and by more canvassing on the doorstep than protest on the streets. This book has touched on drug abuse where there is evidence of it, as in the case of Anthony Eden over his post-operative illness and in the case of President John F. Kennedy over his Addison's disease. Amphetamine, opioids and other drugs are covered as a warning that there are leaders in politics, business and the military, who will strive to increase their performance mentally and sometimes sexually. There are many other drugs with mind changing characteristics that are easily accessible. We are seeing only the tip of the iceberg of what people are doing to their own brains and are I believe too complacent about this. All of these are social and philosophical matters for voters to weigh in the balance against a myriad of other factors.

Trump's personality is complex, he is a narcissist and he has lied on innumerable occasions as President. He has chosen to operate very differently from his predecessors. He called being impeached a hoax and was found not guilty by the Senate. The question is will he be deprived by the electorate of a second term. Evan Osnos in a long article in the *New Yorker* on 8 May 2017 writes correctly, that in by far the majority of cases, 'the history of besieged presidencies is, in the end, the history of hubris, of blindness to one's faults, to deafness of warnings.'

This book does try to learn lessons from the past in the growth of the different types of democracy that have been formed and developed on both sides of the Atlantic. Whereas Prime Ministers in the UK are answerable to Parliament, the so-called fusion of power, in contrast the US system is based on the separation of powers between President and Congress. Prime Ministers can be removed by MPs in their own party, whereas a US President, apart from Congressional impeachment, is not directly answerable for their conduct to Senators or Congressmen. While MPs sustain the executive in the division lobbies in the House of Commons they can throw out a Prime Minister and the government through a vote of no confidence, using the Fixed Term Parliament Act 2011 which requires two votes of confidence separated by a two-week interval. While the legislation makes five-year term Parliaments more likely it reduces the personal power of a Prime Minister as happened in 2019. Boris Johnson will almost certainly repeal this legislation and revert back to the previous situation where a Prime Minister is free to ask the Queen for a General Election at a time of their choosing or if there has been a single motion of no confidence an Election could be forced by Parliament. The traditional justification for the power of MPs to terminate a Prime Minister's tenure, even when they are winning general elections, is that MPs know their leader's strengths and weaknesses and they can detect far earlier than party members or the electorate as a whole whether their leader is not functioning effectively.

In Mrs Thatcher's case, she was thrown out by her own MPs in 1990, having been in office since 1979. The reason was that from

1989 she had acquired hubris syndrome which was impairing her judgement, and a sufficient number of MPs of her own party saw it as their duty to withdraw their support in an inner party vote to force a leadership election. Much the same was done to Tony Blair by his own MPs and for many of the same reasons for he too had acquired hubris syndrome from 2001 to 2007.

Richard Nixon served as the 37th US President from 1969 to 1974. The Watergate scandal, which started with a burglary, had been 'distilled to a single essence' over the White House tapes. John Farrell in his recent biography writes 'every word, every joke, every curse, every tantrum, every flight of paranoia' was recorded. As the Judiciary Committee was debating impeachment the Supreme Court's judgement on 24 July was unanimous; that while the court recognised a doctrine of executive privilege this did not apply to the tapes since the issue was one of criminal behaviour. Had Nixon tried to defy the Supreme Court there would have been instant impeachment. Nixon's only alternative was to resign.[449] Controversially, after his resignation, President Ford, risking his re-election in the process, pardoned him.

Another form of accountability involved two Presidents, Reagan and George H. W. Bush, over the independent council procedure in the Iran-Contra affair from 1986 to 1993. Its history is revealed in the book *Firewall. The Iran-Contra Conspiracy and Cover-up* by Lawrence Walsh, the independent counsel.[450] A saga of how the US, with Reagan's support, attempted to trade arms for hostages held by Iranian terrorists.

Clinton's investigation by independent counsel and subsequent procedures in an attempt to trigger impeachment failed. The process was started because of the importance of not accepting lying by a President to a court, but the proceedings were stalled

449 John A. Farrell, *Richard Nixon. The Life* (Scribe, 2017), pp. 520, 528-9.
450 Lawrence Walsh, *Firewall. The Iran-Contra Conspiracy and Cover-up* (W. W. Norton, 1997).

and ended well short of impeachment with a fine and with a three year disqualification from practising law.

In contrast, the UK completely failed to apply any legal procedures to the alleged contempt of Parliament and breaches of law over the Iraq War during Tony Blair's government from 2002 to 2007. A refusal thereafter confirmed in the light of the Iraq Inquiry. Yet in June 2018, in relation to rendition for the purpose of interrogation and torture, it eventually became clear that the UK had been involved despite denials in Parliament, and yet no judgement or trial is expected. It seems the UK has lost either the will or morality, perhaps both, to hold their leaders to account.

The US and UK have not always worked smoothly together. Yet overall as this book tries to show there have been substantive benefits to both countries from working together and long may it continue. There have been personality differences and much hubris in leaders on both sides of the Atlantic and in specific instances that hubris has acquired the telltale traits of hubris syndrome. Sometimes in the case of Prime Minister Eden and President Kennedy the personality changes stemmed from diagnosable medical illnesses and their drug therapy and their personal abuse. More often the personality differences stemmed from circumstances as in the case of Franklin Roosevelt and Winston Churchill over attitudes to the continuation of the British Empire after the Second World War and limited by the Atlantic Charter. Genuine differences about the merits of British imperialism continuing after the war was ended by the British electorate in rejecting Churchill and electing Attlee, who brought India to independence. Despite Lyndon Johnson's wish to have a friend and ally fighting with US troops in Vietnam, there was a stubborn Yorkshireman's resistance in the shape of Harold Wilson. Wilson understood that the UK would be better able to stay out of the war in Vietnam if he stayed clear of criticising the domestic policies of Lyndon Johnson. The Bush/Blair 'love in', by contrast, over the war in Iraq lead to a hubristic accord that worked against open debate on the conduct of that war.

Theresa May showed the will and need to oppose some international policies of President Trump. Boris Johnson has a better but not a dependent relationship with Trump.

In terms of joint military action for the future and upholding NATO, there is still much to learn from the actions of two very different Supreme Allied Commanders, Dwight Eisenhower and Douglas MacArthur. Also there is much for politicians to learn about the working of the military mind and what the use of force entails. Similarly, the business worlds of Wall Street and the City of London and the hubris of business leaders, which did so much to bring about the 2008 global economic crisis, means we still have lessons to learn that are highly relevant today.

As the US grapples with the aftermath of the rust belt revolt and the Trump presidency and the UK grapples with the aftermath of the people's referendum vote to leave the EU, there are important similarities and lessons to be learnt from each other. Trump and Johnson personally appear to be comfortable with each other. They should meet regularly and not be subject to attacks for doing so. For political reasons they are necessary for international stability. This is not a book about the special relationship, a term which I use now for the first time, but a book about human relations on both sides of the Atlantic. We trade together in a major way, we fight together in wars around the world, we operate under a common language and a common legal system. Yet there are abiding differences that have lived alongside very important friendships and love. I have been married to an American for over 50 years and during that time the Anglo-American relations have changed but we must never stop learning from each other and long may our relationship endure and prosper.

For any UK government, first and foremost, Boris Johnson in 2020 must stay out of the US domestic debate, even if Trump breaks the conventions. Theresa May got a belly laugh from revealing Trump's own plan to handle the EU – 'sue them', but she paid a price in Trump's clear preference for Boris Johnson to replace her as Prime Minister. Narcissists do not like being laughed at. The British media and protesters on the street considered President Trump to be fair game and a Trump-like balloon was floated in the air above London. It may have caused offence, but no one in government can or should ban peaceful demonstrating.

The long-standing tradition for governments internationally, which President Obama flouted, is to stay out of other countries' domestic politics. It dates from the US presidential election of 1888 when the UK's Ambassador in Washington, Sackville-West, wrote a reply to a supposed expatriate stating a preference for the incumbent president, Cleveland. Responding to a newspaper headline, 'British Lion's paw thrust into American politics', Sackville-West was ordered to leave by Cleveland.

Harold Wilson's conduct in relation to President Lyndon Johnson's handling of the Vietnam War was to avoid sending British troops to the unpopular war and restricting his criticism to extending the bombing to the North. (See Chapter 6.)

In the same context any UK government should never lie to a US President: that was Anthony Eden's massive error in handling the Suez Crisis. President Eisenhower deserved the truth; he was a true friend and ally. To keep from him the clandestine military operation with France and Israel was unconscionable. The UK government deserved everything it got back from the US. (Chapter 4.) The Cabinet knew the facts; the decision was not just Eden's, and Harold Macmillan's conduct, in particular, was driven by personal ambition.

The US-UK relationship owes much to a common language and a common legal system: that is why speaking frankly and privately is the bond, break that bond and you break the relationship. Churchill knew this and in 1940 he was determined, in private, to speak the truth despite the President not wishing to hear the message: 'we need 50 destroyers urgently'. Yet by 1941 Churchill knew that in the wording of the Atlantic Charter (Chapter 3), he had been outsmarted by Roosevelt but he had to accept it and he knew Roosevelt had personally designed the wording deliberately to stop his post-war vision of a continued British Empire.

Another example is that Truman did not give Attlee, when he flew to Washington, the pledge he wanted not to use nuclear weapons over the Korean War. Truman said he would try his best to consult but he could not promise to consult without crossing the constitutional powers of the Senate. That reality remains today.

Over the Anglo-American plan for Rhodesia and handling Southern Africa from 1977–79 relations were very close. Yet President Carter's formulation after meeting President Nyerere in Washington that the creation of a military force for a future Zimbabwe during the election would 'be based primarily on the Patriotic Front' presented huge difficulties for both Prime Minister Callaghan and me as Foreign Secretary. Fortunately I got the word 'primarily' removed but Ian Smith was given a lever to use against our proposals which had been more balanced. But that is the risk one takes – a US president can and often does shape Anglo-US and also US-EU policy.

President Clinton's refusal to get behind and enforce the agreement reached on the Vance/Owen Peace Plan (VOPP) for Bosnia Herzegovina on 1 May 1993 in Athens with the Greek Prime Minister Mitsotakis and all three leaders, Milosovic, Cosic and Bulatovic was the end of the road for the VOPP. I understood that Prime Minister John Major and his Foreign Secretary, Douglas Hurd, had by then no other option but to accept the US position. So did the French Prime Minister Balladur accept US policy when in 'co-habitation' in government with President Mitterrand, who was seriously ill with cancer of the prostate. These are the realities of French and of European, not just UK cooperation, with the US.

Even so the reality of power can be difficult. The American Secretary of State publicly said in February 1993 that they would not enforce a peace settlement in the Balkans. Then a few months later, pushed for UN safe areas with insufficient troop numbers – 6,000 instead of over 30,000 which military commanders in the field wanted. This led inexorably to the genocide in Srebrenica in July 1995 and only after that came NATO military enforcement in late August 1995.[451] From then on the public image especially after the Dayton Accords, was of the US rescuing Europe! The truth is the US under Clinton spurned the EU and its European NATO partners which from 1993–95 led to great loss of life and a two way divide in Bosnia Herzegovina in 1995, which is still very unstable in 2020.

Other examples of the lessons of history on UK-US relations are from the Iraq War. In early 2003 a wiser Prime Minister than Tony Blair would himself have examined the option of not being part of the invasion force, put forward by Jack Straw, his Foreign Secretary, but only presented in a personal memo when it was too late, after Blair had flown to the Azores to meet Bush. This was something which George W. Bush had earlier privately made clear to Blair would not damage their friendship and which the Defense Secretary Rumsfeld had publicly floated as acceptable to the Pentagon. The position of the UK by then was clearly an inferior one and we were not part of the military decisions in the way we had been in 1991 as part of the attack on Iraq, in retaliation for their invasion of Kuwait. The UK could have then come in after the US invasion in a major NATO role, reinforcing Baghdad where US troop numbers were totally inadequate. Even so UK military and diplomatic advice on the ground was to move British troops up from Basra in May 2003. This was rejected by the Chiefs of Staff. Sadly Blair did not overrule them. Had he done so Bush would have had to order reinforcements for Baghdad and reject Rumsfeld's advice to actually withdraw 16,000 troops. The UK military would have found it easier in Iraq to assert their views under NATO's command and control procedures, with their knowledge base from Bosnia Herzegovina in late

---

451 David Owen, *Balkan Odyssey* (Victor Gollancz, 1995), pp 81-117 & 217-220.

1995 through 1997, for far higher troop numbers. The transition to democratic elections in Iraq needed more US and UK soldiers on the ground but also more troops from other NATO countries. Fortunately it was President Bush who added to troop levels in Iraq in 2006, realising his earlier mistake.

Sometimes the boot is on the other foot in relations with the US and it is for the UK to pick up the major peacekeeping role. In 1979 my successor as Foreign Secretary, Peter Carrington, persuaded the Prime Minister Margaret Thatcher, that it was right to take up the idea of a Commonwealth military force for Rhodesia to be in position to keep the peace during any election following a successful conference at the end of the year at Lancaster House. The Commonwealth Heads of Government agreed to this in their meeting in Lusaka in 1979. Two years earlier in 1977, I had failed to win support in the Labour Cabinet for a Commonwealth force as being far preferable to the UN force option which we adopted. Cyrus Vance, still US Secretary of State, had rightly preferred all along the Commonwealth option but there had never been any suggestion of a US military contribution. This was a British and Commonwealth military responsibility which we discharged well in 1980.

It is also worth recalling that even President Reagan was, at first, not helpful over British military action to retake the Falkland Islands in 1982 and it was the Pentagon that provided crucial weapons with little support from Washington or the US representative in the UN. It was President Mitterrand who helped over technical information on the French Super Étendard fighter plane with Exocet missiles owned by the Argentines.

Hubristic mendacity is not new. It has been with us for centuries past. What is new is the extent to which our societies accept lying: first in the US with the election of Trump and now with the election of Boris Johnson in the UK. We need a change in substance in the UK Parliament to restore the Profumo practice that lying is no longer acceptable. Slowly, but surely, unless checked, lying will be accepted as will its various manifestations. Lying is increasing in many walks of life. It involves much more than not waiting to check facts or distorting information. It is telling deliberate untruths. We are in danger of developing a mind frame that with social media anything goes. What was unacceptable has become acceptable behaviour. If this continues we will lose an inbuilt brain function where through childhood we develop a virtual filter to stop lying through voice, writing or tweeting. Not just because they are wrong in fact or morally, nor because they are erroneous, disobliging and create misinformation, but because they bring disharmony, upset, pain, disillusionment, envy, hatred and malice. When the filter erodes, then you and you alone judge what is true. Then what you believe overrides everything you do. You start to create a very different community around you, a different country emerges in which you work and play and even a different world in which you live.

When leaders believe in their own truths and believe they are entitled to distort the truth to achieve policy ends, by whatever means, then society itself is endangered. Undermining the truth, undermines the behaviour, the quality of decision-making and the sort of society in which we rub along together despite inequalities, sexual, racial and religious differences.

It is not a minor matter for leaders to lie in any walk of life. Behaviour generally becomes seriously unstuck when leaders distort other people's views and when they distort their own views. When facts are no longer sacred, when opinions reinforce prejudices, then we become in our daily lives strangers to the truth, and we are driving our society towards destruction.

There are different types of proven hubristic mendacity in US Presidents and UK Prime Ministers with different origins. Analysis of what has contributed to leaders lying in office is difficult since these individuals guard their privacy as does the bureaucracy around them. They have died before many truths have been unveiled by history. My conclusions from studying hubris in political leaders over many years however, lead me to conclude that there is a class of lying which I have called Hubristic Mendacity. Proven cases amongst US Presidents and UK Prime Ministers which can be charted.

Hubristic Mendacity.

Cause: Externally administered drugs in excess:
Anthony Eden – Suez (amphetamines)
John F. Kennedy – Bay of Pigs (testosterone, procaine and other mind-changing drugs)
Richard Nixon – Watergate (alcohol)

Cause: Psychiatric illness:
Lyndon Johnson – Vietnam (Bipolar Disorder)

Cause: Hubris Syndrome:
Tony Blair – `Iraq War 2001 – present day (High stress)
George W. Bush – Iraq War 2001-2006 (High stress)

Exposed by Special Prosecutor:
Ronald Reagan – Iran/Contra Affair (Emotional)
Bill Clinton – Monica Lewinsky (Sexual)

Abuse of power impeachment inquiry:
Donald Trump – Ukraine/Joe Biden (personal power)

As of 20 January 2020, according to the *Washington Post* Fact Check, Trump has made 16,200 false or misleading claims in his first three years in office.

President Trump is undoubtedly full of hubris as well as being narcissistic, but does he qualify for the label of acquired hubris syndrome? The answer is I am not sure. We know next to nothing about his mental health. If he had had at some stage in the past a psychiatric illness or mental breakdown he would be excluded from the label of acquired hubris syndrome. One might well ask, has he ever been considered 'normal'? Or has he always been an exception to the norm – 'irretrievably Trump', a description of him by journalist Leslie Marshall in Chapter 11. This is where his Tweets have been discussed in some detail and reference is made to Professor Peter Garrard and his colleagues' work on linguistic analysis of two British Prime Ministers, Margaret Thatcher and Tony Blair, both of whom did develop hubris syndrome and both were removed from office by Members of Parliament.

Garrard and his team's linguistic analysis of Donald Trump's Twitter activities has produced some interesting findings as presented to the Maudsley Philosophy Group in the autumn of 2018. They divided Trump's Twitter output into four epochs: i) before entering politics; ii) the Republican nomination campaign; iii) the Presidential campaign; and iv) the Presidency. They found marked changes across these epochs on a number of measures. His language becomes increasingly formulaic and emotionally negatively charged. Of the linguistic markers of hubris syndrome that they found in Thatcher and Blair, they did see the rise of 'we/our/us' and the decline of 'I/my/me' across the four epochs, though in Trump's case, third person references occur in all three pre-Presidential epochs but disappear after he enters the White House. This gives some evidence that we may be witnessing a gathering hubris in Trump on top of what was there before but in my judgement, there are as yet insufficient grounds to say he has hubris syndrome.

In the words of the eminent American psychiatrist, Allen Frances, 'Trump does not qualify for a mental disorder, but he does present with one of the world's best documented cases of lifelong failure to mature. He is a boy/man who expects everything to go his way and experiences the world as an extension of himself. Other people exist only to do imperious bidding, admire his great deeds, and gratify his enormous wants. . . . The Trump phenomenon marks what I dearly hope will be a bottom in both American tragedy and farce.'[452]

Frances highlights two of the 'most frightening of all Trump's frightening tweets:'

> The FAKE NEWS media (failing @nytimes, @NBCNews, @ABC, @CBS, @CNN) is not my enemy, it is the enemy of the American People!

Trump sets himself up, says Frances, as defender of the American people as he mounts the charge against their most fundamental freedoms of speech and thought. Trump's second-scariest tweet was

> Just cannot believe a judge would put our country in such peril. If something happens blame him and court system. People pouring in. Bad!

He was reacting to court decisions questioning the constitutionality of his banning travellers from Muslim countries and, even more important, his claim that the courts have no jurisdiction on his acts because he is protecting the higher value of national security.

Also, the President is tweeting more than ever. In the first year in office, President Trump posted, on average, about 49 tweets per week. Since May 2019 he has posted, on average, 160 times per week with the second week of October 2019 being the busiest with 271 tweets reflecting his outrage on the House impeachment inquiry.[453]

As to whether Boris Johnson has hubris syndrome, again it is too early to judge. He has a fair measure of hubris in his character but there is humour inbuilt into his make-up, often self-deprecating

---

452 Ibid, Allen Frances, *Twilight of American Sanity* (Morrow, 2018), pp. 97.
453 The power of presidential tweets', *The New York Times*, 13 November 2019.

humour and as yet little sign that power itself is something he cannot handle or that it is corroding his appeal. His problem, like Trump's, is mendacity, but not on the same scale.

All of what has been written in this book raises fundamental questions about how the great democracies choose their leaders and judge or indulge their leaders' behaviour in office. There are fundamental questions of character and behaviour that need addressing urgently. We need more research, greater insight and the courage to admit that the deterioration in both behaviour and character is gathering momentum. But it must go further – the systematic cover up of the elite by the elite has to be ended. The way they appoint each other, to national and also international bodies, the 'revolving door' in and out of government often with insufficient waiting period, easy access to all forms of media, the same schools, universities and clubs. The people are now trying, when others have failed, hence the rust belt revolt and the EU referendum result. How will Parliament and Congress react? Carry on as usual? There is an unprecedented opportunity to learn from past mistakes: to reverse centralisation, in the case of the UK to revive municipal government, redistribute resources and talent from London, regain pride in using and buying good British products through individual choice not government diktat. Where there is bad design, shoddy work, poor service, develop a stronger consumer voice to improve standards. People want to feel they have more influence, greater control.

Wall Street, under Democratic as well as Republican administrations, has been no 'paragon of virtue' and neither has the City of London. Nor have Democrat or Republican campaigns been marked by scrupulous attention to creating a more level playing field between candidates to the truth anymore than Conservative or Labour campaigns in the UK. The voters in the US in choosing President Trump and the voters in the UK in choosing Brexit and Prime Minister Johnson surprised and challenged their elites. Money was not the swing factor, that revolt lay deep in the hearts and minds of voters. The elites neither saw these results coming, nor have many yet accepted the verdicts of the voters in 2020.

No doubt lies were told by both the Remain and Leave campaigns. But I have not seen any evidence they swayed the result. The controversial figure on the Vote Leave bus of £350 million per week paid to the EU was taken from the UK's gross contribution for that year to the EU Budget of £19 billion. I explained in detail launching Vote Leave's NHS campaign in May 2016 that deducting the remaining half of the Thatcher rebate of 1984, the other half having been negotiated away by Blair in 2005, and what money we got from the EU for agriculture and scientific research, left us making a net contribution of £9.9 billion, and this likely meant that £5 billion of this would go extra each year to the UK NHS if we left the EU. It looks as if Boris Johnson will more than fulfil this promise.

I believed Vote Leave, which I supported, would win, reinforced by my campaigning in my home city of Plymouth, where handing out leaflets and holding a public meeting, it was not hard to sense opinion forming for 'out' (never 'leave'). The vote in Plymouth was 60% to 40% to leave. Neither campaign was particularly edifying; few campaigns are in my experience. Yet because they offer a binary choice referendums are in most cases, decisive. Take the French referendum on whether France should join the euro in 1992, which President Mitterrand won by an even closer margin – 51% to 49% – to our UK referendum won by 51.89% to 48.11%. That result was accepted immediately by all in France. In the 1975 UK referendum on staying in the Common Market, that result was accepted too although the winning margin was much greater than the vote to leave in 2016. The result of the referendum on Scottish independence in 2014 was initially accepted by the then SNP leader for a generation. Sadly that was not to last as the SNP began to push for a second referendum. Before that in 1997, the referendum on devolution in Wales, only very narrowly won, was accepted. In 2011, the referendum on changing the voting system to use the 'Alternative

Vote' was rejected and that result was accepted. Why not in 2016? Because the elite could not accept losing.

In the US the Supreme Court ruling on the recount dispute in Florida in the 2000 presidential election, decided in favour of the Republicans and gave George W. Bush a narrow victory and the presidency. The result was accepted with some grace by the losing Democrats and in particular by Al Gore, the losing candidate.

Apart from the serious allegation of Russian interference, why has the election of President Trump been opposed from the start? The answer quite apart from Trump's personality and history, is that he only won in the electoral college not in the popular vote. Elites fear populism and populists and tend to believe they have a right to govern.

What of the Trump phenomenon? An accident of history or history in the making?

On 21 July 2018 in the *Financial Times* interview 'Lunch with Henry Kissinger', Edward Luce managed to entice the 95 year old whom he described as 'the grand consigliere of American diplomacy' to comment on President Trump. He had obviously carefully weighed his answer and may have got closer than probably anyone else, to briefly and perceptively analyse the Trump presidency so far:

> I think Trump may be one of those figures in history who appears from time to time to mark the end of an era and to force it to give up its old pretenses. It doesn't necessarily mean that he knows this, or that he is considering any great alternative. It could just be an accident.

In the US we may be at the end of an era that started with Nixon and Kissinger opening up to China. Trump may not just settle for a trade deal, but be the President who calls out China on its underlying path, its trading practices, its refusal to respect rights to intellectual property, its build-up of military power and repression of minorities.

He may also be the President who forces a measure of realism in the Middle East. He inherited a situation in which President Putin with military force saved Damascus being fought over by President Assad's military against ISIS that was poised in the suburbs, and the unstable coalition of forces that was intent on ousting Assad. Trump has met Putin on a number of occasions in the wider forums of international diplomacy but probably because of the Russian interference in the US Presidential election, tragically the all-important bilateral negotiation over the Russian military action in the Ukraine and the taking by force of the Crimea accompanied by a detailed discussion of the Middle East could not take place until after Trump's impeachment trial. It is hard to see a resolution over the Ukraine or the Middle East without Putin and Trump coming to some form of agreement. In both areas Trump faces the need to give up, in Kissinger's words, "old pretenses". There is, for example, no way that the Russian Federation under any president will give the Crimea back to Ukraine. In the Middle East there is no way that the US dominance established by President Bush Snr will be restored.

It was open to President Obama to have challenged the Russian Federation in both areas but he chose not to. President Trump has largely followed Obama's policies in both areas with two major differences, namely over Iran and Israel, and these two are inextricably linked. Trump decided that the JCOPA [Joint Comprehensive Plan of Action] was not acceptable in its then current form and he pulled out of the plan of action. He believed, and history has shown him to be correct, that Iran was not prepared to stop destabilising the Middle East, particularly in the Yemen and over Israel, around Syria and the Lebanon. It is now very difficult, because of all the other stances that Trump has taken in his own country and in other parts of the world, to give him any credit for his handling of the Middle East. But it is quite possible that history will say that by accident or design he was the crucial figure with

Putin in re-establishing a measure of order in the region. Immediately on taking office, he demonstrated with the use of force that he was not prepared to accept Assad's use of chemical weapons. He followed that by making it very clear in Afghanistan, Iraq and Syria he did not see a future in a long term presence of US troops and where possible he would reduce and eventually withdraw.

The Iranian Revolutionary Guard, under General Soleimani, pursued a sophisticated policy of entrenching men and missiles into Syria and the Lebanon. Trump accepted Israeli air attacks to reduce their effectiveness and only took direct action against Soleimani after the interference with shipping in the Gulf, the use of proxies to attack Arabian oilfields and its Iraq Embassy. For Trump to have continued to ignore these activities would have been to marginalise his influence and exaggerate Putin's. If an eventual settlement is reached, which has Iran, if not a partner at least a player in the stabilisation of the Middle East, Trump may well be seen to have played a major role alongside Putin. Whether there is time to achieve this before the US Presidential election in 2020 is an open question, but I would not rule it out.

In Europe there is some good evidence that we may be at the end of an era that started in 1989 with the fall of the Berlin Wall when the old enemy from about 1946 onwards – the Soviet Union – collapsed; a consequence of the long and broadly successful détente policy, a combination of military containment, ideological engagement and economic competition.

We need more honesty about the process of change from the USSR to the Russian Federation. The Berlin Wall could probably have remained in place for a few more years had President Mikhail Gorbachev not refused to use force to prop up the dying East German regime. President George Bush Sr handled the immediate transition period very well with German Chancellor Kohl. Neither Margaret Thatcher nor François Mitterrand quite caught the mood change in Germany. President Clinton handled Yeltsin well personally but his greatest mistake was to push for NATO enlargement seemingly insensitive to the problems this created for Yeltsin and later Putin particularly over Georgia and the Ukraine.

Neither Blair, Bush, Cameron nor Obama seemed aware of the need to engage seriously with Putin, particularly when he overrode the advice of his immediate entourage and in the wake of 9/11 offered a new strategic relationship to Bush, going as far as closing the Russian military bases in Cuba and North Korea as an indication that he meant business. His offer was brushed aside. Obama's biggest insult was when he described Putin's Russia as merely a 'regional power'. Nothing could have been designed to anger Putin more, but by then he was embarked on his disruptive strategy towards NATO and involvement militarily in the Middle East determined to move Russia away from Europe and towards Asia, particularly China.

The real problem for the Western democracies after the fall of the Berlin Wall was to fail to realise that Yeltsin's market reforms had to be supported with real money not words alone in return for legal reforms. The great mistake was to encourage the unleashing of a rampant market economy in the new Russian Federation without the rule of law. There was no Marshall Plan Mark II for Yeltsin. Too much pretension also that Russia's problems were solved merely by the abolition of communism. Greed followed and encouraged massive corruption. The existing Russian mafia had a field day linking up in ways that were not sufficiently realised with the American mafia and developing its worldwide links.

When Kissinger talks about Trump being a figure in history who appears from time to time to mark the end of an era and forces it 'to give up its old pretenses', it is essential to remember that history. An important book is *House of Trump House of Putin. The Untold Story of Donald Trump and the Russian Mafia* by Craig Unger (Bantam Press, 2018). We learn that the first great boss of the Russian Mafia in America was Evsei Agron from Leningrad who arrived in 1975. He was shot and killed on 4 May 1985 after surviving two previous assassination attempts. His successor Marat Balagula was a modern 'don' who created a multi-million-dollar-a-year criminal enterprise. The book is packed with information, much of it undoubtedly sourced from the CIA, the FBI and MI5 and MI6. It claims with some justification that all of the above organisations, up until the appointment of a special prosecutor to investigate Russian influence on the presidential election of 2016 had, since 9/11, been told to abandon their investigations on what was happening in and around Russia to focus on the US declaration of war on terror and in particular Al-Qaeda. This focus brought with it an understandable readiness to work with Russia in areas of counter-terrorism and it necessarily continued into joint action against ISIS in Iraq, Syria and elsewhere.

In the midst of this, Congress responding to pressure from disappointed Democrats and disillusioned experts, appointed a Special Counsel, Robert Mueller. After Mueller's report was published, amidst much disappointment from those who wanted to impeach Trump, criminality became the focus involving money laundering or other abuses to specified parts of the American legal system. Here Paul Manafort is a key figure for his connections in the Ukraine and Russia and because he was hired by Trump for his presidential campaign. Manafort had previously helped Ford, Reagan, George H. W. Bush and Bob Dole in their campaigns. Besides being convicted on a number of counts not obviously related to President Trump he had agreed to talk to Mueller on that part of his investigation which included 'any links and/or coordination between the Russian government and individuals associated with the campaign of President Donald Trump'. As part of this the Ukraine began to feature and Trump turned to Vice President Biden's role and that of his son in Ukraine. Somewhat surprisingly, it was on this issue that the House of Representatives decided to impeach and somewhat damaged Biden.

The Craig Unger book ends with these words: 'a new era had begun' and so it has. It describes how on the day of Trump's victory

Vladimor Vinokur, Putin's favourite comedian, posted a collage of two photographs on Instagram. One showed Vinokur chatting amiably with Putin. The other showed the Russian comic with Trump. 'We won' it said. 'Congratulations!' That demonstrates the challenge of this new era. The contest will have a new sophistication, not just cyber warfare but showbusiness, humour, social media and dedicated political intent. In that era we have to be very careful about returning to the old Cold War attitudes and techniques in the mistaken belief that Putin's Russian Federation is comparable to Stalin's Soviet Union. But there must be unequivocal determination to end unacceptable practices. Russian killings on the streets of UK or any other country's towns and cities cannot go unchallenged. The use of radioactive substances like polonium and military grade nerve agents with the involvement of first the FSB and then the GRU cannot ignore the involvement of the Russian State.

Yet dialogue between President Trump and President Putin is very necessary and has not yet reached a serious engagement in areas like the Middle East and Ukraine. Nor will it be possible to continue business as normal and lift economic sanctions until Putin signals these practices have stopped. The British government was correct to bring what happened in Salisbury, after a painstaking investigation, to the UN Security Council and both Prime Minister May and Foreign Secretary Johnson were very involved in persuading the EU and US to apply sanctions. Other deaths in the UK of people with connections to Russia are under investigation. If this pattern of Russian state criminal behaviour continues then these matters should be presented in detail to the International Criminal Court in The Hague.

Meanwhile President Trump is right when he states that he has a world to deal with. It is impossible to shut Russia out of a peace settlement in the Middle East, since they saved Damascus from falling to ISIS and other extremists in 2015. Also Russia is a key player if Ukraine is to be stabilised, despite their annexation of Crimea.

Trump's determination to have a dialogue with Putin demonstrates that he is, quite rightly, not going to allow a re-run of the Cold War. Nor a return to the 'Pestilence of "McCarthyism"' that 'marked 1950 as an especially fearful moment in the Cold War, when Alger Hiss, a Russian spy, was convicted on 21 January of that year for perjury in denying he was a spy. Ten days later, Truman announced that in response to the Soviet Union's detonation of an atomic device, the United States would develop the hydrogen bomb.'[454]

We are into a different era and it behoves us to deal with this era using different techniques and skills. Russia is less powerful today in some senses but far more pervasive in terms of business and politics in China, Brazil, South Africa, Eastern Europe as well as the US and the UK.

No doubt there are 'Cold War Warriors' in today's CIA as there may be in the UK's MI6. But fortunately in UK politics, despite the killing of Alexander Litvinenko with polonium and the attempt at killing Sergei Skripal and his daughter Yulia, with a Novichok agent in London and Salisbury, there is still no enthusiasm in the UK for ending all dialogue with Russia despite the death of the woman who picked up the discarded bottle of scent containing the Novichok. Immediate measures like ejecting so-called Russian diplomats 'yes' and in full measure, but stopping trade, and all contact, 'no'. But that mood may change and there are influential voices who want it to change.

I talked to Presidents Gorbachev and Yeltsin about politics but after commencing business interests in Russia in 1996 I never tried to talk to President Putin apart from shaking his hand during a state visit to London in June 2003 and at a Buckingham Palace banquet, believing that foreign business men, particularly when involved in Yukos, should keep a certain distance. It was at the Palace that I was approached by the then President of the Leningrad

---

454 John A. Farrell, *Richard Nixon. The Life* (Random House, 2017) p.144.

region, who was staying there as part of President Putin's entourage. This tall man who at that stage was quite unknown to me came up to me and said, "Are you Lord Owen?" replying "Yes". "Tell Khodorkovsky to get out of politics". He then turned on his heel and left to join other Russian colleagues. At that time Khodorkovsky was the head of Yukos and I was chairman of Yukos International. I arranged for those ominous words to be relayed urgently to Khodorkovsky and then a little later in Moscow reiterated them myself to him emphasising that I did not think there would be another warning like this and that he should reduce his political profile. It became obvious that he was embarked on a course of challenging Putin, with the support of the smaller parties, in the next presidential election, if necessary as a prisoner awaiting trial. He was not prepared to curb his actions and was resigned to an inevitable confrontation. The tragedy was he had little understanding of politics at that stage. I was I believe the only person to make formal representations in the Kremlin to the deputy Prime Minister Shuvalov regarding Khodorkovsky. But the government's position never shifted. He could leave prison and Russia at any time but the two were linked. Looking back I thought business would be the key to reforming Russia. I still believe it will be through business that the rule of law will eventually be established in Russia. But my hopes for a truly democratic Russian Federation appearing quickly after 1989 have receded greatly since the assassination of Boris Nemtsov, the young former Deputy Prime Minister under Yeltsin, on a bridge near the Kremlin, just before midnight on 27 February 2015. Others will have different moments when their hopes of the early 1990s were eventually dashed and many will point to the annexation of Crimea in 2014. But I believe Ukraine has been so inextricably linked with Russia for so long that it cannot be the proving ground for Russian democracy.

What is essential is to rid the Russian Federation of its still inbred culture of lawlessness and lying in government. International business can be the key to a more law abiding Russian Federation but for this to happen the Western democracies will have to be much tougher with their own business communities. Everywhere in the world governments need to bear down harder on criminality, illegality and corruption. On money laundering London has tightened its controls but must do much more.

To reduce any outside interference with democratic procedures around the world the whole issue of the financing of and voting for politicians has to be radically reformed. Politicians will never do it left on their own. We need a non-judgemental worldwide procedure from a forum where there are no vetoes.

Some will say the UN cannot take on such tasks. Certainly at no stage does it make sense to ask a body like the UN to make judgements or adjudicate on any of these political and personal questions. Only individual nations can do this and even they face formidable difficulties in legislating on these issues. The General Assembly could only help by a non-selective, non-judgemental procedural process, like defining what democracy is.

It would be a big step forward if the World Health Organisation issued guidance to all medical practitioners involved with the published health record of candidates to be heads of government.

Democratic politicians as diverse as Woodrow Wilson, Franklin Roosevelt, Churchill, Kennedy, Johnson, Nixon, Blair and George W. Bush have not trusted their electorates with true factual information about their health. Some leaders kept their illnesses secret for years. Openness was the practice of Eisenhower as President but not when in the military. Reagan and Bush Sr in office were very open about their illnesses to their credit.

The time has come for openness about political leaders' physical and mental health. History has shown we cannot rely on their own doctors who lie in order to protect the privacy of their patient, as already described in this book in relation to Woodrow Wilson and Kennedy. Most recently George W. Bush on a period of alcoholism and Blair on cardiac arrhythmia did not tell the truth to the public.

Politicians have long been afraid that the revelation or announcement of any mental illness will damage their candidature. They remember the experience of Senator Thomas Eagleton, who was forced to resign as George McGovern's Vice Presidential candidate before the 1972 presidential race when it was leaked that he had had three depressive episodes. Eagleton had been a highly successful politician in Missouri: in 1960, at the age of thirty-one, he became the state's attorney general and in 1964 its lieutenant governor. Then in 1967 he went to Washington as a senator. Shortly after his nomination by McGovern, whom he did not warn about his illness, amidst mass of rumours, he held a press conference and announced he had been in hospital three times for 'nervous exhaustion and fatigue': firstly in 1960, after his state senatorial campaign, when he had electroconvulsive therapy (ECT); secondly in December 1964, after having been elected lieutenant governor, when he did not have ECT but just rest and treatment for a stomach pain; thirdly in 1966, when he was in the Mayo Clinic from September to October receiving ECT again for depression. Perhaps if he'd been open from the beginning his candidature could have been sustained and he would not have had to withdraw.

On 7 November 2008, in the *British Medical Journal*'s Personal View column, I wrote about the Prime Minister of Norway, Kjell Magne Bondevik, who in August 1998 had a severe depressive reaction. His intention was to resign, but he discussed the matter with his foreign minister, and together they announced publicly that he had depression. After four weeks of treatment and adapting his working practices he returned to his duties. His frankness was greatly respected by the Norwegian people and is widely regarded as contributing to the fight against the stigma that mental illness often carries. Heads of government have a duty to be open about their health, and the media have a duty to expose them when they evade the truth. The cover-up of facts about a President's health as perpetrated by Woodrow Wilson are described in Chapter 2 and are disgraceful: so was President Kennedy's drug abuse covered in Chapter 5. President François Mitterand kept secret his advanced prostate cancer for more than eleven years assisted by French privacy laws, despite the lessons that appeared to have been learned after the death of President Pompidou in office in 1974, whose myelomatosis had also been hidden from the French people. By contrast the openness with which President Bush Sr dealt with his hyperthyroidism or thyrotoxicosis presenting as atrial fibrillation in 1991 was an example of truthfulness. Tragically this has not continued to be the case, with Blair, George W. Bush, French President Chirac and Israeli Prime Minister Sharon all covering up illnesses since then.

How then are democratic societies to ensure that they have the information they need about the health of their political leaders? Or the boards of companies about their CEOs?[455] In the past the public have often had to rely solely on the statements made by the personal physicians of heads of government. But the primary responsibility of a personal physician to their patient means that they cannot be expected to balance the best interests of their patients against the best interests of the country. Personal physicians should not be expected to attempt to combine the two roles. When they do, it usually backfires. Take the example of Lord Moran, Winston Churchill's personal physician, an eminent doctor and a President of the Royal College of Physicians. His attempt to combine the two roles ended in failure. He has rightly been criticised for his misleading public statements about Churchill's health, particularly in 1953. The cover-up by the Shah of Iran's doctors is dealt with in a chapter in my book *In Sickness and In Power*, which also has a chapter on how President Mitterand's

---

455 David Owen, *In Sickness and In Power. Illness in Heads of Government, Military and Business Leaders Since 1900*, pp. 423-444.

physician, Dr Claude Gubler, tried to combine two roles of personal physician and independent assessor but failed.

Often a combination of secrecy and the political limits set on personal doctors results in the treatment for heads of government falling below the highest standards. The best clinical practice, though readily available to a head of government, is simply not utilised because of their fear that the press and public will then discover the truth about their health.

Purists argue that any public statements by doctors about their patients are a breach of the Hippocratic oath.[456] Their view is that doctors should go to their graves with the secrets of their patients and not even leave behind any records for posterity.

If the public cannot rely on personal physicians to keep them informed about the health of their head of government, how should they be informed? One way to find guidance on this question is to look to how practice has evolved in commercial boardrooms. Public companies worldwide have a duty to protect their shareholders from illness affecting their chief executive officers (CEOs). They rely on boards having some independent directors and adopting rules of good governance.

A case in point is Jamie Dimon, the chairman and chief executive of JPMorgan Chase, the pre-eminent US bank, who was told in the summer of 2014, aged fifty-eight, that he had cancer of the throat. It had not spread beyond the original site and the lymph nodes on the right side of the neck. He was assured it was a treatable condition which would need eight weeks, during which he would need to restrict his travel. He immediately told his lead

---

456 There are two versions of the oath, the classical version, 'What I may see or hear in the course of the treatment or even outside of the treatment in regard to the life of men, which on no account one must spread abroad, I will keep to myself, holding such things shameful to be spoken about.' And the modern version, 'I will respect the privacy of my patients for their problems are not disclosed to me that the world may know.'

independent director, Lee Raymond, the former head of Exxon, and several other directors. Full public disclosure then followed.

In 1960, the state of California voted to establish the Judicial Qualifications Commission to deal with judges who might be unfit to continue in office. Of the first ten cases that resulted in retirement, three came about for reasons including severe mental impairment, instability, erratic and perverse behaviour, failing memory, and inability to concentrate or understand what was being said. Judges were ruling on fellow judges and this has become the pattern, with the professions themselves trying to establish mechanisms for checking those whose decision-making can affect the public. In January 2007 the release of the FBI files of the late Supreme Court judge William Rhenquist showed that by December 1981 he had become addicted to the painkilling drug Placidyl, which was discovered when it was withdrawn during hospitalisation for back pain. He was weaned off the drug and this episode was not judged by physicians interviewed by the FBI as disqualifying him from being elevated, in 1986, to the position of Chief Justice. This episode shows that addiction can take hold with few warning signs but also that it can be reversed.

For all candidates for President or Prime Minister, I believe an independent medical assessment, after consultation with a candidate's own doctor, is the best way to determine a person's fitness for office. Had Anthony Eden been subjected to an independent medical assessment before the 1955 general election which he called soon after succeeding Churchill he would probably have been given a relatively clean bill of health.

If John F. Kennedy had known he faced a public independent medical assessment before the presidential election in 1960, he would have decided to reveal far more about his health much earlier, probably soon after Adlai Stevenson had fought and lost the 1956 election, thereby giving the American public time to absorb the facts. He would almost certainly have dated his Addison's disease from his war service. Once that had been done I am not convinced his Addison's disease would have prevented him winning four years later. It might also have altered his own attitude and helped him recognise that as a figure liable to periodic independent medical assessment, he would have to stop his own indiscriminate use of drugs and doctors that brought accompanying mood changes. He might also have come round much earlier to accepting the need for a disciplined approach to his medical treatment for Addison's disease, as well as for his back pain.

If Lyndon Johnson had faced an independent medical assessment in the 1964 presidential election, when his popularity was immense, he would have been able to ride out revelations about his past heart condition. Also, given his nature, he probably would have managed not to reveal any details of his Bipolar depression and paranoia, ensuring any medical notes were not available. Much the same would have applied to Richard Nixon, who was very popular when running for re-election in 1972, had he disclosed he had consulted a doctor who was a psychiatrist.

In Britain, after Harold Wilson was defeated in 1970, he was determined to come back and oust Edward Heath from 10 Downing Street, even though he had private anxieties about his own health. Yet before the February 1974 general election he would probably have been found healthy enough in any independent public medical assessment to go on, and he would have led his party to two narrow victories that year – just as he actually did.

So the past indicates that a system of independent assessment would not necessarily show dramatic results. Where independent medical assessments are likely to have the greatest impact is in persuading those who are ill not to put their medical cover up for the test of having it revealed and exposed by independent examination.

Tony Blair, if he had had a public independent medical assessment before the three general elections which he won, would have had to give all the details of his arrhythmia of the heart but it would probably have had little effect even by the 2005 election, though it would have given Gordon Brown's supporters an additional argument that Blair should go before that election. Again, it is likely that if Brown had lived under a statutory obligation to have an assessment he would have given medical details well before the leadership elections. More openness about his mental health would have done him no harm, depression is a common illness and people are no more sympathetic and this would have meant that subsequent episodes would have had little political impact.

Bill Clinton was relatively open about his health. Senator John McCain, the Republican candidate standing against Barack Obama, had undergone surgery for a melanoma on the left side of his face in August 2000, which was classified on removal as being Stage IIa. In 1999, when challenging George W. Bush for the Republican nomination, McCain gave the public an amazing amount of information about his health, 1,500 pages of medical and psychiatric records that had been part of a US Navy project on former prisoners of war. McCain, a war hero from Vietnam, promised to reveal all the information on his four melanomas when involved in the presidential race with Obama, though this was not done fully before the American people voted on whether he should be their next head of government. McCain's continuing health showed by Obama's second election that his doctors were correct in saying that the melanomas were not then life threatening and he had a vigorous political career before his death in 2018.

According to the *New York Times* editorial of 21 October 2008, 'there was such meager information (on Barack Obama's health) that voters have to take it largely on his campaign's say so that he is in good health'. The Vice President, Joseph Biden, who two decades previously had been operated on for potentially life-threatening aneurysms in the brain, released forty-nine pages of records.

If President Trump wants to end innuendoes and speculation on his health, he should not rely on his White House doctor but submit himself to an independent medical assessment by a doctor judged to be independent by the medical profession, who would report in July 2020 having first consulted his White House doctor.

Another yardstick to apply worldwide would be if the UN General Assembly advised that a country could not be described orally or in writing, in UN forums as democratic if there was no limitation on the length of time a Head of Government could serve. Heads of Government for life have been the source of great evils, hardship, corruption and bad governance. The American maximum of two four-year terms is a very good practice.

At a time when the Russian Parliament was pushing Putin to break the constitutional presidential two-term limit in order for him to run for a third time, Putin was wavering. Knowing Kissinger was due to see Putin soon I flew to New York and urged him to persuade Putin not to change the constitution for the 2008 election. Whether his subsequent discussion influenced Putin neither of us will ever know. But Putin did step down nominally and Medvedev became a one-term President with Putin coming back for another two terms, as their new constitution now allows. In his 2012 election campaign, Putin believed, that Hillary Clinton, as Secretary of State, authorised the CIA to intervene to support his opponents so there is a personal issue involved here. But it goes much wider than this. Antagonism is a feature of both Putin and Trump. Putin developed that characteristic when in the KGB and became head of the FSB. Trump had it in business and both have carried it into politics. Neither are embedded democratic politicians.

In 2020, President Putin announced a new constitution that could in theory, enable him to hold on to power beyond 2024 and even indefinitely, though he says he doesn't want to die in office. Who would? Such leaders believe they are invincible and indispensable.

There is a big question mark over whether President Xi of China, President Erdoğan of Turkey and many other existing Presidents or

Prime Ministers, particularly in Africa, will be persuaded to self limit or legislate to limit their differing tenure arrangements. Only time will tell but pressure for limitations on tenure can and should become a major issue for improving world governance.

The democratic response in 2020 to President Trump for those who disapprove of him and his policies is to defeat him through the ballot box, particularly in the rust belt states, though he could well maintain his previous levels of support and win a second term.

Those of us who do not vote in American elections must respect the decisions of the American people and the UK should continue to work closely with the US. It is very natural for us now to develop a UK-US trade relationship. Firstly, bilaterally, and then perhaps later establishing close links with NAFTA. There are, of course, people who over criticise the US. But there is a fund of friendship between our two countries which can naturally now be matched by an expansion of business and trade. This can be added to the fields of defence and foreign policy where we have long held a structured and close partnership. That partnership not based on party politics but on respect for our jointly held commitment to democratic government.

There are sophisticated commentators today who say and write that politicians have always lied and argue that there is less of it around now than in the past. Perhaps in 1949 with Stalin's USSR and Mao's China when George Orwell wrote *Nineteen Eighty-Four*[457] more people were living under governments who were strangers to the truth: but what is surely troubling and new is the behaviour of our democracies and in particular the two democracies on which this book has focused. I defy anyone to deny that the truth was given a higher priority in 1949 by Truman and Attlee and in 1979 by Carter and Callaghan than by Trump and Johnson in 2020.

---

457 George Orwell. *Nineteen Eighty-Four*. Penguin Modern Classics. 2000, p 244.

It is worthwhile therefore to reflect on George Orwell's warnings on how, in his Party in *Nineteen Eighty-Four*, the act of deception had to be conscious, or it would not be carried out with sufficient precision, but it also had to be unconscious, or it would bring with it a feeling of falsity and hence of guilt:-

"to use conscious deception while retaining the firmness of purpose that goes with complete honesty. To tell deliberate lies while genuinely believing in them, to forget any fact that has become inconvenient, and then, when it becomes necessary again, to draw it back from oblivion for just so long as it is needed, to deny the existence of objective reality and all the while to take account of the reality which one denies – all this is indispensably necessary. Even in using the world *doublethink* it is necessary to exercise *doublethink*. For by using the word one admits that one is tampering with reality; by a fresh act of doublethink one erases this knowledge; and so on indefinitely, with the lie always one leap ahead of the truth."[458]

A senior Trump administration official wrote anonymously in 2019.[459] President Trump 'has been called a pathological liar. I used to cringe when I heard people say that just to score political points, and I thought it unfair. Now I know it's true. He spreads lies he hears. He makes up new lies to spread. He lies to our faces. He asks people around him to lie. People who've known him for years accept it as common knowledge. We cannot get used to this. Think of what we must "trust" a president to do as our chief executive.'

I would not normally quote from a source who was not prepared to use their own name. But I have to admit I have wanted key officials to stay in the Trump administration and do their best to

458 George Orwell. *Nineteen Eighty-Four* (Penguin Modem Classics, 2000), p 244.
459 *A Warning Anonymous* (Twelve, 2019), p. 195.

ensure better governance. It is to their credit that they have stayed and did not resign. Sometimes there is a duty to serve and fulfilling that duty deserves recognition. Eventually I hope we will know the author's name but for now this person, clearly a Republican, urges Democrats to choose as their candidate, someone with as great an appeal as possible to Republican voters.

The democratic response to the rise of populism in many places in the world is to rediscover and reshape what we value in the qualities of our elected leaders and in every place they work whether the US Congress or the UK Parliament or the Russian Duma. Also on the behaviour of leaders in offices, factories, universities, schools, hospitals and their own homes. I have focused on national politicians, business and military leaders. We need to persistently reward and honour wise leaders everywhere, who serve the wider good, enable greater prosperity, provide more jobs and fairer rewards, who respect facts, seek out the truth, eschew bombast, contain their hubris and moderate excess while at the same time showing tolerance and respect across racial, sexual and religious differences.

I leave to the last the most frequent but rarely focused on risk to democracy that has grown up over the last three decades in the US and the UK. It is chronicled in a remarkable book by Michael Lewis, *The Fifth Risk: Undoing Democracy*.[460] It is the casual, ill-thought through, often contemptuous decisions taken by politicians of all parties in government with increasing abandon that coarsen and cheapen democracy. In the Afterword to the paperback edition the author highlights President Trump's decision on 22 December 2018, to sign no more spending bills passed by Congress until they included billions of dollars to build a wall on the border with Mexico. The shutdown lasted 35 days. A physicist from NASA comments, "Everything in space flight is coordinated to the minute . . . when you throw a five-week wrench into that, it'll take years to reset this."

---

460 Penguin Books 2019, p. 224

Index